# Landscape
# Politics and Perspectives

## Edited by Barbara Bender

The term 'landscape' was coined in an emergent capitalist world to evoke a particular set of elite experiences, a particular 'way of seeing'. But other people also have landscapes. The contributors to this book are geographers, anthropologists and archaeologists, and they explore landscape as something subjective, something experienced, something that alters through time and space, that is created by, and creative of, historical conditions and geographic emplacement. The articles range in time from 6000 BC to the present, and in space from Alaska and Melanesia to Belfast and Paris. They show how the cultural and political analysis of landscape cuts across many disciplinary boundaries and how perceptions of the land and its history are created, negotiated and contested.

**Barbara Bender** is Reader in Anthropology at University College London

EXPLORATIONS IN ANTHROPOLOGY
A University College London Series

Series Editors: Barbara Bender, John Gledhill and Bruce Kapferer

Joan Bestard-Camps, *What's in a Relative? Household and Family in Formentera*

Henk Driessen, *On the Spanish-Moroccan Frontier: A Study in Ritual, Power and Ethnicity*

Alfred Gell, *The Anthropology of Time: Cultural Construction of Temporal Maps and Images*

Tim Ingold, David Riches and James Woodburn (eds), *Hunters and Gatherers*

   Volume 1. *History, Evolution and Social Change*
   Volume 2. *Property, Power and Ideology*

Bruce Kapferer, *A Celebration of Demons* (2nd edn)

Guy Lanoue, *Brothers: The Politics of Violence among the Sekani of Northern British Columbia*

Jadran Mimica, *Intimations of Infinity: The Mythopoeia of the Iqwaye Counting System and Number*

Barry Morris, *Domesticating Resistance: The Dhan-Gadi Aborigines and the Australian State*

Thomas C. Patterson, *The Inca Empire: The Formation and Disintegration of a Pre-Capitalist State*

Max and Eleanor Rimoldi, *Hahalis and the Labour of Love: A Social Movement on Buka Island*

Pnina Werbner, *The Migration Process: Capital, Gifts and Offerings among Pakistanis in Britain*

FORTHCOMING:

Christopher Tilley (ed.), *Interpretative Archaeology*

Stephen Nugent, *Amazonian Caboclo Society*

# Landscape
# Politics and Perspectives

**Edited by**
**Barbara Bender**

**BERG**

*Providence/Oxford*

First published in 1993 by
**Berg Publishers**
221 Waterman Street, Providence, RI 02906, USA
150 Cowley Road, Oxford, OX4 1JJ, UK

**Library of Congress Cataloguing-in-Publication Data**
Landscape: politics and perspectives / edited by Barbara Bender.
    p. cm. -- (Explorations in anthropology)
    "Many of these papers were first given within the Department
of Anthropology. University College, London, as part of a
departmental seminar series" -- Acknowledgements.
    Includes bibliographical references (p.   ) and index.
    ISBN 0-85496-373-1 (paper). – ISBN 0-85496-852-0 (cloth)
    1. Landscape assessment. 2. Geographical perception. 3. Human
ecology--Political aspects. I. Bender, Barbara. II. Series.
GF90.L367 1993                                       92-39620
304.2--dc20                                               CIP

**British Library Cataloguing in Publication Data**
Landscape: Politics and Perspectives. –
(Explorations in Anthropology Series)
I. Bender, Barbara II. Series 301
ISBN 0-85496-852-0

ISBN 0 85496 852 0  (hb)
      0 85496 373 1  (pb)

Photograph on frontcover © Alan Lodge.

Printed in Great Britain by SRP Ltd., Exeter

For Jan

# Contents

Acknowledgements                                                    ix

**Introduction: Landscape – Meaning and Action**
    *Barbara Bender*                                          1

1. The Politics of Vision and the Archaeologies of
   Landscape
       *Julian Thomas*                                       19

2. Art, Architecture, Landscape [Neolithic Sweden]
       *Christopher Tilley*                                  49

3. Landscape as Memory: The Mapping of Process and
   its Representation in a Melanesian Society
       *Susanne Küchler*                                     85

4. Intersecting Belfast
       *Neil Jarman*                                        107

5. The View from Below: Paris in the 1880s
       *Felicity Edholm*                                    139

6. Gendered Spaces, Public Places: Public and
   Private Revisited on the North Slope of Alaska
       *Barbara Bodenhorn*                                   169

7. Colonialism, History and the Construction of Place:
   The Politics of Landscape in Northern Australia
       *Howard Morphy*                                       205

8. Stonehenge – Contested Landscapes (Medieval to
   Present-Day)
       *Barbara Bender*                                      245

9. Landscapes and Myths, Gods and Humans
       *Denis Cosgrove*                                      281

10. Sexual Cosmology: Nation and Landscape at
    the Conceptual Interstices of Nature and Culture;
    or What does Landscape Really Mean?
    *Kenneth Olwig*                                              307

**Notes on the Contributors**                                    345

**Index**                                                        347

# Acknowledgements

Many of these papers were first given within the Department of Anthropology, University College, London, as part of a department seminar series on *Landscape: Politics and Perspectives*. I am very grateful to the department for its intellectual, financial and moral support.

# Introduction

## Landscape – Meaning and Action

*Barbara Bender*

This book is about the complexity and power of landscape. Landscapes are created by people – through their experience and engagement with the world around them. They may be close-grained, worked-upon, lived-in places, or they may be distant and half-fantasised.[1] In contemporary western societies they involve only the surface of the land; in other parts of the world, or in pre-modern Europe, what lies above the surface, or below, may be as or more important. In the contemporary western world we 'perceive' landscapes, we are the point from which the 'seeing' occurs. It is thus an ego-centred landscape, a perspectival landscape, a landscape of views and vistas[2]. In other times and other places the visual may not be the most significant aspect, and the conception of the land may not be ego-centred. Many of the papers in this book are about non-western landscapes, and one of its purposes is to deny the primacy of the European 'viewpoint', and to insist that the experience of landscape is too important and too interesting to be confined to a particular time, place and class. True, the word was originally coined in the emergent capitalist world of western Europe by aesthetes, antiquarians and

1. Cosgrove (1989) points to polar landscapes – the most inhuman of natural environments and yet 'the very paradigm of *Boy's Own World* – the setting of British Upper-class male cultural fantasy. Scott's death in 1912 made a corner of Antarctica forever England'.
2. Mitchell (1989) strongly conveys, in a nineteenth-century height-of-the-Empire context, both the objectification of the land and the need to spy out across the surface. He records the bewilderment of the French in Egypt who, seeped in theatrical images of the Orient, find themselves unable to gain the requisite distance, and recoil at the proximity, detail and movement of the lived experience. In an otherwise brilliant exposition, he fails, as so often happens, to gender the gaze. They were French *men* (cf. Massey 1991).

1

landed gentry – all men[3]. It is also true that this coinage is a fine example of how those with power can use language and image to conceptualise and naturalise a particular, and in this case, deeply unequal, way of relating to the land and to other people. But it is inescapably true that even at the historical moment when the word 'landscape' was coined and used to its most powerful effect, there were, at the same time and the same place, other ways of understanding and relating to the land – other landscapes. The poetry of the late eighteenth-century peasant poet John Clare registers a conflict – a tension – between an elitist aesthetic 'viewpoint' (a 'correct', perspectival way of 'seeing'), and an alternative, peasant's, 'close-up' landscape of open field and drove-way; a conflict between the 'viewpoint' of his publisher and his patron in which there was no place for Clare's vernacular or his 'radical slang', and the poet's own need to retain and retell his peasant revolt against enclosure and forced eviction.

Landscape has to be contextualised. The way in which people – anywhere, everywhere – understand and engage with their worlds will depend upon the specific time and place and historical conditions. It will depend upon their gender, age, class, caste, and on their social and economic situation. People's landscapes will operate on very different spatial scales, whether horizontally across the surface of the world, or vertically – up to the heavens, down to the depths. They will operate on very different temporal scales, engaging with the past and with the future in many different ways. Even in the most scientific of Western worlds, past and future will be mythologised. Sometimes the engagement will be very conscious – a way of laying claims, of justifying and legitimating a particular place in the world –, sometimes almost unconscious – part of the routine of everyday existence. Each individual holds many landscapes in tension. Thus, for example, Aboriginal Australians superimpose creation myths upon the land, thereby turning a temporal sequence into a spatial grid.

3. More accurately it was re-coined. There was an earlier Anglo-Saxon useage of the word, corresponding to the German word *Landschaft* – meaning a sheaf, a patch of cultivated ground, something small-scale that corresponded to a peasant's perception, a mere fragment of a feudal estate, an inset in a Breugel landscape. This usage had gone out of vogue by the eleventh century, replaced by words that corresponded to the larger political spaces of those with power – *territoire, pays, domain*. And then in the seventeenth and eighteenth centuries it re-emerged, tightly tied to a particular 'way of seeing', a particular experience, whether in pictures, extolling nature or landscaping an estate (Jackson 1985; but see Olwig (pp. 307–343, this volume) for more detail).

That mythological grid locates the individual and the clan and allows them to renew their ancestral inheritance. At the same time, the grid is a topographic map that locates resources, camps and hunting-grounds. The associated understanding and the necessary rituals and ceremonies are forms of restricted knowledge that require initiation and are therefore part of the way in which people create and maintain status and identity. Moreover, the restricted knowledge is also open to adjustment: 'the ancestral past is subject to the political map of the present' (Morphy 1988). Landscapes are thus polysemic, and not so much artefact as in process of construction and reconstruction.

The landscape is never inert, people engage with it, re-work it, appropriate and contest it. It is part of the way in which identities are created and disputed, whether as individual, group, or nation-state. Operating therefore at the juncture of history and politics, social relations and cultural perceptions, landscape has to be – as this book sets out to show – 'a concept of high tension' (Inglis 1977). It also has to be an area of study that blows apart the conventional boundaries between the disciplines. So the contributors to this book are anthropologists, geographers, historians and archaeologists.

I wish now to draw upon an astonishing novel by V. S. Naipaul that explores, more delicately and precisely than a mere academic could ever do, the complexity and the power of the experience of landscape. It will show how nuanced, and how changing, even one individual's interaction with the land can be.

*The Enigma of Arrival* by V. S. Naipaul (1987) is an autobiographical novel about a rather solitary period in the author's life when he comes to rest in a cottage in the grounds of a run-down manor house close to Stonehenge in Wiltshire. Naipaul uses the landscape, not in the aesthetic sense of pictures or images or perspectives of 'nature', nor in the sense of rural 'scene', but as something dynamic, a way in which to explore: 'the worlds contained within myself, the worlds I live in' (ibid: 135).

*The Enigma of Arrival* is not a theoretical book, it does not define landscape, it simply intimately connects the writer and his material – and often immaterial – world. Often he takes the reader to a particular scrap of Wiltshire landscape – a drove-way, some farm buildings, the edge of the manorial estate. The topography becomes familiar, the relationship of one thing to another becomes known. But each time the walk is made, he – and we – experience the landscape differently.

Naipaul is a foreigner, both in England and in Trinidad. His grandparents left India in the mid-nineteenth century. They came to Trinidad as indentured labourers. His father was educated, and so, in turn, were his sons. For Naipaul, this education means that his ambitions, what he thinks of as his 'centre', are located outside Trinidad, in England – the heart of the Empire. He leaves Trinidad aged eighteen, with a scholarship to Oxford and with preconceived ideas of what it is to be a writer and what it is that he should write about. It takes years for him to discover that writer and man are inseparable and that he has to write out of, and about, his own complex life-history. In *The Enigma of Arrival* he uses his encounters with a Wiltshire landscape and his memories of a Trinidadian one to tease out this life history.

Sometimes his landscapes are about space and scale. Sometimes a sense of geographical scale merges into something more political. When he leaves home, and flies away from Trinidad, the small-scale familial landscape, the dismissed landscape of an ambitious child, are suddenly seen as part of a larger, planned world: 'A landscape of clear pattern and contours, absorbing all the roadside messiness ... the landscape of a real country' (ibid: 97). And then, landing in Puerto Rico, the enlarged world also changes value: 'the world ceased to be colonial ...' (ibid: 101). He watches a black Trinidadian lose glamour and colour as he moves into the American sphere of influence.

Sometimes his landscapes are about time – about historical depth. After leaving Trinidad, and settling in England, he researches a book on the history of his island. Just as the aeroplane taking off created a larger spatial world, his research creates both a larger spatial and temporal world. The island history is part of world history. The Indian indentured labour is part of a long process of conquest and colonisation. His grandparents had arrived at the tail-end of the island's economic depression: 'As a schoolboy I had assumed that torpor to be constant, something connected with the geographic location of the island, the climate, the quality of light. It had never occurred to me that the drabness I knew had been man-made, that it had causes, that there had been other visions and indeed other landscapes there' (ibid: 142).

For Naipaul, historical change holds romance. In contrast, contemporary change threatens. He researches the book, he returns to Trinidad. He wants to *re*-view the landscape as palimpsest: what does the landscape contain of the pre-conquest occupation of the exterminated aboriginal population: 'I had to ignore almost everything that leapt to the eye, and almost everything in the vegetation I had been trained to see as tropical and local, part of our travel-poster beauty – coconut, sugar-cane, bamboo, mango, bougainvillea, poinsettia – since all those plants and trees had been imposed later with the settlement and plantations' (ibid: 146).

But he returns to find that his reconstructed, semi-romantic landscape has been disrupted – the black population are up in arms. Time has moved on; the landscape is in flux. Other people: other landscapes:

> The island meant other things to other people. There were other ways of responding to a knowledge of the world or an idea of the past, other ways of asserting self... The negroes of Trinidad ...simplified and sentimentalised the past: they did not, like me, wish to possess it for its romance. They wore their hair in a new way. The hair that had been ... a source of embarrassment and shame, a servile badge, they wore as a symbol of aggression (ibid: 146).

Naipaul never resolves this conflict between an imaginative (and romantic) sense of time past, one that enlarges appreciation and that is part of the process of change and flux, and a fear of contemporary change – something unfavourable, disruptive, symptom of decay and decline rather than flux. Naipaul (like Hoskins in *The Making of the English Landscape*), can be a radical about the past, and a conservative about the present. The black 'uprising' in Trinidad is: 'Another fake revolution...the wish to destroy the world...to turn one's back on it, rather than improve it' (ibid: 147).

This tension between the neutrality of historical 'change', and the pessimism of contemporary decay is still stronger and more complicated in the Wiltshire setting.

I have taken Naipaul's Trinidadian landscapes first, although the book is not primarily about Trinidad. I have artificially fore-grounded Trinidad because of a misplaced sense that Trinidad *ought* to be Naipaul's primary landscape, the place of his rooted-ness – a misplaced conception based on a European notion that equates home and childhood with a sense of roots. In reality, Naipaul's childhood landscape *lacks* roots. His family harks back to India, and in part he responds: 'I was interested in, had been passionate about, the politics of India, before and after Independence, yet I knew little about my community in Trinidad, ... and ... nothing of other communties' (ibid: 101).

He was interested in Indian, not island, politics. He senses an affinity with the Indian conception of 'a world outside men's control', and yet rejects 'that half-Indian world ... its language not even half understood, its religion and religious ritual not grasped' (ibid; 101). His grandparents hark back to India, Naipaul harks forward to England. So Trinidad, while it is a familiar, first-hand, landscape, is not a rooted landscape.

In contrast, the English landscape of his childhood is a world created from films and literature. When he first arrives in London, he 'sees' what he has read about in Dickens; 'sees' only the large buildings. Years later, when he arrives at his Wiltshire cottage, he notes: 'I saw what I saw very clearly. But I didn't know what I was looking at. I had nothing to fit it into' (ibid: 12). This is not quite accurate; it was not that 'he had nothing to fit it into', rather that he had to unlearn, or to question, his assumptions, his expectations.

He starts by categorising and learning the names of plants and trees, seasons, landforms: flat wet fields with ditches were 'water meadows', low smooth hills were 'downs' (ibid: 11). He matches the 'real' images to ones he had half-imagined: 'The bales unstacked into golden, clean, warm-smelling steps made me think ... of references in books with European settings to men asleep on straw in barns. That had never been comprehensible to me in Trinidad, where grass was always freshly cut for cattle, always green, and never browned into hay' (ibid: 17). He finds memory traces of comparative Trinidadian landscapes. The black and white cows up on the downs remind him of the design on the condensed-milk label from his childhood. They also remind him of the beasts kept by his family, scrawny but revered: 'the big animals on the downs ... even in their beauty, were without sanctity .... No sanctity at birth and none at death: just the covered van' (ibid: 80). He has to negotiate the literary images of his 'English' education. The first person he registers is an old man: '... a Wordsworthian figure: bent, exaggeratedly bent, going gravely about his peasant tasks, as if in an immense Lake District solitude' (ibid: 20).

He has to negotiate his assumptions about the rootedness, the antiquity of the English countryside. Perhaps, indeed, it was not an accident that he came to the Stonehenge area, seemingly that most rooted of English landscapes. Perhaps it was in the hope of finding, as his education had promised him, his own English roots. And perhaps the poignancy of the book is that he has ultimately to accept that it is not possible, that the historical process engages the present as much as the past. Early on, Naipaul focuses on Jack, the farm-labourer working his intricate cottage garden, and turns him into something rooted, something of Old England, a mute figure in a painted landscape: 'the remnant of an old peasantry ... surviving somehow the Industrial Revolution, deserted villages, railways, and the establishing of the great agricultural estates in the valley' (ibid: 22). Only later he comes to accept (albeit rather vaguely) that Jack is not, cannot be, a relic of a past age, that he is probably a newcomer to the valley, that 'he had created his own life, his own world...' (ibid: 87).

Not surprisingly, with Stonehenge just over the hill, antiquity, rootedness, the 'naturalness' of the landscape, are at first passionately accepted. Only slowly the politics of landscape emerge:

> when I grew to see the wild roses and hawthorn on my walk, I didn't see the windbreak they grew beside as a sign of the big landowners who had left their mark on the solitude ... had planted woods in certain places (in imitation, it was said, of the positions of Trafalgar – or was it Waterloo?). I didn't think of the landowners ... I thought of those single-petalled roses and sweet smelling blossom ... as wild and natural growths (ibid: 24).

He touches only lightly on the proprietorial palimpsest of the Wiltshire landscape. And yet it is the politics embedded in the landscape, and his internal conflict about his place in that setting, that forms one of the strongest themes in the book. The landowner who built that windbreak might well have been the father or grandfather of the present occupant of the manor, the recluse suffering from accidie who has given Naipaul the use of a cottage on the edge of his domain. The manor and the garden are all that are left of an enormous estate. Where there had once been sixteen gardeners there is now one. The grounds look ancient, the 'medieval' cottages scattered round the 'green' look ancient. But it is, in fact, an Edwardian folly – evidence of the English at play. It belonged to the same period, expressed something of the same attitude as the restoration of the local church : 'not so much a religious celebration as a sense of history, the assurance of continuity, the sense of something owed to oneself' (ibid: 48).

An Edwardian estate, every detail – the garden door, the greenhouse, the bridges – overspecified, massive, palatial. An estate built on the backs of Naipaul's family, of people moving, being moved, from one part of the empire to another. People who helped make the fortunes of the English landed gentry: 'The colonial plantations or estates of Trinidad, to which my impoverished Indian ancestors had been transported – estates of which the Wiltshire estate, where I now lived, was the apotheosis' (ibid: 52). The estate was part of the empire that had exploited his people, and yet had given him much of his identity: 'An empire lay between us. This empire also linked us. The empire explained my birth in the New World, the language I used, the vocation and ambition I had; this empire in the end explained my presence in the valley, in that cottage, in the grounds of the manor' (ibid: 174). But a Trinidadian Indian could only come to rest on an English estate with the end of empire, and could only feel secure when the sixteen gardeners had gone and the place had begun to revert to wilderness:

> At a time of empire... the builder of the house and the designer of the garden could not have imagined, with their world view, that at a later time someone like me would have been in the grounds, and that I would feel that I was having the place – the cottage, the empty picturesque houses around the lawn, the grounds, the wild gardens – at its peak, living in a beauty that hadn't been planned for (ibid: 52).

For Naipaul, the neglected estate is both romantic and symptomatic of decline. His very presence in the valley is 'part of an upheaval, a change in the course of the history of the country' (ibid: 19). As we have seen before, contemporary 'change' for Naipaul, despite his best attempts, bespeaks decline. Naipaul, a man caught between his English education with its glorification of empire, and his family history – exploited, spiritually disinherited, the downside of empire – uneasily mourns the passing of empire: 'I lived with the idea of decay (... it was like my curse: the idea, which I had had even as a child in Trinidad, that I had come into a world past its peak)' (ibid: 26). His internal confusion is never resolved: 'the history I carried with me ... sent me into the world with a sense of glory dead, and in England had given me the rawest of stranger's nerves' (ibid: 52).

He is not only the grandson of an indentured labourer, he is coloured. His racial identity is hardly ever mentioned directly, it is always this 'raw' nameless thing: 'the rawness of a stranger's nerves', 'the rawness of my colonial nerves' (ibid: 95), a 'raw sense of an unaccommodating world' (ibid: 85), 'a man from another hemisphere, another background' (ibid: 19).

He cannot properly acknowledge his colour because he – unlike the Trinidadian blacks – is of a generation (and a personality) that 'assert(s) propriety, ... wish(es) to live within the old order,... wish(es) to be treated as others' (ibid: 146). He wishes – in his romantic identification with his reclusive landlord – to be part of the Establishment (although he knows that he can never 'see' what his landlord 'sees' – 'his house, his garden, his view, his name').

'Belonging' is a sort of fantasy: the black and white cows on the evaporated-milk labels reappear: 'always on a sunny day on this walk... there was a corner of my fantasy in which I felt some minute, remote yearning had been satisfied, and I was in the original of that condensed-milk label drawing' (ibid: 297). The fantasy is: 'the fulfilment of the child's dream of a safe house in the woods' (ibid: 84).

However, the 'safe' house is threatened at every turn. Just as he had felt both threatened by and intolerant of the black Trinidadians, so he is threatened by and intolerant of an itinerant who camps in the empty 'children's house' on the estate – the man is part of 'a new tide of idleness washing back and forth over the empty spaces of south-western England' (ibid: 250).

I hope that the reader will have gained a sense of the density and the dynamism of Naipaul's landscapes, and will have recognised, more generally, the way in which his landscapes are both spatial and temporal, the way in which, at one and the same time, they serve as palimpsests of past activity, incorporate political action, encompass change – both past and present – , are half-imagined or something held in the memory, are about identity, or lack of identity, roots or lack of roots. Obviously, other people in the same place have quite different landscapes. And Naipaul's landscapes change as his engagement with the land changes. Moreover, his landscapes are more than just reflections of his particular sensibility and circumstances, they act back onto his understanding of himself and onto his actions in the world. You could say that his landscapes are 'postmodern' – fragmented, contradictory. But you could also say that that fragmentation and contradiction are in some measure expressive of, created by, the conditions of a post-imperial world.

Naipaul's experienced world, varied and comparative, is nonetheless contained within a western aesthetic, a western 'way of looking'. Many of the papers in this book are about radically different landscapes involving other ways of relating to and perceiving the world.

Julian Thomas' 'The Politics of Vision and the Archaeologies of Landscape' (pp.19–48) historically contextualises the western perspectival gaze in which the observer is always outside and above the action. He genders the gaze in a way that ties in with Felicity Edholm's contribution (pp.139–168): women are the object of the gaze, men the subjects of identification. He then works through an alternative 'situated' way of experiencing, combining Heidegger's 'being in the world', with its emphasis on social action and subjectivity, with a recognition of the way in which such action and meaning are structurally empowered and empowering. In the context of prehistoric Avebury, Thomas portrays a Neolithic sociality in which artefacts – particularly monuments – become part of a technology of memory. In ways reminiscent of the funerary carvings of the Malangan of New Ireland (see Küchler's contribution, pp.85–106), the tombs and henges become the vehicle for an active reconstruction of remembrance which permits the projection of social relations into the future. Thomas discusses the way in which the physical structuring and restructuring of the monuments, movement within and among them, the sequencing of events/structures, the reordering and reworking of deposited materials work to create sectional and graded fields of knowledge.

In 'Art, Architecture, Landscape [Neolithic Sweden]' (pp.49–84), Christopher Tilley picks up on the hermeneutics of megalithic space, the need to work with perceptions operating on the ground and on a human scale. He investigates the relationship between megalithic tombs and features of the landscape in three different areas of Sweden. Adapting a discourse drawn from studies of modern environmental art, he stresses the manner in which architectural form and topographic features of the landscape play off each other to create a distinctive sense of space. He argues that different forms of megalithic architecture produce different experiences for the people who build and use them. The architecture acts as a lens for perceiving the landscape around the monuments. Its relationship with the landscape may provide a powerful means for legitimising power relations and naturalising the social order. In Vastergotland, for example, where there was no extended tradition of megalith building, the passage graves are intimately linked to the surrounding topography. The mounds are situated to provide maximum visibility towards the mountains. The largest mound and the greatest concentration of mounds cluster close to the highest mountain. The chambers take the axis of the mountain, the low passage directs attention towards both chamber and mountain. The red limestone and sandstone uprights and the igneous capstones mimic the topography of the sedimentary plain and the igneous flat-topped mountains. Through these interconnections the landscape is socialised and drawn into the domain of human negotiation, and as time goes on, social relations become increasingly dependent upon these pre-established physical structures to which people have differential access, both literally and in terms of social understanding.

The theme of landscape as memory informs Susanne Küchler's contribution (pp.85–106). In 'Landscape as Memory: the Mapping of Process and its Representation in a Melanesian Society', Küchler contrasts the western conceptualisation of landscape as inscribed surface from which social and cultural relations can be read off, with the New Irelanders' understanding of landscape as process. The first are landscapes *of* memory, the second landscapes *as* memory. The Malangan art of northern New Ireland takes the form of funerary sculpted images. These elaborate carvings, which are abandoned shortly after they have been completed and exhibited, regulate, through their carved incorporations and exclusions, the transmission of land. Moreover, they make visual the process of landscape formation. They are not, however, some pristine long-term indigenous tradition, but rather the direct consequence of the break-up of clan territory and its replacement by regionally extended land-holding confederations, a process which began in the eighteenth century and intensified with the imposition of German colonial rule in the late nineteenth century. The Germans, intent on breaking up the inscribed landscape, failed to recognise a completely 'other' landscape. They admired the Malangan sculpture as 'art' and attentively collected it for display in museums. Thereby, unwittingly, they permitted – indeed encouraged – an indigenous form of resistance.

In Neil Jarman's 'Intersecting Belfast' (pp.107–138), we move to contemporary Northern Ireland. Jarman maps the politics of a city in terms of sectarian divides and the overarching British authority. We see the neutralisation of the city centre, presented as a 'normal' commercial environment, and the increasing isolation and surveillance of the working class estates. His Belfast, with its ghettoisation and the channelling of communication into new, more easily controlled, radial through-ways, has much in common with Edholm's turn-of-the-century Paris. Jarman then takes us to the murals on the working class estates – both Nationalist and Loyalist. The murals are legitimations *within* communities, defining identities through reference to and appropriation of earlier histories. They are also acts of subversion through which the paramilitaries on both sides of the line create new icons which, through physical juxtaposition with more traditional, ostensibly non-violent images, transform the meaning of both old and new. Both Nationalist and Loyalist murals, with their strong working-class connotations, have in common a resistance to the overweening authority of the ruling middle classes.

The murals stand in sharp contrast with the parades. Any sense of Nationalist/Loyalist parity disappears: the parades, with rare exceptions, are Protestant. They are also male and middle-class, although, again, there are subversions. The Orange parades of the Twelfth of July act to reunify the fragmented communities of Belfast. They also legimate the right to march – to lay claim to the geography of the city and ultimately to the whole of Ulster.

Women are peripheralised in Jarman's Belfast, and again, in Felicity Edholm's late nineteenth-century Paris. Edholm too, in her exploration of Haussmann's 're-modelling' of Paris, charts a geography of repression. In 'The View from Below: Paris in the 1880s' (pp.139–168), she also shows that our perception of Modern-ity, personified in the life-style and writings of Baudelaire, our sense of the individuation, excitement, flux and flow of a great city, with its promise of erotic encounter, is a partial vision, physically tightly located on the boulevards, socially defined by class and above all by gender. Edholm attempts to recreate an alternative experience of the city, that of working-class women, personified by Suzanne Valadon. The attempt is complicated by the inability to encounter Valadon directly. She is identified, yet again, by the middle-class male – writer, painter, sociologist and architect. Rather than despair at the filtering lens that these people offer, Edholm works with the grain, showing how the Valadons of late nineteenth-century Paris were perceived (and feared), how they affected and in part created the experience of those with power. Haussmann's Paris was as much an attempt to suppress, supplant, and make invisible the hated 'other', as to create the conditions for modern capitalist production and consumption. In part, those with power defined Valadon's own sense of identity, forced her to react and interact in particular ways. But their writ was not all-embracing. The back streets of Paris were created by the processes of 'modernisation', but were also beyond the experience and to some extent the jurisdiction of the bureaucrat or *flâneur*. Here the working class woman, whose life was lived to a great extent out on the streets, existed precariously through a network of alliances and exchanges. Here there was some degree of independence, and an experience of the world quite other than that assigned to her by the denizens of the boulevard.

The theme of gendered space is continued in Barbara Bodenhorn's 'Gendering Space: Public and Private Revisited on the North Slope of Alaska' (pp.169–203). She questions the universality of the coupling of private: female, public: male space, and shows that while there may be relatively clear-cut divisions of labour, these, in the context of the Iñupiat, are predicated on a necessary ritual and actual interdependence. Public communal space is not gendered, rather it is culturally defined by those animals that, as communal resources, belong to the public sphere. The physical act of hunting may most often be undertaken by the men, but the whale is caught because it comes, willingly, in spirit, to the hearth of the whaling captain-wife. Hunting, as defined by the Iñupiat, includes the interwoven activities of sewing, butchering, apportioning, music-making and dancing, in all of which women are active partners and most of which take place in the public space.

A secondary theme in this chapter is that, faced with the American way of doing and being, the Iñupiat do not so much resist, as engage in a way that goes with the grain of their own understanding and perception. With their relative autonomy, women as well as men move into wage labour, and, perhaps even more importantly today, the public politics of representing Iñupiat to the State and Nation becomes, like hunting, a joint operation undertaken by men and women. At public meetings women maintain their autonomy and their authority to speak and be listened to. Politically sensitive positions, e.g. State

Legislator, Superintendent of Schools, Executive Director of the Whaling Commission, are not restricted by gender, but by the skills both men and women are acknowledged to possess.

Howard Morphy, in 'Colonialism, History and the Construction of Place: the Politics of Landscape in Northern Australia' (pp.205–243), unravels, in the context of a small land-claim area, first, different visions of white colonial landscape over a period of a hundred years, then changing aboriginal landscapes. Again, the distinction between landscapes *of* memory (represented by the colonial map in which landscape is given value by its place in history, where place-names record the actions of human agents who played a role in transforming the country) and landscape *as* memory (where the place names refer to ancestral action, where the spiritual force that lies beneath the surface of the earth has the capacity to reproduce the present in the form of the past) becomes very clear. Morphy shows how the Aboriginal dreamtime, because it constructs, rather than reflects, continuity, can accommodate change. It is no accident that in the Roper Bar landclaim, the greatest density of Aboriginal names focuses on the same places as the White settlers. Having been forced onto the the cattle-ranches and into the vicinity of white settlement, the Aborigines sacralise and give names to these places. As with the New Irelanders, so with the Ngalakan of Roper Bar, western 'logic' sometimes finds itself helpless and undermined by a different way of engaging with the land.

In 'Stonehenge – Contested Landscapes (Medieval to Present-Day)' (pp.245–279), Barbara Bender charts the way in which for almost five thousand years Stonehenge has been ideologically and politically contested. In prehistoric times the fabric itself was torn down, constructed and reconstructed. The 'final' Bronze Age stone settings represent a rag-bag of 'invented tradition'. For the medieval period she focusses on a contested landscape of church and peasant. It was not the 'magicking' of the stones that created the problem, only the interpretation, and in dealing with a recalcitrant peasantry the Church incorporated the stones into a Christian demonology. The transition from stones cautiously buried in the fourteenth century to stones broken up by fire and water in the sixteenth century marks the change from a medieval cosmology in which nature and culture are still intimately connected, to the increasingly mechanistic philosophy of an emergent capitalist world. In discussing the seventeenth and eighteenth centuries, Bender produces an array of alternative voices: antiquarian, landowner, peasant, Welsh Nationalist, all mobilising different histories and differentially empowered. For the contemporary period she charts the physical coralling of the site, tensions within the 'Establishment' as it attempts to image and sell the past, and the Establishment confrontation with those whose life-styles and conceptualisations offer resistance to its way of appropriating both the land and the past.

Bender's chapter is, in part, about changing western sensibilities. The last two chapters in the book intertwine with each other and explore the roots of western 'modern' sensibilities and conceptualisations of landscape.

Denis Cosgrove, in 'Landscapes and Myths, Gods and Humans' (pp.281–305), draws out the mythic nature of landscape in a western context. He explores the way in which, in Greek and Roman myth, the natural world and the human beings that engage with it as landscape are given meaning and purpose. Gaia, the surface of the land, results from an elemental union between Ouranos, the sky, and Chthon, the depths. The earth's surface changes with the seasons, responding to the eternal cyclical sky clock. As Gaia partakes of sky and earth, so humans yearn towards Apollo and Dionysus. In the gendering of gods and humans, male Apollonian rationality and sociality subsumes, and makes possible, the natural Dionysian fecundity. On the horizontal, landscape axis, human intervention follows the same cyclical movement from 'nature' (wilderness) to culture, from gatherer-hunter through pastoralism and the cultivated garden to the city, and then, through violence and warfare, back to wilderness. Cosgrove shows how these cyclical myths are reiterated and mapped across a series of discourses especially in the Renaissance and beyond – spatial, social, gender, physiological and artistic.

In the contemporary setting of present-day Britain, this mythic axis, from London through rural England to the rude 'wilderness' of the upland fringes, still structures landscape meanings. And the contemporary reworking of the Gaian myth, with its emphasis on subordination to rather than domination of nature, bypasses the post-Renaissance mechanical philosophies, the controlling lord-of-all-I-survey interventions, and seeks a return to an earlier mythic world, a world in which humans, like the Greek

Daedalus, are always perilously poised, their strivings threatened by hubris and nemesis.

In 'Sexual Cosmology: Nation and Landscape at the Conceptual Interstices of Nature and Culture; or, What does Landscape Really Mean?' (pp.307–343), Kenneth Olwig explores a double narrative. He first analyses the changing meaning of key words like 'nature', 'nation', 'culture', 'scape', 'land' and the way in which they play off each other. He then contextualises the changing meanings and suggests that they are interlinked by a sexual dialectic embodied in a pre-modern cosmology which persists through to the present. Like Cosgrove, Olwig examines classical myths and metaphors that generate an entire cosmology. He too stresses the gendering of the land, the interaction of culture and nature, the tension between the desire for rational explanation and organic biological wisdom, between city and pastoral, state and community.

He then contrasts this with post-Renaissance configurations touched upon by many of the chapters in this volume. The social and economic conditions through which, by which, landscape is flattened into scenery. Celestial nature – increasingly invested in man – controls terrestrial, female nature. The map facilitates the transition from a vertical cosmology to a horizontal cosmology of landscape projected through a square frame. Visual perception is privileged over bodily participation, the male gaze over the female form. All this occurs as the land becomes alienated and commodified.

Finally, we watch the reworking of both Virgilian and post-Renaissance myth in the context of the New World. The native Indian dismissed, the new 'untouched' territory echoes Virgil's pastoral paradise, and, in Jefferson's vision becomes a land of small homesteaders. But where land is commodity, the Jeffersonian dream cannot hold: the 'virgin' land waits to be exploited, and the Jeffersonian grid clamps the contoured surface of the land. Ultimately, Olwig points out, in the burgeoning national parks, the city people return to the 'wilderness' from which both Indian and cultivator have been excluded.

Words define experience, experience takes its meaning from time and place. Words empower action (or inaction), they 'naturalise' social relations. But they are also the product of social relations. We need to know how their meanings have been constructed and used. We can then begin to democratise them.

The reader may be perplexed at the seemingly eclectic coverage offered in this book – prehistoric, historic, contemporary, the overdeveloped and underdeveloped world, town and country – and by some of the juxtapositions. The intention is to force a recognition of the multiplicity of experience through time and space, and at any given moment of time and place; to relativise 'our' own experiences and to recognise both their particularity and that they are part of a process and therefore continually open to change; and, finally, to permit an exploration of the ways in which people, differentially engaged and differentially empowered, appropriate and contest their landscapes.

## Acknowledgement

I would like to thank Danny Miller for introducing me to Naipaul, and for discussing with me what 'roots' might mean to a Trinidadian Indian at the end of Empire.

## References

Cosgrove, D. 1989. 'Geography is everywhere: culture and symbolism in human landscapes', in D. Gregory and R. Walfrid (eds) *Horizons in Human Geography*, London: Macmillan.

Hoskins, W. 1985. *The Making of the English Landscape*, London: Penguin.

Inglis, F. 1977. 'Nation and community: a landscape and its morality', *The Sociological Review*, ns 25, 489–513.

Jackson, J.B. 1985. *Discovering the Vernacular*, New Haven: Yale University Press.

Massey, D. 1991. 'Flexible sexism', *Environment and Planning D: Society and Space*, 26, 31–57.

Mitchell, T. 1989. 'The world as exhibition', *Comparative Studies in Society and History*, 31, 217–36.

Morphy, H. 1988. 'Maintaining cosmic unity: ideology and the reproduction of Yolngu clans', in T. Ingold, D. Riches and J. Woodburn (eds) *Hunters and Gatherers. Property, Power and Ideology*, Oxford: Berg.

Naipaul, V.S. 1987. *The Enigma of Arrival*, London: Penguin.

# Chapter 1

## The Politics of Vision and the Archaeologies of Landscape

*Julian Thomas*

### Introduction

One of the tendencies which might be discerned within the history of archaeology is a gradual shift away from the antiquarian focus on the alienated artefact, towards a concern with social and spatial context. In the present century, this has resulted in both the establishment of a distinct 'social archaeology' (Renfrew 1973; Barrett 1988a), and a widening interest in the settings within which artefacts are encountered. This latter has taken a number of different forms. Ecological and geomorphological approaches have been employed to elaborate the natural circumstances of archaeological sites (e.g. Vita-Finzi 1978), while a behaviouralist tendency has shifted the focus away from the 'site' as a unit of analysis, introducing a concern with 'offsite archaeology' (Foley 1981a, 1981b). Thus the landscape as a whole comes to be seen as a continuous record of human behaviour, co-varying with ecological conditions. Other approaches have drawn upon more developmental traditions of ecological investigation (Godwin 1975; Hoskins 1955) in order to cultivate archaeology as a form of landscape history (Jones 1986). In Britain in particular, a highly empirical school of 'landscape archaeology', dedicated to the surveying and mapping of upstanding cultural features (boundaries, field systems, deserted villages) emerged as a complement to excavation, often helping to fill in details of medieval rural life unavailable from documentary sources (Aston and Rowley 1974). Similar work on the prehistoric periods gradually began to develop a picture of clearance and cultivation before the Romans,

notably in the upland areas (Bowen and Fowler 1978). More
recently, the appearance of greater conceptual sophistication in
this tradition has led to impressive results (e.g. Williamson 1987;
Fleming 1988).

While many of these perspectives concentrate on the environmental or economic conditions surrounding past communities,
this interest is not exclusive. It has long been recognised that the
spatial configuration of archaeological traces must be in some
way related to social realities (Hodder 1978), and contact with
several generations of human geographical theory has resulted
in investigations of past social landscapes, from the spatial-sci-
entific (Clarke 1977) to the structuralist (Fritz 1978). Further, an
awareness of ethnography, and of the character of non-western
cosmologies, has made prehistorians in particular willing to consider ritual or symbolic landscapes (e.g. Bradley 1984; Burl 1987).
At least one recent collection attempts to bring several of these
approaches together, under the rubric of 'Landscape and
Culture' (Wagstaff 1987). It is interesting that at a time when the
different aspects of archaeology (scientific and ecological, social
and cultural, or empirical and historical) are drawing apart from
each other and defining rather different research agendas, the
notion of 'landscape' seems to reunite them on occasion.
Whether this is because it presents a genuine horizon for integration and cooperation, or whether it is simply that the concept is
sufficiently vague (or indeed vacuous, at least in archaeological
usage) that it provides room enough for all is a question which
could be debated. In this contribution, my aim is rather to
express some unease over the use of the landscape concept within archaeology, and to suggest that it be subjected to a degree of
critical scrutiny. In particular, I will stress that landscape is not a
universal concept, applied in the same way by all people at all
times, and thus cannot represent a definitive way of apprehend-
ing the world. In so doing I will rehearse a series of arguments
drawn from various sources. Over these arguments I claim no
authority: I present them in order to consider their implications
for the practice of archaeology. It is quite possible that these
approaches would ultimately prove mutually incompatible,
although in one particular they show some affinity: the claim
that the modern West has developed a particular and distinctive
way of looking, which is deployed against place as it is deployed
against other phenomena.

## Cosgrove on Landscape Painting and the Landscape Idea

The first strand of the argument begins with representation. It is notable that prehistoric and non-western art very often depicts place less in terms of outward appearance than as impression, feel, significance or meaning. These are places experienced from the inside. Yet art history since the Renaissance in the West has been dominated by an imperative to depict the world as realistically as possible. But realism is not simply a self-evident reproduction of reality, and a quantity of pigment arranged on a canvas cannot give direct access to a place. Realist painting freezes place as seen from a particular point of view: it holds out the promise of an imaginary relationship with the world while engaging us in the symbolic (McCabe 1985: 66). The realism of landscape art is one which Denis Cosgrove (1984) has described as being both illusory and ideological, and moreover the product of a particular phase of history. It is the contingent character of a particular way of looking at the world which I want to draw from Cosgrove's account, and the richness of his argument must necessarily lose something in paraphrase. What perhaps needs to be stressed is that his project can be seen as genealogical, in Foucault's sense of the word (1984), charting the trajectory of particular ways of looking and thinking and investigating the emergence and transformation of concepts, rather than presenting a monolithic picture of the western mentality. Seeking to steer such a course through the history of cultural manifestations does not necessarily mean the reduction of history to a single variable, nor does it exhaust the potential of those materials.

The emergence of landscape art is connected with the development of linear perspective, perhaps first used by Brunelleschi and formalised in Alberti's treatise of 1435, *Della Pittura* (Cosgrove 1984: 22). The significance of this development was that it allowed painters to represent a three dimensional world on a two dimensional surface, through a technique which organised represented objects in relation to each other. Yet this technique was regarded not as an artifice, but as a means of revealing truth. Perspective art represents a form of visual control, which freezes time and presents things as they empirically appear to be. At the same time, perspective establishes not merely a set of spatial relations on the canvas, but a fixed relationship between object and subject, locating the viewer outside of the picture, and outside of the relationships being depicted. The viewer is thereby rendered transcendental, outside of history. Landscape painting is thus a representation of place which alienates land, such that it can be appropriated by a gaze which looks in from outside. As such, it privileges vision over the other senses, a tendency which can also be recognised in Renaissance theatre, cartography, and later in Cartesian philosophy, which associates consciousness with vision (Jay 1986). Together, these developments indicate the desire of early modern westerners to render the world intelligible to the eye. Landscape, land appropriated by the disengaged look, is thus a notion which emerges at a particular point in history.

Distance and position construct a particular impression of the world, but are at the same time denied and the view is taken as universal, taking in everything. Because landscape art presents the world from the point of view of the outsider, that which is inside the frame takes on the passive role of object, represented, manipulated and alienated, denied any agency of its own. It is laid bare to the eye, which scans at will across the painted surface. That this form of representation should be established in fifteenth-century northern Italy and Flanders, argues Cosgrove, is no accident. It involves the emergence of a new 'way of looking', a new politics of vision. This politics lies in the development of social relations which allowed land to be looked on as a commodity, disengaged from hereditary patterns of tenure, able to be bought and sold at will. Thus, landscape painting and the idea of landscape emerge hand-in-hand with capitalism.

This prioritisation of vision, its separation from and privileging over the other senses, can be detected in other areas of life, substantiating the claim that we live in a 'specular civilisation'. In discussing the emergence of the modern prison, Foucault (1977: 201) draws special attention to the Panopticon, Jeremy Bentham's design for a circular penitentiary arranged about a central control tower, from where the warders look out unseen into the cells. He says 'the Panopticon is a machine for dissociating the see/being seen dyad: in the peripheric ring, one is totally seen, without ever seeing; in the central tower, one sees everything without ever being seen' (idid.: 202). This laboratory of discipline functions for Foucault as a metaphor for state power in the modern era: watching, cataloguing, collecting data, analysing, defining and dividing up classes of person. The hospital, the school, the factory and the social security system are all varieties of Panopticon, in which the power of the gaze is revealed as more pervasive than domination and repression (Foucault 1979). Similarly, in his book *City of Quartz*, Mike Davis presents a terrifying picture of contemporary Los Angeles as a 'carceral city', dominated by surveillance and racial segregation (Davis 1990: 254). Here the Panopticon serves as the model for the shopping mall, while closed-circuit cameras guard the apartments of the wealthy. Again, this demonstrates not simply the importance attached to vision in our world, but its investment in particular strategies of social control.

### The Gaze, Totalisation and Gender

As a dominant mode of perception within our civilisation, the gaze aspires to be all-seeing, to gather everything in and make it visible. It seeks a total view of social reality. Thus the era of classical natural science is dominated by the notion that making things visible leads to their being understood – the emergence of pathology in medicine being a case in point. Yet as Rosalyn Deutsche (1991) points out, this totalisation under the gaze is a *dream* of unity, for just as the landscape painting sees a place from the position of a single observer, vision is always situated. This recalls Foucault's criticism of 'totalised history': that the claim to be able to present the past as a completed development which can be grasped as a whole requires one to stand outside history itself (Foucault 1984: 87). In a sense, history only remains history when we are ourselves inside it, having inherited a particular set of circumstances, yet able to act to change them. There is a very important tension here between accounts like Harvey's (1989), which claim that political action rests upon an analysis which can understand and explain the world as a whole, and others which require that we act on the basis of imperfect, provisional and local knowledge. These latter might appear to embrace a dangerous relativism, but there remains a very real difference between the recognition that there is a real world and maintaining that it can be totally appropriated metally within a limited set of concepts (Gellner 1985: 84). This distinction becomes particularly important in the debate about postmodernism. There are those who see the postmodern world as one in which the modernist project has collapsed, where all certainty and authenticity are replaced by conditions of ultimate possibility (Lyotard 1984). Others would see this free play of images as no more than a floating superstructure hiding the ever more rapacious mechanisms of capital in an era of flexible accumulation, transnational credit and post-Fordist industrial practices (Jameson 1984). Thus the seductions of hyperreality merely displace legitimation (Massey 1991: 33). Yet between these two positions another argument, made by many feminists, is possible, which allows the significance of a cultural politics. It certainly is important to resist the notion that nothing exists beyond an endless series of groundless images. But at the same time, the world is too complex to fold back in on itself until one is left with the single word 'capitalism'. We live in a capitalist civilisation, in which the mechanisms of capitalist reproduction have intertwined themselves with all aspects of human society: this does not mean that they can all be *reduced* to capitalism as a universal source. In particular, one might suggest that capitalism and patriarchy are deeply bound up with each other, and even that capitalism dictates the form which patriarchy takes at present, without holding that patriarchy is a manifestation of capitalism (Massey 1991).

Claims to 'apocalyptic objectivity', to a transcendental reduction, are shown to be both partial and situated by recent feminist criticism. In particular, the gaze is gendered, ours is a distinctively male way of looking. Dealing with the case of cinema, Laura Mulvey discusses the way in which society's sexual imbalance determines the character of looking (Mulvey 1989). She points to the psychoanalytic insight that visual pleasure may take either the form of scopophilia, 'taking other people as objects, subjecting them to a controlling and curious gaze' (ibid.: 16), or of vicarious association. Thus women on screen become objects of pleasure in looking, while men become subjects of identification. Visual art, too, it has been argued, demonstrates the way in which a particular way of looking structures the representation of the human body, so that women are defined by their to-be-looked-at-ness (Pollock 1988: 54). Like landscape, women are painted by men to become visual commodities, consumed by other men. The male gaze is thus the gaze of the voyeur, taking pleasure without engagement, and the objectivity which it promotes as the basis for a privileged knowledge becomes questionable.

In a recent paper, Susan Ford (1991) has drawn some of the strands of these arguments together, arguing that the way in which we characteristically look at landscape is through the medium of the male gaze, yet positing the possibility of a subversive female way of looking. If we think for a moment about the ways in which archaeologists look at landscape, it may be that we have to face the same charges. The means by which we characteristically represent place, the distribution map, the air photo, the satellite image and the Geographical Information System, are all distinctively specular. They all imply a considerable distance between subject and object, and they all present a picture of past landscapes which the inhabitant would hardly recognise. All attempt to lay the world bare, like Eliot's 'patient etherised upon a table', or like the corpse under the pathologist's knife. In the same way, we seek to dissect landscape, to probe into everything and to make it all visible. Our ideal, then, is a simultaneous perception of all of the significant features of landscape – a kind of intellectual appropriation. Knowledge and power are here closely connected. Given that these methodologies have much in common with modern technologies of surveillance and control, we seem to be seeking to monitor and discipline the past. At best this runs the risk of reproducing a sectional view of that past, biased in favour of the powerful, and of representing it as the whole story, the full picture. At worst, it seems likely to construct an outsider's view of a society in which there were no outsiders, a wholly modern fabrication.

## Archaeology and Specular Landscapes

It is, perhaps, unfair to point to a particular work of archaeology to demonstrate these points, but simply for the sake of argument, let us briefly look at Michael Aston's *Interpreting the Landscape* (1985). The intention here is not to single the book out for disapprobation, since it remains a singularly clear introduction to 'landscape archaeology'. As such, it provides a good example of the approach to past human lifespaces advanced by many archaeologists. In characteristically specular fashion, Aston describes the landscape as a palimpsest of boundaries, mounds, abandoned villages and field systems laid out before us. These are the products of generations of human actors, yet we can only gain a knowledge of them through their works. The people, then, have only a hypothetical status: by awarding the material evidence a status of being more 'real' than the society which produced it, Aston constructs an empiricist position. Nonetheless, he insists that 'we must not lose sight of them and their labours. Our studies must be of people in the landscape, how they have lived, worked, died and worshipped over the millennia' (Aston 1985: 154). However, his examples of these 'people' are a manuscript illustration of a peasant and a 'prehistoric man' labouring on the Somerset Levels. These are individuals rather than social beings, and we are only aware of their existence teleologically, through their works. So while the presence of human beings is accepted, it is only in the anecdotal sense of glimpses and vignettes of past ways of life, scattered amid the dead things of the past. What is missed is any sense that these relics are bound together and given significance by a continuous flow of human conduct.

For Aston, the task of the landscape archaeologist appears to be to detail the titanic forces which surrounded these individuals – population levels, climate, land use patterns, technology, settlement patterns and the organisation of focal places. 'Looked at against this background of natural and technological changes, what can we say about how people lived, what sorts of settlements they inhabited, and what field systems they employed?' (Aston 1985: 151). The kind of ecological/systemic analysis implied sets up a huge Heath-Robinson apparatus, within which human beings have the metaphysical status of the ghosts in the machine. This is thus a 'top down' analysis which seeks to lay out a whole functioning system, detailing a series of constraints which between them define a space in which the missing term in the equation – the people – can one day be made to appear, stepping out of the black box. Structures, fields, climate, soils are all fitted into place, in the belief that given a totalising knowledge of all other factors the missing term in the equation, the absent human presence, must emerge. Yet this is a vain hope: the apparatus remains so much wreckage. As Wylie (1991: 32) demonstrates, it is this insistence upon the primacy of the empirical which has held back any archaeological consideration of gender: women are only added to our picture of the past where osteology or iconography conclusively demonstrate their presence.

## Dwelling and Resisting

Let me now turn from critique to something more constructive. Firstly, I do not suggest that we throw away our distribution maps and air photos because they are tainted with surveillance and voyeurism, but rather that we should recognise that this way we have of looking down on the past as a map laid out for simultaneous perception is only one among many ways of looking. There are two lines of argument which I would like to suggest might lead us to other ways of looking at place, beside what we might call a 'landscape perspective'. The first draws upon the insights of hermeneutic phenomenology and its rejection of the notion that the places where we live are purely external objects (Relph 1985). Such an approach is explicitly concerned with many of the problems which have been voiced here. As Relph suggests, 'To think about the world or the entities within it as abstract things is to render them subject to observation, to make them the object of casual curiosity and to distance oneself from them' (ibid.: 17). There are clear problems in an uncritical acceptance by the archaeologist of what has frequently been derided as a 'touchy-feely' approach to human geography. In particular, the way in which the human subject is often presented as an unproblematic entity to whom the phenomena of the world are disclosed can lead to a decontextualised voluntarism. Hence it is absolutely necessary to place an experiential perspective in the context of historical contingency (Heller 1984: 28). As Heller's work demonstrates, there is no necessary contradiction between a concern with the material conditions of human social life and an emphasis on the structures of preunderstanding which underlie the experience of those conditions by the subject. One might well suggest that such an approach finds an echo within the canonical texts of phenomenology (e.g. Heidegger 1977a), even if the resulting position is one which remains to be worked through in its implications (see Bourdieu 1990, for an attempt to lay some foundations).

This leads us back to the argument concerning totalisation. We have noted the charge which Jameson and Harvey level against recent social theory, that in relinquishing any claim to be able to grasp reality as a conceptual totality, it also surrenders the analytical strength of Marxism to a postmodern conceptual anarchy (see

Jay 1984 for a consideration of the notion of totality in western
Marxist thought). However, it is now possible to flesh out a middle
position which steers a course between the extremes of reduction-
ism and relativism. As already indicated, to deny that we can
appropriate reality within a relatively stable set of linguistic categories is not to deny that there is a real world 'out there', or that this
world is held together by a very complex and changing set of relationships. Nonetheless, the grasp of this world which human subjects achieve is always an imperfect and situated one. For the
subject, the 'worldhood' of the world lies not in a set of scientifical-
ly and geometrically defined relationships, but in meaning and significance (Heidegger 1962: 138). Moreover, the so-called 'objective'
and scientific understandings of the world which we achieve are
elaborated out of and on the basis of these pre-scientific understandings. Where one might part company with phenomenology
would be in insisting that power is deeply implicated in the production of even the most primordial knowledge of the world. In
starting to think about the relationship between past people and
the places which they inhabited, the nature of this everyday experience and understanding of existence is of cardinal importance. We
cannot simply draw out a mapping of structures and boundaries
and hope that their simultaneous spatial relations will inform us
about past people. Space is not merely a container around us, and
buildings are not just geometrical orderings of planes and solids
that surround us. Rather, we *dwell* through these places, we abide
alongside them. Heidegger's term 'dwelling' succinctly describes
the way that people *are* on earth, it is a verb which conveys a sense
of a continuous being which unites the human subjects with their
'environment'. Heidegger intends that by this term we understand
a staying with things, cultivating, building, but also the frame of
mind that arises from being alongside things and 'letting them be'.
We do not dwell because we have built, the world we construct
around us is a part of our dwelling (Heidegger 1977b: 326).
Dwelling involves a lack of distance between people and things, a
lack of casual curiosity, an engagement which is neither conceptualised nor articulated, and which arises through *using* the world
rather than through scrutiny. Our immediate world is characterised by its inconspicuous familiarity – not by its to-be-looked-at-
ness. So it is impossible to begin to look at traces of past human
presence without seeing them from the first as bound up with
human social action and subjectivity. The structures which we

excavate have not simply been affected by discontinuous human actions, they are both the outcome and the site of generation of human projects, and are meaningless if divorced from the structure of *dwelling*. This is not to advocate some form of empathy with past people: the contents of past minds are clearly lost to us. But it is to assert that the relationships which hold past material things together are social relations structured by meaningfulness, not mechanical relations between things. Human beings cannot be 'made to appear' at the end of the analysis: places exist through and for them. Distanced, geometrical, 'outsider's' approaches to space can claim no priority over the social and the experiential, and the one perspective which they offer may be that of a dominant group.

Secondly, if an objective and distanced perspective on landscape has much in common with strategies of monitoring and surveillance, we have to remember that even in modern urban society these strategies are countered by tactics of resistance. Spaces may be produced by faceless powers, but can be consumed by individual subjects in unintended and oppositional ways. Underpasses become skateboard parks, concrete buildings give shelter to buskers. Always fleeting, uncoordinated and momentary, these practices are not integrated through global simultaneous perceptions of space, but sequentially, in personal projects of self-realisation and self-production (Gregory 1990). The ways in which people weave their way through spaces, encountering and interpreting the world, gaining new understandings and recalling past connotations form spatial narratives, individual stories which cannot be encompassed by totalisation (De Certeau 1984). In the same way, we cannot assume that past landscapes were inhabited by integrated and smoothly-running social systems. More likely, we should imagine struggles played out across the tiniest aspects of day-to-day existence. We need to recover the 'spaces of resistance', not just the dominated landscape. People in the past would have used, understood and moved through places in a variety of different ways. Equally, in the present, we cannot privilege one perspective as a total and definitive understanding.

## A Case Study: The Neolithic Landscapes of Avebury

Much of what has been said so far would appear to many archaeologists to be rather abstract, and even removed from their concerns in investigating prehistoric and early historic sites in a broader context. For the sake of illustration, I will briefly discuss the development of the area around Avebury in north Wiltshire during the Neolithic and earliest Bronze Age, the period roughly 3200 to 1600 in uncalibrated radiocarbon years bc (4500–1800 calendar years BC) (1). Elsewhere (Thomas 1991, Chapter 7) I have worked through this material in greater detail, but my aim here is to emphasise the way in which the concerns which I have voiced in this chapter can transform our understanding of prehistory. Specifically, I will stress the way in which the emergence of the monumental complex cannot be understood entirely from plans and distribution maps, but requires a consideration of the positioning of persons in relation to the monuments. Moreover, it has to be recognised that this positioning is differential and graded. Vision is important for the appreciation of these monuments, but in terms of the interplay between what is open to view and what is concealed, which is instrumental in the reproduction of privileged positions with respect to social and cultural knowledge. Thus what is seen has to be understood in the context of movement from place to place, and that of non-visual experiences. Thus my account is not one which seeks to do away with vision, but which emphasises 'being-there', the contextual character of interaction. It follows that I pursue an approach which assumes the presence of people in these places as a first principle: they are not merely an absent presence to be pieced together through analysis.

The modern village of Avebury, set within the huge prehistoric henge monument, lies at the headwaters of the River Kennet. Topographically, it is situated within a block of chalk upland from where the land drops abruptly to the north and west, into the Thames and Avon vales (See Map 1.1). The chalk rises somewhat to the south, onto the Bishop's Cannings Downs, before dropping into the greensand Vale of Pewsey, while to the east are the higher Marlborough Downs. The Avebury region is thus a relatively definable topographic unit which corresponds with a remarkable concentration of prehistoric monuments, set on and around the low chalk spurs which rise from the Kennet. While these monuments date to the Neolithic period, it is clear that the area had been frequented by hunting and gathering groups in the preceding Mesolithic. Whittle (1990a: 107) suggests that in the Mesolithic the main focus of settlement had been on

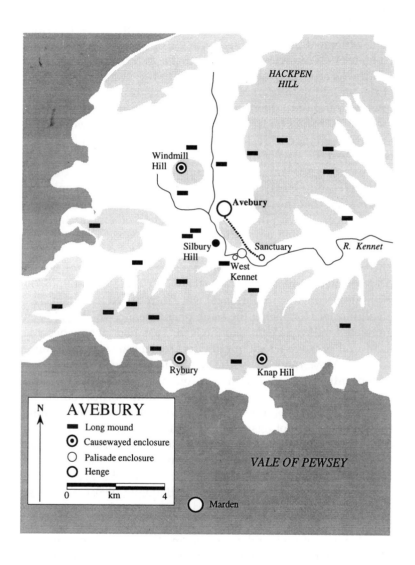

**Map 1.1 One way of looking at Avebury. The distribution of major prehistoric monuments in the Avebury area. Land above 183m and below 152m shaded.**

the lower reaches of the Kennet around Hungerford, with the Avebury area forming a peripheral zone, sporadically visited for hunting and flint extraction. The infilling of the area for permanent settlement thus coincided with the opening of the Neolithic. Holgate (1988), however, indicates that a shift of population onto the downs around Avebury had already begun in the latest part of the Mesolithic, as part of a general move away from the damp lowlands and onto the downs of Hampshire and Wiltshire and the Upper Thames terraces. If this were the case, the evidence for an abrupt change in residence, land use and thus subsistence economy at the start of the Neolithic would be reduced.

This is significant in that recent accounts (Thomas 1988a; Entwistle and Grant 1989) have questioned the conventional assumption that the opening of the Neolithic in Britain is essentially concerned with the wholesale adoption of a mixed farming economy, to which cultural innovations are secondary (Case 1969; Dennell 1983). In contrast, we might now see this phase as one in which a set of interlinked cultural practices (of which domesticated animals and plants were only one element, initially of limited economic importance) were introduced to Britain. The Neolithic, far from being the same phenomenon which had been generated millennia before in the Near East, had by now become a cultural package which might effect social transformation once adopted. Most importantly, the Neolithic 'package' was not composed entirely of abstract ideas, but was sedimented in and reproduced through a series of material culture forms: communal tombs and other monuments, pottery vessels, new forms of stone tools. As anthropologists have begun to point out, the social importance of material things in pre-literate societies is often that they are futural. Artefacts assume a projection forward of social relationships, and often seek to influence the character of connectedness between past and present (Battaglia 1990: 6). They are 'vehicles for the active reconstruction of remembrance, lending that inherently fluid process an aura of stability' (ibid.: 10). The maintenance of social relationships involves a remembering, of debts, obligations, genealogies, which are themselves narratives. The cultural innovations of the Neolithic were, among other things, a technology of memory which was inserted into existing social relations. Material things condense the social history of a community, the stories of individuals, and through their persistence and materiality project them forwards. Importantly, many of the new artefacts of the Neolithic are connected either with food or with the dead. New foods (grain and domestic beef) and ways of eating (from pottery vessels) intervened into events of people coming together to eat, transforming them into occasions for the learning and remembering of cultural rules. Similarly, monumental tombs introduced the ancestral dead into the habitual space of a community, and the practice of feasting outside the tomb drew together the remembrance of the dead with the remembrance of ties among the living.

The Avebury area contains both purely earthen long mounds, sometimes containing timber mortuary structures, and mounds of the Cotswold–Severn type, with a stone chamber at one end (Barker 1984). Very often, these kinds of monuments appear to have been located on sites which had already been occupied in the Mesolithic (Thomas 1988b: 551). At the site of Hazleton North on the Cotswolds, for instance, the mound had been constructed over the remains of a Mesolithic camp with evidence for tool preparation, as well as a Neolithic midden and timber structure (Saville 1990: 13–22). In the Avebury area, excavated monuments like South Street and Horslip have similarly provided traces of a Mesolithic presence (Ashbee, Smith and Evans 1979: 218, 269). Smith (1984: 114) interpreted these as an indication of Mesolithic involvement in early agriculture, but this may be making too much of rather ephemeral evidence (Whittle 1990a: 103). We might suggest that Mesolithic communities had built up a particular habitual way of moving across the downs in hunting and procurement of raw materials, and with it an understanding of place. Just as the Neolithic introduced new artefacts into domestic and communal transactions, tombs were introduced onto the land in locations whose significance had already been produced by an existing pattern of life. So while the Neolithic can be seen as bringing about a transformation of indigenous society, it was a transformation which took place through the insinuation of new cultural media into existing rhythms of movement and understandings of the world.

One tomb in particular in the Avebury district has provided a rich body of information concerning the activities associated with these monuments: the West Kennet long barrow (Piggott 1962). The careful excavation of a particularly large and well-preserved site sets the barrow apart from others in the area, although the particular features of the enhancement and elaboration of the external fabric of the monument and a complex filling of the chamber area are by no means unique. At the more ruinous site of Millbarrow, Whittle's excavation demonstrated that the mound had been constructed in two phases, each with a separate set of ditches, the later concentric to the earlier. Thus rebuilding had resulted in a more substantial and imposing mound, which had evidently been revetted with a peristalith of upright sarsen stones. The remains of the simple stone chamber contained sherds of later Neolithic Peterborough Ware, indicating depositional activities postdating the introduction of burials to the chamber (Whittle 1989). Both of these features are seen more vividly at West Kennet. It seems likely that an original mound of modest proportions was elongated at some stage, producing a monument which dominates a prominent ridge crest above the Kennet valley floor (Thomas and Whittle 1986: 136). At the very end of the long period of use, the chambers were blocked off by the erection of three extremely large sarsens across the entrance (Barrett 1988b: 34). Paradoxically, this has the effect of enhancing the appearance of the façade, making the monument still more imposing when seen from a distance. One can thus distinguish between the internal and external significance of the monument (Thomas and Whittle 1986: 135). The actions and understandings evoked by the tomb differ according to whether one views it from a distance, takes part in observances in the forecourt, or is granted access to the chamber and intimate knowledge of the chamber contents. The inside/outside division thus sets up a graded field of knowledge (Thomas 1990), and it has been suggested that access to the inner recesses of the tomb and the materials contained there was restricted to a privileged social group (Thomas and Whittle 1986: 137). Evidently, the importance afforded to these different perspectives shifted through time, so that the tomb eventually became a monument to be looked at rather than entered, whose external significance was privileged over a hidden and denied interior.

The initial deposits within the complex transepted chambers at West Kennet consist largely of human bones (Piggott 1962: 24–6). It seems likely that some of these were deposited as articulated and fleshed bodies, and that individual bones were later removed (Thomas and Whittle 1986: 134). This accords with a broader pattern in Neolithic Britain, in which the bones of the dead (principally longbones and skulls) passed from hand to hand and place to place as objects of considerable symbolic importance (Thomas 1991: 112–3). Later, 'secondary' deposits in the West Kennet chambers consisted of alternate layers of clean chalk and burnt organic soil containing potsherds, flint tools and animal and human bones. It has been suggested that these represent the remains of repeated ritual practices carried out inside the chambers, and indicate a continuous if sporadic use of the tomb interior from the time when the original deposits were introduced (Thomas and Whittle 1986). As Barrett points out (1991: 8), these practices would have involved a repeated reordering and reworking of the deposited materials in the course of the reproduction of sectional knowledge. Indeed, ritual activities frequently involve a practical remembering effected through the experience and manipulation of symbolic material items (Barth 1987: 75). Objects which condense aspects of cosmology enable meanings and practices to be recreated. At the same time, things which are polysemous and networked into multiple schemes of classification are inherently mysterious and require explanation. Thus a secluded and restricted space like the chamber of a megalithic tomb is an ideal site for the recreation of, and initiation into, arcane and restricted social knowledge. Again, this emphasises the distinction between the monumental exterior of the tomb as a landmark freely available to view from the valley, and its hidden, enigmatic contents.

If the bodies of the dead were introduced into the chambers whole, and then partly or wholly disordered, it follows that the tomb was less a place of resting than a site of transformation. In being broken down into their constituent parts, the remains were being changed into a different kind of being. In this respect, there is a further element of continuity of intent shown in the secondary deposits which fill the chambers. The distribution of sherds of particular pottery vessels, in particular Piggott's (1962: 38–40) P12 and P15, suggests that they were deliberately smashed against the forecourt and passage orthostats before individual sherds were introduced into the chambers (observation based upon material and notebook in Devizes Museum). Moreover, many of the sherds from the chambers have fresh breaks (Thomas and Whittle 1986: 145). This deposition of large numbers of sherds of Peterborough Ware, together with animal bones, may well be connected with feasting activities in the immediate vicinity of the tomb, but the important point here is that the later deposits in some way mirror and repeat the original treatment of human bodies in the first use of the monument. The pottery vessels may or may not have actually represented symbolic substitutes for human bodies (broken into pieces, their contents 'spilled', reduced to bones or sherds which might then be reordered), but the repeated destruction and deposition allowed the possibility of a periodic recreation of the significance of the tomb, through a series of actions which mimicked the primary treatment and circulation of human bones. Elsewhere in the region, deposits of large numbers of smashed pots have been located, preserved beneath the later burial mounds of West Overton G6b and Avebury G55 (Smith 1965a; Smith and Simpson 1964). These traces indicate that the destruction of pots (both here and in the forecourt at West Kennet) was a relatively 'public' and visible practice, in contrast to the deposition and reordering of remains inside the tomb. In the case of West Kennet, then, 'visible' outside and 'hidden' inside were united through ritual practices which withdrew materials from circulation in the outside world (pots, dead people), and then performed a series of operations upon them in seclusion whose details were known to a restricted group within society. In a way, this reflects the treatment of human bodies within a number of Cotswold–Severn tombs, where the corpse would be laid out in the relatively public space of the passage entrance and allowed to rot down, before individual bones (especially skulls and longbones) were moved through to the chamber and rearranged in stacks or lined up along the chamber walls (Thomas 1988b: 547). This uniting of the universally known and the exclusive through a transition from public to private space is a principle which we will see repeated in a number of later monuments. Socially, it is clear that the power attached to ritual knowledge derives in part from the awareness of the community at large of the existence of 'secrets' which they are denied (Barth 1987).

The sequence of secondary deposits in the West Kennet chambers displays a process by which the space in which the deposition of pottery and other materials is gradually restricted, eventually coming to focus on the north-east chamber alone (Thomas and Whittle 1986: 148). At the same time, a number of other tombs in the vicinity including Manton Down and Millbarrow were filled in or otherwise blocked. These phenomena together suggest a process in which the available 'theatres' for the reproduction of secret knowledge, and thus its circulation within society, were further restricted. In the middle part of the third millennium bc, at least two new long mounds were built in the Avebury area which contained no burial deposit, at Beckhampton Road and South Street (radiocarbon dated to 2517 ± 90 bc and 2580 ± 80 bc respectively) (Ashbee, Smith and Evans 1979). Thus as some of the older monuments were blocked off as places to be entered, and their 'inner' significance effaced at the expense of their outer form, new structures were built which were *exclusively* to be looked at from the outside. These new monuments are located on the Kennet floodplain, south-west of Avebury (where no monument yet existed). Thus they, the elaborated mound at West Kennet and the huge barrow at East Kennet would all have been visible as one moved through the valley bottom towards the enclosed site at Windmill Hill, which appears to have become a pre-eminent location by the mid-third millennium. From this time onward it can be argued that visibility as one moves along the valley floor became a major factor in the location and character of monumental constructions.

Three causewayed enclosures had been built in the Avebury region in the earlier part of the third millennium: Rybury and Knap Hill overlooking the Vale of Pewsey and Windmill Hill facing north-west across the Avon plain. Elsewhere (Thomas 1991: 32–8), I have suggested that the causewayed enclosures of southern Britain were commonly built in transitional locations, away from areas frequented in everyday activities. As such, they served as places for seasonal gatherings of large numbers of people, where practices perceived as hazardous or polluting (the acquisition of goods brought from a distance; the treatment of the newly dead; communal feasting and the associated slaughter of livestock; dealings with strangers) could be engaged in within a bounded space. The layout and situation of Windmill Hill accord with this interpretation. The site consists of three concentric circuits of interupted ditches, which effectively create a hierarchical division of space, and possibly of any congregation of people entering the monument (Evans 1988: 92). The most likely entrance route lies to the north-east, where the slope of the hill is steepest and where the ditches are most closely-set in relation to each other (ibid.: 90). At this point, strangers admitted to the site would be most able to appreciate that they were entering a nested series of concentric spaces defined by banks and ditches. The ditches themselves represented more than a mere quarry for bank material, constituting receptacles for the highly formal and structured deposition of cultural materials (Smith 1965b: 9). It is suggested that these acts of deposition served to enhance the symbolic importance of the ditch circuit as a barrier or demarcation. A cultural repertoire which included potsherds, animal bones and human skull fragments was drawn upon in order to produce a conceptual ordering of space. All of these materials are elements in the Neolithic cultural system which we have already discussed, deployed here as a means of eliciting a particular understanding of a place. The awareness that these were remnants of past meals and gatherings, and of dead people again played upon memory, reminding visitors that this was a place in which particular kinds of behaviour were expected and appropriate.

While Windmill Hill may have been the place at which both inhabitants and strangers gathered at auspicious junctures during the mid-third millennium bc, in the period 2200–2000 bc new monuments were constructed on the valley bottom. Silbury Hill, the largest mound of human origin in Europe, appears to have been built in four continuous stages over the period 2150–1850 bc (Atkinson 1970; Whittle, forthcoming). Despite its imposing size, it is notable that its position to the south-west of Waden Hill is by no means prominent (Whittle, forthcoming). It could easily have been placed in a more suitable location to dominate the surrounding country. The failure of a series of excavations to find either a burial or any form of mortuary structure beneath the mound has also caused some consternation. I suggest that, like Beckhampton Road, South Street and the later phases of the West Kennet long barrow, Silbury Hill is a monument which was intended to attract the eye of the onlooker from a distance, as he or she passed up the valley. Moreover, Silbury was so positioned that it could not be seen from all directions at once: it is actually invisible from much of the area north and west of Waden Hill. Thus by the end of the third millennium the monuments of the Avebury area were intended to be seen in sequence rather than simultaneously, forming a kind of spatial narrative, each structure revealed in turn. Intriguingly, the very top of Silbury Hill would have been visible from the Obelisk, a large upright stone inside the Avebury henge (Devereux 1991: 895), prompting the question of whether activities in the stone circle and on top of the mound were intended to be intervisible.

The construction of the Avebury henge, a huge enclosure with four entrances and a bank set outside of the ditch, was roughly contemporary with that of Silbury Hill. There are indications, however, that the monument was built in two phases. The structure today contains a large stone circle, which itself surrounds two lesser circles (see Figure 1.1) and is linked to an Avenue of paired stone uprights which runs for roughly 2.5 km down the valley away from the henge. However, recent geophysical survey has revealed traces of a possible timber circle in the north of the north-east quadrant of the site (Ucko *et al.* 1991: 227), while Gray's excavation of the bank produced evidence that it had been constructed in two phases, separated by a turf-line (Gray 1934). Gray's archive also contains a section drawing which shows the ditch cutting an earlier feature, possibly a less substantial ditch (J. Pollard, personal communication). This evidence indicates that in its first phase, Avebury represented a bank and ditch enclosure with internal timber settings, similar to the henges at Durrington Walls, Wiltshire, and Mount Pleasant, Dorset (Wainwright and Longworth 1971; Wainwright 1979). The earliest structure at the Sanctuary on Overton Hill, which consisted of a series of concentric timber circles, was probably roughly contemporary with this monument (Cunnington 1931). If, as seems likely, the early features at Avebury are dated by the radiocarbon assay of c. 2100 bc (Whittle 1991: 260), then the redigging of the ditch, the replacement of timber uprights with the stone circles, the introduction of stones to the Sanctuary and the construction of the Kennet Avenue linking the two monuments was probably carried out as a single episode of building, no more than two centuries later. As Pollard (1992) points out, the timbers of the Sanctuary were probably still standing when the stones were erected, elaborating rather than replacing the wooden monument. While the pottery from under the bank at Avebury includes sherds of the Ebbsfleet style of Peterborough Ware, that from the 'occupation site' on the Kennet Avenue (which is held to be contemporary with the erection of the stones: see Smith 1965b: 212) includes sherds of the later Fengate style. In addition, Gray states that sherds of Beaker pottery were found among the packing stones of one of the uprights of the Longstones Cove, a structure which may have been linked to the Avebury henge by a second avenue (Gray 1934: 101). On balance, it seems unlikely that the connection of a number of monuments in the Avebury area by avenues of stones took place before about 2000 bc.

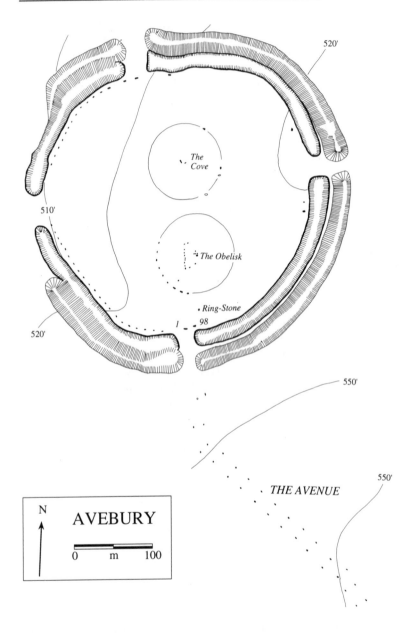

520'

510'

520'

The
Cove

The Obelisk

Ring-Stone

98

550'

THE AVENUE

550'

N

AVEBURY

0          m          100

**Figure 1.1  The Avebury henge and the final section of the Kennet Avenue.**

**Figure 1.2** A reconstruction of the view into the Avebury henge through the southern entrance (based on a scanned image of the present-day landscape).

The significance of this development is that while the monuments of the later third millennium may have been laid out in such a way as to be disclosed in a given sequence, the construction of what amounts to a processional way ties and defines the route to be taken more closely. Entering from the east, the Sanctuary would represent a distinctive mark of the start of the progress towards the henge. As a circle to stone and timber uprights *without* a ditch, it may have been intended that one moved through it in a particular way (Pollard 1992), but its unbounded character suggests that its role was to admit rather than to exclude. From here, the Avenue prescribes a path around Overton Hill, in sight of West Kennet and Silbury, before turning northwards towards the henge. As such, it acts as a guide to the approved way of moving through the valley (*not* carrying on west to Silbury), insinuating rather than forcing a particular passage. Like all of the architectural and symbolic cues which we have discussed, the Avenue served as a guide to the correct way to act for those submitting themselves to approved rules of order, rather than forcing particular acts upon the unwilling. For much

of the course of the Avenue, the Avebury henge is invisible.
Along the stretch which leads past the east side of Waden Hill,
the bank of the monument is effectively hidden by a low ridge
which rises to the east of the Avenue. Only when the Avenue
starts to rise up above about 540 feet above sea level does the
bank suddenly become visible. It is at precisely this point, about
400m from the entrance to the henge, that the Avenue abruptly
changes its direction, swinging round to the west. This path takes
one onto a flank about 250m outside of the south entrance to the
henge. Moving in this direction takes one across the entrance,
and if one turns one's head towards the monument, very little
can be seen of the interior. Much is hidden from here by the pro-
truding eastern bank terminal. About 85m outside of the
entrance, the course of the Avenue again swings to the right, back
towards the entrance (see Figure 1.2). Possibly, given the relatively distant spacing of the stones at the change of direction an
option exists between carrying on around outside the monument,
or turning and entering. If the latter course is taken, one now has
the first opportunity to look in through the entrance to the henge.
However, one's view is restricted by the particularly close-set
banks, and beyond this is impeded by the especially large stones
1 and 98 of the outer circle. It is particularly notable that these
two stones and the uprights of the southern inner stone circle
effectively shield the Obelisk from view from the Avenue and
entrance. If one today stands at the site of the Obelisk and looks
south, the whole of the area between the bank terminals is
obscured by standing stones. Entering between banks, ditches
and stones, one would now face the southern stone circle. Ahead
and to the right would be the Ring Stone, or perhaps a rather
larger stone which originally stood in the same socket (Smith
1965b: 102–3). If this constituted a barrier of any sort, one would
again have been faced with the same choice as on entering the
earthwork: enter the circle or carry on past on the left hand side.
At the focus of the south circle stood the Obelisk, a monolith of
considerable size (Smith 1965b: 198). To the north of this upright
were a number of small pits, of prehistoric date but containing no
artefacts. If the digging of these pits (and deposition of organic
materials?) were to have been part of ritual practices undertaken
within the circle, they would have been hidden from the view of
anyone entering the henge from the Avenue by the Obelisk itself.
Passing by the circle, its uprights would now only partially

impede vision, but inside this and surrounding the Obelisk was another, more angular and more close-set arrangement of uprights. The Obelisk thus stood at the centre of a series of nested spaces, separated by barriers which impeded rather than totally closed off access, and which rendered activities at the centre obscure and partial to the gaze rather than totally invisible. The impression one gains is again one of access to spaces and to knowledge being graded rather than there being a binary division within society.

North from here stood the northern stone circle, again focused upon a central stone setting. Here the central feature was a cove of three large stones, defining three sides of a box open to the north-east. Approaching from the south entrance, and particularly from having passed by the southern circle, vision into the Cove would be restricted by the stones of the circle and of the Cove itself. Interestingly, Burl (1990: 7) suggests that stone coves may derive from the orthostatic chambers of megalithic tombs. Just as the arrangement at West Kennet sets up a distinction between the restricted chamber space and the forecourt, the 44 square metres of the Cove represent the most restricted space within a hierarchy of zones (Cove<Northern Circle<Inside Henge<Outside Henge). Thus the Avebury henge serves to draw in far more people than the chambered tombs through its sheer size, but at the same time its architecture functions to classify them more rigorously through their movements and access to knowledge and performance. As with the tomb, the architecture of the monument allows a complex set of practices to be carried out at a given time, in such a way as to produce simultaneously an impression of social unity and yet reproduce differential access to knowledge. A similar situation may exist with the newly-excavated palisaded enclosures on the floodplain beneath the West Kennet barrow (Whittle and Smith 1990; Whittle 1991), of rather later date than the Avebury henge. The larger of these, of c. 200m diameter, consisted of two concentric timber palisades, while the smaller contained an internal two-ring palisade structure, 40m in diameter (Whittle 1991: 257). In each case, animal bones had been packed around the substantial posts of the palisades, recalling earlier practices at Windmill Hill, while a number of radial fence lines extended from both structures. Evidently, the intention was to construct a set of conceptually separate and mutually secluded contexts for action.

## Conclusion

While the treatment of the Avebury material has been brief, it has, I hope, demonstrated the importance of a recognition of a continuous human presence among the structures studied by archaeologists. I have suggested that in a period of gradual social hierarchisation, power was at least in part vested in access to certain forms of knowledge. This knowledge was made possible by the introduction of a set of cultural resources to Britain at the start of the Neolithic period, resources which were elaborated and transformed over time in accordance with local power strategies. Differentials in access to both power and knowledge in these societies were not absolute, however, and we might imagine each individual subject positioned in a web of power/knowledge relations. Thus while particular individuals might gain entry into the more secluded parts of these monuments, and be initiated into the cardinal secrets of the community, those denied these privileges would have understandings of their own. The potential which this implies for tension and conflict between social orders is an aspect which I have barely touched on here. It should be clear that since this monumental architecture and ritual practice serves to guide movement and recall cultural meanings, resistance, disobedience and alternate understandings could easily emerge. The possibility of a polyvocal 'reading' of a prehistoric monument is an interesting one.

## Acknowledgements

I would like to thank Chris Philo, who provided access to much of the literature, and Susan Ford, whose paper originally started me thinking along these lines. Neither should be held responsible for the wayward direction I have followed.

## References

Ashbee, P., Smith, I.F. and Evans, J.G. 1979. 'Excavation of three long barrows near Avebury', *Proceedings of the Prehistoric Society* 45, 207–300.

Aston, M. 1985. *Interpreting the Landscape: Landscape Archaeology in Local Studies*, London: Batsford.

_____Rowley, T. 1974. *Landscape Archaeology: an Introduction to Fieldwork Techniques on Post-Roman Landscapes,* Newton Abbot: David & Charles.

Atkinson, R.J.C. 1970. 'Silbury Hill, 1969–70', *Antiquity* 44, 313–14.

Barker, C.T. 1984. 'The long mounds of the Avebury region', *Wiltshire Archaeological Magazine* 79, 7–38.

Barrett, J.C. 1988a. 'Fields of discourse – reconstituting a social archaeology', *Critique of Anthropology* 7 (3), 5–16.

_____1988b. 'The living, the dead, and the ancestors: Neolithic and Early Bronze Age mortuary practices', in J.C. Barrett and I.A. Kinnes (eds) *The Archaeology of Context in the Neolithic and Bronze Age,* 30–41, Sheffield: Department of Archaeology and Prehistory.

_____1991. 'Towards an archaeology of ritual', in P. Garwood, D. Jennings, R. Skeates and J. Toms (ed.) *Sacred and Profane,* 1–9, Oxford: Oxford University Committee for Archaeology.

Barth, F. 1987. *Cosmologies in the Making: A Generative Approach to Cultural Variation in Inner New Guinea,* Cambridge: Cambridge University Press.

Battaglia, D. 1990. *On the Bones of the Serpent: Person, Memory and Mortality in Sabarl Island Society,* Chicago: University of Chicago.

Bourdieu, P. 1990. *The Political Ontology of Martin Heidegger,* Cambridge: Polity Press.

Bowen, C. and Fowler, P. 1978. *Prehistoric Land Allotment,* Oxford: British Archaeological Reports.

Bradley, R.J. 1984. *The Social Foundations of Prehistoric Britain,* London: Longmans.

Burl, H.A.W. 1987. *The Stonehenge People,* London: Dent.

_____1990. 'Coves: structural enigmas of the Neolithic', *Wiltshire Archaeological Magazine* 82, 1–18.

Case, H.J. 1969. 'Neolithic explanations', *Antiquity* 43, 176–186.

Clarke, D.L. (ed.) 1977. *Spatial Archaeology,* London: Academic Press.

Cosgrove, D. 1984. *Social Formation and Symbolic Landscape,* London: Croom Helm.

Cunnington, M.E. 1931. 'The 'Sanctuary' on Overton Hill, near Avebury', *Wiltshire Archaeological Magazine* 45, 300–5.

Davies, M. 1990. *City of Quartz,* London: Verso.

De Certeau, M. 1984. *The Practice of Everyday Life,* Berkeley: University of California.

Dennell, R.W. 1983. *European Economic Prehistory,* London: Academic.

Deutsche, R. 1991. 'Boys town', *Environment and Planning D: Society and Space* 9, 5–30.

Devereux, P. 1991. 'Three-dimensional aspects of apparent relationships between selected natural and artificial features within the topography of the Avebury complex', *Antiquity* 65, 894–9.

Entwistle, R. and Grant, A. 1989. 'The evidence for cereal cultivation and animal husbandry in the southern British Neolithic and Bronze Age', in A. Milles, D. Williams and N. Gardner (eds) *The Beginnings of Agriculture*, 203–15, Oxford: British Archaeological Reports.

Evans, C. 1988. 'Acts of enclosure: a consideration of concentrically-organised causewayed enclosures', in J.C. Barrett and I.A. Kinnes (eds) *The Archaeology of Context in the Neolithic and Bronze Age: Recent Trends*, 85–96, Sheffield: Department of Archaeology and Prehistory.

Fleming, A. 1988. *The Dartmoor Reaves*, London: Batsford.

Foley, R. 1981a. *Off-Site Archaeology and Human Adaptation in East Africa*, Oxford: British Archaeological Reports.

_____1981b. 'A model of regional archaeological structure', *Proceedings of the Prehistoric Society*, 47, 1–7.

Ford, S. 1991. 'Landscape revisited: a feminist reappraisal', in C. Philo (compiler) *New Word, New Worlds: Reconceptualising Social and Cultural Geography*, 151–5, Lampeter: Saint David's University College.

Foucault, M. 1977. *Discipline and Punish*, New York: Vintage Books.

_____1979. 'Governmentality', *Ideology and Consciousness* 6, 5–21.

_____1984. 'Nietzsche, genealogy, history', in P. Rabinow (ed.) *The Foucault Reader*, 76–100, Harmondsworth: Peregrine.

Fritz, J. 1978. 'Palaeopsychology today: ideational systems and human adaptation in prehistory', in C. Redman *et al.* (eds) *Social Archaeology: Beyond Subsistence and Dating*, 37–60, London: Academic Press.

Gellner, E. 1985. *Relativism and the Social Sciences*, Cambridge: Cambridge University Press.

Godwin, H. 1975. *The History of the British Flora*, Cambridge: Cambridge University Press.

Gray, H. St. G. 1934. 'The Avebury excavations, 1908–1922', *Archaeologia* 84, 99–162.

Gregory, D. 1990. 'Chinatown, part three? Soja and the missing spaces of social theory', *Strategies* 3, 40–104.

Harvey, D. 1989. *The Condition of Postmodernity: An Enquiry into the Origins of Cultural Change*, Oxford: Blackwell.

Heidegger, M. 1962. *Being and Time*, Oxford: Blackwell.

_____1977a. 'Letter on humanism', in D.F. Krell (ed.) *Martin Heidegger: Basic Writings*, 189–242, London: Routledge and Kegan Paul.

_____1977b. 'Building dwelling thinking', in D.F. Krell (ed.) *Martin Heidegger: Basic Writings*, 319–40, London: Routledge and Kegan Paul.

Heller, A. 1984. *Everyday Life*, London: Routledge and Kegan Paul.

Hodder, I.R. 1978. 'Social organisation and human interaction: the development of some tentative hypotheses in terms of material culture' in I.R. Hodder (ed.) *The Spatial Organisation of Culture*, 199–270, London: Duckworth.

Holgate, R. 1988. *Neolithic Settlement of the Thames Basin*, Oxford: British Archaeological Reports.

Hoskins, W.G. 1955. *The Making of the English Landscape*, London: Hodder and Stoughton.

Jameson, F. 1984. 'Post-modernism or the cultural logic of late-capitalism', *New Left Review* 146, 53–93.

Jay, M. 1984. *Marxism and Totality: the Adventures of a Concept from Lukács to Habermas*, Berkeley: University of California.

――1986. 'In the empire of the gaze: Foucault and the denigration of vision in twentieth-century French thought', in D.C. Hoy (ed.) *Foucault: A Critical Reader*, 175–204, Oxford: Blackwell.

Jones, M. 1986. *England Before Domesday*, London: Batsford.

Lyotard, J.F. 1984. *The Postmodern Condition: A Report on Knowledge*, Manchester: Manchester University Press.

Massey, D. 1991. 'Flexible sexism', *Environment and Planning D: Society and Space* 9, 31–57.

McCabe, C. 1985. 'Theory and film: principles of realism and pleasure', in C. McCabe, *Theoretical Essays: Film, Linguistics, Lierature*, 58–81, Manchester: Manchester University Press.

Mulvey, L. 1989. 'Visual pleasure and narrative cinema', in L. Mulvey, *Visual and Other Pleasures*, 14–26, London: Macmillan.

Piggott, S. 1962. *The West Kennet Long Barrow*, London: HMSO.

Pollard, J. 1992. 'The Sanctuary, Overton Hill, Wiltshire: a reassessment', *Proceedings of the Prehistoric Society* 58, 213–20

Pollock, G. 1988. 'Modernity and the spaces of femininity', in G. Pollock, *Vision and Difference: Femininity, Feminism and the Histories of Art*, 50–90, London: Routledge.

Relph, E. 1985. 'Geographical experiences and being-in-the-world: the phenomenological origins of geography', in D. Seamon and R. Mugerauer (eds) *Dwelling, Place and Environment*, 15–32, New York: Columbia University.

Renfrew, A.C. 1973. *Social Archaeology*, Southampton: Southampton University.

Saville, A. 1990. *Hazleton North: The Excavation of a Neolithic Long Cairn of the Cotswold–Severn Group*, London: English Heritage.

Smith, I.F. 1965a. 'Excavation of a bell barrow, Avebury G.55', *Wiltshire Archaeological Magazine* 60, 24–46.

――1965b. *Windmill Hill and Avebury*, Oxford: Clarendon.

―― and Simpson, D.D.A. 1964. 'Excavation of three Roman tombs and a prehistoric pit on Overton Down', *Wiltshire Archaeological Magazine* 59, 68–85.

Smith, R.W. 1984. 'The ecology of Neolithic farming systems as exemplified by the Avebury region of Wiltshire', *Proceedings of the Prehistoric Society* 50, 99–120.

Thomas, J.S. 1988a. 'Neolithic explanations revisited: the Mesolithic-Neolithic transition in Britain and south Scandinavia', *Proceedings of the Prehistoric Society* 54, 59–66.

――1988b. 'The social significance of Cotswold–Severn burial rites', *Man* 23, 540–59.

_____1990. 'Monuments from the inside: the case of the Irish megalithic tombs', *World Archaeology* 22, 168–78.

_____1991. *Rethinking the Neolithic,* Cambridge: Cambridge University Press.

_____and Whittle, A.W.R. 1986. 'Anatomy of a tomb: West Kennet revisited', *Oxford Journal of Archaeology* 5, 129–56.

Ucko, P., Hunter, M., Clark, A.J. and David, A. 1991. *Avebury Reconsidered: From the 1660s to the 1990s*, London: Unwin Hyman.

Vita-Finzi, C. 1978. *Archaeological Sites in their Setting*, London: Thames and Hudson.

Wainwright, G.J. 1979. *Mount Pleasant, Dorset; Excavations 1970–71*, London: Society of Antiquaries.

_____and Longworth, I. 1971. *Durrington Walls: Excavations 1966–1968*, London: Society of Antiquaries.

Wagstaff, M. (ed.) 1987. *Landscape and Culture*, Oxford: Blackwell.

Whittle, A.W.R. 1988. *Windmill Hill 1988: Preliminary Report on Excavations of the Neolithic Causewayed Enclosure*. MS.

_____1989. *Millbarrow 1989: Preliminary Report on Excavations of the Neolithic Chambered Tomb*. MS.

_____1990a. 'A model for the Mesolithic-Neolithic transition in the upper Kennet Valley, north Wiltshire', *Proceedings of the Prehistoric Society*, 56, 101–10.

_____1990b. 'A pre-enclosure burial at Windmill Hill, Wiltshire', *Oxford Journal of Archaeology* 9, 25–28.

_____1991. 'A late Neolithic complex at West Kennet, Wiltshire, England', *Antiquity* 65, 256–62.

_____forthcoming. Silbury Hill, Wiltshire: excavations in 1968–70 by R.J.C. Atkinson.

_____and Smith, R. 1990. 'West Kennet', *Current Archaeology* 10, 363–365.

Williamson, T. 1987. 'Early co-axial field systems on the East Anglian boulder clays', *Proceedings of the Prehistoric Society* 53, 419–32.

Wylie, A. 1991. 'Gender theory and the archaeological record: why is there no archaeology of gender?', in J. Gero and M. Conkey (eds) *Engendering Archaeology: Women and Prehistory*, 31–54, Oxford: Blackwell.

# Chapter 2

## Art, Architecture, Landscape [Neolithic Sweden]

*Christopher Tilley*

### Introduction

In this chapter I wish to consider megalithic tombs in two contrasting ways. The first, is to consider these monuments in terms of a phenomenology of our contemporary experience, the manner in which we perceive megaliths today. The second is the way in which these stone structures can be understood to have acted in terms of their past life-world. There is, of course, some considerable tension between such different interpretative projects. But rather than being simply left with a sense of incoherence and incompatibility I want to try and suggest that the former perspective feeds into and helps develop the latter and vice versa. Both require a consideration of the relationship between the *art* of situating architectural form in relation to the landscape.

### Towards a Megalithic Phenomenology

Considering megaliths dispassionately, they most usually consist of a few tumbled chunks of unworked stone in a field encircled with brambles, nettles and rank grass. They are frequently difficult to find and unsignposted. The hazards of getting to them may involve braving the dangers of bulls, electric or barbed wire fences, tumbling walls, barking farm dogs, farmers brandishing shot guns and so on. After a strenuous walk the stone, or stones, may, given luck, be encountered. It is almost always raining. The architectural experience of a megalith might be described as minimalist. One unhewn stone rests on another, there is little finesse. After a few minutes, and perhaps a photograph, you have seen that site and...on to the next? Why should anyone possibly be interested? Why do they appeal? Why are they worth visiting? What is it that has captured the European imagination in such places, and motivated the innumerable trips of antiquaries, artists, archaeologists, tourists?

The obvious answer is that these are ancient places. They respond to a modernist historical sensibility. The earliest in Sweden are some 5,600 years old. They were utilised as ossuaries for the remains of the ancestral dead, as social landmarks, focal points and centres for ritual activities, places in which social memories became encoded. The first monumental stone-built architecture constructed around the Atlantic coasts of Europe from Spain to Sweden, megaliths have survived the ravages of time. Built to last while traces of contemporary settlements have long since vanished, they are today the primary signifiers of the Neolithic past, of the first farming populations who transformed the natural environment on a large scale rather than simply living in it.

This is an academic reason for an interest in these places. There are others of equal importance. Megaliths lack immediate historical and cultural referents in a manner not shared with many other architectural remains. In visiting a Roman villa one will perhaps remember Anthony and Cleopatra or Julius Caesar. A Hollywood epic may spring to mind. Megaliths, by contrast, are not enwrapped by a web of film and media images, characters and historical plots. Isolated in a field there is a lack of things leading up to them: no entrance fees, guidebooks, guides, gateways, slide shows, hype. They are almost encountered as if by chance in the landscape. I would argue that this is their primary appeal. The stones, unburdened by a weight of contemporary referents are left simply as *sculptures* in the landscape. They have a mass, a shape, form, colour, size and volume. The dark passage entrances leading into the tombs seduce and entice. My eye is being directed as I enter and leave the tomb.

There has been much recent discussion of contemporary sculpture in the landscape, sometimes referred to as 'environmental art', 'earthworks' or 'landscape art' (e.g. Davies and Knipe 1978; Beardsley 1984; Morland 1988; Alloway 1976) from which we may learn something of use about megaliths. The examples range from the early post-war work of Moore and Hepworth in Britain to the Grizedale Forest sculpture project in north-west England to the work of Richard Long, David Nash and Ian Finlay. In the United States the enormous earth moving sculptural projects and constructions in Arizona, Nevada, Texas and Utah of Heizer, Smithson and others spring to mind. Common to all this work is a sense that the process of creating sculpture in the open rather than in the studio is fundamentally different. The wooden sculptures in the Grizedale Forest or those making up the Milestones project in Dorset are not commissioned and then sited somewhere. Instead the process of creating the sculpture is an integrated one in which the artist lives and works in the locality out of which, they all say, the sculpture 'grows'. These artworks become effective because they embody a sense of place, of belongingness. Landscape is a great defeater and unless the sculpture works with it, exploits natural form, it looses a great deal of its potential effect. The important thing is that the sculpture be worked on site and becomes part of it to create a special identity. Inspiration comes from the place. These sculptures are intended to establish a resonance with their settings by distilling certain aspects of them. Applying thought to the landscape through sculpture encourages further thought and use of it. Morland (1988) summarises the aims of the Dorset Milestones sculptural projects as to:

a. deepen understanding: draw on and highlight hidden aspects of the place
b. express cultural and social aspirations
c. respond to the particular place: encourage pause and reflection
d. generate discussion and stories
e. create a sense of community
f. interest and intrigue people in poetic and imaginative ways
g. create a sense of pride and ownership

The sculptures will ideally work on interwoven layers of meaning and reference differing according to the persons who view them. Such modern late twentieth-century outdoor sculptures are, however, only the most recent additions to the land-

scape in its 5,000-year alteration since the first farmers constructed the megaliths. The forms have changed as have some of the
aspirations. What has been rediscovered, perhaps, is the inspiration the landscape provides to create a sense of social identity
through its appropriation in sculptural and architectural form. It
is this that I wish to explore further.

In Falköping, a small town in Västergötland, central southern
Sweden, sixteen megalithic tombs have been preserved.
Krykerör, one of the largest, stands in a park near to a café and
the tourist information bureau. A few blocks away a few stones
of another tomb are visible in the back garden of a block of flats
making up a rockery around which shrubs and flowers have
been planted. Lusthögen is near to a busy petrol station. Remains
of the stones of other tombs are visible jutting out of manicured
lawns in the gardens of modern houses in the northern outskirts
of the town. Walking along Erik Dahlsbergsgatan one comes to a
small sloping patch of wasteland between prosperous and expen-
sive looking houses. In rough grass, obviously not tended by the
Parks Committee, Kung Björn's grave, now functioning as a
child's den, may be entered at the place where a chamber side
stone is missing. Scheelegatan bends curiously at the point at
which it meets Torstensonsgatan: here is another megalith forming a kind of traffic island, bedecked with shrubs and brightly
coloured flowers. Next to the passage entrance there is a STOP
sign (see Figure 2.1). On the southern fringes of the town more
megaliths are located in an industrial estate. One stands on a
slight rise next to a large Volvo car salesroom.

Falköping is essentially a modern town, although one with a
long history, as the megaliths testify. They all occur in areas built
up from the 1930s to the present day. Remarkably, they all have
small information signs on or near them, even a tomb of which
the only visible remains are two stone slabs jutting out from a
patch of grass by a bungalow. Falköping has dutifully preserved
and recorded its prehistory. I spent a day looking at these tombs
and became depressed. I saw all the tombs – but one was really
enough.

A megalith in an urban environment does not work, it has no
aura. It is as if the modern buildings surrounding the tombs
detract from them as signifiers of the past, deconsecrate their
space. Krykerör looks like any other piece of park furniture. A
plastic Viking sword left in a niche in Kung Björn's grave is more

Figure 2.1 The megalithic tomb on Scheelegatan, Falköping. Photo: G. Nash

interesting than the tomb itself. Megaliths in a town are never impressive. They are always dwarfed by their contemporary surroundings and there is too much distraction. They might have more meaning in a gallery or museum. Falköping is the only place in Sweden in which megaliths are found today in an urban setting. I had looked forward to the visit, to this juxtaposition between ancient ruins and modern town, relics of the past in an urban field, quite literally the incorporation of past architectural fragments into a modern urban fabric – postmodernism, as it were, but by default rather than by design. Nobody in Falköping that day seemed even to notice the tombs. If anybody stopped in the street or took a glance from a passing car it was to observe me observing the tomb. I had imagined that the buildings surrounding the tombs would have been much older, more picturesque, something which might appeal more to the tourist gaze. On reflection, however old or 'charming' the surrounding buildings the effect would be much the same.

By contrast a megalith in a rural setting, in fields or woods, always has a distinctive atmosphere and character about it. The same tomb changes and alters its character according to the weather conditions, the qualities of the light, the seasons of the year. It is never exactly the same place twice. Such tombs are nowadays best seen alone: a crowd destroys the sense of place, the relationship between the tomb and its setting in the landscape. It is this relationship that I want to explore by examining tombs in different areas of Sweden in their environmental and historical context.

I have been describing a personal experience. It has, perhaps, all the hallmarks of a bourgeois sentiment betraying a yearning for the natural and a past unpolluted by the activities of the present (Barthes 1973). Objectively I know that this sensibility is one that I share with all the professional colleagues and students I have talked to. All have agreed that megaliths 'work' better, gain more presence in the rural landscape. Megalith is to town, then, as nature is to culture? Yet the landscape in which these tombs are found has been transformed by thousands of years of human activity is part of culture rather than of nature. It is a sense of a dialectic between the non-human environment and cultural form which is missing in the town: there is too much artifice. The landscape is as much a human artefact as the town but a sense of it being culturally encoded in relation to monument form is only

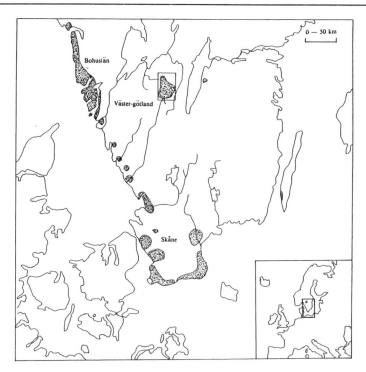

**Map 2.1 The distribution of megalithic monuments in Sweden**

apparent in a non-urban setting. And it is this dialectic in which the landscape becomes a cultural form and the artefact draws from its natural setting to create part of its meaning that, I want to argue, provides the key to understanding megalithic architecture both in the context of the past lifeworlds in which it was constructed and used, as well as in the manner in which we experience these ruins today. It is part of a process in which the natural becomes encultured and the cultural becomes naturalised.

## Megaliths and Landscape in Neolithic Sweden

The visit to Falköping formed part of a much wider survey of megalithic tombs and their relationship to the landscape in Sweden, the results of which are summarised in this chapter. There are at least 470 surviving sites. The vast majority of these occur in three distinct areas: Skåne, Västergötland and Bohuslän (see Map 2.1 ). In each of these regions architectural form differs and so does the siting of the megalith in the landscape. The tombs draw part of their meaning and significance from their relationship to each other and the landscape. At the beginning of this chapter I hinted at an intimate relationship between megaliths and topographic features of the non-humanly created landscape. I want to investigate this relationship further in order to explain the location of the megaliths in these three very different Swedish landscapes and how this might relate to architectural form and social process. I want to argue that through tomb construction the landscape becomes socialised so as to constitute part of a domain of social negotiation. A spatial story is being played out involving an intimate interplay between the tomb and its topographic setting.

I have argued that we experience megaliths as sculptures. By extension the same kind of statement can be made about landscape. It too is a sculptural form – rocks, trees, river courses carving through the land. Its perceived properties alter from day to day and hour to hour and are intimately related to the vantage point of the observer on plain, ridge or valley, halfway up a slope (Higuchi 1983). In an oblique manner, to use another visual metaphor, the point I am trying to make is that if we are to try and understand the relationship between megalith and landscape the focus of our attention must be on modes of visual perception and experience on the human scale. Little is to be gained from the analytical gaze at the distribution map in which megaliths are merely dots in an abstracted containing space. We require, as Thomas has recently put it (1992), an hermeneutics of megalithic space. This hermeneutics, however, has to extend beyond the tomb itself to embrace its relationship with its topographic setting. The starting point for such an encounter must inevitably be our own personal experience of architectural and environmental space and the way they play off each other to create a distinctive sense of *place* (Goldfinger 1941; Norberg-Schulz 1971; Bloomer and Moore 1977).

Megalithic tombs are found in five sub-regional groups in Skåne, the southernmost province of Sweden. They all occur in the most productive agricultural land around the coasts. Linnaeus in his travels of 1749 marvelled at the productivity of the soil – fields of grain stretching as far as the eye could see in a flat or undulating and virtually treeless plain supporting a dense network of nucleated villages. All three major types of megaliths occur: long dolmens, round dolmens and passage graves (see Figure 2.2 ). Broadly,

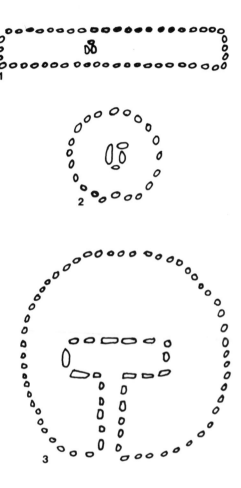

**Figure 2.2  Major forms of megaliths. 1: Long Dolmen; 2: Round Dolment; 3: Passage Grave.**

through time, these three types of monuments represent a succession of architectural forms imposed on the landscape. Based on a survey of 53 sites (just over 50 per cent of the total), four different locations in the landscape can be distinguished. These are independent of monument form. In other words any of the three classes of megaliths may be found in each location. They are as follows:

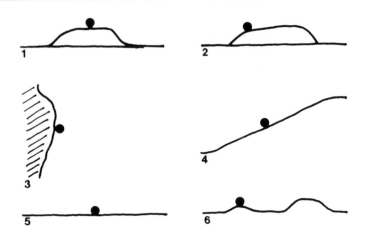

**Figure 2.3** Sketch plan of types of locations of megaliths in Skåne. 1: ridge crest with panoramic views; 2: ridge crest with restricted views; 3: on coast; 4: midpoint on slope; 5: in flat terrain; 6: in undulating terrain but not on highest point in immediate vicinity.

1. The crown of a ridge:
   a) with panoramic views (4 sites)
   b) with restricted views in one direction (4 sites)
2. Directly on the coast overlooking the sea (3 sites).
3. At a midpoint on a slope (4 sites).
4. In virtually flat terrain:
   a) in a completely flat area (29 sites).
   b) in a flat area or on a slight rise with higher land in the immediate vicinity (8 sites) (see Figure 2.3 ).

Despite the flat terrain in which the majority of the megaliths occur the degree of inter-site visibility is not high. The mean first nearest neighbour distance between tombs is about 0.5 km yet from most sites today other tombs (except in cases where they are very closely clustered at distances less than a few hundred metres) are not visible (Hårdh 1982). When we consider that the extent of tree cover must have been vastly greater in the Neolithic than today it is likely that most tombs would not have been intervisible. Considering the relationship of the sites to the local topography it is also evident that, with few exceptions, they are not sited to maximise visibility. Many of those tombs sited in virtually flat terrain are not on the highest point. The land in some cases rises up by as much as 5–10 m in the immediate vicinity of the tomb. Where tombs occur on a slope, or the topography in the surrounding area is undulating, the highest points commanding maximum visibility are invariably occupied by later Bronze Age barrows. This is even the case when megaliths and Bronze Age barrows occupy the crown of a ridge as at Glumslövs backar in north-west Skåne. The megaliths here are sited on the western side of the ridge commanding views over the Öresund to Denmark, and to the north and south. Visibility inland across the ridge top to the east is restricted to about 50 m. By contrast a Bronze Age barrow cemetry occupies the central part of the ridge crown from which there are panoramic views in all directions. Only four of the surveyed sites (7 per cent ) are clearly sited for maximum visibility from the tomb itself in all directions.

All megaliths in Skåne are located either very close to the coast (54 per cent are within 5 km from the nearest coastline) and/or along river courses. In what is, for the most part, a relatively featureless plain both the coast and river channels constitute topographic boundaries of major significance and tombs are located with reference to them, strung out along coastal margins or on the sides of river courses. In this respect it is interesting to note that where the rivers flow north-south the orientation of the mound and/or the chamber differs according to whether it is sited to the west or the east of this natural boundary. Where the rivers run west-east, with tombs located to the north and south, orientation patterns do not differ consistently according to which side of the river the tomb is located (Tilley 1984: 123–5). This suggests that a differentiation between a north-south and west-east axis was of central symbolic significance, a pattern repeated but structurally transformed in other areas in which megaliths occur in Sweden but with reference to marked differences in local topography rather than river channels.

In Västergötland, some 200 km due north of the most northerly area of distribution of megaliths in Skåne, a remarkable concentration of 265 megalithic tombs occurs in an area, which, at maximum, extends only 38 km north-south and 25 km west-east (Hellman 1963; Clark 1977; Sjögren 1986). Both the landscape and the megalithic architecture differs here markedly from Skåne. The central region of Västergötland, where the tombs occur, has been claimed to be one of the most distinctive natural landscapes in Sweden. It is a relatively high flat plateau, c. 200 m. above sea

60 *Landscape: Politics and Perspectives*

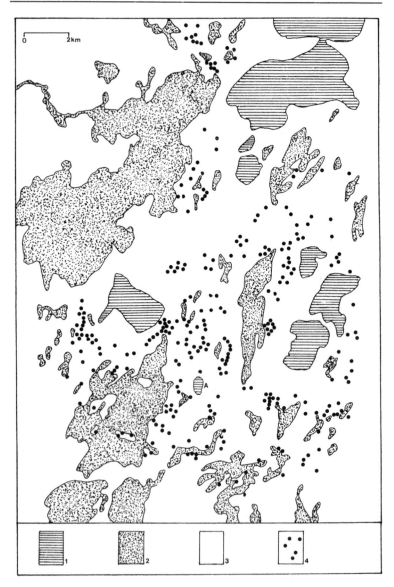

Map 2.2 The distribution of megalithic tombs in Västergotland in relation to landscape features. 1: igneous mountain block; 2: marsh; 3: sedimentary plateau (limestone and sandstone); 4: tomb. A: Ålleberg mountain.

level consisting of sedimentary rocks (limestones and sand-stones) cut up by a series of steep-sided and flat-topped igneous mountain blocks constituting a north-south axis in the landscape. These mountains rise up to 100 m. or more above the level of the flat plain surrounding them. Because the plateau base surrounding the mountains is made up of sedimentary rocks there is an absence of rivers and the mountains constitute the major topographic feature breaking up the land surface. Today, as was almost certainly the case in the prehistoric past the mountain sides are heavily forested and there are extensive bog areas on top. There are in all eleven mountain blocks around which the megaliths are located (Map 2. 2 ). The most distinctive of these in shape, the most southerly, and the highest is Ålleberg. From this vantage point there are sweeping panoramic views in all directions and the mounds and stones of megaliths in the immediate vicinity are clearly visible from the mountain top. There is no evidence suggesting Neolithic settlement on these mountains and megaliths were certainly not built on them. Votive deposits dating from the Neolithic onwards suggest that they were visited rather than occupied. On the plains surrounding the mountains patches of high quality farming land on which all the tombs are located are interspersed with sizeable bog and lake areas so that areas with megaliths originally constituted settlement islands in a watery terrain.

This is a prospect-dominated landscape and views from the megaliths are dominated by the outlines of the granite mountain blocks in the distance. From every tomb at least one mountain block is visible, from some sites up to five mountain blocks can be seen. This is a landscape of break and rupture, plain and mountain, and the megaliths appear to have been deliberately sited so as to maximise the angle of view towards the mountains. Tombs are never found located on the plain edge at the point at which the mountains begin to rise up steeply, and are always some distance away, in the range of 2–500 m from the break of slope (see Figure 2.4 ). This also means, of course, that the tombs can be easily seen from the mountains themselves. Based on the results of a survey undertaken from 30 different sampling points within the area of megalithic distribution it is possible to see Ålleberg from at least 54 per cent of the total number of tombs – the vast majority of those occurring in the southern area of their distribution. Ålleberg is visible from selected vantage points from a distance of

**Figure 2.4** View from the row of megaliths at Karleby towards the Ålleberg mountain, Västergotland. Photo: Gertrud Andersson.

up to 11 km away to the north and 7 km to the south. It can be seen from tombs on the southernmost fringe of the megalith distribution. However vistas from sites closer to it than some of those in the south are blocked by other mountains such as Gisseberg and Gerumsberg to the east.

There are a number of quite striking features about the megaliths in this area as compared with those in Skåne and Bohuslän. They are very numerous: 56 per cent of all documented megaliths in Sweden occur here isolated by considerable distances from those to the south and west. The tombs are densely concentrated and occur in straggling north-south rows of up to 12 monuments with inter-site distances in each group varying only between a few or a few hundred metres. In the centre of the distribution they are more regularly spaced than at the fringes. There is a lack of variability in form. The only type of megalith documented is the passage grave. These are all, with only seven documented exceptions, of a simple T shaped form with a rectangular chamber orientated north-south and a passage with its entrance facing exactly, or almost, due east. The passage and chamber are set in a round mound. The mounds, chambers and passages, are spectacularly large in many cases. Mound diameter approaches up to 40 m and the chambers and passages up to 16 m in length. Any passage grave, even the largest and most impressive in Skåne and Bohuslän, is dwarfed by comparison with the sheer scale and monumentality of some of these sites (Figure 2.5 ). The width of the passage, which may be up to 1.5 m is also considerably greater than that for passage graves in other areas of Sweden where the passage is most usually in the range of 0.7–1 m. wide.

The very largest of these tombs occur in the centre of the area of the distribution in the vicinity of Ålleberg and tomb size tends to decrease on the fringes with a few exceptions. Some of the mounds have a two-tier stepped platform type construction in which the central passage and chamber are set in a mound which is itself surrounded by a lower level mound. This feature was probably generalised but in most cases modern ploughing has removed all but the central part of the mound.

Tomb form is rigidly standardised and this even extends to the use of building materials. The megaliths were constructed from three locally available stones: those from the sedimentary rocks of the plateau, limestone and sandstone slabs, and the igneous rocks (diabase and gneiss) of the mountain blocks.

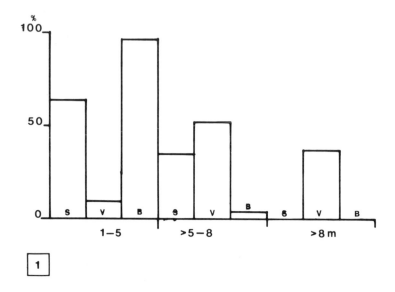

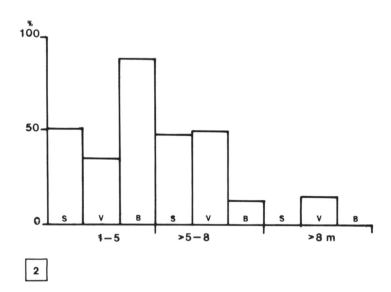

Figure 2.5  Comparison of Chamber length (1) and Passage length (2)
between the passage graves in Skåne (S), Västergötland (V), and
Bohuslän (B).

These rocks contrast in colour (red limestone; light coloured sandstone, grey diabase and gneiss) and form. The sedimentary rocks split into regular and evenly faced surfaces up to 7 or 8 m. in length, 2–3 m in height and 0.3 m. thick. The igneous blocks almost always form irregular or rounded boulders. In the majority of cases the chamber and passage uprights are built of sedimentary rocks and the capstones of both of igneous rocks (Tilley 1991). Even in the few documented cases in which sedimentary rocks were used for the capstones, the final passage roofing stone at the point where the passage reaches the chamber, the keystone, is invariably of igneous rock, usually diabase (Figure 2.6). The difference between chamber and passage uprights and capstones is further emphasised by the occurrence of cupmarks (small carved hollows up to 4 cm deep and 10 cm wide) on the external surfaces of the central chamber capstones and sometimes the keystone. These vary in frequency between one or two and two hundred on individual roofing stones. This decoration strongly suggests that the central chamber roofing stones must have been exposed and visible while the rest of the stone tomb, including the passage capstones, would have been enclosed by its surrounding mound.

In Bohuslän the relationship between megaliths and the landscape differs again and so does their architectural form. This is an irregular landscape, a mosaic of exposed rocks, forests and water. Offshore there is an extensive archipelago of smaller and larger islands. Inland the area is dissected by a series of fjords, rocky forested ridges rising up to around 200 m above sea level, and valleys infilled with sediment. The bare granite rocks are everywhere apparent, smoothed and striated by the ice sheets. Bare rock accounts for up to one-third of the region. Only one-fifth of the area supports cultivable arable or meadow land even after extensive land drainage in the valleys. Land uplift since the last glaciation has transformed the area since the Neolithic. In the south the land has risen by up to 15 m and in the north as much as 25 m. Today the tombs are rarely more than 3 or 4 km from the nearest coastline. At the time of construction they would have been closer to the sea – sited on the inner parts of the archipelago and the outer fringes of the mainland.

Just over eighty megalithic tombs are scattered in the coastal areas of Bohuslän. Half of these are found on the islands of Örust and Tjörn where there is some degree of regularity in tomb spacing. The rest occur individually or in small clusters of two or

Figure 2.6 The megalithic tomb at Rössberga, Västergötland. Note the difference in shape and size of the red limestone sedimentary passage uprights and the igneous keystone. Photo: G. Nash

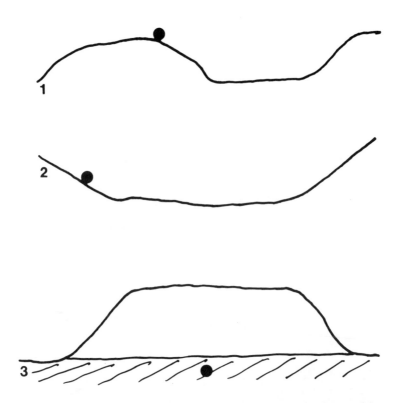

Figure 2.7 Sketch plan of locations of megaliths in Bohuslän. 1: ridge crest overlooking valley or an arm of the sea; 2: valley edge location; 3: below rock dome to north.

three tombs. All the major forms of megalithic tombs occur here: long dolmens (six examples) and roughly equal numbers of round dolmens and passage graves. In no way can any of these constructions be described as 'monumental'. Mounds, chambers and passages are small compared with those in Skåne or Västergötland and passage grave chamber shape is irregular rather than standardised. The majority of the tombs are constructed with a single large capstone covering the chamber which may be contrasted with the use of up to nine capstones in Västergötland. A single chamber upright in Västergötland may be as long as an entire chamber in Bohuslän. Furthermore, these tombs merge into the landscape rather than stand out from it.

Figure 2.8  Remains of the recently excavated small round dolmen at Skredsvik, Bohuslän, high up on a ridge overlooking an arm of the sea. Photo: G. Nash.

Generalising from a survey of 30 sites (35 per cent of the total) three different locations in the landscape may be distinguished:

1) Tombs located on a ridge crest overlooking a valley and/or the sea (13 sites; 43 per cent of the sample).
2) Tombs on a slope in a valley edge location (6 sites, 20 per cent of the sample).
3) Tombs in a valley edge location below a bare rock outcrop immediately to the north of the tomb (11 sites, 36 per cent of the sample) (Figure 2.7).
In all three of these locations long dolmens, round dolmens or passage graves may occur. As in Skåne there is no correlation between tomb type and location in the landscape. Virtually all tombs are near to pockets of arable land that would have been cultivable with a Neolithic technology. Unlike Skåne and Västergötland the majority of them are not located on land that could have been farmed but in locations (the ridge crest) overlooking it or at its margins (tombs in a valley edge location). There is, then, a relative separation between the spaces occupied by the tombs and those that would have been cultivated which does not occur in the other two areas.

The tombs, even those on ridge crests, are not constructed or located so as to be highly visible or to stand out in the landscape. They could only be visible from short distances. Today they are generally in densely forested terrain and are very difficult to find. Often surrounded by bare patches of the rock from which they themselves are constructed they have a hidden quality about them: sites from which one could view but not be viewed (Figure 2.8). Those in valley-edge locations can only be seen from a limited number of directions.

Enter the modern cemetry at Hunnebostrand in northern Bohuslän and there is a striking vista north to an enormous smoothed pink rock dome (Figure 2.9) forming a kind of natural temple, sculpted by ice. The main cemetery path dips down and then leads up to it, terminating at the central point. Neat lines of well-kept graves with granite headstones and flowers are aligned on either side. These are small monuments preserving memories of a loved one, repetitive in form, unimpressive. But there is a mystical quality to this place, an aura of power, created by the rock dome. Walk to the north-east corner of the cemetery and there just below the rock face is a small passage grave, its surrounding cairn now vanished and probably forming part of the

Figure 2.9  The modern cemetery and rock dome at Hunnebostrand, Bohuslän. The passage grave is located behind the bushes in the top right of the photograph. Photo: G. Nash.

cemetry wall. This Neolithic tomb, like the modern gravestones, is hardly monumental. A single capstone covers a small irregularly shaped chamber less than 3 m in length and 1.5 m wide, entered by a short, narrow passage, opening to the south-east (Figure 2.10 ). This type of location, with a small megalithic tomb beneath rocks rising up to the north, (dramatically in this case, sometimes less so ), is repeated frequently throughout Bohuslän. The tombs always occur immediately to the south of a south facing rock outcrop. The passage entrances, or chamber entrances in the case of round dolmens, invariably face east or south-east. In other words, while entering the tomb one must face the rock to its north. The round dolmens here generally have a polygonal chamber, i.e. they are non-directionally orientated, as is their enclosing circular cairn. The chambers of the passage graves have a long axis orientated north-south or NW-SE or NE-SW or at various degrees in between. Whatever the specific orientation the back wall of the chamber is aligned in the same direction as the rock face immediately to its north. Tombs are not found (with one exception in the sample studied) with rocks rising up dramatically immediately to the south, west or east of them. There are no shortages of such locations in Bohuslän!

### Creating spaces, channelling perception

The three different forms of megaliths which occur in Skåne and Bohuslän represent fundamentally different ways of placing the spatial form of architecture into the landscape. The earliest monuments, the long dolmens, are outward focused. These constructions consist of a large barrow with surrounding kerb stones entirely enclosing a small rectangular stone chamber which could contain no more than a few bodies or ancestral remains. The most imposing feature of these monuments is the linearity and size of the mound which must be viewed from a side angle. These long dolmens cut across the landscape, the orientation of their long axis establishing a sense of directionality with which to perceive the space beyond the mound itself. They are only frequent and large in the relatively undifferentiated flat landscape of Skåne. They line up, as it were, one's view in this landscape, creating a visual spatial pathway through it.

The form of the round dolmens and passage graves represents

**Figure 2.10** The passage grave in the Hunnebostrand cemetary. Photo: G. Nash

a total break with this manner of creating a sense of space. There can be no greater contrast than that between the long dolmen, a line across space, and the round dolmen and passage grave both of which have circular or non-directionally orientated mounds looking the same from all directions except at the entrances. The visual field of such monuments, particularly the passage graves, appears inward focused in that attention is inevitably drawn to the entrances in the mound leading towards the internal chamber. One is supposed to approach such monuments from a particular direction and, when leaving the internal chamber, the manner in which one sees the surrounding landscape is inevitably funnelled, the reverse view to that obtained while entering the monument. These tombs thus channel views across the landscape but do not themselves directly establish an orientational axis in it. The long dolmen itself imposes a form, establishes a direction through space. The round dolmens and passage graves perform a similar role but a sense of directionality is instead created in relation to the people using them. The difference here is between a monument itself producing an axis for spatial vision and the monument channelling movement into and out of itself creating a similar effect, but through the medium of the human body. This latter form of spatial orientation is much more subtle, for it works directly through the movements of the body rather than being a feature which an individual might independently observe as something existing beyond the body. In this connection it is pertinent to note that it is only from the passage graves that we have evidence of collective burial on a large scale requiring the tomb to remain in use over hundreds of years as a repository for ancestral remains. Activities largely took place around the long dolmens. At the passage graves it also required repeated use of the internal space of the monument.

Considering available radiocarbon dates relating to megalith construction in Skåne and Denmark there are strong indications that the long dolmens are the earliest and the passage graves the latest. On typological grounds the round dolmens are intermediate in date. Some very recent dates from Västergötland indicate that passage graves began to be built there very early, perhaps when long dolmens were being constructed in Skåne (Hedges *et al.* 1992; K.-G.Sjögren personal communnication). In both Skåne and Bohuslän there is rich evidence of Mesolithic and early Neolithic occupation in the areas in which the megaliths were constructed. This does not seem to be the case in Västergötland where the rather dry and probably densely forested limestone plateau would not have been an attractive environment for hunter-gatherers in the areas where the tombs were built. Mesolithic evidence is confined to a few lake-shore sites on the fringes of the megalithic settlement area. Early Neolithic evidence is limited to some stray axe finds. It appears, then, that in Västergötland the tombs occupy a new settlement area towards the end of the early Neolithic. Skåne has the most complex sequence of monument construction with a succession of different tomb types as opposed to Bohuslän with only a few long dolmens but many round dolmens and passage graves, and Västergötland with only passage graves.

Given the nature of the flat terrain in which the majority of the tombs occur in Skåne the presence of other monuments and settlements in the landscape seems to be of fundamental significance in the structuring of space. In building a new tomb reference would have to be made to pre-existing structures and patterns of activity. Recent excavations (Strömberg 1971: 107–11) suggest that many, if not most, of the passage graves were built on previously cultivated land or on abandoned settlement areas. Outside the entrances to many of the passage graves and round dolmens massive concentrations of highly decorated smashed pottery and broken axes occur in, on and under stone platforms. There is no correlation between the amount of this material and the size of the tomb as, perhaps, might be expected. This can be explained in terms of the cultural history of land occupation and use. The power and significance of the tomb is, in other words, intimately related to the past history of the tomb-using group.

For example, at Vastra Hoby, in western Skåne, three monuments occur within a few metres of each other on flat land by the southern bank of the river Lödde. The land rises up considerably to the south of the monuments which are not therefore positioned for maximum visibility or to dominate the landscape. Two of the monuments are long dolmens. One orientated along a north-south axis is 20 m long, the other, orientated northwest-southeast, is huge – over 50 m in length (Figure 2.11). The third monument is a rather small passage grave outside which an enormous quantity of pottery – over 50,000 sherds has been recovered (Forssander 1936). At this site there was evidently no need to construct a large passage grave since the social group using the tomb

Figure 2.11  The large long dolmen at Västra Hoby, western Skåne. Photo: C. Tilley

had already constructed two long dolmens. The passage grave gained part of its significance and power by its direct association with the previously built monuments. In this connection it is interesting to note that the passage axis duplicates the NW-SE orientation of the largest dolmen mound axis: one structure is being linked in with a previous one to articulate space in a similar manner.

The situation in Västergötland contrasts markedly with that in Skåne. Here there is no architectural tradition of building monuments of different form and only the latest type of megalith to be built in Skåne and Bohuslän , the passage grave, occurs. In constructing such tombs, reference could not be made to previously constructed monuments in the landscape. Lacking such a cultural referent the topographic contrasts in the landscape were utilised to symbolically empower tomb building. The passage graves here directly mimic or duplicate the landscape in a very direct way:

1) They are arranged in north-south rows along the axis of the landscape as defined by the igneous mountain blocks.
2) The chambers are orientated north-south along this same axis.
3) The stones used to construct the tombs, sedimentary uprights and igneous capstones duplicate the low/high contrast between the sedimentary rocks of the plateau on which the monuments stand and the igneous mountains in the distance.
4) The orientation of the east- west passage axis is such that a person moving down the passage towards the chamber would, in effect, be approaching the mountains.
5) The passage by which the chamber is approached is narrow and low by comparison with the spacious chamber. A person entering the tomb would have to stoop down the passage and could only stand up in the chamber.

There are thus two axes of fundamental significance in the internal space of the tomb: the low, narrow and confined east-west axis created by the passage and a high, spacious north-south axis of the chamber. The megaliths, in effect, represent the macrocosm in microcosm. They are the landscape in miniature. The internal spatial organisation of the tomb makes an individual entering it experience this effect. It is not hard to suggest that the mountains in Västergötland were of central symbolic and sacred significance. A place where earth meets sky, they were the home of the ancestral spirits mediating between the populations using the tombs and the cosmos. The tombs are deliberately sited so as to afford a maximum angle of view of these mountains. In the south of the area the Ålleberg mountain, with its very distinctive profile, was undoubtebly the most important of them, a place that must have been visited on ritual pilgrimages by the populations using the surrounding megaliths. In this respect it is interesting to note that there is a wealth of mythology surrounding this mountain. No others in Västergötland have such a wealth of folklore associated with them. Ålleberg is said to have been the site on which the gods slept waiting until they should be called to save the motherland, a site of powerful underground rivers and hidden caves, home of mountain trolls (Sandberg 1956).

From the excavations that have been undertaken in Västergötland we know that large quantities of disarticulated human bones, representing up to 100 individuals of all sexes and ages, were stacked up in niches in the tomb chamber (Montelius 1873; Retzius 1889; Cullberg 1963). The only artefacts contemporary with these human remains are amber beads, most of which are shaped in the form of axes. Outside the passage entrances relatively small quantities of pottery were deliberately crushed and deposited along with broken, and sometimes fire-cracked, flint and ground-stone axes. Here another process of encompassment is at work. The miniature amber axes inside the tomb chamber duplicate or mimic the real axes outside the tomb entrance.

It seems very unlikely that the idea of building a passage grave would occur independently in Västergötland, with Mesolithic hunter-fisher-gatherer populations moving into a new area and beginning to construct passage graves. We are probably dealing here with a group of people who arrived from the south and built passage graves either around the same time, or perhaps earlier than they were being constructed in Skåne and Bohuslän. We know for certain that both amber and flint do not occur in this area naturally and must have been imported from their natural area of distribution in southern Sweden or Denmark. The pottery found outside the Västergötland megaliths is very similar to that found in Skåne. A north-south symbolic axis in the landscape as defined by river channels was of symbolic importance in Skåne. This is also duplicated in a transformed manner in Västergötland. The megalithic monuments of Västergötland encoded social memory, an ancestral track of movement from south to north. The bones of the ancestors of the populations using the monument were deposited in the chambers along this north-south axis. The east-west passage orientation has obvious solar significance. One enters the tomb from the east where the sun, source of light, rises, and passes west to the dark chamber containing the ancestral bones. The passage creates a liminal space between the world of the living outside the tomb and the world of the dead inside the chamber. The chamber is a higher place both literally and metaphorically, its roof and its orientational axis representing the sacred mountains. The axis along which the bones of the dead are placed thus becomes sedimented into the landscape itself. An individual entering the tomb would be undertaking a metaphoric passage in which the secrets of the relationship of the social to the natural order and the historical origins of the ancestors from the south would be revealed. The construction of the tomb follows a 'divine' model which must be faithfully followed, hence the striking degree of regularity in the details of the megalithic architecture in this region. Grounded in nature, in the very topography and geology of the area, the tomb establishes an enduring sense of identity and would have provided an ideological sense of solidity in the presence of an intrusive social group providing a historical and transcendental justification for the occupation of the land, relationship with neighbours and appropriation of resources. The artefact, the tomb, is naturalized through the landscape and the landscape is encultured through the artefact.

As I have noted the location of megaliths in the landscape in Bohuslän is far more variable. The tradition of monument building is longer here than in Västergötland. The chambers of the passage graves are far more variable in shape than in either Skåne or Västergötland, and most megaliths are small and rather inconspicuous. The monuments of Bohuslän do not duplicate the landscape; their role appears, rather, to be a commentary on it and the topographic features of the landscape always seem to be ultimately more important than the monument itself. I distinguished three typical locations. Common to each of these, in contrast to the situation in Skåne and Västergötland is that the monument is not being sited in the middle of highly productive agricultural land but at its margins, either overlooking it from a ridge crest or on a valley edge. In this connection it is interesting to note that fishing, hunting and gathering are likely to have been a far more important feature of the local economy in this area than elsewhere (Clark 1977). The monuments rather than being in the middle of settled and farmed areas were at their margins, in many cases perhaps hidden away. The tomb itself is in a liminal space set apart from day-to-day existence. Here there is, perhaps, a different attitude to the ancestral spirits – beings considered dangerous and potentially malevolent – separated from the world of the living rather than integrated as ancestors placed back into the soil through burial in the tomb. The amount of material deposited in these tombs or around the entrances to the passage graves is very small, indicating that they were not places where repeated offerings on a large scale were made. The most dramatic of the monument locations are those such as Hunnebostrand, discussed above, where the megalith is placed beneath a towering rock dome. Here, again, as in Skåne and Västergötland, a north-south axis in the landscape is of great importance. The entrances to the passage graves and round dolmens face south or south-east so that the individual would be positioned facing the rock outcrop and in moving down the passage towards the chamber would approach it. The lack of scale of these monuments, which are dwarfed by the rock domes that rise above them, suggests that their purpose is to draw attention to the rock itself. The monuments mark the landscape, making its natural sculptural qualities more visible. Entering the tomb is thus a symbolic passage permitting entry into the rock dome beyond it. In Bohuslän the monument does not imitate the natural topography as in Västergötland. It is not imposed on it as in Skåne, but rather is constructed so as to belong to nature itself. The tomb becomes a signifier for the setting beyond it.

### Conclusion

The megaliths in Sweden were evidently designed and located so as to relate to their spatial settings in different ways. A sense of sheer scale and monumentality may be communicated as part of the sense of place, as is the case in Västergötland and occasionally in Skåne. For other tombs this is not the case: the topography rather than the megalith creates the place. Or both topography and built structure may be of equal importance. Whatever the precise importance of topography or architecture, each always interacts with the other. A dialogue is being undertaken. This is because the very presence of the architectural form constantly activates what otherwise is a socially neutral space. Building a structure produces a visual effect in the landscape to which and from which attention is directed. In so doing the architecture of the tomb and its site become interdependent. Form and setting mediate each other, creating a focus for social activity and for the channelling of visual perception. Megaliths thus form part of a visual code providing an architectural apparatus by means of which people become actively involved in the natural and the social environment surrounding them.

Criado has made a crucial link between megaliths and their settings by stressing that these tombs are always events or happennings of *thought*. They reflect not only a sense of spatiality and temporality but a particular order of thought. It was by means of the tomb and its setting in the landscape that people thought through their world ( Criado 1989). Following Lévi-Strauss (1966) he draws a distinction between 'savage' and 'domesticated' thought and suggests that megalith building is an expression of the latter. They represent a will to dominate and control nature. In savage thought nature is a condition of culture and vice versa and there is no dividing line between these two categories. They are thoroughly merged. The land is bountiful and provides. It is a subject rather than an object of labour. The 'domesticated' mind, by contrast, imposes order and form onto the natural world and part of this imposition in the Neolithic is monument construction. A new space-time becomes constructed and part of this process is a separation of culture from nature, humans from the natural world. Thought no longer attempts to reflect the world but actively constructs new spaces in it. This distinction, however, seems somewhat overdrawn. Hunter-gatherers may impose order just as much as farmers. The important point is that building megaliths establishes a particular form of ordering and domesticating in the landscape bound up with stressing ancestral presences through architectural orders.

Clearly part of such a development in Sweden is the use of natural signifiers to produce this fresh spatial configuration and relationship between people and their natural environment. Repetitive links are constantly being set up between megaliths and the local topography, especially natural limits or borders: river courses, valley edges, rock outcrops. In this manner the natural order of the environment could be incorporated within the social organisation of the landscape. The tombs incorporate and exploit the symbolic powers of their settings to create specific experience effects on populations entering, coming out of and moving around them.

One purpose of the monuments must have been to form and channel impressions of their environmental settings, to draw attention to their settings. They made the landscape and its characteristics visible, alerted populations using the tomb to an unseen landscape, a landscape that remained unseen until its perception became focused through the lens of the architectural form of the megalith. The tombs formed part of a process in which populations got to know a stretch of land. Their ideas about the land which they inhabited and their relationship to it evolved from the megalithic architecture which itself must have been evoked as a response to a specific place. The construction of groups of megaliths clearly required people to walk between them and around them involving changing orientations and differing perceptions of the monuments in space, as seen from near or from far away, from different viewpoints, angles, horizons. In this sense the monuments were catalysts, drawing attention not only to themselves but to other monuments and the landscape. Exactly where the monument was located in the landscape determined how, from where, and from what distance it could be looked at and what could be seen from it. It is presented in a setting and in turn its siting determines how that setting appears to an observer. The megalith establishes a stable framework for viewing the world and prevents that world from blowing away visually. The process for siting a megalith is analogous to that for siting a contemporary sculpture or hanging a picture. You may put the picture where it will be seen best. You don't hang a picture in bad light or put potted plants in front of it if you want to look at it. Different types of pictures, with different associations and meanings, of course, need different settings. A picture appropriate for a living room may not work in a bedroom, one appropriate in a church may not seem right at home and so on.

Humanly created space is the space of social reproduction. It follows that control over the creation of that space must confer power over the form that reproduction takes and that control over space is crucial for the maintenance of power relations within and between individuals and groups. Returning to the theme of 'domestic' thought, the construction of megaliths ushers in a new history of landscape perception in which societal relations become increasingly dependent on a pre-established permanent artifical spatial structure as a focus for movement and gaining knowledge of the world. Social power, in such a context, resides in the ability to govern and control both the movements of individuals in space-time and their understanding of their situation in the social and natural world. Personal biographies are formed through encounters with particular places in the cultural landscape and the recognition and understanding of the panoply of codes constituting their meaning. Megaliths constructed personal biographies which in turn constituted the meanings of these places and their settings. Those groups or individuals who were able to control the movements of people around, into and out of the tombs would also be in a position to control the secrets and knowledge embedded in the tomb and its setting which were no doubt deemed essential for group reproduction.

## Acknowledgements

The data on which the observations of the location of the megalithic tombs in the landscape in Sweden was made was collected during a survey undertaken in September and October 1991. This was partly made possible by a grant from the Pantyfedwen Fund administered by St. David's University College Lampeter for which I am most grateful. Notes on tomb landscape placement were made on site and a video record made of the landscape around each tomb which was later analysed. I would like to thank George Nash for helping and encouraging me, undertaking the video camera work, and taking most of the still photographs published in this chapter. I would like to thank Karl-Göran Sjögren for providing a series of constructive comments on an earlier draft, some of which are incorporated here. Thanks are also due to Barbara Bender for waiting for the result, and for her enthusiasm for the subject, which helped to develop my own interest in the social significance of the landscape.

## References

Alloway, L. 1976. 'Site inspection', *Artforum* XV 10, 49–55.

Barthes, R. 1973. 'The Blue Guide', in R. Barthes *Mythologies*, London: Paladin.

Beardsley, J. 1984. *Earthworks and Beyond: Contemporary Art in the Landscape*, New York: Abbeville Press.

Bloomer, K. and Moore, C. 1977. *Body, Memory and Architecture*, New Haven: Yale University Press.

Clark, J. 1977. 'The economic context of dolmens and passage graves in Sweden', in V. Markotic (ed.) *Ancient Europe and the Mediterranean*, Warminster: Aris and Phillips.

Criado, F. 1989. 'We, the post-megalithic people...', in I. Hodder (ed.) *The Meanings of Things*, London: Unwin-Hyman.

Cullberg, C. 1963. *Megalitgraven i Rössberga*, Stockholm: Allkopia

Davies, P. and Knipe, T. (eds) 1978. *A Sense of Place: Sculpture in the Landscape*, London: Ceolfrith Press.

Forssander, J. 1936. 'Skånsk megalitkeramik och kontinentaleuropeisk stenålder', *Meddelanden från Lunds Universitets Historiska Museum*, 1–77.

Goldfinger, E. 1941. 'The sensation of space', *Architectural Review*, 129–31.

Hårdh, B. 1982. 'The megalithic grave area around the Lödde-Kävlinge river. A research programme', *Meddelanden från Lunds Universitets Historiska Museum* New Series Vol. 4, 26–47.

Hedges, R., Housely, R., Bronk, C. and Van Klinken, G. 1992. 'Radiocarbon dates from the Oxford AMS system', *Archaeometry* 34 (1), 149.

Hellman, G. 1963. 'Västergötlands gånggrifter', *Falbygden* 18, 63–74.

Higuchi, T. 1983. *The Visual and Spatial Structure of Landscapes*, Cambridge, MA: The MIT Press.

Lévi-Strauss, C. 1966. *The Savage Mind*, London: Weidenfeld and Nicolson.

Morland, J. 1988. *New Milestones: Sculpture, Community and the Land*, London: Common Ground Press.

Montelius, O. 1873. 'Undersökning af en gånggrift vid Karleby kyrka i Vestergötland, *Kongl. Vitterhets Historie och Antiqvitets Akademiens Månadsblad*, 10–13.

Norberg-Schulz, C. 1971. *Existence, Space and Architecture*, London: Studio Vista.

Retzius, G. 1899. *Crania Svecica Antiqua*, Stockholm: Aftonbladets Tryckeri.

Sandberg, E. (1956) 'Sägner om Ålleberg', *Falbygden* 11, 73–75.

Sjögren, K.-G. 1986. 'Kinship, labour and land in neolithic south-west Sweden: social aspects of megalithic graves', *Journal of Anthropological*

*Archaeology* 5.

Strömberg, M. 1971. *Die Megalithgräber von Hagestad*, Acta Archaeologica Lundensia 9, Lund.

Thomas, J. 1993. 'The hermeneutics of megalithic space' in C. Tilley (ed.) *Interpretative Archaeology*, Oxford: Berg.

Tilley, C. 1984. 'Ideology and the legitimation of power in the middle neolithic of southern Sweden', in D. Miller and C. Tilley (eds) *Ideology, Power and Prehistory*, Cambridge: Cambridge University Press.

———1991. 'Constructing a ritual landscape' in K. Jennbert , L. Larsson, R. Petré and B. Wyszomirska-Werbart (eds) *Regions and Reflections*, Acta Archaeologica Lundensia No. 20, Lund.

# Chapter 3

## Landscape as Memory: The Mapping of Process and its Representation in a Melanesian Society

*Susanne Küchler*

In our consideration of landscape we are imprisoned by long-standing assumption about its nature as a record of, or stage for, significant human actions. The landscape of the western tradition is an inscribed surface which can be measured, described and depicted. Defined in terms of landmarks of ecological, historical or personal validity, landscape becomes the most generally accessible and widely shared *aide-mémoire* of a culture's knowledge and understanding of its past and future.

The conception of landscape as inscribed surface implies a link between mapping and image-making which dates back at least to Ptolemy's *Geography* whose text became part of Renaissance verbal and pictorial tradition.[1] The difference in pictorial conception in Italian and northern Dutch Renaissance, however, lead to distinct developments of landscape art; the Italian Albertian perspective posited a viewer at a certain distance looking through a framed window to a narrative, substitute world, whereas the so-called distant point method favoured by workshops in the north established pictures as record of a great range of knowledge and information about the world.[2] Painted landscapes of the western

---

1. Claudius Ptolemaeus 1883.
2. For a detailed discussion of landscape art in the Northern and Italian Renaisance see Alpers 1983: 133–42. Also: Gombrich 1966: 107–21.

tradition are thus landscapes *of memory*, they seize upon and validate personal or social memories.[3]

Outside the western context, landscapes of memory are rarely to be found.[4] The alternative to landscape as inscribed surface and *aide mémoire*, is a perspective which holds landscape to be implicated as template in the process of memory-work. Following this perspective of landscape *as memory* (process), rather than inscription of memory, image-making practice and its visual forms are implicated in the process of remembering and forgetting and thus are shaped by memory-work rather than by accounts of distinct memories.[5]

Using the ethnography of Malangan art of New Ireland as a basis, I want to argue that image-traditions of the latter kind are not just part of a cosmologically defined view of the world that is symptomatic of indigenous cultures.[6] Rather, generalising from the Malangan material, these traditions have emerged under specific conditions surrounding the appropriation and transmission of non-territorially conceived land. In New Ireland, those conditions, involving the break-up of clan territory and the formation of regionally extended land holding confederations, were the result of western colonialism. The issues over the transmission of land came to be formulated in visual terms, yet because these terms negated western conceptions of landscapes, the misrepresentation of Malangan as 'art' made possible the development of an indigenous legal system which remained veiled and operational into post-colonial times.

3. Finley 1980.

4. The intimate relation between mapping and image-making practice seems to be, when found, a distinct phenomenon of colonial culture. For a discussion of this point for South-America see Miller 1991.

5. The most prominent example of such traditions is Australian Aboriginal Art with its graphic denotation of a landscape which bears the imprints of ancestral actions; c.f. Munn 1973, Sutton 1988, Morphy 1991. Aboriginal landscape, however, is not conceived as a natural or historical construct, but as a memory construct or template which enables the infinite and efficient reproduction of ephemeral imagery and its interpretation in terms of relationships over land; Howard Morphy's elaboration on the method of 'cross-hatching' for ancestral paintings as founded upon the experiential dimension of blood-letting in initiation rituals is a case in point (1989). Aboriginal bark- or sand paintings are therefore not 'landscapes' of historical or personal memory in the western sense, but visualise in complex ways memory-work as such, that is the emotions and beliefs which govern the mnemonic transmission of land-based relationships.

6. Bastien 1985, Munn 1986 (ch. 4).

## Geographical/Historical Background

New Ireland is a 300-kilometre long and (in parts of the North) only 5 kilometre wide island to the North East of Papua New Guinea (see map 3.1). Of volcanic origin, the island was uplifted and twisted during geological formation. The uplifting was most pronounced along the north-west coast and has left its mark in sharp ascending reef formations which leave only a narrow coastal strip of land. The interior of the North is dominated by mountains which rise in three places to formidable limestone formations, each between 400 to 600 hundred metres above sea-level. Towards the centre of the island the mountains rise even further to a plateau known as Lelet, about 1000 metres above sea-level. South of Lelet Plateau, the mountains fall to sea-level and give rise to the wide expanse of southern New Ireland which is separated only by a narrow passage from New Britain.

These differences in the landscape are mirrored in linguistic and cultural distinctions; New Ireland language encompasses three sub-groupings which coincide with the geographical divi-

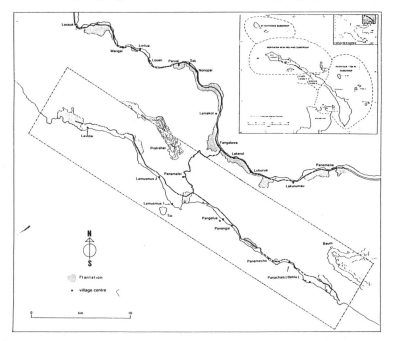

**Map 3.1**

sion of the island into North, Centre and South, each sub-group featuring a distinct ceremonial system surrounding death and initiation – *Malangan* in the North, *Uli* in the Centre and *Tumbuan* in the South. Malangan and Tumbuan are flourishing institutions whose activities centre upon the production of carved, woven and moulded sculptures in the North and fibre masks in the South.

The island is among the northern most islands of the Bismarck Archipelago and is situated north-east of Papua New Guinea between the islands of New Hanover and New Britain. Archaeology has provided evidence of ancient trade routes which connect New Ireland not just with its adjacent islands, but also with the distant Solomon islands to the far south. Since the late eighteenth century, partly because of the prominence of its position and size, and its covering of coconut groves, the Bismarck Archipelago became the prime target of western exploration, trade and colonisation. New Ireland itself was first placed on the map in 1527 and named in another exploration in 1769 when the narrow isthmus separating New Ireland from New Britain to the South was discovered. The island was subsequently exposed to persistent and rapidly expanding indirect trade, followed by unofficial trade networks and the establishment of official trading posts in 1840.

The imposition of German colonial rule in 1885 coincided with the growing alienation of large stretches of fertile coastal land to foreign owned plantations. Around the turn of the century, a highway named after the German official Boluminski was built along the east coast to connect the plantations with the two major administrative centres and ports in the north and the south of the island. In 1904, the German colonial government imposed a head-tax on both men and women with the double aim of enlisting the local population in the construction of the road and achieving a measure of control over the settlements in the interior. Around 1910, government reports mention the formation of temporary settlements along the coast during the dry months of the year in which road construction took place. Gradually over the next twenty years these settlements became more permanent as people deserted their dwellings in the interior. Around 1930, the mountains were deserted with the exception of one village in the North on the east-west track across the narrowest point on the island. All villages along the coast, therefore, are the outcome of a process of resettlement during the first two decades of this century which was heavily constrained by the already established alienation of coastal land which continued until late 1960s. These new villages were formed around coastal settlements or places used by the interior population for fishing or sago production prior to resettlement. The former geographical separation of the population into mountain people (*uru*) and coastal people (*keleras*) came to be replicated in the internal subdivisions of villages which remain a prominent feature of present day social organisation.

A contemporary village such as Lamusmus on the north-west coast, for example, which comprises forty-five nuclear settlements, is divided into Lamusmus 1 and Lamusmus 2. Lamusmus 1 thinks of itself as having formed around a coastal settlement, whereas Lamusmus 2 was formed around the fishing place of a former interior settlement. Each subdivision is divided in turn into two parts of which one has long-standing affinal relations with other 'coastal' clans, the other with other 'mountain' clans. The memory of where and with whom one settled prior to the formation of the new villages structures cooperation in gardening and ceremonial activities, with a prevalence for marriages to be formed between Lamusmus 1 and 2.

Early twentieth century resettlement was just one of many colonial interventions which, like the alienation of large stretches of coastal land, focused attention on relationships over land, labour and loyalty. But it would be highly misleading to present a picture of stability in residence patterns prior to resettlement. The establishing of indirect trade soon after the island was officially placed on the map of explorers in 1769 led to an escalation of warfare and mass migration of people. Territorially organised matrilineal clans which inhabited centralised villages on the limestone formations in the interior were broken up and scattered across the island. The North, on which I will be concentrating in this chapter, became a 'refugee camp' accommodating clans from the New Hanover island as well as from central and southern New Ireland. This process led to the breakdown of the moiety system which had regulated relationships over land. Thus, in the North, a new institutionalisation of relationships over land, labour and loyalty emerged prior to the imposition of colonial rule, testified by the fact that this part of the island did not have to be forcefully appeased by the colonial government. Relationships over land

had come to be institutionalised in mortuary exchanges which
henceforth governed the response made to the artificially created
land shortage around the turn of the century.


## Image, Body and Land

In contemporary northern New Ireland, the right to cultivate and
harvest on village land is not restricted to those inhabiting the village. On the contrary, graded into different categories of ownership, land use is extended to inhabitants of other villages in the
same and neighbouring language areas by virtue of relationships
that are articulated with reference to the memory of exchange.
The right to use land outside the village is acquired through the
presentation of currency, shell-money, and sculpted images
whose generic name *Malangan* is applied to the mortuary
exchanges for which the images are sculptured.

Malangan sculptures are carved from wood, woven from fibre
or moulded from clay. The carvings in particular have come to
constitute one of the largest collections of artefacts in western
museums (Figure 3.1). Some five thousand objects were collected
from the island between 1840 and the present day. These items
were assumed to be part of an extremely complex art tradition of
ancient origin, threatened by western influences. In reality, the
sculpting is inseparably bound up with the institutionalisation of
land rights and their transmission. Malangan art is historically
situated in the colonial and post-colonial culture.

The sculptures visualise a stock of named images which are
transmitted between those who share access to land. The way in
which an image is recalled for sculpting is informed by the type
of land usage to be certified in the mortuary transactions.[7]

The sculpted image, however, is not just a token exchanged for
the use of land and an *aide mémoire* of relationships over land:
Conceptually and stylistically, image-making practice is profoundly shaped by, and thus visualises and renders intelligible,
the process of landscape formation which provides the experiential foundation of the system of landrights.

---

7. For more detailed explications of the mnemonic transmission of Malangan imagery, its
political and economic background and social-cultural implications, see Kuchler 1987, 1988,
Kuchler and Melion 1991.

On the one hand, land is circulated as a movable commodity which can be shared, divided and loaned over periods of time in accordance with the transmission of Malangan images. On the other hand, land is, like the Malangan image, shaped by the process of its transmission in that, after every mortuary ceremony which witnesses sculptural production and the reallocation of land, the surface appearance of the land is restructured according to a map laid down in memory; former garden land is periodically replaced by settlements, and settlements become gardens and later secondary forest. We will see that sculpting articulates a process of the embodiment which results from an inversion and merging of 'inside' and 'outside'.

Both the surface of the sculpture and the surface of the land allude to an invisible, hidden, and remembered pattern whose reconstruction is the main objective in the negotiation of relationships pertaining to the ownership of land and images.[8] This pattern takes the form of a template which governs mnemonic reproduction in all its complexity; it is image based, meaning that there is an inseparable and complex relation between sculpted images and the memory of a past landscape.[9]

Despite its intrinsic and complex relation to land, sculpting in northern New Ireland did not develop into anything like landscape art. It is not possible to read off from the shape and motif arrangement of sculpted images which place or whose land is negotiated in the mortuary exchanges.[10] The rich iconography of Malangan sculptures seemingly invites just this kind of interpretation, as it suggests a relation between the sculpted object and what is represented. The formal properties of the sculptures, however, do not reflect what is represented, but a process of representation which is inseparable from the act of remembering. Visually and conceptually, because of the sculptures' contextualisation in

8. See Remo Guidieri and Francesco Pellizzi on the ephemerality of sites and images, forgetting and the creation of ancestors in Malekula: 'It would appear that the New Hebridean memory keeps negating itself, it "remember(s) much forgetting", as the poet said; it exerts itself tirelessly to wipe out the trace that could form its strongest support. In more than one sense, then, once again, this is a memory that recalls and represents, only the better to forget.'(1981:15). One might add that recall and representation are founded on prior forgetting (see Connerton 1989).

9. Bartlett 1932.

10. The prevailing analysis of Malangan art has consisted of attempts to establish the emblematic nature of style by attempting to assign the ownership over specific visual forms to certain clans; cf. Powdermaker 1932; Lewis, 1969; Wilkinson 1978; Brewer, 1979; Gunn 1982. This has lead to the failure to integrate collections into research, but also prevented understanding of the complex relation between land, exchange and imagery.

the ceremonies of the life-cycle, the sculptures thematise representation and remembering as embodiment. Through sculpting, the process of embodiment takes on significance as a general metaphor for processes of transmission. Sculpting in the form we know of through museum collections, therefore, served to institutionalise emerging relations over land, labour and loyalty.

## The Malangan Sculpture as Embodiment

Western artists and collectors were attracted by the objects because of their visual and conceptual complexity. Wooden sculptures can be vertical, horizontal or figurative and are usually between one and three metres long (Figure 3.1). Carved in the round, the soft wood is richly incised and painted. The resulting fragility of the sculpture seems to negate its identity as three dimensional carving; visually, the sculpture is held together by painted patterns that envelop the carved planes, and which thus transform the three-dimensionality of the carving into the two-dimensionality of a painting.[11]

The sculptures are framed by thin, parallel rods connected by short bridges. Contained within this frame is an assemblage of carved motifs comprising different kinds of birds, insects, fish and shells, and also mythical personages and musical instruments with magical qualities such as the pan pipe (Figure 3.2). Each sculpture depicts between two and seven of a total of twenty-seven motifs, which are arranged around the main body of the sculpture and are sometimes even carved from separate pieces of wood.

The richness of design seems to suggest a heightened importance of the sculpture in the indigenous culture. Yet, though the process of production can last up to three months, the finished work is exhibited no longer than a few hours before it is left to the wind and the rain, which rapidly erase all trace of the craftsmanship. The sale of the carvings to western collectors is a welcome alternative, as money has come to play a prominent part in the present-day economy. Nevertheless, sculptures continue to be produced not primarily for sale, but for the ritual climax in the Malangan mortuary ceremonies.

11. For a more detailed discussion of the visual and conceptual aspects of Malangan art see Kuchler 1987, 1988, Kuchler and Melion 1991.

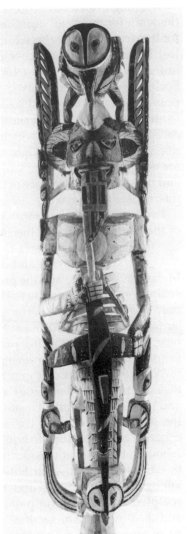

**Figure 3.1 Malangan, museum
für Volkerkunde und schweiner-
isches museum für volkskunde
Basel. ca. 1932.**

**Figure 3.2 Museum für
Volkerkunde und schweiner-
isches museum für volkskunde
Basel ca. 1910.**

The long drawn out process of carving the Malangan 'finishes the work for the dead' (*haisok ine mamat*); it is the final ceremony for the dead who have been buried in the local cemetery since the last Malangan. The process of sculpting is described in the indigenous language as *tetak*, literally 'the making of skin'. Sculptures are thus conceived as 'skins' that replace the decomposed body of a deceased person and thus provide a container for his or her life-force (*noman*). The 'making of skin' serves to recapture the life-force which was freed as a result of bodily decomposition; inscribed into the material, the life-force is transformed into an image. The sculpted image is, like the human eye and the skin, the outer trace of the (usually) hidden, invisible, and internalised life-force.

In New Ireland, as in most Melanesian cultures, the condition of the bodily skin and of the eyes is thought to reveal the condition of the life-force (*noman*), that is of the state of health and creativity.[12] The pervasive and dominant motif of the eye in the Malangan sculpture and the profusion of painted patterns on the sculpture similarly points to the fact that the sculpted image is only seemingly a fixed surface, but that it is something that has surfaced and is constructed in terms of a hidden, interiorised pattern. Likewise, the carving practice takes for granted a hidden form which is thought to emerge during sculpting.

When exhibited on the grave, the sculpted image is thought to be 'hot', intensely dangerous and alive. It embodies raw energy and thus must be 'killed', leading to the ritualised destruction of the sculpture. Following the notion that all death, except death occuring after returning to liquid foods in old age and after being rehoused before death inside the funerary enclosure, is caused by the stripping of skin – attributed to spirit beings or sorcery –, the killing of the sculpture is undertaken by transferring the 'skin' or sculpted image to a group of mourners in exchange for money and shell-money. The sacrifice of the sculpture is thus articulated as an exchange of the sculpted image between those who have carved it in the present instance and those who take on the right to reproduce it in the future.[13]

The definition of the sculpted image as 'skin' (*tak*) seems at first glance to describe the surface treatment of sculptures whose

---

12. cf. O'Hanlon 1990.
13. See also S. Kuchler 1988, Kuchler and Melion 1991.

carved planes are enveloped by painted patterns, as well as the conceptual and visual likeness between the sculpture and the body. *Tak*, or skin, however, is not just the surface of the body, but also the outer trace of life-force (*noman*) together with other body parts ending in 'ak' such as the eyes (*merak*), the throat (*vuak*) and the hands (*mak*), all of which are vivid in a healthy person. The merging of inside (life-force) and outside (skin) is made visible in the sculpture through the inseparability of carving and painting and through the tightness of the overlap between the two.

## The Land as Embodiment

*Tak*, moreover, refers not just to the sculpture, but also to the cultivated land and to affinal relations directed outward to siblings and cousins who are addressed with terms ending in 'ak'. There is a complex relation between kinship terminology, its moral codes, and the body. Affines, as relations of exchange, for example, are constrained in the use of body parts ending in 'ak'. They may not use their own hand (*mak*) for giving, but have to pass things on through a 'neutral' other. They may not look at each other with their eyes (*merak*). They may not speak (use their throat, *vuak*) to each other, and they may not touch each other's skin (*tak*). Constrained in this manner, transmission is thus of key concern in the formation of *korok*, the generalised category of affines whose capacity to generate movable wealth decides the political and economic strength of a residential group. *korok* are 'of one skin' as a result of ritualised acts of consumption, of food grown in gardens and of images inscribed into Malangan sculptures. They habitually garden together and occasionally bring each other special food parcels wrapped in banana leaves, such as sago which is rare in the north of New Ireland. They also assist each other in all their funerary obligations, particularly in the preparation and execution of Malangan ceremonies and payments.

The link between cultivated land, called *laten* or 'the place of the skin', the sculpted Malangan image and affines is odour (*musung*). Odour, a hidden and invisible substance which trigers memory yet is itself not recollectable, is thought to originate on an island beyond the horizon which is believed to be the seat of forces associated with earthquakes (*meruli, moroa*). Attracted to the gardens through magical spells, odour comes to reside in taro tubers. Taro tubers are classified into named types by the smell they emitt when roasted over the fire, each type being associated with certain clans and yet significantly shared by those who call each other *korok* and who garden together. Taro tubers are consumed by the carver (*tetak* or 'the maker of skin') who thus channels odour into the wood during carving which it releases when the sculpture is left to rot in the forest; the area where the sculpture is left to rot is marked by the distinctive odour of excrement.

Odour is thus transfigured from an invisible substance into an object of remembrance, ie. into the taro tuber and into the sculpted image. Both taro tuber and Malangan image are infinitally reproducable and desirable on account of their generative potency. This relation between odour and the material world is essential for an understanding of 'land' and 'landscape' production.

It was some time into my fieldwork before I realised that the relation between garden land and settlement is not fixed, but subject to a process of inversion. The reason for my slowness was that, when under Australian administration, villages were forced to take on a camp-like structure with houses clustered around a central cemetery. The dispersed style of settlement, with scattered house sites surrounded by gardens, coconut palms and secondary forests of various heights, has only gradually reoccured since independence in 1975, and then only where space actually permitted the expansion of the village. Mercifully I was told one day when sweating in the sun drawing maps of a village on the north-west coast, that nobody could understand what I was doing because what I was drawing would soon disappear. Instead, I was instructed not to draw the village as I could see it, but to notate a mental map of places which once were house sites and now were gardens or had been gardens some time ago and were now covered by secondary forest.

Whenever decisions are made about where to relocate a settlement, it is this mental map of 'forgotten' places to be recollected which is drawn upon. In the absence of any emphasis on genealogy, the history of social relations is embedded in the process of mapping. Mapping is the product of place transmission which, together with the transmission of personal names and skills, effects the virtual reconstitution of social relations over time.

The map incorporates a process of inversion from house sites, called *larune* or 'the place of the womb' into gardens called *laten* or 'the place of the skin', and from gardens into house sites. At any one moment in time, the land which serves for gardening and for habitation is thus conceptualised as a body: the communally shared land or 'skin' associated with affinal relationships surrounds the houses or 'womb' which are the domain of the women and the matriline.

However, this physiological structure imposed on the social landscape is not fixed, but is blurred and made indistinguishable in the process of restructuring house sites and garden areas, with house sites associated with particular matrilines being rebuilt on affinally owned garden land. In this process, 'inside' and 'outside' become merged, so that the surface or 'landscape' testifies as much to what lies buried beneath the forest, to what is imagined and remembered, as to what is visible and known.

The Malangan sculpture visually elaborate upon this process, in that the carved image, or 'skin', alludes to the named template from which the image is derived. This template, of which there are not more than six for wooden sculptures, is called *wune*, a term which literally translated means 'womb', 'water-well', and 'smoke'. *Wune* are originated through dreaming and transmitted through sculpting. The polysemic term itself alludes to a generative and inherently connecting process of 'mapping' which proceeds from a hidden, interior source and creates only passing impressions. As the impression of a template onto a sculpture is subject to a process of the recollection of an interiorised and temporarily forgotten image, so landscape is made subject to this process of transmission and transformation.

The social landscape is indeed *the* subject matter of social memory. Sculpting plays a key role in this process of remembering both in metaphorising recollection as embodiment and in providing the forum for negotiating landscape as shared, yet disputed, memory.

## The Dismantling of the Body and the 'Forgetting' of Place

For landscape to become subject to recollection, it has to be rendered absent and handed over to forgetting. The periodical erasure of inhabited and worked upon landscape is the product of the funerary process, commencing with the burial of a person and culminating in the desertion of the settlement and burial place. In effect, it is the transformation of settlement into burial place with the rooting of bodies in the ground which foreshadows the creation of 'burial places of memory'.[14]

Every settlement has its own burial place. Like settlements, burial places have become artificially arrested under colonial administration. Given, however, the conditions which allow for the break-up of the camp-like structure of settlement, burial places are abandoned and reused in accordance with the process of shifting settlements.

The burial place is composed of two adjacent enclosures, one used for presenting and 'drying' the body prior to burial and for sculpting, the other for the burial of the body and the exhibition of the sculpture. The enclosures, distinguished as 'outside'/'visible'/'ephemeral' (*sebedo*) and 'inside'/'invisible'/'permanent' (*uve*), form one side of the settlement. *Sebedo*, a bamboo fence, is built on the former house site of a deceased member of the settlement next to a stone wall or *uve* marking a communal grave in which all inhabitants of the settlement used to be communally buried prior to missionisation.

Following the burial, two main and a large number of subsidiary ceremonies trace the decomposition of the body in the grave. Ritual consumption is the main theme of these ceremonies which erase any trace of the person's labour on the land; ripened planted produce is eaten in the enclosure adjacent to the grave.

About two years after the funeral, when all the produce of the deceased's garden land has been consumed in this way and the garden itself is overgrown by secondary forest, a larger ceremony takes place attended by everybody from the surrounding villages who has plots in the gardens of the deceased's village. This ceremony (*a gom*), lasting two days, marks the burning of the house. The spot where it was standing becomes the place for the construction of cooking houses during the Malangan ceremony. After about a further two years, determined by the time it takes to rear a sufficient number of pigs, a major ceremony (*a gisong*), lasting three days, is performed. The body in the grave is thought to be completely decomposed at this stage. At the ceremony, the mourners meet in the former garden land of the deceased person and walk back to his or her settlement with its funerary enclo-

---

14. For an insightful analysis of the relation between funerary and memory work see Feeley-Harnik 1991, on Madagascar. For the relation between forgetting and the transmission of culture see MacDonald 1987.

sures, singing songs about a land crab that peels the bark off coconut palms. Running along on either side are men with axes who cut down any tree or palm planted by the deceased along the wayside, thus finalising the process of the eradication of traces of the deceased's work on the land.

Between this ceremony and the final Malangan, years can pass in which nothing happens. The interval is longest for men and women between adolescence and seniority, and shortest for those dying after they have been rehoused inside the funerary enclosure (*sebedo*) as a mark of seniority.[15] During this interval, the life-force of the deceased which was dismantled in the first phase of the mortuary cycle is thought to grow in strength. In its dissociation from the body, the life-force is thought to be arrested at the mythical place *Karoro*. It is this place that is addressed in magical spells which are performed at the outer edge of the reef during a ceremony called *musung*.

*Musung* means both the 'calling of smell' and as well as 'flames' and is performed just prior to the planting of ritual gardens whose produce will be distributed to those participating in the exchanges of the Malangan image. The crops are placed on platforms where they emit the musty smell of decay until they are cooked during the final days of the Malangan-ceremony.

Odour, as the disembodied agent of recollection which always depends upon some form of container, transform the burial place into the burial place of memory.[16] During the final days of the Malangan ceremony, the distinct smell of heated stone-ovens effuses without interruption from the cooking houses which are built on the spot where the house of the deceased once stood. The food is distributed minutes after the display of the sculpture and the transaction of the right to the reproduction of its image. Laid out in heaps apportioned to each assembled nuclear family, the cooked food is collected and immediately taken home to be consumed.

As people leave the burial place, they leave behind a settlement which is, like the Malangan sculpture after its symbolic destruction and like the human body after death, a shell which

---

15. The death of women, children and adolescents is marked with a woven, round Malangan called *Warwara*, if they are not included in a Malangan ceremony which is already being prepared at the time of death. Knowledge about *Warwara* is handed down inside the matrilineal clan.

16. See Sperber 1975: 115–49; Gell 1977.

will gradually fall apart. As the forest overgrows the traces of past habitation, the place becomes memory. When encountered again, a nut or fruit tree, a plant or a piece of wall, like an odour, may trigger a recollection of social relations and of past social conditions.

The secondary forest and the garden land surrounding each settlement offers an extended journey into the burial places of memory. The pathways which connect gardens, settlements and villages connect also past settlements, so that each journey done by foot is a journey in which buried, forgotten landscape is quite literally re-collected as nut and fruit trees are harvested by the passers by.

One can interpret this refusal of an empirically founded perspective on land and landscape in cosmological terms; given, however, the colonial experience of northerners with dispersion followed by mass alienation of land and resettlement, the perspective on landscape fashioned in Malangan has a distinctively political overtone. It has regained significance in the present postcolonial phase of the registration of land-titles which the now independent government attempts to impose on villagers. Malangan carving and the shifting of settlements has experienced a resurgence on a scale and intensity which matches the millenarian movement, known as the Johnson cult, in New Hanover island to the North, in which many of those who are active in Malangan are also involved.

## The Political Economy of Memory

Every man and woman can trace the trees of former gardens which were started by them and the trees of gardens in which they used merely to have a plot. What appear to be just trees among trees in secondary forest figure as memoriae *loci* that can be used to retrace relationships of considerable time-depth since rights to former garden land are passed down the generations.

Such claims to land are, however, heavily contested, with the monthly village court dealing in almost every session with some form of dispute. The dispute is the occasion for elaborate reconstructions of relationships whereby the pattern imposed upon the landscape in the form of planted trees, funerary enclosures and other signs of former habitation emerges as a kind of memory template enabling and governing the account of land ownership. The most frequent cause for dispute is the banning of garden land owing to an expressed fear that fallow periods are not adhered to and that it is used for gardening by too many people from other villages.

The impression shared by most northerners that land is a scarce good is not just the result of historically constituted ecological conditions, but is also the result of the transaction of land rights via imagery in the mortuary exchanges: The wider a settlement extends its right to use land, to villages in the same and different language area, the more it is considered to be in control of the production and circulation of valuables. Yet by implication, the more expansive the rights to land exerted by a settlement, the more people will also make a claim to the land of the settlement. The efflorescence of Malangan exchanges was thus accompanied by the formation of a regional social organisation with un-bounded, ego-centered and expanding networks which came to replace kinship-based modes of integration.

Both men and women in contemporary villages have a number of independent ties of cooperation in gardening which stretch across several adjacent villages and even language areas; it is common for a married couple to have plots in several gardens of neighbouring villages and to take up residence for extended periods in further removed places for the purpose of gardening. In addition to extended rights to garden land, every settlement has rights to harvest fruit-carrying trees of various sorts in other villages. Entirely dependent on this system of extended and graded land ownership is the production of cash crops, since village land is not sufficient to accommodate coconut groves of the size required by the demanded output.

The extended system of land-ownership in the North enabled people to meet the challenge of land alienation and resettlement. Under colonial conditions, it also became the framework of ritual confederations which cut across villages and language boundaries and encompassed a number of scattered matrilineal sub-clans. I call these expanding, ego-centred social groupings ritual confederations, because the regulation of relationships over land, labour and loyalty is virtually independent of clan identity and marriage. The sharing of land which is the determining criteria of a ritual confederation implies mutual responsibility in assisting each other in the work on the land and the work for the dead (*haisok ine mamat*). This bond is articulated with reference to the joint memory of an image which once was seen engraved and painted in a Malangan sculpture during the climax of a mortuary ceremony. Those who share land on account of sharing the memory of an image call each other 'of one skin' (*namam retak*).

The ritual confederations are fluid and in constant process of refashioning as they are a product of the political economy of memory surrounding the transmission of land and images. The efflorescence of image-production, itself governed by certain conditions such as the rise in mortality during early colonial impact, must be seen as a key factor in disseminating Malangan-based practices and concepts of transmission across the war-torn North. The scale of image-production around the turn of the century can be deduced from museum collections of Malangan sculptures whose size is comparable with other large collections such as the collection of north-west coast American artefacts.

Summarising the evidence of collections against the background of an understanding of the way in which images derived from templates are circulated, one can say that there is a relation between the distribution of matrilineal clans and named templates, with sculpted images leaving a village as a result of their transaction being channelled along intra-clan ties between villages. Ritual confederations, which define themselves in terms of the sharing of once sculpted and remembered images derived from particular templates, reconstitute in this way matrilineal clans and their relationships. The biography of an image, that is the path taken during its circulation, is thus also the story about the migration of a clan, or a group of two or three intermarrying clans, and this migration has inscribed itself into the landscape in the form of deserted stone-walled cemeteries and planted fruit and nut trees.

The migration histories of clans thus complement the ritual knowledge of the distribution of images and the expansion of ritual confederations. Everyone knows where clan members live and with which clans they intermarry; because of attending ceremonies, which are often far afield, there is also a widespread awareness of what kind of images are to be found where and how they are to be placed in relation to each other.

The ravages of warfare, however, did not simply have social consequences such as the break-up of territorially bounded clans. They also led to a shift from a concern over the transmission and accumulation of life-force (which used to govern the practice of killing neighbouring tribes), to a concern over the transmission and accumulation of land. In fact, life-force and land only became inseparably intertwined in a climate of imagined and actual threat of extinction which was heightened by the rising death toll and decreasing birth-rate which continued to be of concern until the 1950s. This fusion of life-force and land led to the development of sculpting as we know it through museum collections.

The pre-colonial type of funerary monument, called *Kambai*, is still used on the island of New Hanover; it is a wooden log which serves as platform for dances carried out by women. In northern New Ireland, some time around the beginning of the nineteenth century, this log was incised and fashioned as 'skin', that is as something which bears, like the cultivated land, the imprint of social relations. Thus produced, not just as a monument to the dead, but as a gift, sculpting provided the framework for the institutionalisation of land, labour and loyalty which could no longer be adequately addressed by the social organisation.

Inscribed into the experiential dimension of death, the newly evolving system of regulating relationships was successfully veiled from colonial introspection.[17] Even anthropologists interpreted the sculpting undertaken for the final mortuary ceremony as purely commemorative in function, that is as expressive of the deceased's position in the system of social relationships disrupted by death. The production and exchange of Malangan images was allowed to emerge unhindered as an effective indigenous legal system, because it appeared to be nothing more than a memorial to the dead which encoded at most a statement about status, and as the articulation of a mythology which allegedly had been 'lost' during acculturation.

## Conclusion

Our approach to both western and non-western art tends to be based on a prevailing assumption that the relation between landscape and memory results from the capture of memories on the land in the form architectural or other visual landmarks. 'Recollecting' landscape through visual or other modes of repre-

---

17. See also Feeley-Harnik 1985 on political economy of memory in Madagascar.

sentation is thus held to be a primarily private and self-oriented act of appropriation. Landscape is, consequently, seen as a fixed, objectifiable and measurable description of a surface which is not affected by the project of its representation and remembrance. In a sense, one might see landscape and our dominant perception of it, as it is revealed in visual and verbal representations, as a by-product of a change in the perception and status of memory; from a deeply enculturated process of remembering to a personalised, internalised and measurable capacity.[18]

With the example of Malangan art of New Ireland, I argued that by imposing our assumptions about landscape and memory on non-western art we might miss its political and historical significance. We also cannot recognise the dynamic of landscape formation in its peculiar cultural context. When shifting our attention from the encoding of memories to the process of remembering, landscape can be seen, like other form of representation, as the product of this process which is forever being transformed in accordance with a culturally constructed template.

The visual representation of landscape as memory, that is as part of a process of remembering, is, I argue, far from being a general phenomenon of 'non-western' culture. On the contrary, the Malangan material shows that the articulation of the process of landscape formation in visual modes of representation is inseparable from the emergence of a political economy of memory under specific social and historical conditions.

## References

Alpers, S. 1983. *The Art of Describing,* Chicago: Chicago University Press.
Bartlett, F. C. 1932. *Remembering,* Cambridge: Cambridge University Press.
Bastien, J.W. 1985. 'Quollahuaya Andean body concepts: a topographi-cal-hydrological model of physiology,' *American Anthropologist,* 87, 595–611.
Brewer, E. 1979. 'A Malangan to cover the grave', PhD dissertation, University of Queensland.
Carruthers, M. 1990. *The Book of Memory: A Study in Medieval Memory.* Cambridge: Cambridge University Press.
Casey, E. 1987. *Remembering: A Phenomenological Study,* Bloomington:

18. See Yates 1966; Casey 1987; Carruthers 1990.

Indiana University Press.

Connerton, P. 1989. *How Societies Remember*, Cambridge: Cambridge University Press.

Feeley-Harnik, G. 1991. 'Finding Memories in Madagascar,' in S. Kuchler and W. Melion (eds), *Images of Memory: on Representation and Remembering*, Washington, DC: Smithsonian Institution Press.

Finley, G. 1980. *Landscapes of Memory: Turner as Illustrator to Scott*, Berkeley: University of California Press.

Gell, A. 1977. 'Magic, perfume, dream.', in I. Lewis (ed.), *Symbols and Sentiment*, London: Academy Press.

Gombrich, E. 1966. 'Renaissance theory of art and the rise of landscape,' in E. Gombrich, *Norm and Form*, London: Phaidon Press.

Guidieri, R. and F. Pellizzi 1981. 'Shadows: nineteen tableaux on the cult of the dead in Malekula, Eastern Malekula,' *Res*, 2.

Gunn, M. 1982. 'Tabar Malangan,' Unpublished report on fieldwork in Tabar island.

Howes, D. 1987a. 'On the odor of the soul: spatial representation and olfactory classification in Eastern Indonesia and Western Melanesia,' *Bidragen tot de Taal-Land en Volkenkunde 14 (4)*, 84–113.

_____1987b. 'Olfaction and transition: an essay on the ritual uses of smell,' Rev. Canad. Soc. and Anth., 24 (3), 398–415.

Kuchler, S. 1987. 'Malangan – art and memory in a Melanesian society,' *Man* (N.S.) 22, 238–55.

_____1988. 'Malangan – objects, sacrifice and the production of memory,' *American Ethnologist*, 15 (4), 625–37.

Kuchler, S. and W. Melion (eds) 1991. *Images of Memory: on Representation and Remembering*, Washington DC: Smithsonian Institution Press.

Lewis, P. 1969. 'The social context of art in northern New Ireland,' *Fieldiana, Anthropology* 58, Chicago: Fieldmuseum of Natural History.

MacDonald, R. 1987. *The Burial-Places of Memory*, Amherst: University of Massachusetts Press.

Miller, A. 1991. 'Transformations of time and space, Oaxaca, Mexico 1500–1700,' in S. Kuchler and W. Melion (eds), *Images of Memory*, Washington, D.C.: Smithsonian Institution Press.

Morphy, H. 1989. 'From dull to brilliant: the aesthetics of spiritual power among the Yolngu,' *Man* (N.S.), 24 (1), 21–41.

_____1991. Ancestral Connections: Art and an Aboriginal System of Knowldege. Chicago University Press.

Munn, N. 1973. Walbiri Iconography, Ithaca: Cornell University Press.

_____1986. *Fame of Gawa* Chicago: Chicago University Press.

Powdermaker, H. 1932. *Life in Lesu* London: William and Norgate.

Ptolemeaus, C. 1883. *Geographia*, (ed.) Karl Muller, Paris.

Sperber, D. 1975. *Rethinking Symbolism*, Cambridge: Cambridge University Press.

Sutton, P. 1988. *Dreamings: the Art of Aboriginal Australia*, Asia Society

Galleries, New York: George Braziller.

Wilkinson, G. 1978. 'Carving a social message: The Malanggans of Tabar,' in M. Greenhalgh and V. Megaw (eds), *Art in Society*, London: Duckworth.

Yates, F. 1966. *The Art of Memory*, London: Routledge and Kegan Paul.

# Chapter 4

## Intersecting Belfast

*Neil Jarman*

The violence of the past twenty-odd years has brought dramatic changes to the city of Belfast. The apparent permanence of the conflict and the lack of any solutions acceptable to all parties, has meant that the ideological divisions have increasingly become a concrete part of the physical environment, creating an ever more militarised landscape, in which besieged communities turn their backs on their neighbours while attempting to continue life as normal.

The conflict is concerned with the status and allegiance of six of the nine counties of Ulster, maintained since 1921 as a part of the British state when the rest of Ireland was given independence, and whether they should remain within Britain, unite with the Irish Republic or even become an independent Ulster. There is little internal debate, Unionists and Nationalists concentrate on maintaining their existing support rather than moving towards compromise solutions. [1] The civil and military authorities meanwhile continue to pursue a policy of containing the violence and opposition, rather than striking at the root causes, while the paramilitaries on both sides remain excluded from any dialogue.

1. There are a number of names used to describe the two parties to the conflict in Ulster: Protestants, Unionists or Loyalists, and Catholic, Nationalist or Republican. They are usually treated as paired opposites, i.e. Protestant:Catholic, Unionist:Nationalist, and Loyalist:Republican, in which the labels refer to an increasingly specific and radical political orientation. Protestant and Catholic are the most generalised and apolitical of the terms, since it is possible to be a Protestant Republican (like many of the leaders of the United Irishmen in the eighteenth century) or a Catholic Unionist. Throughout this chapter I have switched between the three possible alternatives depending on context, whereas the difference between describing an estate as Catholic or Nationalist is slight (and says as much about the author as the subject, see Burton 1978, ch. 2 on 'Telling') that between a Republican mural and a Catholic one is immense.

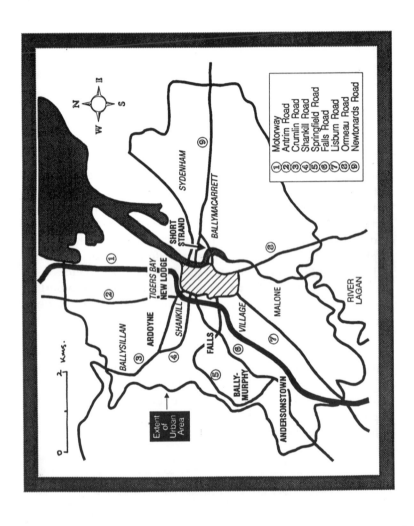

The view from outside, largely mediated by television and newspaper photographs, is presented mostly as bomb-damaged buildings, endless parades and colourful paramilitary murals, and ignores their context within the more extensive transformations of the urban environment. It also ignores the complexity of fragmentation within the two dominant communities. The predominant use of the terms 'Protestant' and 'Catholic' obscures the internal ruptures, in which the voices of the paramilitaries and their political organisations maintain an essentially working-class critique of Establishment organisations, while the coded voices speaking from the walls of the working class estates and the music of the parades are also increasingly those of youth. Whereas in the past muralists and bandsmen were respected craftsmen, today they are more likely to be unemployed and unskilled, but self-taught. The redefinition of traditional icons is thus a product of those excluded from power by age as well as class.

In spite of these internal critiques, the landscape remains a product created not only by sectarianism but specifically by men. All the practices considered below are male-dominated, while women remain substantially excluded both from the activities and the images that are restructuring the fabric of the city.

\* \* \* \* \* \* \* \* \* \* \* \*

It has been estimated that in the early years of the Troubles, between 1969 and 1976, up to 15,000 families in Belfast (approximately 60,000 people or about 12 per cent of the population) were forced to move house as a result of the violence (Boal and Murray 1977). Although some of these people resettled in the expanding satellite towns such as Antrim or Craigavon, the majority were relocated within the city (Doherty 1988). The rioting, intimidation and destruction of those years was overwhelmingly played out in the working-class estates. The effects were particularly pronounced in mixed residential areas and at the interfaces of Protestant and Catholic districts as people sought the safety and security of their co-religionists. As a result, an already existing pattern of sectarian residential segregation was reinforced and extended.

Ever since the early expansion of the city in the late eighteenth century, when Catholic residence was confined to the western areas outside the city proper, segregation developed as a feature of Belfast life. Regular spells of violence and rioting from the mid-nineteenth century onwards entrenched this basic pattern (Boyd 1987; Millar 1978): by 1911, 41 per cent of Catholics and 62 per cent of Protestants lived in streets in which over 90 per cent of residents were of similar faith. Although no rioting occurred between 1935 and the late 1960s, this pattern of living continued to harden, by 1969 the proportions had increased to 56 per cent and 69 per cent respectively and by 1972 to 70 per cent and 72 per cent (Boal 1982). While violence remained the major factor in this repatterning of residential life, the authorities also took the opportunity created by slum clearance and road improvement programmes to relocate some communities. The removal of the small, isolated Catholic population around the Docks in the north of the city was an early example of this policy.

Although denominational segregation has been the dominant factor structuring urban life, it is particularly a feature of the working-class areas. Middle-class residential areas, while less dominated by sectarianism, remained distinct and separate. But here, wealth, status and a more private style of life have helped to neutralise tensions. However, the middle-class streets in the Antrim Road area of North Belfast, have suffered from their proximity to the more violent estates, and, as many residents have moved to more secure addresses (often to more distant suburbs or satellite towns), the area has been lowered in status (Doherty 1988).

Belfast emerges from the dry equality of the map as a patchwork of distinct communities, divided by class and faith, often dominated, even in the 1970s, by ties of kinship (Wiener 1980), and still further fragmented by the physical landscape and the infrastructure of industrial capitalism.

Sited at the southern end of Belfast Lough, in the valley of the River Lagan, the city can be divided into three major sections. The area east of the river and south of the shipyards, Ballymacarrett and beyond, is overwhelmingly Protestant, apart from the small Short Strand district. Opposite, on the west bank, south of the Docks, is the commercial and administrative heart of the city which stretches southwards to include not only the University and the middle-class areas along the Malone and Stranmillis Roads, but also the inner city working-class Protestant districts around Sandy Row, Donegall Pass and Donegall Road. Finally, the west and north of the city is an area of working-class estates. The bulk of the Catholic population live in the streets adjacent to

the Falls Road, which links Divis on the edge of the City Centre to Andersonstown in the south-west, among the foothills of the Black Mountain. North of the Falls are the Protestant Shankill and Woodvale areas and further north, the Catholic Ardoyne and New Lodge estates together with the Protestant areas of Tiger's Bay, Skegoneill and Ballysillan. It is within these areas to the north and west of the Centre, where the sectarian divide is most tightly intermeshed, that much of the rioting and violence have historically been, and continue to be, played out.

The violence that marked the beginning of the Troubles was expended on property as much as on people. Boundaries between differing faiths were reinforced by the firing of homes and erection of barricades across streets. Dereliction became the hallmark of the interfaces. As the violence continued, more elaborate and permanent divisions between estates were established. While the prime agents of this action were the civil and military authorities, it was clear that these moves were supported by many of the local residents (Dawson 1984). Although the barriers reduced ease of movement, they also became focal points for ran-

dom projectile-throwing, and houses immediately adjacent
became the front line. The first of the 'peace lines' was erected
between the Catholic Clonard district of the lower Falls and
Protestant Shankill areas in 1969 (Conroy 1988). Initially made of
corrugated iron, over the years it has been extended in length and
height until it now consists of a brick wall up to four metres high
surmounted by corrugated sheeting and barbed wire. Similar
peace lines have been built at various other insecure interfaces in
West Belfast, from Cliftonville in the north to Suffolk in the south.

In East Belfast the redevelopment of the Short Strand area
involved surrounding the new estate with a wall and metal fence
structure, facing houses inwards rather than outwards onto the
major road, and reducing the number of through roads and
access roads into and out of the area. The redevelopment of this
isolated Catholic enclave east of the river, despite the landscaping of security measures with shrubs and trees, enhanced and
reinforced the sense of difference and isolation. In spite of concerns for security, both the Catholic and neighbouring Protestant
communities were resolute in their desire to hold on to whatever
was perceived as their traditional territory. Although many houses were lost as a result of road development, more radical
schemes that would have obliterated much of the Short Strand
area were abandoned (Dawson 1984).

In other areas, where derelict terraces continue to provide the
major barrier, security is often increased simply by bricking up
door and window openings and blocking road access. This may
involve total closure with steel fences, or the installation of pedes-
trian access gates, or it may simply involve the emplacement of
level-crossing-like barriers which may either be left open or locked
closed, depending on the general security situation. Controlling
vehicle access is the primary aim of these structures, which force
traffic to use major thoroughfares. The creation of cul-de-sacs and
no- through roads is intended to reduce the use of cars in terrorist
attacks. With knowledge of the sectarian geography of the city
such an integral and necessary part of routine behaviour (Burton
1978), it has been relatively easy to commit random sectarian mur-
ders simply by categorising potential targets by their location
(Dillon 1989). Even without these physical changes to the environment, individuals have been forced, for personal security, to adapt
their behaviour and patterns of movement to accommodate perceived changes in the landscape. This may involve such apparent-

ly simple decisions such as which bus stop to use, where to get a taxi or on which side of the road to walk.

The Victorian grid-style road layouts had offered a logical and easily comprehensible structure to, and between, estates. The destruction of these patterns and the creation of circuitous routes and dead ends aimed both to reduce attacks and ease the work of the security forces not only in pursuing terrorists, but also in seal-ing off areas for blanket house searches and similar activities. Such security considerations were also more generally incorpo-rated into the structure and layout of newer estates, such as Ballymurphy, and later redevelopments, where features such as armoured- vehicle-bearing foundations were laid under over-wide footpaths (De Baroid 1990). Such an approach to estate planning is not particular to Belfast (Matrix 1984): the advantages of combining redevelopment with the control of potential conflict have long been recognised (Benjamin 1983; Schorske 1981; Edholm, this volume).

The security forces have become a major agent in the restruc-turing of the Belfast environment. Although their input into defensive planning and reconstruction has already been referred to, the full extent of this role in the planning process can only be surmised (Dawson 1984). However, apart from these interventions, the security forces have made a major impact on the landscape in their own right. Army posts have been installed at strategic locations while police stations have become increasingly fortified. Both utilise one-way observation posts and cameras in otherwise featureless walls, protected from car attacks by speed ramps and huge boulders, while lookout towers bristling with a plethora of panoptic electronic devices peer over the neighbouring streets. In some cases, like the Divis Tower, military observation posts have been installed on top of a residential block, while in the Ballymurphy area army posts were initially (in 1969) established in the Henry Taggart Memorial Hall and the adjacent Vere Foster School. In the 1970s larger installations were constructed around the Ballymurphy estate, the first of which was Fort Pegasus on the Whiterock Road. Later, in November 1979, the Army occupied the locally initiated Whiterock Industrial Estate and built Fort Jericho, forcing local businesses to move elsewhere. Each base, established to aid control and surveillance of the Catholic population, in turn became a regular target of local protest and resistance (De Baroid 1990). Although observation and surveillance equipment has become a general feature of many buildings, and not simply military installations, it is these military installations that are the most intrusive, most obviously in the presence of the helicopters circling like buzzards over West Belfast. And while the military presence is all too familiar to local residents, structures such as Army positions and the Crumlin Road Prison, unlike police stations, are not included on maps of Belfast. Officially, they do not exist.

While the ostensible aim of such measures is the control and containment of violence, the effect of these permanent structures is to further institutionalise the seperation of the two communities. They physically impose themselves on the landscape and make visible a distance otherwise confined to temporary events and less tangible practices. They also reduce the possibility of denying the difference when it stares one in the face. Although segregation has always been a response to sectarian violence, the process has been one of oscillation, of entrenchment of difference in troubled times followed by some degree of reintegration. The permanence of the present peace lines and the ready acceptance of 'defensive planning' in the wider redevelopment of the city

admits to a pessimism regarding any solution. It also confirms a willingness to settle for what Reginald Maudling (when Northern Ireland Minister) described as an 'acceptable level of violence', as long as it does not affect long-term commercial prosperity.

This strategy of control and containment imposed on the working-class estates contrasts with the attempts to normalise the situation in the commercial Centre. In the early 1970s following an intensive bombing campaign by the IRA (Irish Republican Army), the City Centre had the appearance of a besieged citadel. Surrounded by a ring of steel security gates through which everyone had to pass and be searched, shut down to all but pedestrians and security vehicles, it resembled a ghost town after dark. Its commercial prosperity was further threatened by the growth of more convenient and seemingly secure out-of-town shopping complexes (Brown 1986). However, the 1980s have witnessed a regeneration of the commercial infrastructure through new building developments and a cosmetic landscaping at the margins. The heart of the city has been transformed by rebuilding, by new shopping and office developments and by the pedestrianisation of the Centre. The skyline, although still dominated by Goliath crane in the Harland and Wolff shipyard and by the buildings of the City Hospital, is steadily being raised. Despite the high levels of unemployment and continued decline in the textile, shipyard and engineering industries, high levels of central government subsidies to maintain at least some jobs in traditional industries (whose workforce is overwhelmingly Protestant), an enormous security industry, growing service sector and low housing costs have enabled the city to boom (Gaffikin and Morrissey 1990).

The state's approach to the Centre is undoubtedly linked to changes in IRA tactics, but is also part of its wider strategy of Ulsterisation, which principally involves criminalising the Republican movement while emphasising the uninterrupted continuation of daily life. The City Centre is the key to this approach, with the projection of an air of normality, accessibility and prosperity central to attempts to attract both British and foreign investment. A principal element in this strategy has been to remove the visible security presence and especially the sight of armed troops on the streets. Today, the visible military presence has largely been reduced to security cameras. The ring of steel has been removed, except at state buildings which remain protected by fences and security gates, while the overt military presence has shifted outwards concentrically.

Historically, rioting in the western residential districts could easily spill over into the City Centre. While the estates to the east were seperated by the river, with only restricted crossing points, those to the west and north were linked to the Centre by an extensive network of streets, since there were no natural barriers. Throughout the 1970s plans were made to take advantage of the large-scale redevelopment and slum-clearance programmes of the lower Falls and Shankill areas, and link up the motorways coming into Belfast from both north and south. Plans for a high-level carriageway were vehemently opposed by Shankill residents and were eventually abandoned (Wiener 1980). Instead the Westlink road that was eventually built in the 1980s was channelled for much of its route in a cutting, thus creating a moat-like barrier around the Centre. The road further extended the fragmentation process by slicing across Donegall Road, dividing the Protestant Village area and the Grosvenor Road district of the Falls, and elsewhere seperating the Shankill from the small Catholic Unity Flats complex. In place of the network of connecting roads, the western working-class estates are isolated

from the Centre and the inner-city areas, linked only via the major radials.

Thus, with the river to the east and the Westlink extending and enforcing the existing barriers of the Blackstaff River and the railway, the City Centre has become relatively insulated from the most troubled and impoverished areas of the city. On the map, it sits at the apex of a triangle extending southwards into the University and Malone districts and out to the Protestant heartlands of Lisburn and Craigavon. The demilitarisation of the core emphasises the neutrality and impartiality of the commercial and administrative activities. The Centre is projected as an area above and beyond the sectarian conflict, an aspect that is further reinforced by the absence of any visual political displays or slogans (apart from a large 'Ulster Says No' under the domed tower of the City Hall).

In contrast (both symbolically as well as practically), West Belfast is increasingly isolated from the planned reorientation of the Ulster economy. Just as the Catholic majority in Derry, and in the west of the province in general, have suffered by an orientation of development towards the eastern predominantly Protestant counties of Antrim, Armagh and Down, so Belfast's geography mirrors Ulster's in miniature. Catholic West Belfast remains underdeveloped, its underemployed population occupying ever more densely populated estates, pushed further into the foothills of the Black mountain, and growing increasingly marginalised both economically and ideologically.

* * * * * * * * * * * *

Although the city and its surrounding estates have been dramatically transformed by redevelopment and security measures, events since 1969 have generated a popular response which has also radically altered the environment. Resistance to major road developments and support for peace walls has already been referred to, but these are largely responses to the initiatives of others. Elsewhere, in areas like Ballymurphy, the Troubles have been influential in forging a commmunity with a sense of identity and worth in an area that in the late 1960s was little more than a transit camp and dumping ground for the most disadvantaged (De Baroid 1990).

It is, however, the production of hundreds of large murals painted on the gable walls of terrace houses that is perhaps most distinctive of contemporary Northern Ireland. In Britain, scarcely a news report or documentary on Ulster is complete without a panning shot of a large paramilitary mural. At a time when the voices of the paramilitaries and their legal supporters are excluded from television and radio, the murals have come to be used as a short hand, alluding to the continued importance of the gunmen in the urban areas. Yet the murals themselves remain little more than an elaborate backdrop for the cameras, and are never explained or even referred to; instead, the impression is created that one is confronted by them in all parts of the city, and that the murals are part of the sectarian conflict. In reality, murals remain exclusively a feature of the working-class areas, and it is possible to live and travel within Belfast and scarcely be aware of them. Nor are they painted as provocational statements directed towards the other side. Rather, they should be seen and understood as part of an inwardly focused propaganda which largely ignores debate.

Murals have been a feature of Belfast life since the early years of this century (Loftus 1990), and until recently have been predominantly the preserve of the Loyalist community. Rolston

(1987, 1991) attributes this to the close identification of the Loyalist workers with the Unionist-controlled Stormont Parliament, encapsulated in the proclamation of Ulster as a 'Protestant state for a Protestant people'. Secure in the protection of an almost exclusively Protestant police force and Reserve, the Loyalist people proclaimed their support and loyalty with murals commemorating the battles of the Boyne and the Somme, and depictions of monarchy. In 1954, any display of Irish emblems or colours was made illegal under the Flags and Emblems Act, and acts of cultural resistance within the Nationalist community were increasingly channelled into sports and music. Throughout the 1960s and 1970s mural painting and other activities stressing Loyalist supremacy declined in popularity, as first liberal rapprochment policies, and later the Troubles and direct rule from Westminster, undermined the Loyalist hegemony.

The present florescence of painting exploded in the Nationalist estates in 1981 during the Republican hunger strike. As *graffiti* and slogans of support became more elaborate many of the images and styles developed by prisoners in the H-Blocks were transferred onto walls. The emergence of a body of Republican murals in turn seemed to act as a catalyst to Loyalist painters, stimulating many new paintings and new subjects (Rolston 1991). Although the intensity of painting produced in the early 1980s has not been sustained, there are at least 150 murals at any one time, while new ones continue to be painted.

The murals are only found in the working-class estates. The majority are in an arc running south-west to north, from Andersonstown round to the New Lodge and Tiger's Bay areas, with a second large concentration in Ballymacarrett, east of the river. Isolated examples can be found in most estates. The boundary areas of estates, as with the middle-class and neutral parts of town, usually have no display of political affiliation: the lines are too well-drawn and demarcations too well-known to demand delineation. The first visible signs of affiliation are often kerbstones and lamposts either painted red, white and blue or green, white and orange. During the summer marching season or at other times of commemoration or celebration, streets will be decorated with flags and bunting visible from a greater distance, but the murals, the most elaborate of the political statements, are only accessible to those who venture into the heart of the estates. In part, this is due to the risk involved in painting political statements in exposed locations – at least one youth has been killed while painting slogans (Rolston 1991) – while the murals themselves are also the target of attacks, with paint bombs being a favoured weapon. [2] But, more importantly, their location is due to their function as objects which confirm beliefs rather than challeng those of other people.

Although they are still referred to as gable-end murals, any available wall space is a potential site and some murals are even painted on boards and erected only temporarily. Some have occupied the same site for many years. The Rockland Street King Billy (the local name for William III) mural in the Village area, has been regularly repainted since its first appearance in the 1920s. In Derry a mural in the Loyalist Fountain area, also dating from the 1920s, was removed along with the wall on which it was painted, and relocated during redevelopment, while the famous Republican 'You are now entering Free Derry' mural today

---

2. Bottles filled with paint are an easy means of defacing murals. Many older murals are damaged to some degree in this way. Republican murals are frequently vandalised by members of the security forces. Rolston (1991:102) relates how after one mural in Derry was attacked, a plaque was erected commemorating its destruction.

stands isolated on a dual carriageway. Redevelopment of many areas and the removal of terrace houses, has changed the nature of the space available, so that many murals now occupy low garden walls or are adapted to more constricted spaces. The Northern Ireland Housing Executive, which is responsible for all municipal housing, has while forbidding paintings on its property, nevertheless apparently instructed *graffiti* removal squads not to remove existing murals.

While Loyalist and Republican murals depict very different political ideals, the subject matter and even the images are often similar. Loyalist murals fall into two main groups. The first group includes historical subjects, such as King William III (whose victory at the Boyne in 1690 established the Protestant ascendancy in Ireland), and events relating to the time of the Home Rule and Partition crisis between 1912 and 1916. The second group consists of murals supporting the Loyalist paramilitary groups, the UDA (Ulster Defence Association) and the UVF (Ulster Volunteer Force).

The range of historical images constitutes a continuation of the traditional mural subjects, but the paramilitary murals are a direct product of the present Troubles. While the UVF was formed in 1966 and the UDA in 1971 (Nelson 1984), both have utilised murals to tie their existence to earlier Loyalist traditions of paramilitary resistance to Home Rule. The UVF (motto: 'For God and Ulster') claims an ancestry in the organisation of the same name founded in 1912. Thus, a large mural on the Shankill portrays an historical and a contemporary gunman on either side of a map of Ulster, under the slogan 'They Fought Then For the Cause of Ulster We Will Fight Now'. Others link the UVF with the 36th Ulster Division who fought at the Battle of the Somme in 1916. The UDA, unable to trace a line of ancestry, has adopted a heraldic-style design on a shield, with a Latin motto (*Quis Separabit*). This is generally depicted over the crossed Union Jack and the Ulster Red Hand flags. Hooded gunmen are a consistent feature of paramilitary murals but, as with the portrayals of King Billy, the figures adopt a heroic and defiant pose abstracted from any sign of conflict or enemy (Jarman 1992).

Increasingly, however, the two groups are brought into conjunction, as paramilitary murals are painted next to, or among Williamite and Orange emblems. The Rockland Street King Billy now has a mural of the Red Hand Commandos, complete with flags and emblems beside it. In Percy Place, off the Shankill, a sequence of seven large murals depicting traditional Orange themes such as King Billy, a Crown and Bible and Ulster symbols with slogans of 'No Surrender', 'One Faith, One Crown' and 'God Save the Queen' has been appended by four smaller paramilitary murals whose masked gunmen assert 'We will never accept a United Ireland – Ulster still says No'. In both these cases the traditional symbols of the Orange Order, Establishment and religious in their emphasis, have been co-opted by the paramilitaries. While Orangeism has always acknowledged a certain ambivalence in its relation to the British state, if not the Crown, it remains, publically at least, opposed to the use of unauthorised violence. The muralists have shifted the orientation of the Orange symbols away from themes of civil and religious liberties and glorification of past victories, as shown on Orange banners, and instead emphasise the need for, and legitimacy of, armed defence. It is not simply a matter of one range of subjects being replaced by more contemporary ones, but rather, by their conjunction on the walls, becoming transformed in meaning.

Republican murals largely relate to the campaigns of Sinn Fein and the IRA against the continued British presence in Ireland. In this, they differ from the Loyalist work in that they are more orientated to specific events or campaigns. Although some King Billy murals are regularly repainted, many Loyalist paintings are simply left to fade away. In contrast, Republican mural sites are frequently reused, new murals being painted on top of old: as a result there is much less duplication of images than among Loyalist works. Many of the images aim to emphasise the legitimacy of the armed struggle by presenting the IRA as the legitimate inheritors of the aspirations of the Easter Rising of 1916 that brought about at least partial Irish freedom from British colonial rule. This was strongly emphasised throughout West Belfast in 1991 on the 75th Anniversary of the Rising, at a time when the government in the Republic was playing down the event and the importance of 1916 was under increasing examination (Ni Dhonnchadha and Dorgan 1991). Within this group of historical images one might also place a number which draw on Celtic mythology, a linkage invoked within the broader Nationalist movement since the late nineteenth century (Sheehy 1980). An elaborate mural, now demolished, near the New Lodge area, incorporated images from the Irish mythic saga *Tain Bo Cuailnge*, with silhouetted Neolithic dolmens and portraits of the IRA Volunteers killed at Gibraltar.

Besides this historical continuity, others link the aims of the IRA with those of the PLO or the American Indian Movement, while on the wall of the Sinn Fein offices in the Falls Road a large portrait of Bobby Sands faced a mural of Nelson Mandela until this was removed in late 1992. Many Republican murals focus on contemporary events in a way that is avoided in Loyalist murals. The 1981 Hunger Strike was an obvious example: among the images produced at the time were several which adopted the iconography of Catholicism, exploiting the Jesus-like appearance of the hunger strikers after years on the no-wash blanket protest for the return of political status. At a time when the Church was attempting to stop the strike, the murals combined popular support for the strikers with more widespread religious sentiments. Most of these classic images have long been removed, replaced by less dramatic contemporary causes, such as anti-extradition or electoral campaigns.

Both Loyalist and Republican murals include a number painted as memorials to individuals killed in the Troubles, frequently former paramilitary comrades. The tenth anniversary of the Hunger Strike produced many murals to the dead, particularly in and around their home areas, and some, like the mural to hunger striker Joe McDonnell, near his family home in Andersonstown, were unveiled at a formal opening ceremony. This mural was paint-bombed by the security forces only three days later (*An Phoblacht* 25.7.91).[3] While remaining as memorials, the murals may also become a focus for more ritualised activities: in Woodvale, a mural to UVF gunman Brian Robinson, killed by the security forces after he himself had shot an unarmed man in the back, was the site of a short commemoration by the Brian Robinson Memorial Flute Band on the morning of the Twelfth parades. In the Ballymurphy area an elaborate memorial to the eight IRA men killed by the SAS at Loughgall was the site for an IRA last salute to Patricia Black who blew herself up in a premature explosion at St Albans in November 1991 (*An Phoblacht* 21.11.91).

3. *An Phoblacht* is the weekly newspaper of Sinn Fein. The *Belfast Telegraph* is a daily commercial paper, with a soft Unionist line. The *Orange Standard* is the monthly paper of the Orange Order.

Others, besides the paramilitaries, have also used murals. From 1977 to 1981 Belfast City Council sponsored a mural programme which employed students to work with local community groups in the summer. The aim was to brighten up depressed areas. The majority of murals produced in this scheme were of the cartoon or rural idyll type, but few have survived (Rolston 1991; Watson 1983). More recently the Catholic Church has taken to sponsoring a number of large Madonna and Child murals in the Nationalist estates, which contrast dramatically with adjacent Republican images. One huge Madonna and Child sits sentinal-like at the bottom of the Falls Road, seeming to attempt to counter the Republican presence within.

Although the murals stand as the boldest and most emphatic of political statements, other more discreet and permanent reclamations of the environment have been made. While mention has already been made of the increasing number of memorial murals, a number of estates have constructed permanent memorials to the dead. These are largely a feature of the Nationalist estates, although at least one, constructed in marble, has been erected to the dead of the Loyalist Woodvale area. In the New Lodge estate a carved and engraved marble Celtic cross, with the names of the dead of the area, stands at the end of a cul-de-sac behind an iron fence. A similar cross memorial can be found in the Ardoyne, while elsewhere plaques have been mounted on walls, commemorating either all the dead, or sometimes specifically IRA Volunteers killed in action.

Another, more specific, act of opposition to British rule has been the renaming of streets in Nationalist areas with Gaelic names. This practice dates from the early 1980s, and most streets now have an Irish name-plate. Usually these are placed adjacent to the English name, but in some cases only the Irish name remains (De Baroid 1990). Other roads have been renamed completely: Beechmount Avenue, off the Falls Road, has long born the name RPG (Rocket-propelled Grenade) Avenue (named after one of the IRA's favoured weapons).

Naming has long been recognised as an important part of the act of claiming and confirming possession over space. The *Tain Bo Cuailnge*, the classic early Irish tale, which tells the story of Cuchullain as he defends Ulster against the forces of Medb and Ailill of Connacht, is as much a description of the landscape as a hero myth. Throughout the tale emphasis is continually laid on the importance of the name of any place, which is generated by the deeds acted out at the site, and thereby creates and defines both its physical presence and spiritual essence (Kinsella 1970). Similarly, the conflict in Ireland is reflected in the multiplicity of names, both of the place and of the people. Ulster, Northern Ireland, the North of Ireland, the Six Counties, the Republic, Eire, the South and the Twenty-Six Counties are all terms used to describe a small area inhabited by Loyalists, Unionists, Protestants, Catholics, Nationalists and Republicans. Each name has its own political nuance, defining its user as well as the place and subject (Deane 1990).

All these are activities which define the identity of the estates. The difference of faith and politics between areas is literally written on the walls, yet the similarities between the actions on either side of the sectarian divide also affirm them as redefinitions in the face of norms and values imposed by outside authority. Feldman (1991) has stressed the importance, and the changing nature, of the concept of sanctuary as a space of safety and security, not only from physical violence, but also from ideological incursion. As the Troubles erupted, the sanctuary space – specifically the space of residence, family and children – was physically protected by the paramilitaries behind

makeshift barricades. Later, as the military attempted to assert its authority and the no-go areas were reintegrated into state-controlled territory, the peace lines demarcated the interface of opposing sanctuaries. But, as well as being a sanctuary from the excesses of the violence, the heart of the estates also provides visible reassurance of the certitude of one's own faith among the competing ideologies. As the open demonstration of the paramilitary presence was increasingly restricted and they were excluded from the more powerful media of communication, it was left to the very bricks and mortar to confirm that there would be 'No Surrender' or that 'Tiochfaidh Ar La' (Our Day Will Come).

While Loyalist and Nationalist areas proclaim their difference from each other, they also distance themselves from the hegemony of their respective ruling classes. As well as being sanctuaries from the violence, the estates are also distanced from the neutral parts of town, where business continues as usual. They are part of the zoning pattern of front and back regions with their associated practices of disclosure and enclosure, through which less powerful groups are able to sustain and generate resistance to dominant and orthodox ideologies (Giddens 1985). The Loyalist paramilitaries' appropriaton of the symbols and icons of middle-class Orangeism is balanced by the Republican use of the imagery of the crucifixion and the Catholic Church. In both cases,it is recognised that, while it is impossible to break completely with tradition, it is also possible to force those traditions to take on new meanings, in order to represent changed circumstances. The activities in the estates thus function on two planes, one sectarian and the other class.

\* \* \* \* \* \* \* \* \* \* \* \*

The impetus for much of the mural painting and other forms of display is the approach of one or other of the commemorative marches, which are held regularly across the province over much of the year. Although the high point of the Marching Season are the summer months of July and August, commemorations begin at Easter, when Republicans celebrate the Rising and Loyalists the Siege of Derry, and continue into December, when the closing of Derry's Gates is remembered (Bell 1990). The 1991 RUC Chief Constable's Annual Report recorded that 2,379 parades were held across Northern Ireland that year. The vast majority organised by the Loyalist Orange Order (2,183 Loyalist to 196 Republican).

The Order dates back to 1795, and though formed in the recently industrialised rural Armagh, it was soon established among the workers of Belfast's linen mills and shipyards. Developing as an alliance between the Protestant middle class, the gentry and the workers, it aimed to ensure the continuation of the Protestant ascendancy, established after the Battle of the Boyne, and to preserve the relative advantages of the Protestant workers over their Catholic counterparts (Beames 1983; Gibbon 1975; Millar 1978). This alliance has been maintained via the Orange Order ever since. In the 1980s, this male-only organisation had an estimated membership of 100,000 in Ireland.

Parading, as a regular feature of Irish society predates the formation of the Order. From the 1770s at least, competing vengence groups marched with bands before engaging in mock battles throughout the rural areas of Ulster (Gibbon 1975). Williamite parades are recorded as being held in towns throughout Ireland in 1778 (Millar 1978), and in 1796 the Orange Order took up this practice. Characterised by violence from the beginning, the summer parades often initiated the sectarian rioting which polarised

Belfast residential life, and for much of the nineteenth century were banned by act of Parliament (Boyd 1987; McClelland 1990).

The Twelfth of July, the anniversary of the Boyne, remains the centrepiece of the Orange calendar. The day is a public holiday and parades are held in some eighteen centres across the province. In all areas except Belfast, the location of the march changes annually. The capital hosts the largest parade, on which some 15–20,000 people walk, the majority of whom are Orangemen, predominantly middle-aged and eminently respectable. The parade is structured in quasi-military manner, with each Orange Lodge being led by its colour party and officers and preceded by a flute-and-drum band, which are increasingly independent of any larger organisation. Most band members are young and, in contrast to the rest of the parade, many are female. The bands introduce colour and noise into the event, while frequently displaying discreet emblems of support for the paramilitaries. Besides the walkers, thousands more line the streets – those too young or too old to take part in addition to the women who, excluded from membership of the Orange Order, cannot march.

Preparations for the Twelfth begin long before that day. In the evenings of late June and early July a series of small parades are held around Belfast to mark the First of July, the anniversary of the Battle of the Somme. Central to the celebrations is the decoration of the residential areas with flags and bunting, and the repainting of kerbs and murals. In past years, huge decorated arches were built across streets, and although few are erected these days, one still marks the entrance to Sandy Row, outside the local Orange Hall. While this arch seems rather to mimic the industrial cranes of the shipyards, its origins are claimed to be in the arch of Solomon, an Orange symbol of unity and brotherhood. The focal point for local celebrations is the building of huge bonfires, sometimes forty feet high, which are lit all across the city at midnight on the Eleventh.

The parade starts early on the Twelfth, with the Orangemen and bands meeting at their local headquarters before marching to the main assembly point at Carlisle Circus at the bottom of the Crumlin Road. From here they march into the City Centre, where they are joined by lodges from East Belfast and then the West Belfast Orangemen. As a body they parade through the commercial centre (all shops are closed for the day), southwards past the Dublin Road headquarters of the Order, and then out of town up the Lisburn Road, before finally reaching their destination, the Field at Edenderry, some five to six miles away. During the two-hour stay at the field lunch is taken, a service of Thanksgiving held and finally a public meeting expresses resolutions of loyalty to the Crown and Protestant resistance to political change. The men then march back into the town. In contrast to the seriousness of the morning, the atmosphere of the return is much lighter, almost carnival-like, as the marchers are welcomed by the thousands of people lining the route.

The day is an exclusively Loyalist occasion, celebrating 300 years of Protestant dominance and righteousness. It is a day on which the Catholic people are excluded, not simply from the celebrations, but also from the city itself. The present route of the march does not take it close to major Nationalist areas, except where the parade passes each end of the Unity Flats estate at the bottom of the Shankill. Here a heavy military presence is provided, the roads are closed off and the residents enclosed behind 5-metre-high screens. In other areas, less extreme measures are taken, but increased security and checks are in force, discouraging people from venturing far.

One section of the population is confined as the other is permitted to occupy the heart of the city. Although, for the most part, the commercial centre excludes any display of politics, on the Twelfth the position is reversed, businesses remain closed and the space is taken over by the Orange Order. Portraying itself primarily as a religious body and as an organisation which brings together all Protestant sects, it is, and always has been, enmeshed within the political life of Ireland: all but a handful of Unionist MPs have been Orangemen (Farrell 1976; Gibbon 1975; McClelland 1990). Marching through and occupying the heart of Belfast city reasserts Protestant power over that space and also the primacy of religious values over the commercial and administrative practices carried out there.

Protestant power is consolidated by the fact that traditionally only the Protestant organisations have been able to march through the centre, while Republican or oppositional marches are confined to outer areas. In March 1991 a parade celebrating International Women's Day attempted to enter the City Centre but was stopped by police on the grounds that a banner (in

Irish) at the head of the procession might cause offence (*An Phoblacht* 14.3.91). Eventually, after months of trying, the Right to March group was permitted, on Sunday 26 July, to march and hold a rally in front of the City Hall, for the first time in the 70 years since partition (*An Phoblacht* 1.8.19). Two weeks later, on August 11, a march from east Belfast, crossing the city to join the main Internment Commemoration rally on the Falls, also managed to parade past the City Hall (*An Phoblacht* 15.8.91).

The contrasts are marked. The Nationalist marches were held on Sundays, causing little disruption, and the police did what they could to prevent the marches going ahead and little to exclude hostile spectators. However, in July, when Tyrone Orangemen proposed to hold their Twelfth parade through Pomeroy, a town with a 95 per cent Nationalist population, the RUC gave permission, claiming it would cause no offence, a decision eventually upheld by the Court of Appeal (*Belfast Telegraph* 12.7.91). For the Loyalists, a key feature in asserting their power in their Protestant state is the right to march where they will, when they will, a right that cannot be extended to others. Nationalist parades, which focus on the Easter Rising and the introduction of Internment (which have replaced the Catholic Lady's Day parades on 15 August in importance), are therefore largely confined to West Belfast, as are the numerous funerals which proceed to the Milltown and City Cemeteries located on the Upper Falls Road.

While the assertion of control of space is an important feature of Orange parades, the events are less about confrontation with the Other than with ignoring them. The Twelfth parades are inwardly focused, concerned with reaffirming the unity of the Protestant people. The banners carried by the Orangemen, with their depictions of historical and Biblical events, ignore contemporary political issues and recent events and instead dwell on the need for vigilance against a general, abstract evil (Jarman 1992). The parades are thus both a statement about Protestant supremacy and an act of reunification in face of the fragmented geography of Belfast.

The Orange Order is organised into lodges which are coordinated within a geographical and hierarchical structure. Individual local lodges are organised into Districts which are in turn linked at County level and then at national level in the Grand Orange Lodge of Ireland. Although individuals may join any lodge, the norm is to join one in which one has links through family or geographically through work or residence. The Belfast

lodges are organised into ten geographical districts which embody the entire city. It is as fractions of these districts that lodges parade. Although the ten districts vary considerably in the number of lodges they contain – from 42 to 6 – each has equal standing, and each district leads the parade in turn.

A philosophical emphasis on egalitarianism is incorporated within the hierarchical structure and reasserted at each level. Individualism is denied through submersion into a collective identity, reinforced through the adoption of the formalised dress of dark suit, bowler hat and sash. When Orangemen parade, they do so not as individuals but rather as members of a lodge, as a body, and as a body incorporated into a larger structure. The parade represents a drawing together of the fragmented Protestant communities of Belfast in which individual members can be interpreted as embodied geography. The socially and physically fragmented spaces of the city reunite, and as a single entity confirm and exercise their power over Belfast. A similar process occurs across the province as in each of the 18 parades an act of unity and equality is expressed in recolonising the land. Rather than marking out and confirming boundaries and interfaces as has been suggested (Feldman 1991), the Orange parades ignore boundaries, whenever possible since within the Border there are no places from which Protestants will accept exclusion.

The entire Twelfth celebrations can be seen as an act mirroring in a spatial manner the Orange structure of hierarchy and equality. In the days leading up to the eleventh night activities are focused in and around the residential districts. The 'mini-Twelfth' parades in early July delineate these territories in a way the main parade will ignore, while bonfire building represents a localised focus in which the main actors are children and young adults. The lighting of the fire draws all together at the minute at which the Twelfth begins. In the morning the focus shifts, as the adult males take centre stage and the action encompasses the city as a whole, the march to the Field recreates the march to the Boyne, with the victorious forces welcomed back again in the evening. At the same time it represents an abandonment of the city and its profanities for the purity of the countryside, where spirits are refreshed away from women and heathens. Renewed in their fortitude, the men can recolonise and reassert control over the city for another year.

On the next day, the thirteenth, the focus shifts yet again, south to rural Scarva, where the Royal Black Preceptory, sister organisation to the Orange Order, but senior and almost exclusively religious in its iconography, hosts a parade and the Sham Fight, a costumed recreation of the Battle of the Boyne. Apart from small parades of Black Preceptories in Lurgan and Bangor, Scarva is the focus of all attention with massive crowds of spectators, estimated at 100,000 in 1991 (_Orange Standard_, August 1991). Over the three days of commemoration and celebration there is a shift of focus outwards from the residential areas, to the level of city or district and finally to the single event, at which the Sham Fight symbolises the unity of the Ulster Protestants. Played out in a rural setting, it refutes the position of the city as dominant force. Parallel with the increasing geographical incorporation is a shift in focus from young to old and from the politicised iconography of the murals to the Old Testament images of the Black Banners (Buckley 1985–6). As a totality, it reaffirms the importance of their history as settlers and colonists, and of their tradition and religion as a means of maintaining control over the territory of Ulster.

* * * * * * * * * * * *

This essay has explored some of the ways and means in which different interest groups build up and use the fabric of a city, and considered how various constructed facets of the built environment interlace and depend on one another. Much of the writing on this subject, both theoretical and empirical, has focused on the dominant role of industrial capital as a conditioning agent. Henri Lefebvre in particular, has stressed the importance of capital in creating a landscape which is of necessity fragmented, homo-genised and hierarchical (Harvey 1989; Shields 1991; Soja 1989). But these processes also need to be understood in terms of the actions of individuals and communities, which in occupying spaces within the built environment, must not only interpret and adapt to them but also challenge and redefine them. In considering the emerging nature of Belfast, I have largely ignored the economic factors underwriting spatial organisation and have preferred instead to concentrate on the events of the past 20 years, which are euphemistically known as the Troubles. Rather than being regarded as unique to the situation in Northern Ireland, the practices of containment, surveillance, resistance and redefinition are unique only in their intensity and concentration. Many of the tactics of the state and the armed forces developed in Ireland have since been utilised elsewhere in

Britain, while acts of resistance, from barricades to elaborate wall art, have similarly appeared on the mainland. What is unique to Northern Ireland is the continued prominence of sectarian divisions, now cemented into the physical landscape. The peace walls may serve as a short- term palliative and provide security for some, but they serve only to further entrench divisions.

Although divided by political aspirations, the response to violence and conflict in both Loyalist and Nationalist working-class estates is similar. In both cases, the traditional authority of the middle classes, as expressed through bodies like the Orange Order and the Catholic Church, has been challenged and their norms redefined, while in both cases the organisations that are instrumental in expressing the new values remain excluded from attempts to create long term solutions.

* * * * * * * * * * * *

## Photographs

The theme structuring the choice of, and order of the photos is that of a walk. This takes one through the Falls and Ballymurphy areas of West Belfast, along the Springfield Road, which for much of it's length forms the 'peace-line', before crossing into, and passing through the Shankill until one arrives at the next boundary zone in North Belfast.

Page 111  Military surveillance post on top of the Divis Tower.
Page 113  Social Security Office on the Falls Road.
Page 115  Republican mural with quote from Padraig Pearce, Beechmount Avenue/Falls Road.
Page 117  Ballymurphy murals, Anti Censorship, King Nuala and Loughgall memorial.
Page 119  West Circular Road-Springfield Road junction.
Page 121  Security between Springfield Road and Upper Shankill.
Page 123  Security between Springfield Road and Upper Shakill.
Page 125  Security between Springfield Road and Upper Shankill.
Page 127  Peace line in the Clonard area of the Lower Falls.
Page 129  One of twelve murals in Percy Place, Shankill.

Page 131 UDA-UFF mural on the Crumlin Road.
Page 133 Security zone in the Oldpark Road area.
Page 135 Peace line between Ardoyne and Ballysillan.

## Acknowledgements

I would like to thank Barbara Bender for her support and encouragement while writing this essay, Richard Stubbs for the computer work on the map, Hazel and Gerry, and May and Lou for their hospitality in Belfast and Maggie McBride for talking through many of the ideas with me.

## References

Beames, M. 1983. *Peasants and Power, The Whiteboys Movement and their Control in Pre-Famine Ireland*, Brighton: Harvester Press.

Bell, D. 1990. *Acts of Union, Youth Culture and Sectarianism in Northern Ireland*, London: Macmillan.

Benjamin, W. 1983. *Charles Baudelaire, a Lyric Poet in the Era of High Capitalism*, London: Verso.

Boal, F.W. 1982. 'Segregating and Mixing, space and residence in Belfast', in F.W.Boal and J.N.H.Douglas (eds) *Integration and Division: Geographical Perspectives on the Northern Ireland problem*, London: Academic Press.

Boal, F.W. and Murray, R.C. 1977. 'A city in conflict', *Geographical Magazine* 44, 364–71.

Boyd, A. 1987. *Holy War in Belfast,* Belfast: Pretani Press.

Brown, S. 1986. 'Crisis-Response and Retail Change in Belfast City Centre', *Irish Geography* 19, 83–91.

Buckley, A.D. 1985–6.'The Chosen Few, Biblical texts in the regalia of an Ulster secret society', *Folk Life*, 24, 5–24.

Burton, F. 1978. *The Politics of Legitimacy; Struggles in a Belfast Community*, London: Routledge and Kegan Paul

Conroy, J. 1988. *War as a Way of Life, a Belfast Diary*, London: Heinemann.

Dawson, G.M. 1984. 'Defensive Planning in Belfast', *Irish Geography*, 17, 27–41.

De Baroid, C. 1990. *Ballymurphy and the Irish War*, London: Pluto Press.

Deane, S. 1990. Introduction, in *Nationalism, Colonialism and Literature*, A Field Day Company Book, Minneapolis: University of Minnesota Press.

Dillon, M. 1989. *The Shankill Butchers, a Case Study of Mass Murder*, London: Hutchinson.

Doherty, P. 1988. 'Socio-spatial change in the Belfast Urban Area, 1971–1981', *Irish Geography*, 21, 11–19.

Farrell, M. 1976. Northern Ireland – the Orange State, London: Pluto Press

Feldman, A. 1991. *Formations of Violence, The Narrative of the Body and Political Terror in Northern Ireland*, Chicago: University of Chicago Press.

Gaffikin, F. and M. Morrissey. 1990. *Northern Ireland, the Thatcher Years*, London: Zed Books.

Gibbon, P. 1975. *The Origins of Ulster Unionism*, Manchester: Manchester University Press.

Giddens, A. 1985. 'Time, Space and Regionalisation', in D. Gregory and J. Urry (eds) *Social Relations and Spatial Structures*, London: Macmillan.

Harvey, D. 1989. *The Urban Experience*, Oxford: Basil Blackwell.

Jarman, N. 1992. 'Troubled Images, The Iconography of Loyalism', *Critique of Anthropology*, 12:2, 133–65.

Kinsella, T. 1970. *The Tain*, Oxford: Oxford University Press.

Loftus, B. 1990. *Mirrors, William III and Mother Ireland*, Dundrum: Picture Press.

McClelland, A. 1990. *William Johnston of Ballykilbeg*, Lurgan: Ulster Society.

Matrix. 1984. *Making Space, Women and the Man Made Environment*, London: Pluto Press.

Millar, D. 1978. *Queen's Rebels, Ulster Loyalism in Historical Perspective*, Dublin: Gill and Macmillan.

Nelson, S. 1984. *Ulster's Uncertain Defenders*, Belfast: Appletree Press.

Ni Dhonnchadha, M. and T. Dorgan. 1991. *Revising the Rising*, Derry: Field Day.

Rolston, B. 1987. 'Drawing Support: political wall murals in the North of Ireland', Paper read to the British Association for the Advancement of Science Conference, Belfast.

———1991. *Politics and Painting, Murals and Conflict in Northern Ireland*, London and Toronto: Associated University Presses.

Schorske, C. 1981. *Fin-de-siècle Vienna: Politics and Culture*, Cambridge: Cambridge University Press.

Sheehy, J. 1980. *The Rediscovery of Ireland's Past*, London: Thames and Hudson.

Shields, R. 1991. *Places on the Margin*, London: Routledge.

Soja, E.W. 1989. *Postmodern Geographies: the Reassertion of Space in Critical Social Theory*, London: Verso.

Watson, J. 1983. 'Brightening the Place Up?', *Circa* 8, 4–10.

Wiener, R. 1980. *The Rape and Plunder of the Shankill; Community Action the Belfast Experience*, Belfast: Farset Press.

# Chapter 5

## The View from Below: Paris in the 1880s

*Felicity Edholm*

I am writing a biography of Suzanne Valadon, the painter. She was born in 1865 in the Limousin, the illegitimate daughter of a 35-year old peasant woman, Madeleine Valadon. Shortly after the birth, mother and daughter went to Paris and settled in Montmartre where they lived for the rest of Madeleine's and all of Suzanne's life. This is virtually all that is known until Valadon became an artist's model when she was sixteen or so. In 1883, aged eighteen, she gave birth to her only, and illegitimate child, Maurice Utrillo. Given her origins, the lack of information is not surprising. Madeleine and Suzanne were part of the silent, semi-literate, if not altogether illiterate, mass of inhabitants of Paris in the last quarter of the nineteenth century.

Part of the exploration of Suzanne Valadon's early life involves an attempt, in the absence of any first hand information, to get some idea of how she would have experienced Paris, how she would have seen and understood the landscape of the city. What, for example, would it have been like for her to walk down a Parisian street in the early 1880s? The interest in getting her into the street was inspired by the extensive literature on late nineteenth-century Paris and, in particular, the writings by and on Baudelaire.[1] Baudelaire's walks through Paris are used to map and describe the

---

1. Nearly all discussions of modernist consciousness in the context of the urban refer extensively to Baudelaire. I have drawn specifically here on: Adler 1989; Benjamin 1976; Berman 1984; Buci-Glucksmann 1986; Clark 1985; Harvey 1985; Pollock 1988; Sennet 1974; Timms and Kelley 1985; Wolff 1990.

experience of modernity. His experience seems to have been taken as representative of a whole sensibility, an attitude to and a perception of the modern. Despite some acknowledgement in this literature of the fact that there were other ways of experiencing the city, it is still Baudelaire's experiences that are taken as most representative of the modern view. It is as though he is the only one able to appreciate what the city is really about, as though different responses to the city were not picking up on what was distinctively modern about it. The experience of the modern is tautologically defined as Baudelaire's experience. But, although this certainly tells us something about the ways in which Valadon might have seen the modern city, it is clear that she could not have shared his vision, and that her experience would have been very different. A recognition of this quite different perspective on the city forces a rethinking of the characterisation of the experience of modernity.

Janet Wolff, mapping a view of the city from the perspective of the bourgeois woman in the suburbs, makes just this point:

> ...the literature of modernity ignores the private sphere, and to that extent is silent on the subject of women's primary domain. This understanding is not only detrimental to any understanding of the lives of the female sex; it obscures a crucial part of the lives of men,too...Moreover the public could only be constituted as a particular set of institutions and practices on the basis of the removal of other areas of social life to the invisible arena of the private. (Wolff 1990: 45)

Thus any account of modernity, in this context, has to include the experiences of bourgeois women. The argument must, however, be extended to take account of class. The public and private spheres, with their concomitant gendered identities, could only take the form they did because of the existence of the quite differently constituted world of the impoverished urban working class. Only through identifying the major lines of social difference and recognising their interdependence, and trying to identify some of the factors which shaped the experiences and the different consciousness of individuals in such groups can we begin to think through the multiple meanings which comprise the modern. No one experience or perspective is adequate.

Baudelaire and Valadon came from the opposite ends of a classed and gendered hierarchy. He was a man in his early forties from the property-owning classes. His widowed mother remarried a general, and he lived on, and dissipated, a small personal fortune. In his reliance on an independent income and freedom from the necessity to sell his labour he is representative of a significant sector of the Parisian upper classes. Valadon is female, in her late teens, working class and working. His is a view from above, hers a view from below, his the perception of a small, albeit extremely powerful elite, hers of a significant section of the majority of the city's population.

Two caveats could be made about juxtaposing these two views. First, Baudelaire is walking the streets in the late 1850s and early 1860s in the heyday of the Second Empire, Valadon twenty or so years later at the beginning of the Third Republic. However, the Baudelaire experience is never seen as specific to the 1850s and 1860s so it does not seem unduly cavalier to link them in this way. The city he wrote about is in most ways the city Valadon lived in. Second, between the two dates came the the Commune of 1871. Despite the massive physical and human destruction that the suppression of the Commune entailed, there is little evidence to suggest that the city itself, and relations within it, changed in any fundamental way. The impact of the Commune on the structure of social relations in the city seems relatively insignificant when placed against the massive and fundamental changes that Paris had undergone as a result of Haussmann's reconstruction, which officially began in 1853. In many ways it could be argued (although I am not aware that it has been) that the defeat of the Commune permitted and completed some of the processes that Haussmannisation set in motion, particularly in relation to the way that class relations were structured in the city.

Since any experience of the Paris street from the 1850s onwards rests very largely on these processes I begin with a brief account of Haussmanisation and some of the implications of the changes that took place, before considering in more detail the ways in which Baudelaire and Valadon might have experienced the city.

## Haussmannisation [2]

In 1853, two years after the coup that brought him to power, the Emperor Napoleon III decided that 'his' capital had to be cleaned

---

2. This discussion of Haussmannisation is drawn from a wide range of accounts, the most relevant have been the references above and: Berlanstein 1984; Chevalier 1973; Couperie 1970; Fuchs 1984; Gaillard 1977; Pinkney 1958, Reff 1982; Shapiro 1985; Vidler 1977.

up and redesigned. Baron Haussmann was appointed préfet of the Seine and given the brief of restructuring the city. Much of this was in essence achieved by the time the Empire collapsed in 1870. It was arguably the most radical urban redevelopment programme ever carried out.

The demand that Paris had to change, that her constitution was diseased, had become increasingly insistent from the 1830s onwards. Contemporaries viewed Paris as crushed by its mass, stifled by its own 'respiration, transpiration and excreta' (Vidler 1977: 35). It was agreed that the city was in a state of physical collapse, unable to provide the most basic amenities for its inhabitants and, more seriously for those in power, unable to meet the physical demands of the developing capitalist economic order.

Until the early nineteenth century, the city had been relatively compact and highly centralised. All political, economic and leisure activities were concentrated in the centre and people lived near where they worked. Residence was characterised by vertical rather than horizontal segregation, rich to poor going up a city house. Although some *quartiers*, (small neighbourhood areas) were exclusively working class and others far more affluent, many were quite socially heterogeneous. This pattern began to break down at the end of the eighteenth century. New and old industries moved from the old overcrowded central locations to areas to the east and north of the city, and labour followed and settled. The bourgeoisie and the propertied classes moved to more exclusively residential quartiers to the west. Work and domesticity, working class and middle class became increasingly separated physically. The pattern of a more or less uniformly working-class east and north and a 'middle-class' west began to emerge. Meanwhile, the rural immigrants who had begun to swarm into Paris from the early nineteenth century onwards moved into the already crowded, decaying, central districts. In 1831 the population of Paris was 576,000, by 1851 it had nearly doubled. In 1860 the peripheral communes were annexed to Paris doubling the area of the city and adding significantly to the population. By 1881 over 2,270,000 people lived in Paris. Working-class accommodation in central Paris, never very adequate, was already by the 1830s and 1840s appallingly overcrowded and insanitary. Most *quartiers* in the centre were slums, effectively no-go areas to anyone other than their residents. An 1848 police ordinance identified the causes of 'insalubrity' as overcrowding, cohabitation with animals (many households still lived with pigs, chickens and rabbits in their rooms), unkept privies, stagnating household waste, the absence of windows. (Shapiro 1985: 15)

By the 1830s there was a real sense of panic about urban conditions, expressed in the literature as a paranoid fear of 'the people'. The labouring classes, the honest decent workers, were perceived as being overwhelmed and dominated by the dangerous classes, the dishonest, lazy, immoral, casual workers. The conspicuously evident poverty of the working class as a whole was considered to be the result of profligacy, laziness and intemperance. The workers, it was argued, drank their wages away on Saturday night, were still sleeping the drink off on Monday mornings, and then spent all week in the cabarets. This dark mass threatened all moral and political standards and ultimately civilisation itself. Underlying this fear was the reality of revolution. 1789 was still a living memory, and the uprisings of 1830 and 1848 confirmed the fear. The Paris mob and the urban working class mesmerised politicians, businessmen, social commentators, theorists and the literati throughout the century. The great popular novelists from Sue and Hugo to Zola were obsessed by it.

The urban milieu itself was seen as pathological, producing a population with 'withered bodies and corrupted habits: the human debris of a deteriorating environment' (ibid: 14). The notion of an urban poverty syndrome was developed: 'Dark, humid, exiguous lodgings drove the worker to the cabaret; family life crumbled; the wife was forced into prostitution and the children to the streets, the city spawned a generation of vagabonds, pariahs living outside of social norms whose lodgings were sites of infection and sedition.' (ibid: 16) The imagery used to describe the working class inhabitants of the city remains very similar throughout this period: the slum-dwellers were 'urban nomads', 'veritable cave dwellers', 'barbarians', 'savages', 'ferocious beasts' (cf. Chevalier 1973). They were non-human, non-civilised, constructed as either the animal or the human 'other'. Fear of the masses was further fuelled by the terror of contagious diseases. Cholera epidemics in 1832–5 and 1848–9 killed thousands. Like other contagious diseases cholera was believed to be carried in the respiratory system, and spread by the contaminated air of the slums. Syphilis, which in the later part of the century replaced cholera as the great fear, was also seen as having been brought to the middle classes by prostitutes, by the women of the working class. The working classes were the carriers of death.

Napoleon's and Haussmann's project for dealing with the diseased and 'pathological' city was described in medical, and, most powerfully, surgical terms. Haussmann himself was quite explicit about the cause of the disease and the implications of the remedy. He argued that, in part, the plan was designed to 'disembowel' the quartiers that had been the home of uprisings and barricades. For Napoleon, the emperor who had come to power through a *coup d'etat* in the wake of the 1848 revolution, the fear of another uprising that would remove him from power was always close. Getting rid of the people and destroying the places seen as fermenting revolution was one way of cauterising the fear – the surgical solution for the political gangrene that was the Paris mob.

It was primarily the working-class areas in the centre which went. Great wide roads, the boulevards, too wide for barricades to be easily set up in and wide enough for the army to move swiftly through them, were driven through the cramped, narrow, medieval streets, severing whole quartiers, deliberately destroying the working-class communities that inhabited them, leaving small sections marooned between the boulevards and the grandiose monuments. In the language of Haussmannisation, these boulevards were the arteries of the city. Economic ends were achieved by the same means. The boulevards provided for the first time easy access throughout the city, they connected the stations to the central markets, the stock market and the newly constructed department stores. Their width was not only barricade proof but also provided efficient, fast and free-flowing traffic. They were the first step in the creation of an infrastructure that was appropriate and necessary to the new capitalist economic order. As one contemporary observed, Haussmann's boulevards were laid down as 'humble servants to industry and trade' (Pinkney 1958).

The boulevards fulfilled another important function. Lined with cafes and restaurants, shops and the newly created vast department stores, they were dedicated to consumption, fashion and display. Patterns of consumption for those who had the means to consume were revolutionised. Haussmann and Napoleon III turned the city itself into something to consume. The emperor was intent, as many French heads of state have been, on leaving his aesthetic and cultural mark on the capital.

Paris was to be the fitting monument to the greatness of 'his' France. The Opera, the huge vistas and monuments, the bridges, the streets and boulevards laid out so that they focused upon a public building, a statue, a monument – these were the public and visible manifestations of state power and ambitions. It was the age of the spectacle. And the inhabitants of the city were part of the spectacle. The cafes and restaurants along the boulevards, with their great glass fronts and their extravagant lighting, were not only symbols of unimaginable luxury, but were designed for maximum visibility, those outside could see in, those inside could look at the world going by, the pageant of the street. Paris was on view, displayed, to be seen. It was self-consciously presented to the onlooker, it became part of the leisure industry and increasingly a centre for tourism.

Haussmann's redevelopment ordered and accelerated the process which had already begun to divide the city along class lines. As far as possible all traces of labour were to be removed from the centre of the city. Working-class housing was not included in the redevelopment plans for the centre. Acres of working-class housing were removed and not replaced, thereby forcing thousands of workers out of the centre. Free trade, no-planning zones, designed to attract large scale enterprises, and to take the workers with them, were located in the peripheral areas to the east and north of the city, in Belleville and on the *plaines* of St Denis, St Ouen and Clignancourt. The market, according to Haussmann, was to provide for the needs of the people, but money was not made by building working-class accommodation and the inhabitants of the new areas to the north and east lived either in very inadequate housing or in shanty towns of tar-paper and plaster. Despite the lack of working-class housing in the centre, thousands also remained, employed in the workshops that had stayed in the centre, and which were so important to the economy of the city, or providing the labour for the destruction and construction of the city. At one point in the 1860s it was estimated that one in five of the labour force of Paris was involved in the rebuilding works. These workers had either to commute between suburb and centre, or, if they had stayed in the centre, live in overcrowded, degenerating housing stock or in all kinds of unauthorised infilling, the instant slums that mushroomed in the spaces behind, between and alongside the grand bourgeois apartment blocks along the boulevards.

The city continued to grow. The trains that brought in goods from all over France also brought in immigrants. By 1861, just under two-thirds of the population of Paris had been born outside the city. They all had to be housed somewhere. Between 1851 and 1856, while the population increased by more than 250,000, the number of houses decreased by 600 (equivalent to accommodation for 24,000 people). Rents spiralled, increasing by a third between 1852 and 1855. Overcrowding in the centre became unmanageable. Haussmann's phasing out of the welfare provisions that had been available to the indigent through the city authorities exacerbated poverty. Such suppport as remained tended to be controlled by the Church and strict sanctions were applied. Well over half of all Parisians were so poor that they paid no taxes and 80 per cent of them went to paupers' graves. Seventy-five per cent of the population of Paris in 1860 owned 0.06 per cent of the wealth, and official estimates, including those of Haussmann himself, put nearly half a million living at and below the level of destitution.[3]

The effects of the programme were clear. The heart of the city, although still inhabited by the working class, had essentially been appropriated by the bourgeoisie, the state, and the interests of the new economic order. The way in which the city had been changed was revealed by the quartiers and areas which offered most resistance to the army which was sent in to crush the Commune in 1871. The uprisings were mainly in the *cordon rouge* – the outer ring of working-class areas. Many of the quartiers that had traditionally been the centres of revolution in central Paris had been eliminated. The bourgeois areas of the centre and the west were threatened not so much from within as from without.

Haussmann's physical restructuring of the city was only one part of a much wider process which imposed particular kinds and forms of control and order on the use of space and time by the working class. These processes changed the way this class inhabited and used the city and the extent to which it was therefore visible to the bourgeoisie. The processes most relevant to Paris were the de-skilling of craftwork, the increasing organisation of production in large factory systems, the imposition of fixed regulated work time, the separation of the rhythms and rituals of work from those of leisure. For example, the 'Sainte

3. See Berlanstein 1984, Couperie 1970, Shapiro, 1985.

Lundi', the day workers used to take off, declined in favour of employer-imposed Sundays. All but a very few, very powerful workers lost their right to impose their own definitions of proper leisure and labour time. Working-class street culture, so conspicuous in the city in the eighteenth century, had not only been undermined by the destruction of many of the old *quartiers* but was, until the very end of the Second Empire, deliberately suppressed through heavy licensing and censorship laws. These laws were repealed in 1867–8 in a desperate attempt by the emperor to maintain his authority. But even though street entertainment and balladeering re-emerged almost immediately, and indeed flourished, it also began to change its form and content and cater for a different audience. Street culture became more general, more homogeneous, more professional. Increasingly, working-class pleasure and leisure was found and taken in places of organised, commercial entertainment, in dance halls and cafe concerts. Increasingly, bourgeois pleasure and working-class, popular culture overlapped. By the end of the century the bourgeois fashion was to slum it in the cafe concerts of Pigalle and Montmartre.

## Baudelaire's Paris

It is through this Paris that Baudelaire, and later Valadon, walked. There are remarkably few direct references in Baudelaire's descriptions to Haussmannisation, and the physical destruction of the city, despite the fact that the experiences that he describes can only be fully understood in the context of the changes that had taken place in Paris. I want to discuss three different aspects of these which seem to be central to his experience of the city: the cafe, the boulevard and women.

One of the most quoted of Baudelaire's prose poems is *The Eyes of the Poor*. It is written to his mistress to explain why he had hated her that day (and is one of the few poems which does, in fact, make a direct reference to the changing city).

> That evening as you were tired, you wanted us to sit on the terrace outside the cafe at the corner of a newly built boulevard which was still littered with rubble but already making a lavish display of its uncompleted spendours. The cafe glittered all over with lights. The new gas jets cast their incandescent novelty all round..." (Baudelaire 1989: 111)

He describes the ornate interior of the cafe and then the way that, directly opposite to where they were sitting, a man and two children were standing. All three were in rags. Their:

> faces were extraordinarily serious, their six eyes fixed on the new cafe all with equal amazement and admiration, their expressions slightly dfferent according to their age. The father's eyes seemed to be saying what a beautiful sight ...it's as though all the gold in our poor world has been spread over those walls, the little boy's eyes were saying how beautiful..but this is a house where only people who are not like us are allowed...the youngest just looks with an expression of profound and stupid pleasure. (ibid: 111)

Baudelaire is moved and feels a little ashamed of: 'our array of glasses and decanters all so much bigger than our thirst'. He turns to share this response with his mistress, but she, at the same time, turns to him to say: 'I find those people unbearable with their eyes as wide open as gates. Can you ask the waiter to tell them to move on.'

There are many possible readings of this rich poem [4] but, in this context, what it says about the restructuring of the city is of particular interest. Baudelaire's view of the family and his interpretation of their response to the cafe is arguably sentimental – he is willing to enjoy the delights of the new bourgeois consumption-oriented city but not to take on board the social implications of that luxury. His lover's reaction is far more appropriate to the new city. She is asserting the confidence of the bourgeois consumer, that she has total power in and over the boulevards, the public spaces of the city. Unlike Baudelaire she does not feel uncomfortable about the ostentatious display or conspicuous consumption. She is prepared to be seen, to be part of the spectacle of the city, but only by those who can consume the city as she herself does and can. She is not prepared to be an object to be looked at by the dispossessed, those who should, according to the ambitions of the Haussmann project, have been removed from the city.

Her response challenges one of the notions implicit in the modernist version of the city, that it is somehow democratised, that it is available equally to all its inhabitants, that there is one urban experience. The boulevards in particular have been seen as the place of the crowd, which is by definition heterogeneous,

---

4. See Berman 1984, chapter 3 for a very interesting reading of the same poem.

composed of anyone in the city. In reality the boulevards were designed precisely to exclude the mass of the inhabitants of the city from doing much more than use them as routes to and from their places of work. They were unable to consume what the boulevards had to offer.

What the family sees is a world, a city, to which none of them has access. The message they receive is clear: this city belongs to those who have the ability to consume it. What is interesting is the way in which Baudelaire represents their response to this realisation: they are overwhelmed and awestruck by the very existence of this form of public, conspicuous consumption and they are defeated by it. They do not feel anger, their response is passive, resigned. They are no longer representatives of the dangerous classes, they bear no relation to the urban mob. It is significant, too, that the family is shown as isolated, not part of a class or group, not members of the threatening animal mass. They are pathetic and disempowered, and it is to this that Baudelaire sentimentally responds. They are, finally, presented as consumed by the same desire and admiration for the wonders of the city as those who can possess and consume it. They share the same values, they do not experience or represent a different, critical perception of what the city is.

The most influential aspect of Baudelaire's vision of the city essentially derives from his walks through the streets, or more specifically the boulevards, the place of the crowd. One of the most important aspects of these walks is that he is alone. He can in this way concentrate on what surrounds him and on his own sensations and experiences. His relationship to the crowd is not shared with nor mediated by anyone else. The experience he has would be impossible with someone else. Baudelaire describes the ecstasy of giving himself to the crowd. He talks of 'the indescribable supersensual pleasure, the saintly prostitution of the soul when it yields itself entire in all its poetry and all its charity to the epiphany of the unforeseen, the unknown passer-by.' (Baudelaire 1964) The *flâneur*, the urban promenader, according to Baudelaire, 'sets up house in the middle of the multitude, around the ebb and flow of movement, in the midst of the fugitive and the infinite.' (ibid: 9) Baudelaire and all modernists after him stress the flux, the ebb and flow of the street, heterogeneity, fragmentation, the passing encounters, the delight in chance and accident, the endless possibilities the city offers.

This experience is essentially private, the sensual pleasure is a solitary one. This isolation is characteristic of much of Baudelaire's represented experiences. In the relationships he describes his feelings are never represented as shared, and often, as in *The Eyes of the Poor* his feelings are indeed quite different from those of the person he is with. He is the extreme representative of the sensibility of the age of individualism: the *flâneur*, the detached observer, able to view the passing world with his refined, cynical eye. Deliberately, explicitly, he feels no solidarity or identity with anyone except in these fleeting, fragmentary moments of fantasy in the crowd. The confidence with which he assumes his right to survey also derives from his relationship to others, it implies distance, leisure, and therefore money and power. The sense of ownership and control, the absolute, unchallenged right he feels 'to be away from home and yet feel oneself everywhere at home', can only be that of a male member of the dominant class, the bourgeoisie. It is an experience that is gender- and class-specific.

Baudelaire's experience of the city also has much to do with its physical restructuring. A man of his class walking the city a quarter of a century earlier, in the 1820s and 1830s, would only have felt at ease in the very limited area of the boulevards that already existed and above all in the arcades. They were in the centre of Paris, and were virtually the only areas that were illuminated, relatively clean and inhabited predominantly by the leisured classes and their immediate dependants. It would have been impossible to walk at the speed of a leashed turtle, as the Arcade *flâneurs* of the 1840s did, in the narrow, dark, confused, intertwining streets of the central quartiers (Benjamin 1976: 54). But, in the 1850s, Baudelaire inhabited a different kind of urban space, the Haussmann boulevard, and his confidence was therefore directly related to the security it offers.

The structure and form of the boulevards were designed to reassure and privilege the bourgeois and to offer a vision and experience of the world that corresponded to his position of power within it. They were wide and straight and brightly lit, there was space to avoid and light to see what and who was there and who was coming. The regular architecture of the boulevards, the straight lines of houses, trees and benches, the elaborate, luxurious and decorated, but uniform, façades spoke of a rational order, implied an overall plan, physically defined a sense of purpose, control and direction. The vast and imposing monuments, the churches, 'mairies' and statues to which the boulevards led, were a physical reminder of the authority and ever-presentness of the state and the increasing centralisation of power. This city was the antithesis of the old impenetrable working-class quartiers with their unsurveyable curving and narrow streets, lack of view and perspective, plan and coherence. The confidence of the urban bourgeois promenader in such a context is, then, not surprising. It is worth noting, too, that the Impressionist representations of the city are essentially of these boulevards, not of the old city. As Meyer Shapiro argued, their work reflects the conditions of a sensibility closely related to those of the urban promenader and the refined consumer of luxury goods, and celebrates this world of changing bourgeois leisure, a world portrayed as harmonious and reassuring(quoted in Clark 1985: 3).

The final aspect of Baudelaire's experience of the city that I want to consider is the way he eroticised the walks he took in the city. This relates directly to his attitude to sex, to the prostitute and to women. For Baudelaire, not only is the encounter with the crowd as a whole eroticised ('the supersensual pleasure') but the flux and chance encounters of the street are seen as offering the possibility of meeting the unknown, infinitely desirable woman and realising the dream of the fulfilment of desire. It is in the streets that you come close to, touch, see the other whose life overlaps with yours for a fleeting moment. This is most explicitly stated in his poem *To a Woman Passing By*: 'O fleeting beauty, whose glance brought me suddenly to life again in a second birth, shall I never see you again except in eternity?...For whither you flee away I know not; nor do you know whither I am bound – O you whom I could have loved, O you who knew it! (Baudelaire 1961: 221)

The crowd in the city, on the boulevards, offers the endless possibility of such pleasurable erotic encounters. Perhaps the most graphic depiction of this kind of fantasy is Renoir's *Les Parapluies*. In the midst of a crowd a young working woman stops and gazes directly out of the canvas into the eyes of the spectator, while behind her a young bourgeois attempts to offer her the protection of his umbrella. The promise, the appeal, the possiblities of the chance erotic encounter are all there, with the very special touch of Renoir's soft-focus sentimentality. For Baudelaire the eroticism is much sharper. It is a mixture of pleasure and repulsion, and is closely connected to and identified with prostitution. The boulevard was for him, and for most late nineteenth-century commentators, the place of the prostitute. So the boulevard offered not just the fantasy, but the reality of sexual encounter. Just to be in the street on her own implied that a woman was not respectable. So any woman on her own, or even with others, might or might not be a prostitute, but would almost certainly, in various other ways, be designated as available.

## Valadon's Paris

Baudelaire's Paris comes to us first-hand through his writing. He is both representative of a particular male bourgeois attitude and an individual. With Valadon we do not have the luxury of her own account. She was illiterate, working-class and female; her point of view is never represented. It is only through indirect sources that we can gain some idea of how she experienced the streets and boulevards, what she thought about the cafes and their clientele and how she responded to assumptions made by men of Baudelaire's and Renoir's kind about her availability and sexuality. There is an immediate problem in going to such sources since the extensive contemporary representations of working-class women in literature, painting, 'sociology', political debate and moral tracts are nearly all produced by bourgeois men. What we have, then, are the fears and fantasies of the dominant class and gender. Their vision is, of course, important, for it defines and imprisons Valadon and women like her in very particular ways: in terms of how they were seen and treated; how they would, in part, have seen themselves; and how we have been taught to see and expect them to be. In their understanding of themselves and in their experience of their daily lives, they lived and thought in ways this literature cannot begin to understand, let alone represent.

I intend, then, to discuss the ways in which such women were represented, to question these accounts and finally to try to identify some of the other factors which might have been significant in shaping the experiences and responses of a woman like Valadon to the city she inhabited. [5]

5. For discussions on women and prostitution in France in the second half of the nine-teenth-century I have drawn on a range of texts, the most relevant in this context are: Adler 1989; Bernheimer 1989; Coons 1987; Corbin 1986; 1990, Harsin 1985; Lipton 1986; McMillan 1981; Perrot 1979, 1980, 1984, 1987; Pollock 1988; Scott 1988; Wolff 1990.

The literature of the period, radical or conservative, was remarkably consistent in its representation of the ideal woman. She was *La Reine du Foyer*, the Angel at the Hearth. A woman's sphere was the domestic and private, her role to care for men and children under the protection and authority of men, the superior sex. Women's qualities and attributes were complementary and distinct to those of men, each sex occupied different and separate spheres to which they were naturally fitted and destined. Women should not enter men's sphere nor men women's. Women who worked, particularly married women (and well over a quarter of married working-class women in France did work, a far higher proportion than in Britain at the same period) had therefore entered the male world and thus endangered their identity as women. Work corrupted women. Jules Michelet, one of the most influential writers of the period, stated, and he was endlessly quoted, that 'the very word ouvrière was sordid and impious.' (McMillan 1981: 45). Work deformed woman's true nature, her natural role as mother and wife, and the natural hierarchy of authority in the relations between men and women, husband and wife. This latter argument is well represented in the trade unionist discussions of women and work (Scott 1988)

The implications of the corruption of work went even further. Proudhon neatly summed it up by stating that women were either housewives or whores (McMillan 1981). This sexualisation of working women was fundamental to any definition or discussion of women. Once women were outside individual patriarchal control, outside the structures which kept them in order, they were defined (and presumably experienced) as dangerously free, and this freedom was read as sexual freedom. By implication, then, all working women were sexually available. They were therefore the legitimate sexual targets for men of any class. Their lack of respectability meant that they were themselves responsible for these sexual attentions. Male sexual interest and sexual rights over working women was assumed and legitimated. One means, the central means, whereby men sought to control working women – women who seem not to be under male control – was through sex.

Femininity, the proper behaviour and constitution of women, was defined not only in opposition to what 'man' was and did but to what women of another class were and did. Class was built into definitions of gender. The myriad and complex rules which governed what bourgeois women could do, where they could go and with whom, how they could move, what they could look like, what spaces they could enter, and so on, are only fully understandable in relation to the threatening presence of the coarse, unregulated, uncontrollable, immoral, working-class non-woman. The contemporary descriptions of working-class women, too, only make sense if they are seen as negative representations of bourgeois women. The mirror reflects back and forth. Bourgeois women were the opposite of working-class women, who were the negation of bourgeois women. The working-class woman was the classic 'other'. Women, in general, were seen as closer to nature, to feeling, than men. They were, in Baudelaire's terms, 'natural, that is to say abominable' but working-class women were closer to animal nature. Descriptions of working-class women are invariably couched in animal imagery. Baudelaire's prostitutes have the eyes of animals, sometimes beasts of prey, they are also astonished, blank, alert. Novels of the period abound with descriptions of working-class women fighting each other, out of control, excited, animal. Here, in the *Vatard Sisters* by Huysmans:

> ...wine bottles dripping saliva and wine were passed around from mouth to mouth... two women who began to shout obscene insults at one another. Grabbing them by their hair coils and their tattered dresses, their companions held them apart, but they twisted and shouted, chins stuck out, teeth bared, slavering, hurling themselves at one another, arms in the air, the hollows of their armpits visible beneath their torn blouses. (Huysmans 1987:2)

This imagery is not confined to novels but permeates the language of daily life. The dancers at the ballet, so exhaustively portrayed by Degas and others, were known, for example, as the little rats. The Degas sculpture of the *Little Dancer of Fourteen Years* was described in an 1881 review in *Le Temps* in these terms: 'With bestial effrontery, she thrusts forward her face or rather her little vicious muzzle, and the word is entirely appropriate for this poor little girl is an incipient rat'. Other reviewers likened her to a real rat, a monkey and an expelled foetus. (McMullen 1985: 338–9) This language is not exceptional. The imagery is often metaphor not simile, working-class women are not just like animals, they are animals.

The notion of the animal had all kinds of resonances in the bourgeois world which so valorised control, rationality, rules and order. The animal was constructed in opposition to the social, the human, the civilised and cultured. It was also associated with all kinds of defiling and polluting bodily functions. The overwhelming association was, however, with sexuality. Sexual activity was, by definition, animal, out of control, irrational and thus very frightening. For Baudelaire the great tension in man was between his contradictory leanings towards God and Satan, or animality. Weber saw sexuality as a non-, even anti-, social force 'The desire that most firmly bonds man to the animal, the irrationality of the sexual act.' (quoted in Davidoff 1983: 20)

The implications of these connotations were complex. Sex was in many ways incompatible with the dominant constructions of the domestic sphere, the bourgeois home and its symbolic centre: the angel of the hearth. It was, perhaps inevitably, forced out of the private into the public sphere, onto the streets. The counterpart of the 'angel' is the prostitute, and this explains in some measure the obsession with prostitution, the combination of fear, horror and fascination, and the sense of its all-pervasiveness. It is an obsession apparent in the arts, poetry, painting, novels, and in the way the prostitute was extensively used as a symbolic representation of the corruption and decadence of society (Alexandre Dumas *fils* even blamed prostitution for the defeat of the empire at Sedan in 1870). It was also apparent in the ordinances of control and regulation of prostitution and the extensive research that was undertaken.

Baudelaire's attitude to prostitutes was the same mixture of fear, contempt and desire characteristic of other bourgeois men of the period. They are for him 'evil with the beauty of evil, the beauty of the horrible' and with characteristic venom and disgust, he describes 'the innocent but monstrous fatuity...of prostitutes...heavy, sad, stupid,absurd, their eyes glazed with brandy and their foreheads bulging with the force of their own obstinacy'. (quoted in Clark 1985: 85). Huysmans describes a painter:

> 'He specially liked rendering prostitutes where they abound: yawning in the evening in front of a glass of beer at a concert hall; on the prowl at a cafe table; out hunting in the streets, laughing full-tilt over little nothings, making themselves idle in order not to scare away the timid...swearing and yelling in jealousy or drukenness, their bloated faces raised in the air.' (Huysmans 1987: 80).

Degas shows prostitutes in the cafe concerts, on cafe terraces, and in his private work in brothels. Consummate portraitist of women though he is, he is unable to see these women except in terms of the stereotypes, his prostitutes are coarse, graceless and unreal. He conveys exactly the same visual contempt for his subjects, although none of the sexual excitment, as the novelists do. Such women are not fully human. All the misogyny and class hatred comes out, cross-cut with powerfully ambivalent feelings about sex.

Paris in the last quarter of the century became increasingly notorious as a centre for sexual consumerism. This was part of its attraction as a tourist centre, part of the spectacle and display of the boulevards. The official attitude to prostitution was complex and contradictory. On the one hand its social importance was recognised, and indeed sanctioned, by the official and self-appointed moral guardians of society. The prostitute was a necessary social evil. Parent Duchatelet, the great classifier of, and researcher into prostitution, argued that without public women men 'who have desires, will pervert your daughters and your servants... (they) would bring trouble into your households.' (McMillan 1981) The prostitute protected the body social from ill; she also protected respectable women from the pollution of sex and the family itself from danger. On the other hand, prostitutes were seen as socially disintegrative. They spread and bred corruption, both physical and moral. Syphilis (as common as the common cold according to Flaubert) was responsible for over 15 per cent of deaths per annum at the turn of the century, and, as an inherited disease, was also seen as leading to the degeneration of the race. Prostitutes were blamed.

All kinds of attempts were made to control prostitution, and none succeeded. A *Police des Moeurs*, set up specifically to supervise prostitutes, was active throughout the century and had extensive powers of intervention. It was able to register professionals and force them to operate in officially regulated brothels, subject them to medical tests and pick up women suspected of illegal prostitution. Parent Duchatelet's research had revealed that a very large number of prostitutes worked casually. They were working women who turned to prostitution to make ends neet and were therefore difficult to control and identify. This casual prostitution was a source of extraordinary anxiety to the authorities and the bourgeoisie, especially since large numbers of registered prostitutes and those apprehended as unregistered prostitutes, worked, or had worked at some time, as domestic servants. As a result working-class women were subject to constant harassment by the police and some 30,000 women were picked up each year, the majority of whom were almost certainly not even casual prostitutes, but merely working women.

The increased discussion of, and anxiety about prostitution which is evident after Haussmannisation can again be linked to the redesigning of the city and in particular to the boulevards, with their emphasis on display, consumption and leisure and their intentional exclusion of the working class. Professional prostitutes inevitably used the boulevards and their cafes and were conspicuously visible. The working class in its masculine form had been removed and had become the observer of the rich and of the commodity, but its female form had penetrated the respectable world via the prostitute, as a commodity. The fear of pollution and corruption as represented by the prostitute was heightened by the fact that she broke all the rules surrounding women and commodities. She was consumed but she was never fully owned. For although she was, like any *bourgeoise*, totally dependent on men, and was there to service them, unlike a wife, there was no way of binding her, she did not vow obedience, she was not forced into subordination and there was always another client. She was not fully under men's control, and indeed revealed their dependency and weakness.

The elision of prostitute and working-class woman, of sex and class is very clear in the literature. Joan Scott has indeed argued that at this period sex becomes the metaphor for all other bourgeois fears of the worker (Scott 1988: ch. 7). Working class women were also, after all, the least directly supervised of workers. They were predominantly employed in casual jobs, in small scale enterprises, often working at home, and were therefore not easily subjected to the kinds of discipline exercised in more organised workplaces. The rights of the *Police des Moeurs* to pick up suspected prostitutes can in this way be seen as an attempt to control and police working-class women as a whole. It is not irrelevant in this context to note the real hysteria generated, in the aftermath of the Commune and the repression of the working-class population of the city, around the figure of Louise Michel and the *petroleuses*. These latter were supposedly hordes of working-class women who systematically set fire to the city when the army moved in.

Historians who have worked through the trials of the Communards have found virtually no evidence to indicate that such women were anything other than figments of the fevered imaginations of the paranoid authorities, but many women were killed and transported for such crimes. [6] In the imagery of the period the out-of-control, hysterical crowd is always female (Barrows 1981).

Contemporary social commentators also assumed that many poor working-class women were, however casually, involved in prostitution. Women's wage rates and the cost of living were used as evidence. Jules Simon argued that in the 1850s and 1860s the most a woman could earn was 600 francs per annum (Fuchs 1984: 101). Since it was also estimated that survival necessitated at least 2 francs per day per household member, women were assumed to be dependent on a man's wage, and even then there was no guarantee that this would be adequate to maintain a household. It was therefore argued that prostitution was the only way single women and married women with inadequate incomes could survive.

Such claims, and the statistics upon which they are based, have gone largely unexamined and are still used, relatively uncritically, by many historians. It would seem wise to treat them with caution and see them as, to some degree, part of the discourse which identified the working-class woman with sex, the commodity form, and pollution. However, to challenge such claims means having evidence for the existence of alternative survival strategies for working-class women. Historians have only recently begun to explore this area. Berlanstein's work on fostering in Paris is particularly relevant in this context (Berlanstein 1980). His examination of reports of the visits made by the authorities of an orphanage in Paris to the homes where children had been fostered demonstrates that many female-headed households were able to satisfy the (suspicious and critical) authorities that they were able to provide the care considered appropriate and necessary. In one case a single seamstress who worked an 18-hour day was seen as a very adequate 'mother', surviving in economic circumstances that most contemporary commentators deemed impossible without resorting to prostitution. A study on the recipients of welfare describes elderly women living on less

6. See Barrows 1981, Gullickson 1991, Thomas 1966.

than a franc a day (Coons 1987). Women lived in great poverty, and survived in poverty without selling their bodies. More generally, the work of Michelle Perrot on working-class Parisian women indicates, as similar work on London does, that women survived through establishing networks of support, of lending and borrowing and sharing. [7]

Perrot's focus is particularly relevant to the whole notion of the spaces that urban working-class women occupied and the kinds of relationships and dependencies women were effectively forced into by the conditions in which they lived. The appalling overcrowding of the centre, the almost total lack of amenities and the fact that most working class women did some form of paid labour (albeit much of it casual outwork and manual work) meant that almost inevitably a great deal of their time was spent outside the squalid rooms they inhabited with their kin – and often shared with other non-kin. Most of the activities required to maintain a household were done outside the 'home'. There were no internal amenities, water had to be queued for at the public fountain, food bargained or scrounged for at the market, washing done at the local laundry. Activities assumed to be synomymous with the private, domestic sphere, also took place outside: privies were public; many households had no cooking facilities so food was cooked, sold and consumed on the street; and, for want of privacy, people made love in alley ways, on waste ground, in dark, secluded, detritus-filled corners.

The important factor here is that the notion of a home, a hearth, a foyer was, for most working-class women effectively non-existent. Where you lived was where you slept. Bourgeois and petit-bourgeois women were increasingly confined to and defined by the home, the private sphere, but working-class women had, in this sense, no private sphere. Lives were lived in the street. While Baudelaire talks, boasts, of 'setting up home in the street' working-class women had to do precisely that.

Perrot also indicates that working-class women spent most of their time within a quite tightly defined local area and would, within this area, be part of a community of women. Ellen Ross describes similar kinds of localised networks of female relationships in the late nineteenth-century East End of London, within

7. For discussions of urban working-class women see references in note 5 above and: Farge 1979; Fuchs 1984; Garrioch 1986; Hilden 1986; Ross 1982, 1983; Shapiro 1985; Walkowitz 1984; Weston 1979.

which extensive and elaborate systems of borrowing, lending and support for destitute households or individuals operated. She also describes the kind of power and authority such women were able to exercise in their neighbourhoods, and the considerable separation between men's and women's lives (Ross 1982 and 1983). Zola in *L'Assommoir* gives a flavour of the same kind of female interdependence and sociability when he describes how Gervaise managed to find work and accomodation after she has been abandoned by her lover with no money and two children. The women she meets at the laundry give her all kinds of advice and help about work, rooms and so on (Zola 1970). The network of support provided for women in this way is almost invisible and certainly not statistically quantifiable, but has to be taken into account if we are to begin to question the stereotypes and get some idea of how women survived in extreme poverty and experienced the cities they lived in.

In what way can factors such as these enable us to begin to imagine what it might have been like for a young woman like Valadon to walk through the streets of the city she lived in, and how does this experience differ from Baudelaire's? To compare the two experiences, Valadon has both to be on her own and in the same kinds of places he would have walked. The fact of being on her own is immediately highly significant. The combination of her class and gender would have meant that she was, as an unaccompanied woman defined in very specific ways by others on the boulevard. To the bourgeois and petit-bourgeois male and female she would have signalled non-respectable, and her sexual availability would probably have been assumed. She would have been the object of bourgeois – and possibly other – men's erotic fantasies. Various forms of direct and indirect, predominantly sexual, harrassment was therefore inevitable. Moreover, men, particularly bourgeois men, had the power not only to define but to treat working-class women in particular ways, and women had very little power in this context to protest or challenge, directly, the way they were treated. Working-class women had no legal and social rights, particularly in terms of their sexuality. Women were seen as responsible for the sexual relations they were involved in, regardless of circumstance (Fuchs 1984 ch. 2). They were afforded no protection. The diaries of John Munby in late nineteenth-century London reveal that in the streets he would frequently, and with absolutely no evidence of self-consciousness, accost young working women he thought looked interesting, and ask them about their work and their lives. Nearly all the young women would stop and answer with suitable deference. His interest was in fact not explicitly sexual but this would not have been immediately apparent. Other diaries reveal similar interactions. [8] There was, too, always the threat of the ubiquitous *Police des Moeurs* who were by this time concentrating on the surveillance of the streets. They were 'obsessed with soliciting' (Corbin 1986:211) and able to apprehend women on the suspicion of an improper glance.

There was obviously a range of different strategies that could be adopted in response to this kind of behaviour. Without any first-hand evidence from the 1880s, however, we can only assume that some of these would be similar to those adopted by women in cities a century later: avoidance (only possible for a few and in particular contexts), solidarity in numbers, or various ways of being aware and alert and taking defensive action. On her own in the boulevards, Valadon, aware of the possibility of male sexual interest would therefore have been alert and self-conscious, concerned to avoid eye-contact and the attention it might bring. There is no way that she could have assumed the detached and separate persona of the *flâneur*. She could not have surveyed the crowd before her, could not have stopped and stared or abandoned herself to the flux and flow, the heterogeneity that Baudelaire found so erotically stimulating. The crowd was more likely to have signified fear and danger, the heavy hand of the *Police des Moeurs*, the invasion of unsolicited sexual interest. The Renoir painting of *Les Parapluies* seems in this context to be entirely a work of male fantasy. That any solitary young woman would have stood and, innocently and trustingly, gazed in that way at a stranger in the crowd is unlikely.

The boulevard was the people in it, and also a world of cafes and restaurants, shops, stalls and entertainments to which Valadon would on her own have had no access. She could only have looked, a spectator to the consumption and pleasure of others. But even the status of spectator, so important to Haussmann's project, was effectively denied to someone of her class and gender. A young woman on her own who stopped to look at what was going on along the boulevard, or into a cafe or

8. See Davidoff 1983; Hiley 1979; Marcus 1966.

restaurant, was inviting interest. She would have been identified as a prostitute, for the boulevards and their cafes were, after all, frequented by prostitutes. To avoid such interest she could not easily have stopped, just looked as she passed by. The only way a young working-class woman could have gained entry into the cafe world, to the world of consumption offered by the boulevard and to this aspect of the spectacle of the modern city, was through a man, by providing sexual services. Zola's Nana was seduced through just such a desperate desire to be allowed to consume, to possess, to enter this world of leisure that was so publicly on offer to those who lived in the city, and so impossibly out of reach to all but a powerful minority, the bourgeois men who set the terms which gave some women access to this process of consumption (Zola 1970: 357).

It is hard to imagine that the architecture of the boulevards, the uniformity and order, the sense of wealth, luxury, leisure and power could have represented either security, or a sense of identity to someone like Valadon. In *L'Assomoir* Zola (who hated what Haussmann had done to Paris) tries to imagine precisely this situation: a working-class woman's perceptions of the boulevard. His Gervaise reacts in several ways: she feels cheap because it has become so grand, she feels overwhelmed by its size and length, she feels alien and out of place. It is huge and uniform and endless. It is not a space that she, a working-class woman, can inhabit with any ease (Zola 1970: 392).

Paris was, however, more than the boulevards, it was also the streets: the roads behind, the spaces in between the boulevards. They, too, were part of the modern city and indeed were essential to its functioning. The very existence of the boulevards depended on them. Valadon came from these streets, and we can reasonably assume that she must have felt 'at home' in them, and was able to read them in ways that would have been unimaginable to a Baudelaire. She would have recognised and understood what was going on, who people were, why they were there, and would herself have been identified by others in the streets, the circumstances of her life known and understood. She would inevitably have been defined differently by men and women (and potentially have represented erotic promise to the men) in the streets, but the context, and therefore her possible responses, would have been very different from her experience in the boulevard. The differences would have been not only the result of shared class, but of the ways in which the street was inhabited and possessed by those who worked and lived in it, particularly women. The fact that women in working-class areas had considerable presence and authority in the street and were able to exercise some degree of control over social relations in the immediate areas they lived in must have provided some sense of security for other women. There is also evidence to indicate that young women would have been brought up in these streets to be assertive and tough (the realist novelists' descriptions of fights between women possibly reflect the existence of such incidents, whatever their interpretation) and to some extent self-sufficient. In this working-class, and for much of the time predominantly female world, Baudelaire could only have felt an outsider. Here, despite the power and privilege given him by his class, he was the 'other'. Those who inhabited the streets were those who lived, worked and consumed there, people who shared the same conditions of existence, and who were to some extent united by this.

This is not to sentimentalise the street or poverty, nor to romanticise class relations. It is clear that the conditions which forced people to live so much of their lives in the street were intolerable. It is clear, too, that there was a great deal of violence and that the close proximity in which people lived, the sharing that was necessary, the lack of privacy and sanitation, caused all kinds of interpersonal tensions. Furthermore, the streets were also the place for drinking. On nearly every street corner there was a cabaret, used almost exclusively by men. Levels of alcohol consumption were extremely high and the drunks were on the streets, with the attendant violence and fear. Again it is Zola in *L'Assommoir* who describes Gervaise having to wait in the street and choosing to sit with a concierge rather than at a table on her own in the cabaret, with a lot of men all round her (Zola 1970: 26). What is important in this context is not only that she, as a woman on her own, wishes to avoid being in what is predominantly a male space, but that the concierge is there to offer space, protection and the solidarity of shared gender. While women did have some control over social relations in these streets (partly because they spent so much time in them) and were thus able to provide each other with support and security, and bring some pressure to bear on men who were seen to brutalise women, this power was inevitably limited.

## Conclusion

The modernist experience of the city offered to us in the literature
is based not on the streets but on the boulevards, the spaces deliberately created by and for those who had economic, political and
social power. An experience of excitement was generated by the
heterogeneity and flux offered by the crowd in the boulevard, the
powerful intoxication of feeling that the world was peopled by
free-floating, atomised individuals who were disconnected from
each other and from the social context which gave them a collective or class identity. Social identity was hard to read, ambiguous, individuals were isolated and to some extent powerless.
They shared space, their lives overlapped only in time, or
through exchange. The excitement was imagining other ways of
connecting while remaining separate and disconnected – the
great erotic charge for Baudelaire. The particular pleasure of this
is available only in the boulevards because they were essentially
the place where exchange relationships predominated, they
were, as Benjamin argued, constructed for the consumption of
commodities, they were devoted to the commodity form. They
were, therefore, designed for those who had the necessary economic and social power to enjoy the commodities on offer and
had the leisure to survey and enjoy the spectacle of the city. It is,
in the context of late nineteenth-century Europe, inevitably an
exclusively male, privileged experience, the view from above. It
is the partial view of a powerful minority, presented as though it
were comprehensive and universal.

This view has to be set against others. The view of bourgeois
women who were excluded from experiencing the boulevards
except from within the confines of the department store, or
accompanied by their husbands in cafes and restaurants. They
did not have access to the boulevard itself on their own, they
could not experience its excitment, flux, heterogeneity. Their
view of the city was predominantly the view from the suburbs,
the world of the private and domestic.[9] There is also the view
from below, that seen by young working class women, those who
were so central to the spectacle and experience of the boulevard
for the privileged consumers of it. For them it was a view powerfully constrained by the identity assigned to them by bourgeois

9. See Adler 1989; Pollock 1988; Wolff 1990.

men (and the police) as objects, primarily of sexual desire and availability. It was this identity that determined what they could see and how they could act in this space which was controlled by those with the power to impose their definitions. But such women also had another place through which they experienced and saw the city – the street. In this space power relations were very different, and social identity much clearer. Working-class women had a right to be, some power to control the ways they were defined, and far greater freedom to see and act and influence what happened. The existence of the streets and the kinds of relations which operated within them are as important to the way in which the boulevard functioned and was experienced by the *flâneur* as the suburb and the existence of the public/private divide. Neither can be ignored in an attempt to map the experience of modernity. Both reveal the ways in which the dominant notion of the modern, urban experience was constructed out of and dependent upon ways of ordering and controlling space that were gender- and class-determined.

## References

Adler, K. 1989. 'The suburban, the modern and 'Une Dame de Passy''', *Oxford Art Journal*, Vol.12, 3–13.

Anderson, S. (ed.) 1978. *On Streets*, London: MIT Press.

Barrows, S. 1981. *Distorting Mirrors: Visions of the Crowd in Late Nineteenth Century France*, Newhaven: Yale University Press.

Baudelaire, C. 1961. *Baudelaire: Selected Verse*, trans. F. Scarfe, Harmondsworth: Penguin.

_____1964. *The Painter of Modern Life and Other Essays*, trans. J. Mayne, Oxford: Oxford University Press.

_____1989. *Baudelaire – The Poems in Prose*, vol. 2 with La Fanfarlo, ed. and trans. F. Scarfe, London: Anvil Press Poetry.

Benjamin, W., 1976. *Charles Baudelaire: A Lyric Poet In The Era Of High Capitalism*, London: New Left Books.

Berlanstein, L. 1980. 'Growing up as workers in nineteenth century Paris: the case of the orphans of the Prince Imperial', *French Historical Studies* 11, 551–76.

_____1984. *The Working People of Paris, 1871–1914*, Baltimore: Johns Hopkins University Press.

Berman, M. 1984. *All That is Solid Melts into Air*, London: Verso.

Bernheimer, C. 1989. *Figures of Ill Repute, Representing Prostitution in Nineteenth Century France*, Cambridge, MA: Harvard University Press.

Buci-Glucksmann, C. 1986. 'Catastrophic Utopia: The feminine as allegory of the modern,' *Representations* 14, Spring 220–9.

Chevalier, L. 1973. *Labouring Classes and Dangerous Classes in Paris During the First Half of the Nineteenth Century*, trans. F. Jellineck, London: Routledge and Kegan Paul.

Clark, T. J. 1985. *The Painting of Modern Life: Paris in the Art of Manet and His Followers*, London: Thames and Hudson.

Coons, L. 1987. *Women Home Workers in the Parisian Garment Industry 1860–1915*, New York: Garland.

Corbin, A. 1990. *Women for Hire: Prostitution and Sexuality in France after 1850*, trans. A. Sheridan, Cambridge, MA: Harvard University Press.

_____1986. 'Commercial sexuality in nineteenth century France: a System of Images and Regulations.' *Representations* 14 Spring, 209–19.

Couperie, P. 1970. *Paris Through the Ages: an Illustrated Historical Atlas of Urbanism and Architecture*, trans. M. Low, London: Barrie and Jenkins.

Davidoff, L. 1983. 'Class and Gender in Victorian England,' In J. L. Newton et al (eds) *Sex and Class in Women's History: Essays from Feminist Studies*, 17–72, London: Routledge & Keegan Paul.

Dufrancatel, C. et al., 1979. *L'Histoire sans Qualites*, Paris: Galilee.

Farge, A. 1979. *Vivre dans la Rue a Paris au XVIIIe Siècle*, Paris: Gallimard.

Fuchs, R. 1984. *Abandoned Children; Foundlings and Welfare in Nineteenth Century France*, Albany: SUNY Press.

Gaillard, J. 1977. *Paris, La Ville (1852–1870)*, Lille: At. Repro. de These.

Garrioch, D. 1986. *Neighbourhood and Community in Paris 1740–1790*, Cambridge: Cambridge University Press.

Gullickson, G. 1991. 'La Petroleuse: representating revolution', *Feminist Studies* Vol 17, 2, 241–65.

Harsin, J. 1985. *Policing Prostitution in Nineteenth Century France*, Princeton: Princeton University Press.

Harvey, D. 1985. *Consciousness and the Urban Experience*, Oxford: Blackwell.

Hilden, P. 1986. *Working Women and Socialist Politics in France 1880–1914: a Regional Study*, Oxford: Clarendon Press.

Hiley, M. 1979. *Victorian Working Women: Portraits from Life*, London: Gordon Fraser.

Huysmans G. 1987. *The Vatard Sisters*, trans. J.C. Baldock, University Press of Kentucky, (originally 1877 Les Soeurs Vatard).

Lipton, E. 1986. *Looking into Degas: Uneasy Images of Women and Modern Life*, Los Angeles: University of California Press.

Marcus, S. 1966. *The Other Victorians: A Study of Sexuality and Pornography in Mid-Nineteenth Century England*, London: Weidenfeld and Nicolson.

McMillan J. 1981. *Housewife or Harlot: The Place of Women in French Society 1870–1940*, Brighton: Harvester.

McMullen R. 1985. *Degas, His Life, Times and Work*, London: Secker and Warburg.

Newton, J.L., Ryan, M.P., and Walkowitz, J.R. 1983. *Sex and Class in Women's History: Essays from Feminist Studies*, London: Routledge and Kegan Paul.

Perrot, M. 1976. 'Léloge de la menagere dans le discours ouvrier francais au XIX siecle', *Romantisme* No 13, 105–21.

———1979. 'La femme populaire rebelle', in Dufrancatel, C. et al. 126–56

———1980. 'La menagère dans l'espace parisien au XIX siècle, *Annales de la Recherche Urbaine* Autumn.

———ed. 1984. *Une Histoire de Femme est elle Possible?* Marseilles: Rivages.

———(ed.) 1987. 'De La Revolution a La Grande Guerre', vol 4 of P. Aries and G. Duby, (eds) *L'Histoire de la Vie Privee*, Paris.

Pinkney, D. 1958. *Napoleon III and the Rebuilding of Paris*, Princetown: Princetown University Press.

Pollock, G. 1988. *Vision and Difference*, London: Routledge.

Reff, T. 1982. *Manet and Modern Paris*, Washington D.C.: National Gallery of Art.

Ross, E. 1982. '"Fierce questions and taunts": married life in working-class London 1870–1914', *Feminist Studies* 8, 575–602.

———1983. 'Domestic Sharing in working-class London', *History Workshop Journal* 15, 4–27.

Scott, J. 1988. *Gender and the Politics of History*, New York: Columbia University Press.

Sennett, R. 1974. *The Fall of Public Man*, Cambridge: Cambridge University Press.

Shapiro, A.-L. 1985. *Housing the Poor of Paris 1850–1902*, Madison: University of Wisconsin Press.

Sue, E. n.d. *The Mysteries of Paris*, trans. uncredited, London: Dedalus European Classics (originally *Les Mysteres de Paris*, 1842/3).

Thomas, E. 1966. *The Women Incendiaries*, trans. J. and S. Atkinson, London: Secker and Warburg (originally published 1983 as *Les Petroleuses*, Paris, Gallimard).

Timms, E. and Kelley, D. (eds) 1985. *Unreal City: Urban Experience in Modern European Literature and Art*, Manchester: Manchester University Press.

Vidler, A. 1977. ' The scenes of the street; transformations in the ideal and reality 1750–1871', in Anderson, 1977.

Walkowitz J. 1982. 'Male vice and female virtue: feminism and the politics of prostitution in nineteenth century Britain', *History Workshop Journal* 13, 77–93.

Weston, E.A. 1979. *Prostitution in Paris in the later Nineteenth Century: A Study of Political and Social Ideology*, PhD. Thesis, Buffalo: SUNY Press.

Wolff, J. 1990. *Feminine Sentences: Essays on Women and Culture*, London: Polity Press.

Zola E. 1970. *L'Assommoir* trans. L. Tancock, Harmondsworth, Penguin (Originally published 1877).
___ ___ 1972. *Nana,* trans. G. Holden, Harmondsworth: Penguin. (Originally published 1880).

# Chapter 6

## Gendered Spaces, Public Places: Public and Private Revisited on the North Slope of Alaska

*Barbara Bodenhorn*

This chapter examines critically the public/private model of gendered space with the help of information given to me by Iñupiat (Eskimos) on the North Slope of Alaska.[1] It questions theoretical assumptions which implicitly equate a sexual division of labour with a gendered division of space, and at the same time, challenges Inuit ethnography which assumes the Inuit world is fundamentally divided into male and female categories.

Hunter-gatherer material has frequently served as a reference point for theoretical discussions concerning the position of women in society, particularly in the feminist/anthropological search for the origins of women's inequality. The model which assigns men to 'public' and women to 'private' spheres in social organisation, was most explicitly suggested by Michelle Rosaldo (1974). Its longest genealogical root, however, is Engels' (1972 [1896]) evolu-

1. Iñupiat is the name of the Inuit who live on the north and northwest coasts of Alaska. The word literally means 'real people'; the singular as well as the adjectival form is Iñupiaq. By Inuit, I refer to all of the circumpolar peoples collectively known as 'Eskimo'; with the Iñupiat, this includes, then, the Yup'ik peoples of southwestern Alaska, the Siberian Yup'iit of Saint Lawrence Island, the Kalaalimiut of Greenland, and so on. Fieldwork material upon which this chapter is based was collected between 1984 and 1986 with the support of the Alaska Humanities Forum, the Iñupiaq History, Language and Culture Commission, the Audrey Richards Fund, the Smuts Fund, Wolfson College and a Chadwick studentship. It also uses information told to me while I was working for the Iñupiaq Community of the Arctic Slope (ICAS) from 1980 to 1983. The chapter itself expands one of several points made in a paper comparing Iñupiaq and anthropological models of gender delivered at the 1989 Inuit Studies Conference in Fairbanks, Alaska. I would like to thank Barbara Bender, Susan Benson, Nurit Bird-David, Ernest S. Burch, Jr, and Frances Pine for comments on earlier versions.

169

tionist argument, put forward in the *Origin of the Family, Private Property and the State*. Social life, according to Engels, began with the 'communistic common household' (ibid.: 474) which endured in the 'East' until the domestication of animals and in the 'West' with plant cultivation (ibid.:463). During this stage, Engels posited a separate-but-equal division of labour in which men ('roving savages', ibid.: 479) went out to chase animals and women exercised 'supremacy in the house' (ibid.: 484). Because there was no private property, there was no private sphere; all labour was social. Domesticated herds were the first form of private property, given over to men to control because they were already associated with animals and 'procuring food'. This then generated the public/political sphere. Woman's productive labour lost out to her purely reproductive role. Her labour became invisible within the house, the domestic/female sphere which was subsumed and dominated by the public/male arena in which social production was controlled (ibid.: 486–89). Rosaldo argues that gendered oppression developed prior to private property. Although she claims to reject biological determinism, she feels that the universal subordination of women in relation to men stems from cultural constructions of the experience of motherhood which connects the former to the domestic sphere (1974: 23–4).[2] Relative equality, she feels, occurs when the productive/reproductive boundaries are blurred, i.e. when women gather more than men hunt and men are incorporated into the child-rearing process. Both Engels and Rosaldo assert that if public/private spheres are clearly demarcated, they will be gendered. At a more basic level, they assume that a clear sexual division of labour entails differential use of space by men and women and consequently a gendering of those spaces.[3] Debate continues as to whether or not the systematic exploitation of women occurs in the absence of private property, just as it continues to ponder the relationship between mothering and gathering. The basic assumptions concerning space have remained.

2. Challenges to this model have pointed out that women occupy multiple roles: wife, sister, mother, etc. (Sacks 1979); that women's productive role may be emphasised over her reproductive capabilities (Collier 1988); and that relative gendered status may change during the life cycle (e.g., Joseph 1974; Silverman 1975). These question monolithic models of 'womanhood', but implicitly accept the idea of gendered space: where domestic space exists, it will be gendered as female space. Weiner (1976) accords Trobriand women an institutionalised moral, as opposed to political, niche in the public sphere.

3. Rosaldo's use of 'domestic' and 'extra-domestic' is an indication of her implicitly spatial model. Engels' article is also replete with references to space without a clear statement to that effect. Thus his 'savage' men 'roam from camp to camp' (p. 479) while the women reign supreme in the house (see above).

Generally speaking, the public/private model is presented as one based on social organisation.[4] Both Rosaldo and Engels talk about what men and women do. I find the analysis of material conditions crucial to most social inquiry. Nevertheless, I agree with Moore (1988) that such an approach is weakened if it ignores the cultural construction of human action. Indeed, Godelier (1980) argues as a Marxist that to understand relations of production, systems of thought must be considered as part of the infrastructure as well as the superstructure. Women work hard in many societies; only when they are *seen* to work hard does this transform labour into 'social production'. I shall argue that for Iñupiat at least, the public sphere is defined by an ideology that incorporates women in two very important ways. First, knowledge is not gendered and *is* defined as a communal resource ('You must tell what you know; that's one of the rules'). Secondly, there is a shared, explicit (and therefore public) ideology that men and women need each other in order to maintain proper relations with the animals on which humans depend. This is marked by marital relations in what I shall call the kinship – or private – sphere and by male/female interdependence in the communal – or public – sphere.[5] Both Engels and Rosaldo suggest that relatively egalitarian relations exist when the borders between private and public are blurred, or non-existent. I shall argue that in this particular case at least, egalitarian relations occur within these spheres which not only exist, but are culturally elaborated. Despite a clearly defined gendered division of labour in relation to hunting, their borders are marked, however, not by gender, but by animals, a distinction that is ritualised throughout the year in 'physical' as well as 'mental' space.

Anthropological models of Inuit social organisation have long assumed male-domination (e.g. Friedl 1974). This is being steadily challenged (Briggs 1974; Fienup-Riordan 1986; Guemple 1986; Guérin 1982); however, the gendering of Inuit space – which has been quite forcefully argued by Saladin D'Anglure (most recently 1986) – has yet to be examined as critically.[6]

4. I am, therefore, not addressing the other dominant model of this era, namely that identifying 'nature' with women and 'culture' with men.

5. I consciously use the term 'kinship' rather than 'domestic' since this sphere extends far beyond the household level on the North Slope. The assertion that a hunting society such as the Iñupiat can be divided into 'kinship' and 'communal' spheres, the latter not defined by kinship, is by no means a given. Establishing the basis of this assertion is the first task of the chapter.

6. Fienup-Riordan (1990), working with Yup'ik Nelson Islanders, and I (1990) have argued from different angles that gender does not carry the same weight as a classification system among Alaskan Inuit as it does in many societies, although neither of us deals with space *per se*.

## The Setting

Barrow, Alaska lies on the shore of the Arctic Ocean, half-way between the Canadian border and the Bering Strait. With a population of about 3,500, it is the major community of the North Slope Borough, an Iñupiat-controlled home-rule borough which covers roughly 88,000 square miles of northernmost Alaska.[7] Permanent settlement in the Barrow region goes back some two thousand years. Three thriving communities: *Nuvuk* (Point Barrow) *Piġniq* (Shooting Station) and *Utqiaġvik* (Barrow), existed in close proximity by the first half of the nineteenth century. *Nuvuk*, the oldest of these, extends out into the Arctic Ocean, directly in the path of migrating bowhead whales whose leisurely movements, docile behavior and tender meat have made them a preferred food for millennia. In addition, seals, beluga walrus, water fowl and fish provided a steady supply of protein from the sea while caribou, fresh water fish and fur-bearing mammals offered further important resources from the land (see Figure 7.1). Boats and dogsleds made travel possible virtually year-round and facilitated a lively system of intercontinental trade which extended from Canada to Siberia and was a source both of staple and exotic goods. Unlike their Inuit relatives to the east, the whaling and trading Iñupiat developed patterns of differential wealth accumulation. Permanent settlement was accompanied by hierarchical social relations through which complex property rights in relation to hunting and trading developed. At the same time, however, generalised access to resources and individual control over labour acted as levelling mechanisms and allowed for a great deal of the individual autonomy which marks so many hunter-gatherer societies (cf. Woodburn 1982). Contact with 'others' broadened to include Euroamericans in the mid-nineteenth century as explorers, Yankee whalers and fur traders came and left. Churches, schools, and government agencies established a permanent presence in the early decades of the twentieth century. None of these threatened Iñupiat autonomy over their land, for the 'outsiders' focus was largely on renewable resource exploita-

---

7. Iñupiat are not a hunting people who were, as some others may have been, pushed to the most inhospitable corners of the land. Although their territorial autonomy is now under threat, the attachment to the land they occupy has a history of millennia rather than centuries.

Figure 7.1 Barrow, early autumn. Houses are generally surrounded by the means to obtain food. Here you see the frame of a whaleboat which will be stored until the spring when it will be covered in walrus skin. Above it seal meat is drying. Nearby is the outboard motor boat used for summer and fall maritime hunting and fishing. Out of sight, but accessible by the ladder in the left hand corner, ducks are hanging above the *qanichaq*, or arctic entry. [ *location in text page 180 – close to description of marine resources*].

tion.[8] Today Iñupiat continue to hunt, and indeed define themselves as whalers. Largely due to the discovery of oil at Prudhoe Bay in 1968, they are also heavily involved in the national and international economies centred on petroleum development. For both military and economic reasons, the land itself has become an issue of 'national interest' and Iñupiat connection to the land has become as much a matter of politicised ethnicity as it is of social identity.

## Social Organisation, Space and Time

One's place of origin and one's kin continue to provide much of the framework for the Iñupiaq experience of space. In this and the following sections, I shall argue that permanent settlements have not 'fixed' Iñupiat in any one place any more than kinship, which is fundamental to Iñupiaq social relations, has 'fixed' Iñupiaq household membership. Communities and households have had – and continue to exhibit – boundaries of great permeability. My earlier assertion that the categories 'community' and 'kinship' do indeed describe discrete spheres must, therefore, be examined. I shall do this by considering social organisation and the physical organisation of space on the tundra and in town, in relation to time, to labour, to distribution, and finally, to ritual.

Kinship is bilateral, includes affines and is exceedingly fluid. One may both establish and deny relatedness in a variety of ways which are used on a regular basis, but having relatives (as opposed to ancestors) is profoundly important. The first and perhaps most important source of the knowledge one needs to hunt remains one's kin: 'you learn to hunt what your family eats', explained Raymond Neakok, Sr. when I asked him why Barrow households followed different hunting patterns. Relatives form the core of one's social world, nourished by the constant reciprocal flow of assistance and one would be unlikely to move to a village where kinship connections could not be established.[9] One way to do this

---

8. For a variety of historical reasons that I do not have the space to explore fully here, the Iñupiaq experience of early Euroamerican contact was not as one-sided as that of many indigenous peoples. Although they too suffered famine, disease and death, competition among the Europeans and highly sophisticated trading practices among the Iñupiat gave the latter considerable room to manoeuvre (see, e.g. Bockstoce 1986; Burch 1988).

9. The 'affinal inclusive' nature of Iñupiaq kinship does not merely include one's spouse. Quite distant relatives can – and do – take advantage of the affinal connection to visit unfamiliar territory and learn about its resources.

is through marriage which may be exogamous and is neo-local.[10] Marriage is easy to enter and equally easy to leave, and may be instigated by either partner. According to Murdoch (1892), couples customarily 'got married' by going hunting together and by 'acting married' on their return, i.e. by living in the same house and fulfilling their gender specific responsibilities toward the other. Today, 'going camping' (hunting which entails staying on the tundra overnight) together remains a marker of a 'serious' relationship. Spouses frequently come from different parts, and indeed men may say that such partnerships give them the opportunity to learn about new hunting territory.[11]

Permanent settlements grew up where bowhead whales passed close to the shore during their spring and fall migrations. They appeared along with the development of technology to hunt, transport and preserve whales as well as the variety of other land and sea mammals already mentioned. Using dogs and boats, in Dumond's (1975:173) words, 'to transport large kit over considerable distances', Iñupiat were able to live in one place and exploit a wide range of resources. This was by no means anarchic. According to Burch (1988), Iñupiat at the start of the nineteenth century formed several 'countries', identified by place name and encompassing clearly bounded territories. Any *Utqiaġvingmiut* ('person-of-Barrow') had generalised access to all of the resources of the region. At the same time, a number of institutionalised ways of gaining access to others' territory existed. People of one territory might arrange to enter another during times of the year when the 'owners' were elsewhere. A system of trading partnerships also developed which connected explicitly non-related individuals from different villages and thus provided regular access to resources not at one's immediate disposal. In addition, seasonal movement often included attendance at one of several trade fairs.

10. Today, as citizens of the United States, Iñupiat may only enter into monogamous marriages. Prior to the interventions of missionaries and federal officials, there were few fixed rules. Monogamy was the norm, but many people also participated in spouse exchange, or what Burch more accurately calls 'non-residential marriage'. These were enduring economic/sexual partnerships between couples. The balanced nature of the marital division of labour meant that multiple spouses, while not prohibited, were relatively uncommon. Polygyny was generally restricted to wealthy men, but they were by no means expected to have more than one wife. Polyandry was not completely unknown, but was certainly the rarest marriage form (Burch 1975). Today, when young people refer to 'Eskimo marriage', they are referring to multiple sexual partners in an enduring relationship.

11. According to Burch (1975, and even more vehemently in a recent personal communication), 'non-residential marriage' was most likely to occur between partners from different Iñupiaq societies, quite explicitly to enlarge one's resource base.

These were held at points along the coast, spanned the region between the Mackenzie River in Canada and the Seward Peninsula in western Alaska and were established well before the first Euroamericans appeared on the scene. Individual access to resources, then, covered a wide geographic area, included a number of strategies and was influenced, but not controlled by community membership. Indeed, individual autonomy of movement was and remains highly valued. Movement was spurred by needs to find food, to trade, to avoid tension, or simply for the enjoyment of change. Early ethnography suggests that residence patterns fluctuated between sedentism, seasonal variation and semi-nomadism (Simpson 1875, Murdoch 1892, Giddings 1967). Some people remained in *Nuvuk* (Point Barrow), or *Utqiaġvik* (Barrow), for instance, on a permanent basis; some followed a seasonal rhythm, moving between shore and inland while others spent entire years travelling the riverine systems to follow the trade fairs mentioned above; still others varied their patterns between years of residence and periods of nomadism that spanned the coast, the inland rivers and the Brooks Range (see, e.g. IHLC 1980). In the late twentieth century, movement continues to be regarded as an acceptable, and often desirable, response to a variety of issues. Permanent settlement, then, has by no means entailed immobility for individuals or for groups, either in the past or in the present.

If one can choose where one lives, with whom one works, with whom one shares the products of one's labour, and if these may change on a daily basis, it becomes impossible to talk of a 'domestic unit', either of production or of consumption. A 'domestic sphere' ceases to be a useful category for analysis. If at the same time, one adds the knowledge that people may choose which relatives they will recognise, that they may choose whether to leave or remain in a particular place, the division of social relations into those of 'kinship' and 'community' might easily seem to depend on anthropological, rather than indigenous categories. To argue that they are indeed powerful Iñupiaq categories, we must turn to other factors.

## Organisation of Space

Although one hunts in the territory one knows, and that is strongly influenced by one's early experiences with kin, access to hunting territory itself is not subject to spatial regulation. When I asked where people 'could' hunt, I was often corrected, as the following example illustrates: 'Since time immemorial, it's been this way – when people travel up there on the land, it doesn't matter if they're from Barrow or from any other place. If they get up there, they can go hunting. This also applies to the oceans.' (E. Kignak, in Bodenhorn 1989: 85; trans. F. Mongoyak)[12]

The only fixed sites are fish camps which belong to individuals while they live. If someone wants to hunt while the camp is in use, they are expected to ask permission (a formality), and to donate a portion of the catch to the camp residents. Otherwise, rules are designed to guarantee rather than to restrict access to animal resources.

In town, space is more clearly defined than on the tundra, both in terms of houses that belong to individuals and in regard to community places. Iñupiaq households are fluid to the point of being exceedingly difficult to define. They cannot be classed as a unit of production. Cooperative labour is central to the activities of men, women and adolescents, but the labour pool is an ever-changing mosaic of related and non-related partners. Nor do they form a unit of consumption, as many fruits of household members' labour move along highly intricate sharing-networks. Indeed, none of the functional, locational or biological criteria set forth in Laslett and Wall (1972), for instance, can be met easily. Meat flows into and out of the household, meals are shared, tools and equipment shift hands at a steady rate. A cousin may come to stay for a month or more; a son or a daughter may decide to go live with a grandparent. For the most part, people under one roof are *ila*, relatives, but beyond that, a single household shape is difficult to pin down. The sharing-networks through which food, children and services regularly flow mark the kinship sphere.[13]

Despite the fluidity of household membership, houses are identified as belonging to someone and they 'say' something. Single adults rarely live in houses on their own and households of conjugal couples without children are only slightly more common. Houses 'should' have children in them, but the children

12. Neakok, Sr put it even more succinctly: 'In our society, you use it, it's yours' (Bodenhorn 1989: 41).

13. People share food with a wide variety of others; 'sharing' is not restricted to kinsfolk. Sharing multiple resources on a regular basis is conducted among those who consider themselves relatives.

themselves move easily between them: to eat, to sleep, to 'visit for a while', to be fostered, or adopted. Husbands and wives are the fixtures. Moving in under one roof signals marriage, moving out indicates divorce. As I shall argue throughout the paper, the marital couple is culturally constructed as the pivotal link between animals and humans. The house is the physicalised locus of that ritualised relationship in the kinship sphere.

This goes directly against a number of people who argue that women, houses and wombs are explicitly linked (Fienup-Riordan 1983; Graburn 1973; Saladin D'Anglure 1986) and that houses are therefore 'female'. I will return to this later, saying here only that from the earliest ethnography (Murdoch 1892; Simpson 1875), Iñupiaq houses were divided into male *and* female spaces. One could, in fact, argue that wombs – which shelter males and females – are associated with houses, and not the reverse. Indeed, Saladin D'Anglure's (1986) informant often describes womb interiors as houses, divided into male and female spheres and furnished with male and female artefacts. Space within the house was gendered. The house itself was, and continues to be, at the very least, ambiguously classified.

The most important extra-household institutions in Iñupiaq communities were the *qargich* (pl), most frequently translated as 'men's houses', which were the focus of social activity until the missionaries suppressed them in the early twentieth century. Although men primarily would work there during the day, they were transformed in the evening into community centres, where men and women participated in singing, dancing, story-telling and shamanic exhibitions. They were the sites of the numerous feasts organised during the Arctic winter nights and provided the venue for inter-village events such as the Messenger Feast.[14] *Qargich* were associated with whaling crews and a community the size of Barrow would have several. Members might be relatives, but whaling crew participation, not kinship, was the recruitment requirement. In addition to these physically defined public places, various ceremonies connected with whaling would occur at any one of a number of commonly recognised sites along the shore. Today the beach sites remain important, but, as we

---

14. See, for instance, IHLC 1981: 559–61 for descriptions as they were recalled in the 1980s. Messenger Feasts occurred when one trading partner sent out (by messenger) a 'wish list' of gifts to be received from a partner. Once the gifts were assembled, invitations were sent out and a massive inter-village feast would ensue.

shall see, other community activities have moved out of the *qar-gich* and into the churches, gymnasium and community centre.

The *qargich*, then, was arguably a physical manifestation of a social category beyond kinship. Other social institutions suggest this as well: trading partnerships which were explicitly conducted between non-kin, and leadership positions which were achieved rather than ascribed. This distinction receives further elaboration in distribution and ritual practice. First, however, I want to introduce the element of time with a reconsideration of Mauss' theory of seasonal changes in Inuit social morphology.

## Space and Time

Mauss (1906) was probably the first anthropologist to discuss Inuit social organisation in terms of space. In *Seasonal Variations of the Eskimo* he suggests that Inuit gather in communities during a winter season marked by richly elaborated ritual. Summer is the time to spread across the tundra, hunting and fishing in smaller kin groups. Mauss's interpretation was that Inuit social morphology shifted from the sacred/social to the profane/individual with the seasons. Although he was wrong to assign a sacred/secular dichotomy to these alternating strategies, a seasonal morphology I believe, has merit, best defined in terms of kinship and community.[15] We therefore turn to the annual cycle and map time onto Iñupiaq uses of space.

The annual cycle in the 1980s is marked simultaneously by customary hunting patterns which echo those recorded by nineteenth century ethnographers and Euroamerican institutions such as church and school events. Spring whaling involves approximately three quarters of the adult community directly and draws a number of Barrow people back to town who work elsewhere during the rest of the year. They may come from one of the non-whaling inland villages such as Atqasuk, or from 'outside' (i.e. a city outside of the North Slope Borough). Crews undertake their preparations in town during the late winter months (February – March);

15. Burch (personal communication) questions Mauss' relevance for Alaskan material, noting that in northwest Alaska at least 'it was very unusual... for conjugal families to disperse in the summer except, perhaps, for a couple of days.' The idea that there is a different moral weight assigned to seasonal activities I find convincing, as shall be discussed. What Mauss missed entirely is that sacred components exist for the activities of each season, primarily because his Durkheimian definition of 'the sacred' is confined to an equally Durkheimian definition of 'community'.

individuals may occasionally go ice-fishing, ptarmigan-hunting and the like, but trips are not usually extended. Whaling itself lasts while open leads in the ice and migrating bowhead coincide, from approximately mid-April to late May.[16] The last weekends of this month as well as early June are the best times to go *nigliaq-*, geese-hunting, an activity that perhaps more than anything else is pleasurably anticipated by married couples. Families – conjugal and extended – take off to 'go camping' for the Memorial Day Weekend and Barrow is often left feeling distinctly 'ghost-town-ish'. The whaling celebrations bring people back to town in mid-June, again attracting Iñupiat with any Barrow connections. This is the last major community event of the season.

Summer is a quiet time. A number of people go out to 'fish camp' – some in family groups, some on their own. A few will spend the entire summer out on the tundra; others will take extended weekends. Still others remain in town, but take advantage of good weather to 'go boating'. Many people have built shelters out at *Piġniq* – site of one of the three original villages, but abandoned as a permanent community since the early decades of this century. It is connected to Barrow by a road and serviced in the summer by municipal transportation. Situated on a narrow neck of land, it is an ideal spot for hunting ducks. The long, bright Arctic nights can well be spent drinking tea, visiting with friends and waiting to take advantage of the occasional flock of ducks already winging southward. Many people will go to Fairbanks in July for the Eskimo-Indian Olympics; a few will travel to Kotzebue during the time of the traditional trade fairs; 'annual leave' from jobs is often taken to travel inland or to neighbouring villages for berry picking and/or fishing. Late summer is the time for walrus-hunting, a village-based activity undertaken by groups of men; autumn caribou-hunting and fishing again call for camping trips which may last from an extended weekend to a number of weeks, depending on needs, desires, availability of time, resources and, of course, the weather. Although the activities follow their traditional pattern, they are often marked by the American equivalent of the bank holiday; just as Memorial Day weekend is the most common time for geese-hunting, so Labour Day weekend (in early September) is popular for a trip inland to 'look around' for caribou. All of these activities are followed by

16. The imposition of whaling quotas by the International Whaling Commission has, since 1978, occasionally shortened the season.

people who work as well as people who are unemployed. As I shall discuss, hunting costs money and a wide variety of strategies exists to meet the need for hunted food as well as the need for cash. For the moment, what I want to emphasise is that individuals may choose one, all, none, or a combination of the hunting activities described above. Hunting partners most probably will shift according to activity; both the region and the resources exploited are a matter of individual decision. With the exception of beluga, which is defined as a communal resource, animals caught will travel along the sharing-networks that are, for the most part, decided upon by husbands and wives and which, again for the most part, mark the kinship sphere.

The autumn brings a new school year and, shortly thereafter, the fall whaling season. From this point until the end of spring whaling, the cycle is punctuated by a series of community-oriented events – again conforming to the dominant American calendar, but performed with a uniquely Iñupiaq twist. Thanksgiving and Christmas are community, not family, occasions, marked by the communal distribution of Iñupiaq (hunted) food, commensality and *aġġi-*, or 'Eskimo dancing'. The period between Christmas and New Year's Day is taken up with 'the games' – traditional Iñupiaq games of skill and endurance when individuals compete against each other within age cohorts, and 'marrieds' are pitted against 'singles' in community-wide teams. These take place in the community centre, finish with an all-night marathon beginning on New Year's Eve, and culminate in another 'Eskimo dance' on the night of January 1. Within the last few years, a new version of the customary Messenger Feast, *Kivgiq*, has been reintroduced in January. Although the original, as I have mentioned, was a competitive give-away feast that matched trading partners against each other in ostentatious generosity, the focus of the 1990s version is once again communal feasting and dancing.[17] February–March heralds the annual Alaska Eskimo Whaling Commission meeting, which concludes with a pot-luck dinner of Iñupiaq food and an Eskimo Dance. This is the time when representatives of all of the whaling communities gather to agree on strategies for increasing and maintaining autonomous control of subsistence whaling. The feasts and dances are a celebration of inter-village hospitality as well as of political cohesion. As the days become lighter but remain cold, a

17. Because of the timing of these events, I have as yet been unable to participate. My information is based solely on accounts given to me by Iñupiaq friends.

day of games, *qitiktitchirat-*, is organised on the frozen lagoon on the edge of town. This too is a 'modern' reintroduction of older forms, not 'pristine' by any means and no less community-oriented because of it. Soon spring whaling begins again; a successful season is celebrated with one or more *Nalukataq* feasts; school lets out and the emphasis on community abates until the fall.

Summer, then, is by no means a time of individual isolation, nor, as Burch pointed out (footnote 12), a time when one's social world boils down to the conjugal family as suggested by Mauss. Rather, it is a time of sociality. People do things together, travel together, play cards, go to parties, and go camping together. But it is not one that is community-oriented – no commensal feasts, nor celebrations of group process such as those which mark the whaling cycle. Winter, on the other hand, is filled with activities that are social in the Durkheimian sense of society; the focus is not only extra-household, extra-kin, but also emphasises participation: dancing, games, eating. It is participation that is defined by Iñupiat in terms of community; it both allows one to become and marks one as a community member.[18]

'Community', then, might be said to be a time, a set of locations, certain kinds of activities, and participation. It is marked by extra-household, extra-kinship institutions and is, by any measure, public. It is now time to add gender to the equation.

## Gender, The Division of Labour and Distribution Practices

Of the 78 households with whom I worked in Barrow, 42 (54%) had at least one household member who hunted regularly; another 20 (26%) hunted occasionally; 58 (76%) of households took a direct role in whaling and 100% were involved in sharing-networks which gave them access to 'real', or hunted, food and, by extension, 'real' identity. Hamburgers, pizzas and Chinese food may be eaten with pleasure; new foods are tested with curiosity, but I repeatedly heard Iñupiaq identity talked about in terms of food. A baby who shows a liking for *maktaaq* (beluga blubber) is pointed

18. This was made quite explicit to me on a number of occasions. When I first began to work at ICAS, in the lull of late August, I was reassured that things would 'start happening' in the fall. It was made clear that it would be 'better' if I took part (as I was of course delighted to do), since so many outsiders – teachers and hospital staff for the most part – did not. If I held back at a communal distribution because I felt I would be taking a valuable resource; if I refrained from taking part in discussions when the 'singles' were choosing their next game at Christmas, I was chided, literally with the words, 'go ahead, you're a member of the community'.

out with a chuckle, 'he's real Iñupiaq, that one'; an adult may say, 'I'm Iñupiaq, I eat Iñupiaq food.' Public hearings on proposed development are filled with impassioned testimony regarding the importance of 'our garden', the sea. Shared food, in fact, forms the core of those networks which are central to the provisioning of Iñupiaq households. Sharing-networks may or may not include a flow of mutual assistance, tools, equipment, child care and/or money; none exists, to my knowledge, without 'Iñupiaq' food.

Barrow in the late twentieth century is a full-fledged member of the US economic system. It costs money to pay for heat, electricity and water, to pay for the cable television which broadcasts twelve channels around the clock, to buy bread, milk or Pampers in the local store, or to purchase an airline ticket to the next village, to one of Alaska's 'big' cities, or to Hawaii for vacation, a popular choice. And it costs money to hunt: $25 (US) for a box of shells, $5,000 (US) for a snow-machine, $700 (US) for a sled, and so on. Many strategies are followed to provision households. In some cases, one person works (not necessarily a household member) and provides another with the wherewithal to go hunting. This may be a spouse, sibling, parent, or child. There is no cultural construction as to who 'should' be earning money. Some people work for short, intensive periods and accumulate enough overtime pay to support long periods of unemployment during which they can hunt full-time. Many others work full-time, building up 'annual leave', and taking 'leave without pay' to go hunting, fishing or berry picking. Kruse (1982) found a positive correlation between education, income, the number of subsistence activities engaged in per year and the amount of time spent pursuing them.

In 1986, 252 Iñupiaq men and 229 Iñupiaq women were working full-time in Barrow; a similar ratio counted themselves unemployed. In the early 1970s, the pattern was for women to work full-time 'pink-collar' jobs while men preferred seasonal construction with flexible time which allowed them to hunt. By 1977, women had started moving into technical and professional jobs, a trend that continues into the late 1980s.[19] Within the past decade,

19. See Bodenhorn 1989; Kruse 1982; Worl & Smythe 1986 for specific numbers and trends over two decades. I was asked by the editor if the predominance of women in 'pink-collar' occupations did not suggest a *de facto* sexual division of labour. Women's increasing participation in 'white-collar' positions, I think, argues against this. Certainly when employing institutions were non-Iñupiaq-run (schools and hospitals), women were hired to do what Euroamericans define as 'women's' work. It is within the past two decades that this pattern has changed, along with the development of more Iñupiaq-run institutions. I was never told that women 'should' do secretarial work.

women have occupied public positions such as magistrate, state
legislator, Executive Director of the Alaska Eskimo Whaling
Commission, school superintendent, city manager, and chair of
the Village Corporation under the Alaska Native Claims
Settlement Act. Access to cash is necessary for survival; access to
*niqipiaq*, real food, is necessary for social identity. What is important here is that the former was not discussed with me in terms of
gender. Earning money was not talked about, either as a 'male'
activity, nor as somehow more 'important' than other forms of
labour. When I asked about 'men's' and 'women's' work, waged
labour was simply not mentioned.

An explicitly gendered division of labour emerges when talk
turns to the complex of activities defined by Iñupiat as 'subsistence'. Men make and maintain tools and equipment, although
women may buy and own them. The former go out after animals
and fish. They may hunt alone, with partners (kin or otherwise),
or with a spouse. Women hunt occasionally, fish, butcher the
meat, transform the hide into clothing, preserve and prepare food
and take care of children – who may or may not be theirs, and
with a great deal of help from male and female kin. Although relatives might be called on to help, the marital relationship was
and is the ideal form within which these services are carried out.
As Belcher Island Inuit said to Lee Guemple (1986), hard work is
something one does *for* (his emphasis) someone of the other gender. This is indeed a gendered division of labour, for it is not con-
strued as 'natural' (see also Briggs 1974; Guemple 1986). Women
who can shoot straight as well as butcher are considered 'skilled',
not 'manly'. By the same token, a man should be able to repair a
rip in his parka if he needs to. All knowledge contributes to survival skills. 'Survival' rather than 'biology' was the most frequent
reason given to me to explain action.

In terms of this division of labour and a gendered use of space,
the historical record suggests that both women and men were
familiar with land and sea. Charles D. Brower, one of the first
Euroamerican whalers to winter over in Barrow, noted that: 'The
women worked in the whaling crews the same as the men, were
just as good at paddling and did not seem afraid of going alongside of a whale...' (n.d.: 117–18). Similarly, Burch (personal communication) pointed out that when men hunted on foot, women
were expected to take the dog team out to collect their husbands'
catch. They were better dog handlers than men, 'often better

trackers' and equally knowledgeable about the land. Knowledge, in fact, was one important factor in the hunting enterprise that arguably was not gendered. As in many hunting and gathering societies, women's observations about the land and animals' movements were actively solicited. Knowledge continues to be constructed as a public resource and one is expected to share what one knows.[20] Beyond the gendered division of labour, few hunting skills are specialised; several couples in fact described how they survived virtually on their own for the first few years of their marriages. Still, most hunting is undertaken with others and larger animals – bearded seal, walrus or beluga for instance – are often pursued in groups.

How resources are distributed in hunter/gatherer societies is increasingly a subject of inquiry (e.g. Altman and Peterson 1988; Ingold, Riches and Woodburn 1988; Wilmsen 1989). Iñupiaq distribution practices distinguish between 'sharing' (an on-going reciprocal process) and 'shares' (a portion of the catch earned by individuals). In general, entitlement to a share, or *ningik*, is earned by contributing towards the means of production, or by furnishing one's labour. Contributing food to a whaling crew, giving a hunter the present of a rifle, helping to butcher an animal, or providing fuel to a group of hunters may all earn one a 'share' of the catch. This is not gendered. A woman who owns the harpoon (a 'male' instrument) used to kill a whale is just as entitled to her *ningik* as she is if she helps to butcher a bearded seal (a 'female' activity). Once the share has been transferred, obligation ceases between the parties involved. Meat that circulates as a function of 'sharing', on the other hand, forms part of the reciprocal process which both binds kin to each other and ties humans and animals together.

I have discussed this distinction between 'shares' and 'sharing' elsewhere (1988; 1989). For the purposes of this study, however, I want to suggest that the animals themselves fall into two categories: animals whose 'shares' are designated only for those who participated in the hunt, and animals whose 'shares' are explicitly meant for the entire community. The former (seals, caribou, walrus, fish, etc.) are divided on the tundra, the ice and in or near the house. How they are divided is a matter for the individuals

---

20. In collecting life histories, it was clear that both boys and girls, for instance, have been exhorted to 'get the white man's education' and to bring it back to the community.

involved. The 'communal' group (beluga, polar bear, bowhead whale) are butchered on community territory and shares are distributed not only to those who have taken part in the hunt, but to all community residents as well. In both cases, people talk about receiving 'their' shares: an entitlement, not a gift.[21]

The whale, the largest of the animals, serves as the focus of the greatest social and cultural elaboration involving hunting, taking hunting out of the kinship and into the community sphere. Bowhead whales are very large animals, one of which may provide up to sixty tons of usable meat to the community. It is possible, but difficult, for a single crew to kill a bowhead; several crews spread along the open lead greatly increase a community's chance for a successful hunt. Led by the *umialik* (lit., 'boat owner') and his wife ('the whaling couple'), a whaling crew endures over time; its members may be, but are not necessarily, related and it includes the specialist position of harpooner.[22] Whaling celebrations encompass both shares (distribution) and sharing (hospitality); they involve explicitly extra-kinship social relations and occur in community spaces.

The whaling season starts as the sun reappears over the Arctic horizon. Men gather to work on the wooden frame of the *umiaq*, the whaling boat, and to make sure their equipment is in working order. As the days rapidly gain light, crews set out to cut ice roads in the direction they hope to camp, somewhere on the edge of the open lead through which the migrating whales will pass. In town, the most expert sewers (women) will be contracted to 'dress' the *umiaq*, i.e. to sew its walrus skin cover which will allow it to travel safely through the spring ice. Radio contact is maintained with other whaling villages along the coast; news of approaching whales and the success or failure of more westerly villages travels instantly through the region. When the moment seems right, the crew sets out for camp.

21. See also Altman and Peterson (1988) who found that the distribution of meat is likewise complicated among the Gunwinggu of Arnhem Land, Australia. Small animals are not subject to the same rules of generalised distribution as are the larger animals such as kangaroos. The explicit right of the hunter to retain small game, the authors feel, thus recognizes the right of the household to ensure its own provisioning.

22. *Umialik* is a position of relatively high status; it is achieved, is based on authority and respect rather than power and is dependent on followership, to echo Collier (1988). People are free to change crews as they are free to change hunting partners or place of residence. As Ernest Burch pointed out (personal communication), many people might achieve the position of owning a boat without becoming an *umialik* who must not only have the resources needed to build a boat, but must also show the proper characteristics of a leader: knowledge, an even-temper, generosity and the like.

Once a whale is caught, the entire community is invited to help pull the whale onto the ice. The crews gather to help with the butchering. One man stands on top of the animal to make sure the correct cuts are being made; the wife, or co-captain, generally directs the cutters where to take each piece of meat or maktak (whale skin and blubber) which is laid out in precise shares on the ice (figures 7.2 and 7.3). There is an ordered division of shares between crews and another one within crews. The latter follows the general rule for the division of game: everyone who contributed material or labour to the crew is entitled to a share, with the captain and his wife (the whaling couple), the harpooner, and the harpoon owner receiving an extra share (figure 7.4). Although women no longer paddle as they did in Charles D. Brower's time, participation may take a variety of forms: women who work full-time may send out coffee and snow-machine fuel; they might furnish a harpoon, bake bread, or go out to camp to help cook, thus earning a share. Half of the whaling couple's share is destined for communal distribution during a series of whaling feasts that mark the annual cycle. Before discussing these feasts, let us turn to cosmology and ritualised space.

## Cosmology, Humans and Animals

Animals, according to many northern hunters, have intent and decide to give themselves up to be killed. Hunting is a sacred act in which all participants must be ritually proper. According to Iñupiat, animals give themselves up to men whose wives are generous and skilful; the men themselves must also treat the animal with proper respect, but it is the woman to whom the animal offers itself. This came to me as somewhat of a surprise, being well indoctrinated in anthropologists' models of hunters in general and Inuit hunters in particular. During the first autumn of my stay in Barrow, I was talking with Ernie Frankson, a whaler from Point Hope, about preparations for the fall hunt and said something about 'only men hunting'. He took a moment and then responded: 'the whale comes to the whaling captain's wife.' When asking a friend about this, she remembered one very successful inland hunter who stated: 'I'm not the great hunter, my wife is'. He was referring to her generosity and skill at attracting the animals, not to her accuracy with a rifle. Other people agreed:

**Figure 7.2 Butchering a whale. Once the whale has been pulled onto the ice, members from all the present crews will help to butcher it.** [ *location: p 195 with discussion of butchering*].

**Figure 7.3** Dividing whale shares on the ice. The butchered meat is first divided into crew shares on the ice. These will be subdivided into further shares for individual crew members once the meat has been taken back to the village. [*location: close to previous photo*].

Figure 7.4 Wainwright Nalukataq, 1985. Distribution of shares. Plastic buckets and plastic sacks are used to collect a household's shares. This year was an abundant one, and each household received shares according to the number of people who regularly ate there. In harder years, each household would receive the same amount. [*location: close to above*].

'Yes, these were very strong beliefs'; 'it has been like that from way back.'

Two major responsibilities that humans must exercise in order to continue the animal/human relationship are first to invite/attract the animals, and then to act as good hosts so that they will want to come again. Customarily wives had ritual responsibility to ask for the animals. Dinah and David Frankson of Point Hope relate how wives would ask the moon for animals and good health. 'Whatever Alingnaq (the man in the moon) put in a woman's bowl, that was what her husband would get during his hunting activities' (Pulo 1980: 15–6). The whaling captain-wife would ask for whales in the spring; all the others asked for game animals throughout the year.

The husband's proper behaviour was, and is, also fundamentally important. A wounded animal, for instance, should never be allowed to wander off and die on its own, for when a man has killed an animal, he must make sure that its *iñua*, its soul, is treated hospitably. Sea mammals would be thirsty after a life in salt water, and so they should be offered a drink of fresh water (by a woman); land animals should have their heads severed so that their souls may return from whence the animals came. The hunter's wife butchers the meat and shares it generously; the animal's spirit is pleased by this and, in reciprocity, will offer itself up again to the hunter. Just as the wife's skill with the *ulu* (woman's knife) allows her to share meat widely and thus attract the animals, so too is her needle an instrument of the hunt. Customarily it was the wife's job to make all of the hunter's clothing; the animal's hide would be transformed into a 'second skin' for the hunter, which if pleasingly done would draw the animals to him (Chaussonnet 1988). Today women no longer clothe their husbands entirely in the skins of hunted animals. But sewing remains a highly valued skill and young women who did not learn how to sew as adolescents, frequently begin after they are married. Wives still make parkas for their husbands; their skill in creating pleasing designs for the 'fancy trim' and full ruff adds stature to the wearer making a public appearance. And a clean, new *qatignisi* (whaling shirt) is still part of the preparations for spring whaling. It is the wife's job to attract the animals, and thus, in Iñupiaq terms, to hunt.

Customarily the spousal relationship was even more ritualised for whaling than for the other hunting. Then, as now, it was not marital couples in general who were responsible for the success of the hunt, but the whaling couple, the *umialik*, the whaling captain-husband-and-wife. I have already mentioned that it was the whaling captain-wife whose job it was to ask for whales in the spring. Rainey (1947, 245, 259–64) also detailed a number of mutual ritual responsibilities which were to be carried out by the couple. The husband was to hire a skilled craftsman to make the wooden pot from which the wife was to offer the whale its welcoming drink of water. The wife would hire an old woman to make mittens which she had to wear when carrying the pot. The husband would keep her left-handed mitten in the boat with him during whaling season; he would wear special boots made for him by his wife, and her belt. By the same token, after helping to launch the *umiaq*, she would place the special pot and her husband's drum by the entrance of the house for the duration of the hunt. Upon the successful catch, the wife would offer the drink of water; after the whale was butchered, she would offer her husband a drink from the same pot. The pot, cooked meat, hunting charms, amulets, the hammer used to make the pot and shavings from the paddles were then placed under a tripod formed by three paddles, over which the wife threw a parka.

If the whales did not come, a ritual marital pair would have to travel to the spirit world to rectify matters. According to David Frankson, 'in the old days', if the ice did not open in time for spring whaling an *angatkuq* (shaman) was sent to the *Itivyaat* (people who lived under ground). The shaman, however, could not do this alone, but needed a partner:

> Whenever a male *angatkuq* was sent to the *Itivyaat*, the wife of a captain was sent to carry the *angatkuq's* divining rod.... The men did not hesitate to give up their wives for this purpose because of the necessity to catch a whale. It is said that Kataliuraq (Frankson's grandmother) was chosen to go to the *Itivyaat*. However, since she was a woman, a captain was named to follow her. In the case of a female *angatkuq*, a man is chosen to follow her... (Frankson in Pulo 1980: 52)

While the men are out on the ice, it is the job of the whaling captain-wife to be welcoming; she must move slowly, think peaceful thoughts and act generously. The whale may then be attracted and offer itself up to her husband. Imagery connecting whales, women and the house is most explicit in a story recorded by Rasmussen (1929: 24–6). Raven is flying over the ocean, becomes exhausted and falls into the sea. He tumbles 'right into a house, a beautiful, lovely house where there was light and warmth. On the platform sat a young woman, busy with a burning lamp.' The woman is the soul of the whale; her lamp is its heart. It is the woman at the hearth that gives the whale life. This provides an important clue as to why the *umialik*-wife's ritual responsibilities are physicalised in the house. The whale-woman in her house sees the whaling captain-woman in hers, senses her welcoming spirit, decides this is a good place 'to camp' and offers herself to the whaling crew.

Missionaries attempted to suppress many of these practices in the early twentieth century, although much of the detail I have just presented (Rainey 1947; Frankson, in Pulo 1980) was gathered in the 1940s or later. During my stay in Barrow clearly marked ways of inviting were less in evidence, but the obligation of the whaling captain-wife to offer an inviting hearth remains strong. It also continues to be the whaling couple who must make sure the whales are treated well. Patrick Attungana, a Point Hope whaling captain, had this to say a few years ago:

> When the whales travel, they know about St. Lawrence (Island), so when they reach there, one of them stop, like they are camping, allowing themselves to be killed... when they reach Barrow, one of them camp, caught by the whalers... When the whale is caught... the whole whale gives itself to all the people... the whale being or spirit never dies... the dead whale's being or spirit return to the live whales.... He tells them that his hosts were good, the married couple were good to it... The whale that had good hosts starts wishing and telling others that it will camp again the following year. The other whale, who did not have good hosts says that it will not camp again. When you hunt in harmony, you don't have problems catching the animals (1986: 16ff).

Once the whale has given itself up, then, it remains the whaling couple's responsibility to provide hospitality. The most important hosting activities are the community feasts which take place several times during the year. The first is immediate. As the whale is being butchered, women prepare *uunaaliit* (literally 'hot things', boiled *maktak*) to serve with coffee out on the ice. Simultaneously, sledsful of meat are being transported back to the whaling couple's house. Women connected to the crew begin to cook all possible parts of the whale: meat, *maktak*, heart, tongue and other organs; others will bring cakes, drinks, bread and the like. When the feast is prepared, the captain's flag flies high over the house. This is an invitation for anyone in town to come and have a meal. Cooked food will once again be served at the end of the whaling season when the crew serves boiled *maktak* to all comers on the beach to mark the moment when the boat is brought off the ice for the last time.[23] Each of the above is an example of 'pure' hospitality. Food is prepared and explicit invitations are sent out to the entire community: the flag flying over the *umialik* house, announcements broadcast over the short-wave radio to 'come get *uunaalik* on the beach'. Each is conducted on a different site: the first on the ice, the edge of the lead through which the whales travel; the second is the whaling couple's house, heart of the community; the third is on the shore, the boundary between land and sea, the point at which the societies of animals and of humans meet.

Throughout the year, the whaling couple have the responsibility to provide meat for people who are in need; today this might include donations to the Seniors' Center in Barrow, or shipments of food to the Iñupiaq inmates in the Fairbanks prison. Their crew should not go out on the ice again until all of their share has been eaten or given away. Three more celebrations occur, however, which involve all community members in the public sphere. These are *Nalukataq*, Thanksgiving and Christmas, feasts which include both the distribution of shares by successful whaling crews and the provision of their hospitality to the entire community.

*Nalukataq*, or 'blanket toss', is held about six weeks after the end of the whaling season; the crews have spent the intervening time hunting ducks and geese, preparing *mikigaq* (whale meat and *maktak*, fermented in whale blood), and in general, getting ready to feed several hundred guests. On the day itself, a windbreak is erected at a traditional site on the beach, tables are set up in the centre, and quantities of food are brought out.[24] A short distance away, the walrus skin 'blanket' has been set up, a trampoline from which people will be tossed into the air. Around noon people begin to appear, carrying eating utensils and plastic sacks to carry home their shares; children try out their skill on the blanket and

23. It is significant that this food is cooked. *Quaq*, or frozen meat, may be distributed as a share, or it may be shared hospitably as part of a meal. Thus, its status is unclear. Shares are never distributed in the form of cooked food which is therefore an unambiguous marker of hospitality.

24. Nalukataq feasts may be held by successful whaling crews either singly or together. The exact organisation of the feasts varies from village to village; this description reflects how I experienced the event in Barrow during the five years I was there.

people sit around and visit, usually in small family groups. Soon the feasting begins. Pairs of male and female crew members serve soup which is eaten on the spot. Then the distribution of shares gets underway. Containers of *mikigaq, maktak,* whale meat and *quaq* (usually frozen fish or caribou) make the rounds, again carried by female/male crew member pairs. In a good year, each household will get shares according to the number of people who eat together; in a bad year, shares are allocated by household, regardless of size. Anyone who is in the community on the day is entitled to a share[25] and the village is usually crammed with North Slope friends and relatives for the event. People eat their fill and pack the remainder to take home. The feast is finished with quantities of hot tea, 'hard tack' and fruit for all and special cakes for the elders. The distribution of shares, then, begins and ends with the hospitable provision of a meal: food that may not be classified as 'shares' and that therefore may only be 'shared'.

Afterwards, men and women show off their skill (and their parkas) on the blanket toss until finally the dancing starts, around mid-evening. The drummers (men) sit tapping quietly on their drums, while behind them is a row of singers (women). The walrus skin blanket is put down before them to form a platform. The music is performed by these two rows of musicians. The dancers come from the audience; they dance in solidarity, in high spirits, but mostly in thanks that the season has been a successful one. Men and women dance together as crew members, as relatives, as friends.

The other two feasts, which take place well after the sun has disappeared entirely, also occur in public places; at one time these would have been the *qargich*, but are now the churches.[26] The food is provided by the whaling captains, the distributors are male/female pairs who have been chosen by the deacons, but the distribution-and-feast pattern itself remains the same. In the evening, everyone repairs to the community centre for 'Eskimo dancing' which will be broadcast over the entire North Slope by the local radio station, complete with running commentary by one of Barrow's elders.

25. My niece was visiting me during the spring of 1987 and had the opportunity to participate in both Wainwright and Barrow Naluktaq feasts. Although we explained that she would be in town only for a day or two, she was firmly given shares in both places.

26. Thanksgiving and Christmas are of course not indigenous to the North Slope. They were, however, allowed by the missionaries and are celebrated at the same time of year, i.e., during the darkest period, that was traditionally marked by much ceremonial feasting.

5

Figure 7.5 'Blanket toss', Barrow Nalukataq, 1985. After the main feast, adults gather around a 'blanket' sewn from walrus or bearded seal skin. As people pull simultaneously, the blanket acts as a trampoline, tossing jumpers high into the air. Those who are skilled carve dramatic poses in the air. At some point, one of the crew members will climb on the blanket carrying sweets which s/he will throw to the assembled crowd. It is one of the last gifts of the day. [ *location: p. 203 – end of description of dance*].

6

Figure 7.6 'Eskimo Dance', Barrow Nalukataq, 1985. The final event of any Nalukataq feast is the dancing. The walrus hide 'blanket' has been spread in front of the musicians to form a platform for the dancers. These will come from the audience, including first whaling crew members and subsequently anyone from the community who wishes to celebrate the successful whaling season.

## Conclusions

Among Iñupiat, work is something that men and women do for each other. Their interdependence is acknowledged and appreciated. The sexual division of labour is culturally constructed as one in which all participants have crucial responsibilities.

'Real work', like 'real food', is connected to hunting. Although this work is marked by gender, the space in which it occurs is not: the tundra, the ice, domestic and communal spaces in town were customarily all accessible to men and women even if their gendered use might differ. Today the inter-gendered use of space continues. There were no areas to my knowledge that were considered somehow 'off-limits' either to men or to women. The intensity of interaction between them has intensified according to some. Supermarkets as well as feasts, basketball games, public meetings and church services are all attended by men and women, frequently as married couples. At public hearings, men and women testify very much as individuals and may contradict the position of a spouse without exciting comment (no politicians' wives here, instructed to gaze lovingly at their husbands when the latter speak in public).[27]

The above are not necessarily ritualised spaces, which are more defined by context than physical location and which therefore may be created anywhere. Space may also be ritualised on the tundra and the ice – where the hunter must treat the animal carcass and its *iñua* properly and where the marital relationship truly begins. It is ritualised in the house where animals are shared and their skins are sewn into pleasing patterns. Although women no longer go out to hunt in the western sense as frequently, they do continue to butcher, to sew and to share – i.e. ritual action that is contained in 'hunting' in the Iñupiaq sense. These spaces include sites that are explicitly recognised as communal: special places on the shore, in the *qargich*, the gymnasium, the churches. Ritual activity within all of these spaces depends on gendered *interdependence*; ritual efficacy cannot be achieved by one gender alone. Within the kinship sphere, however, ritual does not have to be performed together. As long as husbands and wives do what they are supposed to do, their marital/ritual obligations are met and, indeed, many married couples spend much of the day in separate activities. In contrast, ritualised

27. This is, I am sorry to say, part of the US Republican candidates' handbook.

spaces that serve the community are not only marked by gendered interdependence, but by gendered *interaction*. To go to the spirit world – *Itivyaat* – one needs a spouse. To share the whale meat and thus act as good hosts, the whaling couple need male/female pairs to help with the distribution. To thank the animals during *aġġi* – Eskimo dancing – men must drum and women sing. The dances which show thanks may be individual, groups of men or women, or men, women and children together. The final dance of the evening (which is called the welcome dance), should include everyone. It is precisely in the public sphere that the interdependence of men's and women's roles receives the greatest elaboration.

The public/community sphere for Iñupiat, then, is a realm that is ceremonially elaborated. It is culturally constructed as important, but animals, not gender, mark its boundaries. Those animals classified as communal resources belong to the public realm where both men and women must act correctly to maintain the proper relationship between animal and human worlds.

The woman is indeed associated with the hearth, but it is here that she attracts the whale, the animal most bound up with community. It is not any woman, but the whaling captain-wife, in the whaling captain-house, working as the ritual co-head of the whaling crew. She must do this in conjunction with the work of her husband at their whaling camp. In earlier times, he would have worn her belt and kept one of her mittens, just as she would have kept his drum by the door. Today their connection is maintained by virtually constant communication by short-wave radio.

Sewing is skilled labour which, if you are a man out on the tundra may keep you alive; if you are a woman, it may earn you shares from other hunters, or money from itinerant whites. When a woman sews for her husband, her needle creating a second skin to attract the animals, she is acting ritually as wife-the-hunter. It is the ritual, not the labour, that is gendered. And it is the context, not the activity, that creates the ritual. It is the shared ideology that makes this 'public'. The conjunction of ideology (the equation of women's ritual with hunting) and practice (women's ability to earn shares with their labour and their role in distribution) places women at the centre of socially productive relations, not on the periphery as reproducers. They have remained at the centre.

This material suggests that Engels was correct to argue that a sexual division of labour does not in and of itself constitute a system of gender exploitation. It is a critical flaw, however, to assume that such a division genders space as well as labour and it is precisely that point on which the remainder of Engels' logic rests. One could argue that it is the gendering of space – whether mental or physical – that creates exclusion from which difference leads to differential evaluation. The fact that space is thus gendered in many societies is uncontestable. It cannot be taken as a given.

The Iñupiaq construction of the social relations of production has, I think, had important ramifications for the ways Iñupiat have dealt with the economic changes of recent decades. This, in turn, has important implications for models of social relations within a capitalist context. I suggested earlier that women's control over their labour has perhaps allowed them to move more easily into waged labour than has often been women's experience elsewhere. In fact, it is sometimes thought by Iñupiat to have been an easier move for women than for men. Here the spatial context of gendered ritual may be a factor. Waged work has neither been classified as a male domain, nor as somehow more real or intrinsically valuable than hunting, which continues to be defined as 'real work' – the work of maintaining proper animal/human relations. Men must go out on the tundra or the ice to hunt. Earning money is needed for survival, but it conflicts with what men have to do to fulfil their ritual responsibilities to the animals and to their fellow humans. Women, whose ritual work (sewing and butchering) is not restricted spatially, can more easily accommodate 'real work' and jobs.

I suggest as well that gender-neutral ideas about knowledge likewise provide access to the public sphere. Leadership positions such as *umialik*, or *angatkuq* have long been associated with skills and knowledge, neither of which is gendered in the 'natural' idiom of Euroamerican models. Frankson's grandmother possessed shamanic knowledge and was sent 'to the other side' to procure animals. Today a woman with specialist political knowledge may be sent to the legislature to represent Iñupiaq interests.

It seems most useful to argue, not, as Rosaldo might, that the boundaries between public and private are blurred, nor that gender differences are unmarked. On the North Slope, unlike many hunting and gathering societies, an entire complex of social activities has developed around whaling which is explicitly community – not kinship – oriented. All animals must be treated correctly

– the very acts of hunting, butchering, sewing are ritual which should be conducted by husbands and wives. The shares of a bearded seal, or a caribou are earned by participants in the hunt. Most of the meat that will subsequently circulate through sharing-networks will travel to kin who are involved in a series of intensive reciprocities. Some will be shared with 'the people', people in need, people who ask, but the decision of what and how much to share is made at the household level by the marital couple.

With whaling these rituals are brought out of the kinship sphere, onto the beach, into the *qargich*. Here the whaling couple – symbolizing the marital relationship as linking humans and animals – act as ritual husband and wife, representatives of the whole community in their role of 'good hosts'. The other crucial actors are men and women. Gender, then, is important; it is marked by the different things that men and women do. It does not mark the communal sphere which may be clearly separated from the kinship sphere, but is rather incorporated into it. Whales, not men, 'make' community.

### References

Altman, J. and Peterson, N. 1988. 'Rights to game and rights to cash among contemporary Australian hunter-gatherers', in T. Ingold, D. Riches, J. Woodburn (eds) *Hunters and Gatherers*, vol. 2: 75–94, Oxford: Berg.

Attungana, P. 1986. Address to the Alaska Eskimo Whaling Commission, *Uiñiq: The Open Lead*, 1(2), 16ff, trans. Nageak, J.

Bockstoce, J.R. 1986. *Whales, Ice and Men*, Seattle: University of Washington Press.

Bodenhorn, B. 1988. 'Whales, souls, children and other things that are "good to share"', *Cambridge Anthropology* 13(1), 1–18.

———1989. *The animals come to me, they know I share: Iñupiaq kinship, changing economic relations and enduring world views on Alaska's North Slope*, PhD dissertation, Cambridge University.

———1990. 'I'm not the great hunter, my wife is: Iñupiat and anthropological models of gender', *Études/ Inuit/Studies*, 14 (2), 55–74.

Briggs, J. 1974. 'Eskimo Women, makers of men' in C. Mathiesson (ed.) *Many Sisters*, New York: Free Press, 261–304.

Brower, C.D. 1889–1928. 'Diaries', unpublished manuscript, University of Alaska Archives, Fairbanks, Alaska.

Burch, E.S., Jr 1975. *Eskimo Kinsmen: Changing Family Relationships in*

*Northwest Alaska,* New York: West Publishing Company.

_____1988. 'Modes of exchange in Northwest Alaska', in T. Ingold, D. Riches and J. Woodburn (eds) *Hunters and Gatherers,* vol. 2: 95–109, Oxford: Berg.

Chaussonnet, V. 1988. 'Needles and animals: women's magic', in W. Fitzhugh and A. Crowell (eds) *Crossroads of Continents: Cultures of Siberia and Alaska* 209–26, Washington, DC: Smithsonian Institution Press.

Collier, J. 1988. *Marriage and Inequality in Classless Societies,* Stanford: Stanford University Press.

Dumond, D. 1975. 'Coastal adaptation and cultural change in Alaskan Eskimo prehistory', in W. Fitzhugh (ed.) *Prehistoric Maritime Adaptations in the Circumpolar Zone,* The Hague: Mouton.

Engels, F. 1972 [1896]. *Origin of the Family, Private Property and the State,* New York: Pathfinder Press.

Fienup-Riordan, A. 1983. *The Nelson Island Eskimos,* Anchorage: Alaska Pacific University Press.

_____1986. 'The Real People: the concept of personhood among the Yup'ik Eskimos of Western Alaska', *Études/Inuit/Studies* 10 (1–2), 261–70.

_____1990. 'Introduction' to the special edition on 'Hunting, sexes and symbolism', *Études/Inuit/Studies.,* 14 (2), 7–22.

Friedl, E. 1974. *Women and Men: an Anthropologist's View,* New York: Holt, Rinehart and Winston.

Giddings, J.L. 1967. *Ancient Men of the Arctic,* New York: Alfred Knopf.

Godelier, M. 1980. 'The emergence of Marxism in Anthropology in France' in E. Gellner (ed.) *Soviet and Western Anthropology,* London: Duckworth.

Graburn, N. 1973. *Circumpolar Peoples: an Anthropological Perspective,* Palisades Pacific: Goodyear Publishing Company.

Guemple, L. 1986. 'Men and women, husbands and wives: the role of gender in traditional Inuit society', *Études/Inuit/Studies* 10 (1–2), 9–24.

Guérin, Y. 1982. 'La femme inuit dominée, création mythique allochtone?' *Anthropologie et Societés* 6 (3), 129–54.

Ingold, T., Riches, D. and Woodburn, J. (eds) 1988. *Hunters and Gatherers,* vols. 1 and 2, Oxford: Berg.

IHLC (Inupiat Commission of History, Language and Culture) 1980. *Qiñiqtuagaksrat Utuqqanaat Iñuuniaganingisiqun: Traditional Land Use Survey of the Colville River Basin,* Anchorage: North Slope Borough.

_____1981. *Puiguitkaat,* Transcript of the 1978 Elders' Conference, Barrow, Alaska, Anchorage: North Slope Borough, trans. Okakok, L.

Joseph, R. 1974. 'Choice or force: a study in social manipulation', *Human Organization* 33 (4), 150–69.

Kruse, J. 1982. *Subsistence and the North Slope Iñupiat: an Analysis of the Effects of Energy Development,* (Man in the Arctic Series 56),

Anchorage: University of Alaska Institute of Social and Economic Research.

Laslett, P. and Wall, R. (eds) 1972. *Family and Household in Past Time,* Cambridge: Cambridge University Press.

Leacock, E. 1982. 'The place of women in hunting societies', in E. Leacock and R. Lee, (eds) *Politics and History in Band Society,* Cambridge: Cambridge University Press.

Mauss, M. 1979 [1906]. *Seasonal Variation of the Eskimo: a Study in Social Morphology,* trans. J.J. Fox, London: Routledge and Kegan Paul.

Moore, H. 1988. *Feminism and Anthropology,* London: Polity Press.

Murdoch, J. 1892. *Ethnological results of the Point Barrow Expedition* (Ninth Annual Report of the Bureau of Ethnology to the Secretary of the Smithsonian Institution, 1887–88), Washington, D.C.: US Government Printing Office.

Pulo, T. 1980. *Whaling: a Way of Life,* Anchorage: University of Alaska, National Bilingual Materials Development Center.

Rainey, F. 1947. 'The whale men of Tigara', *Anthropological Papers of the Museum of Natural History* 41(2), 231–483.

Rasmussen, K. 1929. *Report of the Fifth Thule Expedition: 1921–24* vol. 10 (posthumous notes on the Alaskan Eskimos, edited by H. Ostermann), Copenhagen: Gyldendaske Boghandel, Norsk Forlag.

Rosaldo, M.Z. 1974. 'Theoretical Overview' in M. Z. Rosaldo and L. Lamphere (eds), *Women, Culture and Society,* Stanford: Stanford University Press.

Sacks, K. 1979. *Sisters and Wives: the Past and Future of Sexual Equality,* London: Greenwood Press.

Saladin D'Anglure, B. 1986. 'Du foetus au chamane: la construction d'un troisieme sexe' inuit', *Études/Inuit/Studies* 10 (1–2), 25–113.

Silverman, S.F. 1975. 'The life crisis as a clue to social function: the case of Italy' in R. R. Reiter (ed.) *Toward an Anthropology of Women,* New York: Monthly Review Press.

Simpson, J. 1875. 'Observations on the Western Eskimo and the country they inhabit from notes taken during two years at Point Barrow', *Arctic Geography and Ethnology,* (monograph) London: Royal Geographic Society.

Weiner, A. 1976. *Women of Value, Men of Reknown,* Austin: University of Texas Press.

Wilmsen, E.N. 1989. *Land Filled with Flies,* Chicago: University Press.

Woodburn, J. 1982. 'Egalitarian Societies' (Malinowski Memorial Lecture for 1981), *Man* (N.S.) 17, 431–51.

Worl, R. and Smythe, C. 1986. *Barrow: A Decade of Modernization* (Technical Report 125), Anchorage: Minerals Management Services.

# Chapter 7

## Colonialism, History and the Construction of Place: The Politics of Landscape in Northern Australia

*Howard Morphy*

One of the reasons that the concept of landscape is beginning to prove so useful is that it is a concept in between. At a time when simple determinisms are breaking down, and the boundaries between disciplines are continually being breached, it is useful to have a concept that is free from fixed positions, whose meaning is elusive, yet whose potential range is all-encompassing. Landscape is a frame for discourse that encourages the development of metaphors, which enables the exploration of old topics in new ways, and which may provide the framework for the construction of new theories. Of course, landscape does not exist in a theoretical vacuum: it takes up the flavours or the sophistication of the age. Today's 'landscape' is inevitably processual and transforming, integral to processes of objectification and the sedimentation of history, subjected to poetic and hermeneutic interpretation and a place where value and emotion coincide.

Landscape has for a long time been a central concept in writings about Australian Aborigines. For much of the time it has been an undertheorised concept, being part of ethnographic focus and description rather than integral to the way people have analysed processes of social reproduction in Aboriginal Australia. However the work of Strehlow (1970), Peterson (1972, 1986) and pre-eminently Munn (1970) can be seen as part of a relatively coherent process of theorising a concept of landscape in different parts of Aboriginal Australia, and indeed echoes of these theoretical positions can already be found in the works of Spencer and Gillen. The coherent theoretical strand that I am isolating is one in which landscape is seen as being both integral to the development of concepts of Self and Other and part of the way in which adaptive relations between people and land have been maintained. In writings on Australia, a cultural conceptualisation of landscape which centres on the development of emotional attachment to place has been a component both of models of the Australian hunter-gatherer mode of production (in particular in the works of Peterson) and of the processes of Aboriginal religion (see especially Myers 1986). The pre-post-modernist in me would argue that it is not a coincidence that many of the issues in the anthropology of landscape are pre-figured in the Australian literature. Just as Debbora Battaglia (1990) argues that the people of the Massim urged her towards a deconstructionist perspective, I would argue that Australian Aborigines made landscape a key concept in the study of their society. Indigenous people have played a far more active role in the outsiders' construction of their societies than some theorists have allowed.

## A Landscape Colonised

A landscape-based cosmology is one of the ways in which Aboriginal identity has been maintained in a post-colonial context and also one of the areas of conflict between black and white Australians. Landscape provides an excellent framework for representing the clash in values and the different interests of Aborigines and colonists. Aborigines and European colonists live in and create quite different landscapes. The creation of the cattle country landscape of northern Australia involved both a physical and a conceptual transformation of the land. The European landscape has been created through a process which involved a change in land use and a break with the previous history of the land, amounting almost to a denial that the land had a previous history. Europeans moved into what (to them) was a previously unutilised environment, their objective being to release its potential. The process is efficiently captured in the title of John Dunmore Lang's 1847 book on Queensland: *Cooksland in North-Eastern Australia; the Future Cotton Fields of Great Britain its*

*Characteristics and Capabilities for European Colonisation*, to which is added, almost as an afterthought, *with a Disquisition on the Origins, Manners and Customs of the Aborigines*. Descriptions of Australia by early explorers are descriptions of what it might become. In the process they had to destroy what was there already. The past of the 'new' land had no existence except as it was reflected through the clashes of the moment. But the colonists also brought with them an 'old' past in the form of distant landscapes that they had experienced elsewhere and which influenced their conceptualisation of, and 'prospect' of, the 'new' land.

I will begin my analysis at this breach in time that was the consequence of colonialism, and consider first the emergent and changing colonial construction of the area centered on Roper Bar in northern Australia (Map 7.1), before looking at Aboriginal conceptions of the same land. European and Aboriginal people have co-existed and interacted in the region over a long period of time, yet in some respects it can almost seem as if they occupied different conceptual space/times (see Munn 1986: 9 ff.). These were not, however, strictly separate, and in their particularities they influenced one another, even if they were constructed on fundamentally different premises: they were carried forward by people occupying the same geopolitical space and the actions of the one group had consequences on the life of the other. The Aboriginal prehistory of Australia created a landscape with places, boundaries, and directions that had an effect on the pattern of European colonisation, which in turn had more obvious consequences on the continued Aboriginal uses of space. The Northern Territory Land Rights legislation brought these different space/times into open conflict as part of the contemporary Australian political process. It is through that process that I have come to know about Aboriginal concepts of landscape in the Roper Valley as part of a historical process that followed a break in time. Hence, although Aboriginal concepts of Australian landscape are in some senses temporally prior to those of white Australians, in the form in which I know them they are subsequent to, if not consequent on, the colonial process.

## The Making of Roper Bar

The processes which created the physical landscape of colonialism and the cultural landscape of the cattle stations developed

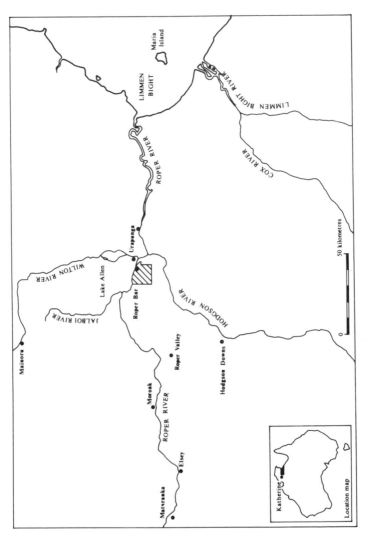

**Map 7.1 The location of Roper Bar Police Reserve.**

together almost without reference to the Aboriginal landscape. Landscape was located as part of the colonial process. Its position changed as that process moved on, as the 'wild' landscape became the 'frontier' and then the 'outback' and finally 'settled' Australia. The speed of the process and the duration of each particular state varied regionally, most of Australia became 'outback' quite early on but some places remain to the present on the frontier.

The focus of this chapter is on one such area: an area of land in the Northern Territory known as Roper Bar Police Reserve (Map 7.1). In the 1980s it was the subject of a land claim under the Northern Territory Land Rights legislation and for a short time it was, for ideological reasons, referred to as Yutpundji-Djindiwirritj (Morphy and Morphy 1981). I will begin with a description of the area by Justice Toohey, the presiding Aboriginal Land Rights Commissioner, in his report which, in effect, represents a judgement on the Yutpundji-Djindiwirritj (Roper Bar) Land Claim:

> The claim area lies south of the Roper River between the Jalboi and the Wilton Rivers, with the Hodgson River to the south-east. The Roper River, with Roper Bar Crossing runs along its Northern boundary. To the West and South of the area lies Roper Valley Station and to the East St Vidgeons Station. The land described has an area of 156 square kilometres, though some excisions made during the hearing and alienated blocks within its boundaries reduce the area accordingly. ... The claim book describes the land as ranging from black soil flood plain country to dry sandstone ridges, with medium forest cover. Coolibah, paper bark and wattle and other eucalypt species predominate. (Toohey 1982)

Roper Bar Police Reserve is a tiny area of land in Northern Territory terms, an area of land that would have probably cost a few thousand Australian dollars to buy if it had been possible to purchase it. However it was an area of land of sufficient significance in white Australian history to be at one stage proposed for inclusion on the register of the National Estate. It was also of considerable significance to the Ngalakan, since it was the only area of their traditional lands that remained unalienated crown land and therefore available for them to claim. The land of the Ngalakan included most of Roper Valley Station, Moroak Station, Urapunga Station and a small segment of the ex-Arnhem Land

Reserve. They were on the edge of the Arnhem Land reserve – the largest block of unalienated crown land in the Territory – and had they been within it the Northern Territory Land Rights Act would have granted them title without even the need to make a claim. However being on the outside of the Arnhem Land had been a significant part of their history for over one hundred years and was part of the same story that made Roper Bar significant in White Australian history (see Morphy and Morphy 1984). Roper Bar was one of the first places on European maps of the Northern Territory, a marker of the colonial frontier, but a marker that remained on the edge of the frontier almost to the present.

Roper Bar (Fig. 7.1) was discovered, for Europeans, by Leichardt's expedition on 24 October 1847. It was originally known as Leichardt's Bar but later on took the name of the river that flowed across it, the river named by Leichardt after George Roper. On maps it is still sometimes referred to as 'Leichardt's Roper Bar'. Leichhardt on his journey from Queensland had come across the river five days earlier and since then had been following its course inland.

> It was the River that Mr. Roper had seen two days before, and I named it after him as I promised to do. The country along its left bank was well grassed and openly timbered with box; hills were on the opposite. Natives seemed to be numerous for their footpath along the lagoon was well beaten; we passed several of their fisheries and observed long fish traps made of rattan. All the cuts on various trees were made with an iron tomahawk. Natives crows and kites were always indicators of a good country. (Leichardt 1847: 143)

Leichardt's journey was significant for the Ngalakan – apart from generalised scientific motives its main aim, as was that of most Australian journeys of exploration, was to mark out routes across country and to assess the economic potential of the land, in particular its agricultural potential and mineral deposits.

There are no records of European visitors to Roper Bar for the next twenty-five years, but it is almost certain that by the 1860s occasional expeditions were following Leichardt's route from Queensland into the Northern Territory. Certainly enough became known of Roper Bar for it to be proposed as the site for the main provisioning station for the Overland Telegraph along its Northern Sector (Figure 7.2). Although the depot was of short duration, lasting from 1871 to 1873, it gave sufficient impetus for

Figure 7.1 Roper Bar crossing at the height of the dry season when the river is low.

Figure 7.2 A ship unloading at the site of the Overland Telegraph supply depot at Narrakarani in 1873. Photograph by Henry Sweet in the South Australian Archives.

Roper Bar to remain a European place until the present. In a matter of months Roper Bar changed from being an occasional stopping place to being the largest European settlement in the Northern Territory (Figure 7.3). The settlement was established two miles South of Roper Bar and at its height in 1872 a sizeable township had developed: 'tents waggons, drays, carts, buggies, horses and bullocks and some 300 men'(Chisolm: 1973). Six years later the European population of Darwin was 198 and of the Territory as a whole 505 (S.A.A. 790/1878: 613).

Roper Bar had the potential to become a key place in the white history of the Northern Territory but it was always in the end too out of place, too close to the edge of the map. It was a place always imminent in white Australian history – a place of visions of a future transformed. But the transformations never came and it remained on the edge. Visions of the future were promoted both by institutions of the State and by individuals who happened through the vagaries of personal history to end up living around Roper Bar. I will give four examples of such visions which reflect changes in the prospective history of the place and a diminution of goals over time.

The first vision of the land, already hinted at in Leichardt's Journals, is the view in the early surveyors' reports. These reports are characterised by dry descriptions of the land, paying particular attention to the nature of the soils and its agricultural potential. The fullest survey of Roper Bar was carried out by Lindsay in 1880–81 and I will quote from the section of his summary report referring to the claim area (AA CRS A1640, 232a 1881):

There is a lagoon under Harts Range 1/2 mile off the track (North side) native name boora moola. Ingram Valley extends from River between Harts range and Charlotte Ranges to the Finnian range and some 6 miles South of Mount McMinn. It is all good country and well grassed and permanent water in Sherwin Creek [Djirriyiga]. Raboo Spring under Mount Valentine and a waterhole Welkajedda under Mt. McMinn and one about three miles South of Mt. McMinn named Pinyatarrawoejaka are permanent waters. From Hell's Gate to the Leichardt Bar the track winds along the foot of Finnians range. Good sound country well grassed. From the bar we went South through scrub and Bay of Biscay country with long grass to waterholes under the range in the gap between Elsey Creek and Finnian Range. The whole country passed over is well suited for grazing and a great deal of it fit for agriculture.

Figure 7.3 A series of engravings from photographs by Henry Sweet illustrating the supply depot at Narrakarani on the Roper. Patterson was the manager of the project in the Northern section and set up the depot on the Roper.

Reports such as Lindsay's and that of McMinn before him were one of the main things to stimulate European colonisation of the region. They provided encouragement for drovers to bring cattle through the region, extending the cattle station landscape ever further North. They operated in the interests of the Government in the South who used the sale and leasing of land as a major source of State income. Indeed it was part of a game that at the end of the nineteenth Century involved much of the Northern Territory. Leases on cattle stations were bought and sold for ever-increasing values, often in places where not even a surveyor had been, and certainly where no cattle or sheep were ever going to be driven. The landscape of the Northern Territory was divided up into sections on largely mathematical grounds creating even blocks of land that were the ideal basis for speculation. The era of speculation was soon over, fortunes were won and lost, and the blocks of land became largely unsaleable. And so they remained for most of the subsequent European history of the Roper Valley, with the exception of occasional periods of speculation when it looked as if political changes would affect land values, or when the price of pet food went up on the world market. Though the image has always remained of it being cattle station country, cattle stations were a mode of colonisation and expropriation, rather than viable business enterprises.

For the second vision of the future I will switch attention away from the surveyors and propagandists towards the people on the spot, the early colonists of Roper Bar. By the 1880s Roper Bar still had a sizeable European population though from Searcy's description it was precisely because of its peripheral status on the very margins of settled Australia that it attracted the population it did. It provided a sanctuary for those who were wanted by the law in other States: 'many had faces that would take the edge off a razor, smash a mirror, or bust a camera' (1909: 111). Roper Bar remained on the main route for cattle being driven from Queensland into the Northern Territory and the Kimberleys gold rush of the 1880s brought many 'diggers' through the area. In 1884 for example it was estimated that 20,000 head of cattle were in transit between Burketown and Elsey station to the west of Roper Bar (S.A.A. 790/1884/1008).

On 16 November 1884 a petition was sent from the residents of Leichardt's Bar to the Government resident in Palmerston (Darwin) (SAA 780/1885/282):

> We the undersigned ... humbly petition you to get the mail service
> extended from Katherine River Telegraph Station to the Leichardt Bar
> Roper River ... the country between the Hodgson Limmen and Roper
> River is being rapidly stocked up ... [we] now travel a distance of 120
> miles to Elsey telegraph station ... a very great inconvenience to us ...
> [and] a source of heavy expense owing to the hostility of the natives,
> it not being safe to send one man alone.

The post office and telegraph in Darwin strongly supported
the petition and noted that though the number of settlers in the
area appeared to be small 'there is every prospect of the settlers
soon increasing.'

The South Australian Government was unconvinced by the
petition and did not at the time introduce a mail service. The relevant memorandum reads

> It appears that the pastoral rents are so low that it is impossible to
> grant this or any similar mail service. Many of the signatories of the
> petition are of no weight, they have nothing to do with the Roper or
> the Gulph country, and one of them is the trooper Wilshire who
> brought over the native police.

This second vision, that of the people on the spot in the 1880s,
is of people whose ambitions are limited, who live in a difficult
world of conflict, who are battling the Government in the South
for the rights they feel they are entitled to as citizens, who live in
a state of near warfare with Aborigines. Wilshire, for example,
was probably responsible for killing more Aborigines than any
other European (though not in his case in the Roper Valley). Their
vision is of Roper Bar becoming established as a township, a
regional centre with a pub and a post office, and just as the government assured them it was good cattle country they are sending back images of a rosy future. The Government does not
respond in the way they had hoped but responds in its own way,
one more suited to its interests.

This brings us to the third vision of the future, and a much
grander one. On 17 March 1887, the township of Urapunga was
proclaimed by the South Australian Government Gazette. To say
that little remains of the township of Urapunga would be an
understatement (Figure 7.4). The township of Urapunga only
ever existed on the books, in the surveyors' plans, in the leases
granted, and in the nine housing blocks sold and still presumably
owned by the descendants of some enterprising Victorian. If any

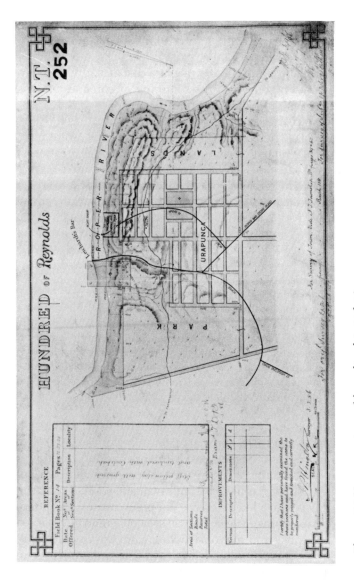

**Figure 7.4** Urapunga township as it exists today!

of the purchasers ever visited Urapunga they left no record behind, nor was any work ever carried out on the township. Indeed as far as Roper Bar was concerned the township of Urapunga was to have as little impact on the land as a game of Monopoly has on land values in Mayfair. The township of Urapunga was drawn up in abstract at a distance, divided into the grid system favoured in the planning of colonial cities, a miniature version of Melbourne and Adelaide.

The township of Urapunga became a myth but it was the kind of myth that elsewhere in the Northern Territory at Mataranka, Katherine and Tennant Creek, resulted in the eventual creation of townships that had more physical expression. But though a myth it was one that had legal existence, the squared off blocks were no longer unalienated crown land in the sense defined under the Northern Territory Land Rights Act, and almost 100 years to the day that they had been marked off on the map, they were excluded from the land available for claim. To quote Justice Toohey (1982: 1)

> In the north-east of the claim area lies the township of Urapunga, pro-claimed in the South Australian Government Gazette of the 17 March 1887. The general location of the town is marked on Exhibit 2 and a more detailed town plan comprises, with a copy of the gazettal, Exhibit 11. The Aboriginal Land Rights Act (Northern Territory) defines unalienated crown land to mean (s. 3(1)) *Crown Land in which no person (other than the Crown) has an estate or interest, but does not include land in a town.'* The town of Urapunga did not form part of the claim as finally presented. [ italics in the original]

Thus a clause that was presumably intended to protect the citizens of Darwin and Alice Springs from Aboriginal claims also protected the rights of lost causes. Although such absurdities of European law usually work against Aborigines they do not always do so. Roper Bar itself became available for claim since in the 1930s it was 'Gazetted a Reserve' for police horses. The police had been campaigning for years for an area of land to be reserved for such a purpose and met obstruction from the Government, presumably because of other interests in the land. However in 1930 the grazing licence on the land at Roper Bar was not renewed and the land concerned was rapidly gazetted a police reserve. It became a reserve for horses precisely at the time that motor vehicles were beginning to replace horses as the main means of transport of supplies, and by the time of the land claim, horses had ceased to be used for any purpose by the police.

It is interesting that a Government that was trying to sell blocks of town land in the region did not consider that the actual European occupants justified services that a town would have required. In a way the township and the petition symbolise the history of Roper Bar at the end of the last century. On the one hand a government at a distance sending out surveyors, dividing up the land, dreaming of a future of developing towns and a prosperous pastoral industry, on the other hand the reality of an extremely marginal pastoral existence on the edge of settled Australia, dependent for its future on the expansion of government services into the region to boost the local economy. The government in the South and the colonists of the North were united in purveying a vision of a prosperous expanding future that probably neither had any belief in.

The township of Urapunga remained unsold and the settlement at Roper Bar failed to develop in the way the colonial optimists anticipated. This was in part because the very geographical factors that had early on favoured Roper Bar as a nodal point of the colonisation of the Northern Territory ceased to be significant. Roper Bar was both the highest navigable place on the Roper River, where quite large paddle steamers could dock, and the crossing point of the main route from Queensland into the Northern Territory. However by the 1890s the need for large steamboats to bring cargo up the Roper River had long since passed, and the opening out of routes to the south meant that the Leichardt route was no longer used for droving cattle. The overland telegraph passing some 120 miles to the west had determined that the main axis for the colonisation of the Northern Territory ran from north to south along it, bypassing the Roper Valley. It might have been expected that the frontier would have moved on further into Arnhem Land, leaving Roper Bar behind as a staging post on the journey north. But the frontier remained almost stationary after the 1890s. There were attempts to develop cattle stations in the heart of Arnhem Land, Arafura station being the most persistent attempt, but they were eventually abandoned, after they had caused the deaths of many Aboriginal people (see Berndt and Berndt 1954). Arnhem Land remained, until the 1930s and even beyond that, the land of the 'wild blackfellows' and a place to be avoided (see Morphy and Morphy 1984: 471). Even the establishment of a police station

Figure 7.5 The police trackers' quarters at Roper Bar police station in 1980. The tree in front is one of the many manifestations of the ancestral kangaroos, *Djadukal*, in the area surrounding the police station.

(Figure. 7.5) at Roper Bar in the 1890s probably did as much to maintain the isolation of the place as it did to encourage any expansion of the European population, if as Searcy suggests, the majority of residents had been until then, fugitives from the law. The police station became the base for occasional expeditions into Arnhem Land, but its main business was in managing the relations between Aborigines and pastoralists and in distributing welfare benefits of food and clothing to its client Aboriginal population.

By the 1920s, in the region as a whole, the relationship between Aborigines and pastoralists had reached something of a steady state (for a more detailed discussion see Morphy and Morphy 1984). The whole of the Roper Valley had long been colonised and the Aboriginal inhabitants had either become the clients and workers of the various cattle stations or moved into Arnhem Land or the neighbouring mission station of Roper River. Aborigines were a major source of labour for the cattle stations but in addition the welfare distribution system had become an important component of the cattle station economies.

My final vision comes from the end of this period of stability and was developed by Bill Harney, a well known character in the history of the Northern Territory, who at the time was a patrol officer for the native affairs branch of the Department of the Northern Territory. His report on the development of a control station for the Arnhem land reserve was written in 1944 when Roper Bar had become a quiet backwater in the Territory. Harney's plans for the Roper Bar region would have had the effect of making the linkage between the European cattle economy and the welfare of Aborigines even closer. He proposed that an Aboriginal township should be developed north of Roper Bar by Mr. J. Gibbs, the owner of Urapunga station and at the time the only white resident of Roper Bar apart from the policemen stationed there. I will cite significant passages from his report.

I have seen Mr. Gibbs and knowing the value of a man who knows both the country and the natives and has cattle and horses I placed before him the idea of developing a native station. He is willing to put all his herd and horses, saddles, pack and riding and other gear on his station onto a selected site. He has 60–70 head of broken horses, 7 riding saddles, 8 pack saddles, goats 1,500 head, pigs, cattle over 1,000 head. Native stockman and all the gear for operating a station. He asks for the following £6 a week wages and rations. £2 a head for

half his cattle, calves to be thrown in. The department will feed the
natives and all non-workers will be forced to walkabout on the
reserve – white missionaries will educate the children under government supervision. The houses shall be built of local timber no persons shall build outside the area and all working Aboriginals shall
live in these areas. Half the cattle shall belong to the native people as
killers etc. The other will belong to Mr. Gibbs as inducement to him
as manager. W. Farrar and G. Conway have each a large plant of
horses and could be brought in to muster [ cattle in the ALR]. A
retaining fee of £2 a week could be paid them and their natives fed,
and for every unbranded beast they mustered they be paid 7/6 a
head.

The ultimate dream however was to use this as the basis for
opening out the Arnhem Land Reserve and moving the frontier
that last step to the sea:

A road would be opened up from Roper Bar to the station. Another
bush road would be cut to Oenpelli Mission, with another station on
route. These would be useful to patrol by utility and from there to the
missions Milingimbi and Yirrkala by horse. By this means the Reserve
will be opened up. Coastal stations could also start to exploit the
marine resources of the shores. Once this place is established we will
be certain of the control and welfare of the natives of this part of the
region.

This last vision of the future contrasts in interesting ways with
the previous three. Roper Bar is no longer a central place but part
of a network of linkages into Arnhem Land, indeed the plan will
lead to its virtual disappearance as the local cattle station moves
north 100 miles. It is also a vision that includes Aborigines as a
central component of the region. Reading between the lines the
basis of the future economy is not the development of a viable
cattle industry, but the development of an industry for controlling Aborigines. But still the impetus to transform the landscape
comes from the cattle station model of Northern Australia as a
land divided into paddocks. Although a similar proposal to this
one was implemented at Maranboi to the West of Arnhem Land,
nothing came of Harney's proposal.

These four visions of the future, all involving different conceptualisations of Roper Bar as a place, represent the trajectory of a
landscape over time, as it moves from beyond the frontier, through

a stage of successful pastoralism, through the development of a township, to a distant outpost in the back of beyond, dependent for its future prosperity on an Aboriginal welfare role. [1]

In the period of time between the 1940s and the 1980s, when the land claim was heard, considerable changes had occurred. Communications had in general been improved. The road between Mataranka and Roper Bar had been partly metalled (though it was still cut off for most of the wet season), there had been a major strike of Aboriginal stockmen which had in theory brought about improvements in their working conditions but in practice meant that in most places they ceased to be employed in any numbers, welfare benefits for Aborigines had been transformed and effective health and education services provided for the first time. However, much remained in continuity with the past. The European population of Roper Bar had been reduced even further with the closure of the police station and now consisted only of the married couple who ran the Roper Bar store and petrol station. The local cattle stations continued to be of doubtful viability: St. Vidgeons was closed, Hodgson Downs had a caretaker, and Roper Valley Station was on stand-by. Urapunga station mustered a few cattle but cattle alone would not have been sufficient for its survival. Both in the case of the cattle stations and the store Aborigines were among the mainstays of the economy. Welfare handouts had long ceased, but the provision of electricity and housing for Aboriginal station settlements, development agency grants, the management of Aboriginal enterprises, as well as the direct provision of goods and services to Aborigines all made a significant contribution to the local economy. One further vision had entered the regional picture and that was tourism. By the 1980s Urapunga station gained a significant amount of its income from tourism.

I will now consider how these European visions of Roper Bar

---

1. It could be argued that all four visions are essentially male visions. However it is difficult to separate out the gender specific components of these views on the development of the Northern Territory from the more general ideologies associated with the processes of capitalism and colonialism. Certainly as far as white Australians were concerned the Northern Territory was primarily a male preserve until well into the twentieth century, and white women were largely absent from cattle-station country, with some notable exceptions including Mrs Warrington-Rogers, who lived much of her life in the Roper Bar area as the wife and mother of cattle-station owners and cattleperson in her own right (for a description of her life see Hill 1951: 388 ff.). On the surface, women writers about the Territory such as Jeannie Gunn and Ernestine Hill, do not present markedly different views from their male counterparts on the matters discussed here, though a detailed analysis may show fundamental differences.

were reflected in images of the landscape at the time of the land-claim hearings. I will use two sources of data: European maps of the area and the kind of objections brought up in the land claim hearings by European opponents to the claim. The first exercise is based on the assumption that place names and inclusions on maps represent one of the ways in which the history of a landscape is passed on, albeit partly through a process of fossilisation. The second exercise is based on the assumption that objections and concepts of detriment reflect values that are located in land and hence the vision of landscape futures at a particular point in time.

## Place Names

The present-day European place names in Roper Bar Police Reserve and the surrounding area directly reflect the early history of colonisation and the development of the pastoral industry (Map 7.2). From the south east, Roper Bar is reached through Queensland Crossing on the Hodgson River, reflecting the main direction of the early droving expeditions. From the west the area is entered through Hell's Gate, a name that should have referred to the punitive massacres of the Ngalakan that followed the death of Charlie Johnson, the manager of Daly Waters station at Roper Bar in 1875, but is said to refer to the danger of attack by Aborigines when passing through the narrow gorge. The religious imagery may also have been prompted by the towering red walls of decaying red sandstone that loom above on either side. Just before Hell's Gate on the open plain is Mount McMinn named after the surveyor for the Overland Telegraph. The Telegraph is also recorded on the other side by Todd's Bluff on the Hodgson River, named after Charles Todd, who managed the operation. The Hodgson River is named after one of Leichardt's sponsors and the Wilton River is named after another. The bar itself is associated with both Leichardt and Roper, one of his expedition members. The cattle industry is represented by Rogers Hill opposite Roper Bar, and by the neighbouring hill Mount Warrington. Both were named after Henry Warrington Rogers who took out the lease on what subsequently became Urapunga Station in 1885, and whose family ran it until the 1930s, when his son John Warrington Rogers shot himself at Mataranka homestead. The only apparently Aboriginal name

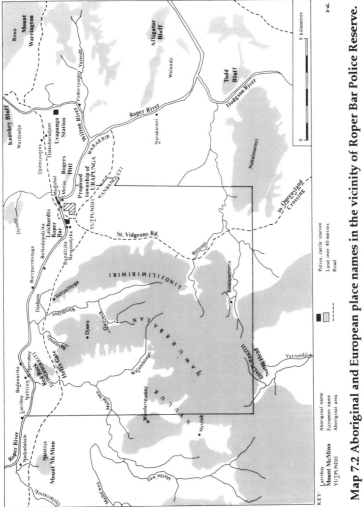

**Map 7.2 Aboriginal and European place names in the vicinity of Roper Bar Police Reserve.**

that entered European maps of the region was Urapunga, the name of the proposed township that became the name of Rogers' station. The name is almost certainly a transformation of Yutpundji, the Ngalakan name for Roper Bar, recorded early on as Yurrapundji. Thus the place names of the Roper Bar region refer almost entirely to the late nineteenth- and early twentieth-century history of the area, with a strong bias towards the early official 'explorers' who 'opened it out' for European colonisation and who clearly ensured that their memory remained in the land. Hell's Gate is the only reference to the bloodshed of occupation and Queensland Crossing refers to that brief period of time when Roper Bar was a central place on the main route overland into the north and north-west of Australia.

## Objections

The main objectors to the land claim represented a variety of different interests, from the Northern Territory Government, through the Northern Territory Historical Society, to mining, tourism and pastoral interests (see Toohey 1982). As far as mining was concerned the area of the reserve seemed unpromising on geological grounds, but mining interests are included in land claims as a matter of principle. The Department of Energy wrote that

> the claim area covers a group of rock formations known to hold only moderate economic interest relating to base metal and uranium mineralisation, but no exploitable deposits have been located. Insufficient exploration has been carried out to dismiss the ground completely and exploration options should be kept open to ensure that possible earth resources in the area are not missed. (Toohey 1982: 32)

Ashton Mining, whose exploration licence application covered the area, also clearly thought that the police reserve was an unpromising source for mining. They had, however, an excellent argument up their sleeves that can make even unpromising areas essential for exploration purposes: 'Information from every sample is of value for assessing the importance of every other sample within an extensive area and gaps in sampling, as would occur if the land claim area was omitted, detract from the value of the effort in the whole area' (ibid: 33). This is an argument that can presumably be extended infinitely.

The objection from the cattle industry was more significant and involved two main issues: the use of the stock route and the mustering of stray cattle from the reserve. The latter objection was a common one. Justice Toohey had argued on a number of occasions that it was an issue which required complementary legislation to be drafted. It was not something that should affect a particular claim. The case of the stock route was more complex. Leichardt's original stock route from North Queensland still existed and had been used for many years by the local cattle stations. Stock routes were unalienated Crown Land and technically could be claimed by Aboriginal traditional owners. However it was also quite possible to recommend in the particular case that they could be excised from the claim. Although this had not been an issue in any previous land claim, it became so in this one since as Toohey (1982: 40) reported 'this is the first land claim in which there is evidence of contemporary use of a stock route.' In this case the pastoralist Ray Fryer of Urapunga Station argued that he regularly used the stock route (Figure 7.6). During the wet season trucks could only go as far as Mount McMinn on the far side of the Police Reserve from his station. In order to load the trucks he had to drive the cattle along the stock route to Mount McMinn. At other times of the year he used the stock route to bring cattle in the other direction from joint boundary musters carried out with Roper Valley Station. This he said occurred three or four times a year. Although this level of use of the stock route was surprisingly high, he was supported in his claims by the Aboriginal head stockmen and in the context of the hearings it was impossible to challenge the evidence presented.

The evidence over the stock route is interesting for present purposes since it involved presenting the landscape from the perspective of the pastoralist. To summarise Mr Fryer's evidence: 'The only place where the cattle can be brought across the Roper is at Leichardt's Bar and Mount McMinn. There are places where the cattle can be swum across but "with swimming cattle you are knocking them around and you have a chance of losing them. They get stirred up and break away on the banks"' (Toohey 1982: 42).

On the Urapunga side the cattle cannot be walked within three miles of the river because of the ridge of hills running down to it; they could be taken inland towards Mount McMinn but would have to be walked single file through some parts and the whole

Figure 7.6 Ray Fryer, owner of Urapunga Station in 1980, towers over his cattle.

journey would take one and a half days. However, using the stock route through Roper Bar would take no more than half a day. Viewed as cattle country, the Roper Bar Police Reserve, despite the optimism of Lindsay's report, was largely of use as a passage-way for droving cattle. The low parts of the area referred to as Bay of Biscay Country were liable to seasonal inundation and useless for cattle for most of the year and much of the southern part of the reserve was waterless sandstone karst. Nevertheless the image of the country as cattle country was a very important one and was taken most seriously by the Land Rights Commissioner.

The detriment to tourism was introduced to the case by the Northern Territory Tourist Board and by Dieter Janushca the manager of the Roper Bar store. The attraction of Roper Bar police reserve for tourism is an obvious one. The bar crossing itself is picturesque and at the end of the wet season is an excellent fishing location. It is the highest point from which boats can be launched to explore the lower reaches of the Roper River and to visit the islands and fishing locations along the coast. The store can supply provisions to the campers and twelve motel units are available. And in addition to these factors it is said to be a major heritage site for white Australians, attractions including Leichardt's Memorial at the Old Police Station, Charlie Johnson's Grave, the grave of John Urqhart who died of a fever on 3 March 1885 (though no one seems to know anything more about him) and a short distance away the remains of the wreck of the 'Young Australian', one of the boats used to supply the Overland Telegraph. Although evidence of actual tourists was equivocal there was no question that much could be made of the potential of the site as a tourist resource. While no-one suggested Aborigines were incompatible with tourism, a strong case was made for excising areas of land at Roper Bar itself and including the site of the old police station for tourist development.

Thus the view of the landscape that comes across from the objectors, which is perhaps inevitably biased towards its economic potential, is that it has value as cattle country, as a tourist spot, and as an integral part of Northern Territory history. An interesting aspect of these valuations of the landscape is that they all have the same focal points: Roper Bar and its immediate surrounds and routes that enable access to it. I will return to consider some of the implications of this later. The vast part of the area was uncontested; the sandstone hills and the blacksoil plains, even though to me they were areas of intense natural beauty, received no mention. The only perspective that saw value in the landscape as a whole was the mining survey!

## The Aboriginal Landscape

I will begin looking at the landscape from an Aboriginal perspective by focusing narrowly on what we can label the 'traditional owners' perspective. The underlying premises of the Northern Territory Land Rights legislation is that Aborigines' relationships with the land are set on a fundamentally different basis from that of Australians of non-Aboriginal descent. The land rights legislation defines traditional owners as 'a local descent group who have common spiritual affiliations to a site on the land, being affiliations that place the group under primary spiritual responsibility for that site and for the land' (see Hiatt 1984, and Maddock 1983 for detailed discussion).

Aborigines have been as much a part of the history of the region over the last 150 years as have white Australians and hence they also have views of the landscape that link it to the processes of white colonisation, to the spread of the cattle stations, and so on. However, I am immediately concerned with the view of the Aboriginal landscape that was presented to the court and which can be most easily opposed to the various European valuations of land. It is not as easy to present a historical perspective as it was in the case of Europeans, since there are few early records of the Ngalakan. Indeed in preparing evidence for the land claim we became the first anthropologists to work specifically with the Ngalakan, though Maddock, Bern, Labarlestier, and Merlan had all done fieldwork in the surrounding region, and had worked with Ngalakan among other groups. Indeed it could be argued that the land claim partly involved the process of the recreation of the Ngalakan. The earliest documents on the Ngalakan were word lists and place names, recorded by the early surveyors. Interestingly enough the word list collected by Lindsay from the Roper Bar area in 1880 was in the Ngalakan language and where we were able to identify them the place names remained the same.

It would be impossible here to present a detailed account of the Ngalakan conceptualisation of the landscape and in many

Figure 7.7 Gadjiwok or Boomerang Rock. The hole in the rock was made by a boomerang thrown in the ancestral past by the uncircumcised boys as they fought their way along the Roper Valley. Where the boomerang landed it created a permanent freshwater spring.

ways it would be redundant since it fits in with the general pattern described for other Aboriginal groups by numerous authors (see e.g. Morphy 1991). The land is the creation of the Dream Time ancestral beings who journeyed across it. Through their actions they created features of the landscape, and they left behind them songs, sacred objects and practices that commemorated their creative acts (Figure 7.7). They also left behind in the ground spiritual forces which are released by ceremonial action and which are integral to the process of spirit conception. The process of spirit conception is part of the way in which continuity is established between ancestral beings, social groups and land. Thus features of the landscape are signs both of people and of the embodiment of spiritual forces.

This can be illustrated by following one ancestral track through Roper Bar Police Reserve and out the other side. The plains kangaroo *Djadukal* travelled in a north-west to south-east direction — almost the direct reverse of the route taken by Leichardt. Plains kangaroo enters the claim area only in the north-east corner, but its presence was crucial to the hearing. I will quote justice Toohey's (1982: 8) description of the *Djadukal's* journey since it has the added authority of mediation through judicial process.

> The major dreaming for this estate is *djadukal* the plains kangaroo which travels from Bermula well to the North of the claim area, through at least three other named places and enters the claim area at Ngalkandari. It then travels east along the Roper River and there is a cluster of sites connected with that dreaming around Roper Bar. Oral evidence was given for the creation of certain physical features along the track – for example, rocks at Bolkodjngodjika are said to be the backbone of the plains kangaroo. The flat rocks at Roper Bar crossing are said to be the place where the plains kangaroo met the boney fish. At Mudpal, Yudpundji, Bawuda, Motjo and other places the plains kangaroo left important trees (Figure 7.5).

Two major *djadukal* sites are in the grounds of the police station. One of these is a main regional ceremonial ground. From Roper Bar the plains kangaroo travelled on east to Narrakarani, the actual site of the Overland Telegraph Depot, and then turned northwards towards the Wilton River which it crossed at Yinbirriyunginy, where the bodies of squatting kangaroos are revealed at low tide as they pause for all time to excrete in the river (Figure 7.8).

Figure 7.8 The bodies of the kangaroos crossing the Wilton River at Yinbirriyunginy begin to emerge as the tidal flow falls.

Links between the present and the ancestral past are continually being recreated. If I may quote from my own evidence to the court: 'It is not simply that the large coolibah trees are manifestations of the *djadukal* but the young trees that grow up and will subsequently replace them are also pushed up by the spirit of the plains kangaroo.'

An example given in the hearings was of a tree at Roper Bar boat landing called Bandu. It was the name of a man who had died some years ago but who was the father of a number of the claimants. Originally the name applied to a paperbark tree nearby but when that tree died the name was transferred to the present coolibah tree. The landscape becomes a mnemonic for past generations and a means of establishing continuity with the present. This shows most clearly in the case of the inheritance of death names. When people die they are for a while referred to by the place of their death plus the prefix *mulu-* (death place). People can inherit the names of their father's fathers and father's father's sisters, and death names are no exception. So one of the claimants was named Muludjayidjayi after Djayidjayi, the place where his grandfather died.

The close spiritual ties between a person or people and the land can be seen from the fact that damage to the land no matter who has caused it can endanger the well-being of the person or the clan. For example in 1978 the Department of Works damaged one of the main transformations of the *Yaliyalinyga* (the uncircumcised boy ancestral beings) by moving a boulder while excavating for gravel. Shortly after two members of the owning clan died and their deaths were attributed to damage caused to the boulder (Figure 7.9). Any transgressions of the religious law associated with the land and any violation of sacred sites causes members of the clan great anxiety.

## Comparison of the Processual Aspects of European and Aboriginal Valuations of Landscape

It may be useful at this stage to draw a preliminary conclusion by comparing the Aboriginal and European processes of locating and creating value in the land. In the case of Europeans, history and landscape progress from outside to inside, history articulates with landscape and releases its potential. Landscape is given a

Figure 7.9 'Old Edna' Nyuwuluk standing beside one of the Yaliyalinyga stones recording evidence for the Land Claim hearings.

value by its place in history and by its economic potential. There is no precise fit between the naming system of land and the progressive shifts of perspective which I refer to as changing visions and which reflect differences in the values located in the land over time. Place names inevitably lag behind. Nonetheless in the case of Roper Bar we are dealing with a landscape that is almost overtly political, a landscape that incorporates a progressive view of change, with history as a record of times past adding to the emotional significance of the place. The European place names record the actions of human agents who played a role in transforming the country in 'opening' it up for future development.

In the Aboriginal case the landscape is equally a political one. However, the place names have a very different relationship to history. Landscape and myth are, in this case, to transform Lévi Strauss' suggestive phrase, machines for the suppression of history. The place names refer to ancestral action when the form of the earth was set for ever. The names signify the spiritual force that lies beneath the surface of the earth and that has the capacity to produce the present in the form of the past, to enable new trees to grow, new people to be born, yet the names and ceremonies reunite the new with the old, blurring distinctions and collapsing generations. As I have shown elsewhere (Morphy 1990) the most conservative part of the system is the totemic division of the landscape and certainly in the case of place names there is remarkable continuity at least since the 1880s when we first have evidence. However the very capacity of the system to mask history means that it has been able to accommodate change, in particular change in the groups that occupy the land and in the constitution of groups that are formed. The name is not, as it is presented, evidence of spiritual continuity, but the very way in which spiritual continuity is constructed. Which brings me on to a consideration of the ways in which the Ngalakan have been part of the process of producing the post colonial landscape, and the way this might have influenced the focus of spiritual life, the densities of dreaming tracks and so on.

Frances Morphy and I have shown elsewhere how, from the beginning of this century, Aboriginal people in the Roper Valley survived by becoming clients of the various cattle stations. Early on they joined the European station men in suppressing the population of the surrounding area, creating a distance between themselves and the 'wild blacks' of Arnhem Land. Those who survived had to be part of the process of pacification of the area. Some took on official roles working as police trackers, others worked for established stations and still others became members of the groups that formed around semi-itinerant white bushmen who became long term European residents of the region. People like George Conway who spent more than fifty years living in the Roper Valley, beginning his working life in the region working for the Eastern and African Cold Storage Company, leading killing expeditions into Arnhem Land (see also Merlan 1978). For the rest of his life he made his living on the margins of the cattle industry, occasionally taking out a grazing licence on a particular stretch of land, acting as caretaker manager of a station for a while, but never successfully establishing the station that was his lifelong ambition. The process was more complex than this bald summary allows, since from the Aboriginal side it involved more complex processes of mediation and collusion. After the initial period of what must have been a nightmare of violence, Aborigines reconstructed their own regional linkages and continually interacted across the boundaries set by Europeans. However the colonial process ended up structuring the Aboriginal population to fit into the landscape as it had been transformed by European settlement and gave the people no option but to articulate with the life of the cattle stations. One of the consequences of this was that the sacred landscape became focused on the cattle stations and their immediate environs. Roper Bar seems to represent an extreme case of this.

The Ngalakan used to occupy an enormous area of land of many thousands of square miles. It is impossible to estimate what their pre-colonial population was but 500 would not be an unreasonable estimate, 1,000 or more a distinct possibility. People identified six clan estates within the Ngalakan lands, though I suspect this is a considerable underestimate. Four of those clans were extinct at the time of our fieldwork. The two remaining clans comprised some 100 individuals and it was they who held the estates in the vicinity of Roper Bar. One way of interpreting this data is to suppose that those who lived in the neighbourhood of the European settlements had a better chance of surviving and passing on their inheritance than those who lived at a distance. Indeed there is evidence that Jalboi, the Ngalakan estate most distant from Roper Bar was one of the centres of operation of the marauders from the Eastern and African Cold Storage Company.

Certainly this may have been a factor early on. What is surprising however is that other people have not moved in to fill the gap, since succession to estates is an integral part of the politics of Aboriginal society. Here I think the answer is that the political and spiritual centre had moved to where people were living. Although knowledge of country elsewhere was maintained, especially if it was included in the regular activity of the cattle station or was land still used for hunting and gathering during the off season, the intensity of interest in land had shifted. This process was reinforced before and after World War II, when the stations became ration depots and centres for the distribution of welfare and the provision of services.

Given the shift of focus to the cattle stations and to settlements such as Roper Bar, then, aspects of Aboriginal religious and political processes would have reinforced linkages to land in those localities. Religious practices such as the naming system, the process of identifying people with the place of their death, the practice of adopting people into clans in areas where they live, and the fact that major regional ceremonies tend to be performed at population centres which in turn enhances the spiritual significance of those places, all contribute to this process. For example one of the main ceremonial grounds for the *Yabadurawa*, which re-enacts the journeys of the plains kangaroo, is within a stone's throw of the police station at Roper Bar. This inevitably means that sites associated with the ceremony within the surrounding area will be frequently visited and knowledge of them maintained and amplified. Roper Bar became the death place for many of the Ngalakan of recent generations who worked for the police or received their rations there. Many of the trees that surround the police station and the boat landing, through their names, link present generations with past ones, and establish continuities in spiritual identity with place.

Another quite independent factor may also contribute to the concentration of sites around European settlements and along the roads and stock routes that connect them. The geographical and environmental logic that made them sites and routes for European colonists meant that they were already centres for the Aborigines of the region. In areas where we have the evidence the distribution of pre-contact Aboriginal religious sites tend to correspond closely to the hunter-gatherer economy and pattern of movement (see Morphy 1977, also Layton 1989: 451). Dreaming tracks tended to follow watercourses and the greatest density of mythological activity appears to have taken place close to major camping sites. And when it is realised that hunter-gatherers in the Roper Valley were semi-sedentary for much of the year, living at a few key resource centres, the possibility of an overlap between Aboriginal and European valuations of the landscape increases. The spaces in between that the Aborigines were being asked to occupy by the colonists, were the spaces in between pre-existing Aboriginal centres. Early reports refer to large populations of Aborigines in the Roper Bar area and it is impossible to imagine that it was not a focal point of regional life. My hypothesis would be that the two factors I have introduced to explain the density of Aboriginal activity around the sites of European settlement interact with one another. Within a particular Aboriginal estate there are likely to be several sites of major religious and economic significance, only one of which becomes the site of a cattle station or a police station, eventually however the colonial process that I have outlined results in that one becoming the main centre of ceremonial activity and the centre of people's religious attachment. By a great irony of the colonial process Aborigines and Europeans developed their strongest emotional attachments to precisely the same places though the attachments are constructed on a quite different basis.

## Conclusion: Conflicts and Competition

The landscape of the Roper Valley is associated with two different cultural constructions of space/time. In the European case land is part of a historical process that leaves certain images, visions, and events behind. Place names, for example, provide a kind of scattergram of historical events with certain densities of historical focus that reflect positions in colonial time – the coming of the Romans, the Norman Conquest, European colonisation. Land use, the attachment of people to land, and the people attached, changes over time. In the Aboriginal case, place and place names are integrated within a process that acts to freeze time; that makes the past a referent for the present. The present is not so much produced by the past but reproduces itself in the form of the past. It is a process which increases the density and intensity of attachment to places where people are currently living. At the same time mechanisms exist for renewing links with places that were until recently abandoned or irregularly visited, or which were occupied by other groups. It is this flexibility in combination with the ideology of timeless continuity that has proved conceptually difficult for anthropologists to grasp and has proved so frustrating for European objectors to Aboriginal land claims. The timeless continuity in itself makes it difficult to reconcile Aboriginal interests which appear long term with European interests which appear temporary. Yet at the same time the Aboriginal past seems to be inconveniently present. It is not possible for a government to move a sacred site or the focus of Aboriginal spiritual interest a few kilometres to the south, though it is quite possible for Aborigines to extend the influence of the site in that direction. The kangaroos that are transformed into a rock in the Wilton River may hop on to other places but in the medium term at least are unlikely to leave places altogether where they have had a strong presence.

European uses of land are often likely to be incompatible with its continued use by Aborigines. The job of the Land Rights Commissioner – apart from deciding whether there are traditional Aboriginal owners for the area of land concerned and determining that it is unalienated Crown Land available for claim – is to make recommendations on detriment to others which basically concern other interests in and valuations of the land. There were two major areas of conflict of interest between Aboriginal claimants and European objectors that had to be resolved, or rather that Justice Toohey had to provide guidance to the Minister of Aboriginal Affairs about. One concerned the stock route, the other tourism. The stock route was most serious since it ran along the northern boundary of the claim area and took in not only most of the sacred sites, but also the two outstations where Aboriginal people lived. Because the owner of Urapunga station had convinced the court that the use of the stock route was integral to the economy of his station a compromise had to be suggested. Toohey's recommendation was that contemporaneously with the grant, a satisfactory agreement can be made for the use of the stock route – 'to protect the position not only of Mr Fryer but his successors'.

The detriment to tourist interests could not be resolved so easily since the Aboriginal claimants were entirely opposed to ceding any rights to tourist interests. Roper Bar itself and its immediate surrounds, which included the boat landing-stage, the police station, Leichardt's memorial and Charlie Johnson's grave as well as innumerable potential camping and fishing sites, was the key area of conflict, since from the evidence it was also of immense spiritual significance to the Aboriginal claimants. To quote Toohey:

> there was evidence of the importance of land around the boat landing to the claimants – I was shown two large gum trees near the boat ramp which were described as ceremony trees, one of which bears the name of one of the claimants. Tex Camfu made the general observation 'why we don't like tourism – you can see the cans they leave, and the names they carve on the trees. They are not our names...'

Toohey continues:

> The difficulty with camping along the river arises from the location and nature of the sites of significance there. With trees dying and new ones growing it may be difficult to locate precisely which trees are of special significance. As Dr. Morphy has said the protection of sites... is not as simple as putting up a fence around certain trees. It is the whole notion of controlling if you like a totemic landscape, which does not consist of a single tree in a particular place ... but is integrated within the whole process of that environment.

In this case Toohey did not recommend a compromise for one already existed through the foresight of the Gazetteers of the township of Urapunga 100 years before. Toohey concludes: 'The best accommodation of interests may be found in the availability to tourists of public roads, the township of Urapunga, the bar, the boat ramp, land on the Northern part of the river, the Southern bank from its top to the water and the river itself.' It is ironic that the timeless alienation of Urapunga township early on in the colonial process made possible the resolution of the irresolvable by making the timelessness of Aboriginal interests in land commensurate with the temporary interests of Europeans. Urapunga, a town that never existed, filled a gap in history.

## Acknowledgements

I would like to thank Frances Morphy who shared the fieldwork and archival research on which this chapter is based, discussed the ideas with me and made many helpful comments on the completed chapter. Only lack of time prevented her from writing the chapter. I acknowledge the assistance of the Australian Archives in Canberra, the South Australian Archives in Adelaide, and the Northern Territory Archives in Darwin. The initial research for this study was supported by the Australian Institute of Aboriginal and Torres Strait Islander Studies, the Northern Land Council and the Australian National University. Writing up has been facilitated by a grant from the Economic and Social Research Council. I would like to thank Barbara Bender for encouraging me to keep writing about landscape.

# References

Battaglia, D. 1990. *On the Bones of the Serpent*, Chicago: University of Chicago Press.

Berndt, R. M. and Berndt, C. H. 1954. *Arnhem Land, its History and its People*, Melbourne: Cheshire.

Chisolm, A. H. 1973. *Strange Journey*, Adelaide: Rigby.

Hiatt, L. R. 1984. *Aboriginal Land Owners*, Sydney: Oceania Monographs.

Hill, E. 1951. *The Territory*, Sydney: Angus and Robertson.

Lang, J. D. 1847. *Cooksland in North-Eastern Australia, the Future Cotton Fields of Great Britain its Characteristics and Capabilities for European Colonisation* London: Longman, Brown, Green and Longmans.

Layton, R. H. 1989. 'Are socio-biology and social anthropology compatible', in V. Standen and R. Foley (eds) *The Comparative Socio-ecology of Mammals and Man*, 433–55, Oxford: Blackwell.

Leichardt, L. 1847. *Journal of an Overland Expedition in Australia, from Morton Bay to Port Essington....During the Years 1844–1845*, London: T. & W. Boone.

Maddock, K. 1983. *Your Land is our Land: Aboriginal Land Rights*, Ringwood: Penguin Books.

Merlan, F. 1978. 'Making people quiet in the pastoral north: reminiscences of Elsey Station', *Aboriginal History*, 2: 70–106.

Morphy, H. 1977. 'Schematisation, communication and meaning in toas', in P. J. Ucko (ed.) *Form in Indigenous Art*, 77–89, Canberra: Australian Institute of Aboriginal Studies.

———1990. 'Myth, totemism and the creation of clans', *Oceania*, 60, 312–28.

———1991. *Ancestral Connections: Art and an Aboriginal System of Knowledge*, Chicago: University of Chicago Press.

———and Morphy, F. 1981 *The Yutpundji-Djindiwirritj Land Claim*, Darwin: Northern Land Council.

Morphy, H. and Morphy, F. 1984. 'The myths of Ngalakan history: ideology and images of the past in Northern Australia', *Man* (n.s.) 19, 459–78.

Munn, N. M. 1970. 'The transformation of subjects into objects in Walbiri and Pitjanjantjara myth', in R. M. Berndt (ed.), *Australian Aboriginal Anthropology*, 141–63, Nedlands: University of Western Australia Press.

_____1986. *Fame in Gawa: a Symbolic Study of Value Transformation in a Massim (Papua New Guinea) Society*, Cambridge: Cambridge University Press.

Myers, F. R. 1986. *Pintubi Country, Pintubi Self*, Washington D.C.: Smithsonian Institution Press.

Peterson, N. 1972. 'Totemism yesterday; sentiment and local organisation among the Australian Aborigines', *Man* (n.s.) 7, 53–68.

_____1986. *Australian Territorial Organisation*, Sydney: Oceania Monographs.

Searcy, A. 1909. *In the Australian Tropics*, London: George Robertson.

Strehlow, T. G. H. 1970. 'Geography and the totemic landscape in Central Australia', in R. M. Berndt (ed.), *Australian Aboriginal Anthropology*, 92–140, Nedlands: University of Western Australia Press.

Toohey, Mr. Justice. 1982. *Yutpundji-Djindiwirritj (Roper Bar) Land Claim*. Report by the Aboriginal Land Commissioner, Mr. Justice Toohey. Canberra: Australian Government Publishing Service.

# Chapter 8

## Stonehenge – Contested Landscapes (Medieval to Present-Day)

*Barbara Bender*

### Introduction

On a small, heavily populated, down-at-heel, off-shore island, with illusions about its position in the world, the past can become oppressive. Fay Weldon, in her *Letter to Laura* (1984), describes what it is like to live in a country with too much past, too little present (though it is a pity that she overlooked the women):

> Every acre of this tiny, densely populated land of ours has been observed, considered, valued, reckoned, pondered over, owned, bought, sold, hedged – and there's a dead man buried under every hedge, you know. He died of starvation, and his children too, because the common land was enclosed, hedged taken from him ... The past ... is *serious*.

She is describing an English, rather than a Scottish or Welsh landscape, one in which, at least from medieval times, armed interventions were short-lived, where appropriations – and contestations – were somewhat more subtly negotiated. She gets the sense of the 'terrible beauty' to be found in many such landscapes, the tension between the pleasure gained from a worked-over, lived-in landscape and the uneasy knowledge of what the working and the living often involved; the way the 'historical rootedness' of the English landscape, the seeming slow evolution, has served to disguise a proprietorial palimpsest, the working out of a long history of class relations.

Not just the land, but the very word 'landscape' has often been used as though it 'belongs' to a particular class. Recently British Rail put up two Intercity posters for First Class travel. One of them began with the words: 'The only Constable you'll see at a hundred miles an hour ...'. The assumption was clear: those who matter know who Constable is, those who might be confused by a seemingly obscure reference to the forces of law and order do not matter and are not being targeted. The other poster, reproduced in Figure 8.1, shows a quiet landscape, monotone, almost monotonous, acceptable to those who know how – and can afford – to appreciate the understatement, and those desirous of joining their ranks. It is a view from a window. You are the observer. It is not your land but it is certainly someone's land. The fields are cultivated, but the cultivators and their machines are not visible. You could perhaps view it as an 'old' landscape with the tree and the hedge standing for something stable and unchanging. Or you might view it as a 'new' landscape in which, in fact, most of the hedges have been grubbed up to make way for 'economies of scale' and agribusiness. There is perhaps, for those in the First Class, a satisfactory elision between old and new so that the changes associated with the new monetarist climate are referenced on symbols of stability and the old order – the old tree – and thereby gain legitimacy.

In this chapter, working with one small (albeit heavily symbolic) corner of the English landscape, I want to explore not only the different ways in which, over a period of a thousand years, those with economic and political power and the necessary cultural capital have attempted, physically and aesthetically, to appropriate the landscape, but also how these appropriations have been contested by those engaging with the land in quite different ways. Elsewhere I have suggested that people's experience of the land is based in large measure on the particularity of the social, political and economic relations within which they live out their lives, while at the same time their individual actions form part of the way in which these relations are constructed and changed (Bender 1992; see also the Introduction to this volume). I am uneasy about the contemporary theoretical emphasis in which 'the cultural' is uncoupled from the political, and the individual from larger historical structures (for a similar sense of unease see Thrift 1991, Jackson 1991). I want to retain the coupling while accepting that there is a complex system of interactions rather than any consistent one-way flow (Williams

Figure 8.1 British Rail Intercity poster.

1973). I want, too, to stress the physicality of 'living in the world', the interlocking *habitus* of action, belief, experience, engagement – a theme reiterated in many chapters in this volume. Finally, perhaps unfashionably, I want to retain the notion of a hegemonic discourse – the imposition by the powerful of particular ways of doing and seeing which often work to disguise the labour process – and to stress that the strategies involved are not only riven by internal factions and tensions, but are dependent upon some degree of acceptance by those 'without' power, and must perforce take on board their reactions, contestations and subversions (Thompson 1974).[1] One can perhaps make use of Bakhtin's notion of positive shape and negative space in his theory of 'the other' (cited in Foch-Serra 1990). Although the 'positive shape' (in this case, the discourse of the powerful) and the 'negative space' (those to whom it relates) are distinct entities, they share the same edges. When you draw one you inadvertently draw the other.

Since I believe that one can only understand the contestations and appropriations of a landscape by careful historical contextualisation, an attempt to sketch the history of the Stonehenge landscape over a period of more than a thousand years in a few pages becomes problematic. What follows is no more than an outline and is piecemeal. I concentrate on the medieval (with a prologue on prehistoric landscapes), the landscapes of the seventeenth and eighteenth centuries, and, finally, in somewhat more detail, the present-day landscape.

For each period the evidence is very different. Where one is dependent upon archaeological remains, the interpretation is particularly tentative. It is not easy to say what the abandonment of a site might mean. A switch in power? In ideology? What would these changes mean for people as they moved around the landscape? For the medieval period, we can draw on both archae-

---

1. As an example of fractured hegemony, Daniels and Cosgrove (forthcoming), annotate the 'alternative' and contradictory landscapes found within the quite narrow, and well-heeled, society of Jane Austen's *Mansfield Park*, while Said (1989) muses on the unmentioned, slave-operated world of the absentee landlord in the same novel. 'Positive shape' and 'negative space' can be illustrated by changes in landscape gardening at the turn of the nineteenth century. Daniels (1988) notes how the smell of revolution in the air provided part of the impetus behind the move from more formal and exclusive forms of landscaping to ones where the boundaries were softened, so that, as Uvedale Price, landscape gardener, carefully explained, 'although the separation of different ranks and their gradations, like those of visible objects, is known and ascertained, yet from the beneficial mix, the frequent intercommunication of high and low, that separation is happily disguised and does not sensibly operate on the general mind.'

ological evidence and literary sources. But the latter are derived primarily from the work of clerics. There are references to the peasants, but only as the (despised) 'other'. As we move on in time, the description thickens, the voices quicken, but always, even in the present, there are unevenesses in the way in which different people can be heard.

## Prologue: Prehistoric Stonehenge

In another study I have talked about the way in which the prehistoric landscape was created and, right from the beginning, contested and appropriated (Bender 1992).

At the beginning of the Wessex Neolithic, c. 3100 BC, there was nothing to mark the site of Stonehenge. The early Stone Age farmers lived in temporary hamlets in woodland clearances. They practised shifting agriculture and herding and were still dependent upon hunting wild game. Their only durable monuments were long mounds that covered the disarticulated remains of many members of the community, and causewayed enclosures, probably the *locus* of inter-tribal feasting and ceremony, sited on higher ground.

The first 'Ur' henge – no stone in sight – was constructed around 2800 BC – a simple circular ditch and bank with wooden structures in the centre (see Map 8.1). Just to the north lay the great parellel banked 'cursus', running for three kilometres across the downs. Everyday life went on right up to the very edge of 'Ur' henge and cursus. The monuments were not isolated and there was no no-man's land (Richards 1984).

The cursus and circle reiterated the shapes of the long mounds and round enclosures, and when the great cursus was constructed, a very large, but empty, long mound was built at its eastern end. It would seem that the potential conflicts and social changes associated with the building of these monuments were already muffled by referencing back to earlier forms, to places long associated with the ancestors or the gods. The endless historical process (still, as we shall see, continuing), whereby particular people, particular ways of doing and thinking, were empowered and sanctified by appropriating earlier sites and earlier activities within the landscape, had begun. Thus, while the long mounds continued to be built, and, from the outside, retained their old form, each

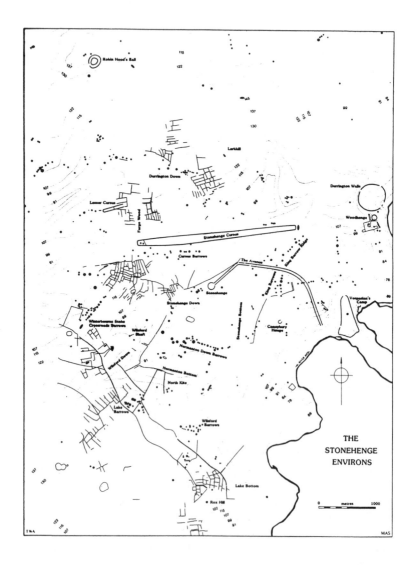

**Map 8.1 Map of the prehistoric Stonehenge landscape (Royal Commission).**

mound now covered just one inhumation – a male – or none at all.
A lot of people, particularly women, were being excluded.

Three hundred years later, c.2500 BC, not just the site of the
'Ur' henge but the surrounding area were virtually abandoned –
the banks tumbled, the ditches silted, the cursus fell into disuse,
the long mounds ceased to be used. Even the surrounding everyday settlement vanished. Settlement and ritual arena moved a
short distance to the east, to the ridge and the river beyond. This
abandonment must surely signal some sort of power struggle, a
rejection and antagonism towards not only the physical siting but
also the ritual order associated with the 'Ur' henge. Almost abandoned, but not quite: Stonehenge was still lodged somewhere
within the landscape of these people. The great wood henges
(Durrington Walls, Woodhenge, Coneybury) on the ridge to the
east were the focus for ritual enactments, but these enactments no
longer encompassed the dead – there were no burials and no
human bones, except for one centrally placed child sacrifice at
Woodhenge. Instead, in the abandoned banks and ditches of the
'Ur' henge, and in newly dug holes around the internal perimeter
of the circle, a few cremations were placed. The sort of grave-
offerings associated with them seem to suggest that the people
involved, both living and dead, were not marginalised people
(prehistoric 'travellers') excluded from the main settlement area
to the east, but rather, some part of that community that, for
whatever reason, made their way down from the ridge to bury a
few of their dead.

Several hundred years later, c. 2100 BC, in the Early Bronze
Age, the action reversed. Eastern ridge and river were abandoned, and the 'Ur' henge was rebuilt – in stone. There then followed an extraordinary period during which members of a
more restless and competitive society laid claim and counter-
claim to the construction of Stonehenge. Stones were put up,
taken down, rearranged, added to. The claims on the past were
no longer muffled legitimations, but rather an aggressive piecemeal appropriation. The wood henges to the east were left to
rot, but the wood-working construction techniques were carried
over to the site of Stonehenge. Some of the bluestones used at
the revamped Stonehenge were probably transported from
another ritual site which lay far to the west. The large sarsen
stones were dragged over thirty kilometres from the Avebury
area.

At the earlier Avebury henge the stones had been used in their natural state; at the new Stonehenge the stone was worked, controlled. The occasional carved motifs on the stones at Stonehenge go back to an earlier tradition usually associated with megalithic tombs. The skyward orientation of the earlier 'Ur' henge – seemingly unused for at least five hundred years – was resuscitated and elaborated. The surrounding Early Bronze Age burial mound cemeteries often focused upon a long mound, the last of which had probably been constructed a thousand years earlier. In this Early Bronze Age a ragbag of deliberate, if eclectic, archaisms was pulled in from a thousand years of earlier landscapes (Hobsbawm and Ranger 1983).

Finally, in the later Bronze Age, through the Iron Age and the Roman period, the Stonehenge area seems to have been more or less abandoned, or perhaps avoided. The monuments lose their official power – they are no longer an arena in which power is legitimated by being linked with the ancestors or the gods. But perhaps the stark abandonment speaks for an *unofficial* and unofficiated power, perhaps Stonehenge remained a 'dangerous' place, to be avoided in the course of everyday activities. We find, when the record reopens, that the Anglo-Saxons, who rarely bothered to rename natural landscape features, have laid claim to the Celtic *Choir Gaur* – it has become Stan Hencg. Of course, given the prominence of the stones, they could have been incorporated into folk culture by different people, at different times, on an *ad hoc* basis, with little sense of continuity. Alternatively, it is conceivable, as Piggott (1941) tentatively suggests, that they were part of an enduring, if syncretic, local folk culture.

## Medieval Stonehenge[2]

The record opens briefly, then closes again. The next mention of Stonehenge is in the later medieval period, in the middle of the

---

2. In this medieval section, there are many allusions to Avebury, the other great stone circle that lies thirty miles to the north. Avebury is less well known, though for some, like John Aubrey, it 'did as much excell *Stoneheng*, as a cathedral does a Parish church' (cited in Hunter 1975: 158). A medieval village straddled part of the Avebury circle, and the church, built sometime after ad, 900 was located just beyond the bank and ditch. Because of the proximity of church and village to the stones, there is often more detailed information about Avebury than about Stonehenge. Obviously there were differences between these medieval landscapes but also much that was similar.

twelfth century. Now the stones express the conflict between Church and peasant.

For most of the medieval period the Stonehenge downlands were marginal land, probably common grazing land. The open fields and the villages straggled the valley bottom and lower hill-slopes of the river Avon to the east. The stones lay on the edge of the familiar world, beyond lay the 'wilderness' (Anglo-Saxon *Wylder ness*, nest or lair of a wild beast) (Stilgoe 1982: 10). For the medieval peasant, the landscape, both familiar and unfamiliar, was imbued with magic – half-pagan, half-Christian. The stones in their liminal setting were revered and believed to have curative and procreative powers. In the villages, houses had to be protected from witches. Sometimes a carved rowen post would be set to one side of the hearth. Sometimes the post, carved with St Andrew crosses, was set in place by the local priest who, rarely a man of letters, trod a fine line between the old and the new religion (Stilgoe 1982). The higher echelons of the Church could protest. As early as the eighth century, King Canute could claim that 'It is heathen practice if one worships idols, namely if one worships heathen gods and the sun or the moon, fire or flood, wells or stones or any kind of forest tree, or if one practices witchcraft' (cited in Burl 1979: 36). But, as Le Goff makes clear, the Church authorities, faced with the power of passive resistance, negotiated, trimmed, and adapted their doctrines (Le Goff 1980: 160–88; Gurevich 1988: 5). The peasants did likewise. In many ways their positions were not so far apart. For both, 'the material world was scarcely more than a sort of mask, behind which took place all the really important things. ... Nature ... in the infinite detail of its illusory manifestations ... was conceived above all as the work of hidden wills' (Bloch 1962: 83). Both Church and peasant imbued the landscape with magic – there were plenty of 'magical' Christian sites and relics. The problem was how to interpret the magic. Where the Church saw the hand of God, the peasants, in their fearful encounter with the wilderness, confused Satan with Pan, and continued to relate hoary tales of the wild hunt when '... on moonless nights, and especially Walpurgis-nacht (May Day eve), Satan and his hounds coursed through the forest, pursuing with a terrible roaring and baying all the wild creatures and any humans unlucky enough to stumble in their way' (Stilgoe 1982: 8).

The Church, heir to the Graeco-Roman tradition, was more prone to define good and evil, true and false, black and white magic. The old religion – more precisely the 'traditional culture of folklore'– was more equivocal, more ambiguous: forces were good and bad at the same time, natural forces were to be propitiated and thereby rendered beneficial (Le Goff 1980: 159–88).

The Church, embedded in the hierarchical relations of a feudal society, preached of a 'natural order' homologous to feudalism; the pyramidal social relations were reiterated in the hierarchy of heavenly relations and in material representations. Demarcations – social, material, ritual – were to a large extent played out within a single body of space rather than, as later on, between distinctive, class-differentiated, spaces. The inside of a church, of a manor, even a poor man's long-house, were physically 'open', but socially and mentally heavily demarcated (Johnson, forthcoming). In this world of interdependencies, the peasants, the worshippers of stones, were represented as 'the other' – their labour necessary, their visage hideous. They also acted as a foil for the qualities of wealthy men and saints, as 'fodder' for the redemption of the upper classes (Le Goff 1980). There is little that is positive about the peasants in the writings of the clerics, and much that is passed over in silence. Our sense of their world is filtered through the contortions, concessions, and supressions of the Church.

The Church physically 'appropriated' the stones. Amesbury, close to Stonehenge, housed a religious order; at Avebury the Anglo-Saxon church was built alongside the great bank and ditch. The stones and mounds were also 'intellectually' appropriated and adulterated. They became a malignant part of a Christian iconography, the work of the Devil – Devil's Den, Devil's Quoit, Devil's Chair. The great cone of Silbury Hill, near Avebury, became the place where the Devil had dropped a spadeful of earth. The Heel Stone at Stonehenge compounded a diabolical and Arthurian etymology. It bore, supposedly, the impression of a holy father's heel struck by a stone thrown by the Devil when angered by Merlin, King Arthur's magician, who had magicked the stones into place (Burl 1979: 36).

The medieval Church vacillated between attempting to appropriate the stones, and destroying them. One of the earliest accounts of Stonehenge, c.1136, by the Welsh cleric Geoffrey of Monmouth, embedded in his *History of the Kings of Britain*, combines 'pure legend and a sense of the marvellous that is sometimes still completely pagan' (Bloch 1962: 100).

In Monmouth's account, Aeneas, arriving from Troy, con-
quered the giants that inhabited 'Albion'. Later, a Celtic King,
Emrys (Ambrosius), brother to Ythr (Uther Pendragon, father of
Arthur), intent on establishing a memorial to kinsmen killed at
Amesbury by Saxon treachery, enlisted Merlin's help in transporting the great stones from Ireland and erecting them at
Stonehenge (see figure 8.2). According to Geoffrey, these stones
had originally been brought by giants from Africa to Ireland.[3] In
a matter-of-fact way, he cites Merlin's description of the magical
power of the stones: 'whenever they felt ill, baths would be prepared at the foot of the stones; for they used to pour water over
them and to run this water into baths in which their sick were
cured. What is more, they mixed the water with herbal concoc-
tions and so healed their wounds. There is not a single stone
among them which hasn't some medicinal value' (Geoffrey of
Monmouth 1966: 196).

In later medieval times such benign empowering of the stones
was forbidden and the Church moved to obliterate their magic.
At Avebury, in the early fourteenth century, the Church authorities made the local inhabitants destroy the stones. Nevertheless,
the destruction was done with caution. The stones were not broken up; instead, the villagers dug large holes and tumbled the
stones into them, 'handled almost with reverence, covered without hurt to the sarsen, doing God's work without upsetting the
Devil' (Burl 1979: 37). Compare this with the late seventeenth
century, when the local farmers broke up the stones, partly for
purely utilitarian reasons, partly, as we shall see, as part of the
Protestant backlash against paganism and popery. Now they
were broken by fire and water, and were incorporated into local
buildings (see figure 8.3).

## The Seventeenth and Eighteenth Centuries

Ucko *et al.* (1991: 163) suggest that by the end of the seventeenth
century, the peasants no longer worshipped the stones, and
broke them with impunity. But perhaps this is too simple a read-

3. Piggott (1941), much impressed by this part of Monmouth's saga, suggests that it indicates that Monmouth was heir to the Welsh bardic tradition that, in faint outline, resonated
with millennia-old traditions recounting the movement of the bluestones from Wales to
Wessex.

**Figure 8.2 Merlin (British Library Egerton ms. 3028 fo. 140v).**

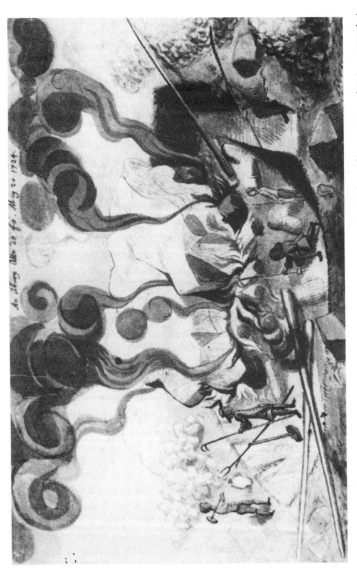

**Figure 8.3 Stukeley: Atto [*sic*] de Fe. Fire-setting at Avebury, 20 May 1724 (Bodleian Library Gough Maps 231 f.5).**

ing. There remains a tension, right through the seventeenth and into the eighteenth century, between the stones seen as something utilitarian, a source of building material or an encumbrance to be got rid of by farmers 'chiefly out of couvetousness of the little *area* of ground each stood on' (Stukeley, cited in Ucko *et al.* 1991: 249), and the stones invested, however vestigially, with supernatural power. While the Nonconformist preacher harnessed all the populist rhetoric at his disposal to force a disassociation between 'pagan' ritual and festival and true Christian piety, he also, in repudiating the 'emotional calendar of the poor', drove a wedge between the teachings of the Church and everyday life, between 'polite' and 'plebeian' culture. In attempting to destroy the 'bonds of idolatry and superstition – the wayside shrines, the gaudy church, the local miracle and cults – ' (Thompson 1972), he undermined traditional remedies against the devil and his agencies, and made witchcraft and pagan practices appear both more powerful and more menacing (Hill 1982). Added to which, by the end of the seventeenth century, with the acceleration of the enclosure movement, many a member of a church congregation had been cut loose not only from the land, but also – a negative freedom – from traditional forms of obligation and service (Thompson 1974). There was, thus, not only a degree of political anarchy, but also a considerable residue of superstition. Indeed, it was not unknown, in the late seventeenth century, for preachers attempting to 'tame' their congregations by threats of 'petrification' for those that danced on the Sabbath, and several stone circles were attributed to just such divine intervention (Grinsell 1976). *Fools Bolt*, an anonymous diatribe also from the late seventeenth century, both threatens, and remains threatened by the power of the stones at Stonehenge:

> these forlorne Pillers of Stone are left to be our remembrancers, dissuading us from looking back in our hearts upon anything of Idolatry, and persuading us ... so to deride it, in it's uglie Coullers, that none of us ... may returne, like Doggs, to such Vomit, or Sows to wallowing in such mire' (cited in Legg 1986: 18).[4]

There are many mentions of the magical properties of the stones in the seventeenth and eighteenth century. John Aubrey, in the

---

4. Various guesses at the authorship have been made: J. Gibbons perhaps (Piggott 1985: 86), or Robert Gay, a Parliamentarian rector (Legg 1986). Whoever he was, the author was exceedingly scornful of Inigo Jones – 'Out-I-goe Jones' – and of his Romano-British origin for Stonehenge.

1660s, notes, in the context of Stonehenge, that 'it is generally averred ... that pieces of powder of these stones, putt into their wells, doe drive away the toades ...' (cited in Olivier 1951: 157); while the Rev. James Brome noted in 1707: 'if the stones be rubbed, or scraped, and water thrown upon the scrapings, they will (some say) heal any green wound or old sore' (cited in Burl 1987: 220).

In the 1740s Stukeley records that people chipped off bits of bluestone because they were thought to have medicinal purposes. And when John Wood, also in 1740, attempted to survey the stones and a violent storm blew up, the locals reckoned he had raised the devil (Burl 1987: 182).

In the longer term, the old ways, the old superstitions, the last vestiges of a 'deification of nature', were undermined by what Marx called 'the great civilizing influence of capital' (quoted in Thomas 1983: 23). The change in people's attitudes towards the natural world occurred in piecemeal fashion, depending upon who they were and where – economically, politically, socially – they were located. An illiterate peasantry (slowly being commodified into farm-'hands') abandoned more slowly the notion of 'a natural world redolent with human analogy and symbolic meaning, and sensitive to man's behaviour' (Thomas 1983: 89). It was the literate classes that embraced the concept of nature as something detached, 'to be viewed and studied by the [male] observer from the outside, as if by peering through a window ... a separate realm, offering no omens or signs, without human meaning and significance' (Thomas 1983: 89 – my parenthesis; see Thomas, Olwig this volume), and – more sinisterly – as something 'to be put to the question' (Bacon), and racked for its secrets and treasures (Gold 1984).

The more pronounced attempts by the Church, in the seventeenth and eighteenth centuries, to impose Christian teachings, and Christian marriage, upon the vestigial paganism and easier-going sexual mores of the countryside, were only aspects of a greater intervention in the lives of ordinary people by both Church and State. Having followed through the contestation between Church and peasant, I have to backtrack in order to discuss the way in which the State interceded, and the importance of Stonehenge in the context of an emerging national, and then regional, identity.

Already in the fifteenth century, the Church had begun to lose its exclusive hold on the past: history was no longer a matter of

ecclesiastical precedent. 'Time' ceased to be the gift of God and
became 'the property of man' (Le Goff 1980: 51), and 'Time's
arrow' began to replace the repetitive cycles – the endless chain of
cause and effect – of earlier history. Instead, historical predecents
and 'genealogies' became part of the process of internal pacification and state-nation consolidation. As early as the fourteenth century Stonehenge begins to be drawn into a nationalist diatribe.
Langtoft tells the story of 'the Wander Wit of Wiltshire', who:

> rambling to Rome to gaze at Antiquities, and there skewing himself
> into the company of Antiquarians, they entreated him to illustrate
> unto them that famous monument in the contry called Stonage. His
> answer was that he had never seen, scarce ever heard of it, where-
> upon they kicked him out of doors and bad him goe home and see
> Stoneage. And I wish that all such Episcopal cocks as slight these
> admired stones and scrape for barley cornes of vanity out of foreigne
> dunghills, might be handled, or rather footed, as he was (cited in
> Olivier 1951: 156).

Under the Tudors, historical and archaeological precedents
were used to formalise 'custom and tradition into instruments of
government and a defined code of laws' (Piggott 1985) and at a
time when the Act of Union (1536) extended the English law of
the land to Wales and menacingly set out the need 'utterly to
extirpe all and singular the senister usages and customes dif-
feringe from [the Realme of Englande]' (cited in Jones 1990), the
myth was created that the inhabitants of England and Wales
were one people with a common ancestry and shared history
(Piggott 1985: 16). Henry VIII, intent on breaking with Rome and
on seizing the Church lands, employed Leland to ride around
the country, mapping, collating, and 'spying'. And Leland, professing himself 'totally enflammed with a love to see thoroughly
all partes of your opulente and ample realme' thereby to expose
'the craftily coloured doctrine rout of Roman biships', rode
around the land: 'By the space of these vi yeares paste that there
is almost nother cape, nor bay, haven, creke, or peere, river or
confluence of rivers, breches, washes, lakes, mere, fenny water,
montaynes, valleis, mores, hethes, forestes, woodes, cities,
burges, castelles, principal manor places, but I have seene them'
(Chamberlin 1986: 69). *Inter alia*, he mapped and described
Stonehenge, appending, without comment, Geoffrey of
Monmouth's 'explanation'.

Compilations, categorisations and a comprehensive mapping of Britain became increasingly important during the seventeenth and early eighteenth centuries. Refinements in surveying and mapping were part of a changing technology of power, integral to the development of mercantile capital and to the opening up of the New World. Control of knowledge, control of resources, control of nature.

By the late seventeenth century, as the 'county naturalists picked their way through all the legends of prognosticatory springs, portentous birds and similar marvels', popular and learned views of nature significantly separated out (Thomas 1983: 78). James I demanded that Stonehenge be made to give up its secret, and ordered his court architect, Inigo Jones, to map and explain it – giants and Merlin were no longer sufficient. Inigo Jones, steeped in Italianate landscapes, claimed Stonehenge for the Romans. It was, he said, as he manipulated his plans, built c.AD 79 by British chieftains subject to Rome, and was based upon Vitruvian geometry. The king encouraged the Duke of Buckingham to dig the monument, causing – as, a little later, Aubrey laconically noted – the 'falling downe, or recumbancy of the great stone'.

With the influx of capital into the countryside, with 'new' families competing with and marrying into the older aristocracy, and with both the old and new aristocracy hastening to enclose open field and common land in order to 'improve' their land and their fortunes, the mapping and description of land-use, natural curiosities, and the genealogies of local families, helped both to create and to legitimate the new class and property relations. Aubrey, the 'discoverer' in 1666 of Avebury (the peasants of course had been there a while) and of the Aubrey holes at Stonehenge, was the first to propose that Stonehenge was not Roman or Danish but rather Celtic and (probably) associated with the Druid religion. He was also not reluctant to admit that he was recording with the explicit intent that knowledge be made available to those who might find economic advantage (McVicar 1984). Walter Charleton, three years earlier, was in favour of a Danish origin and proposed it as 'a *court royal*, or place for the *Election* and *Inauguration* of their Kings', and, in the same vein, dedicated it to Charles II (Ucko *et al.* 1991: 15). And John Smith of Boscombe, in the later eighteenth century, noting that Stonehenge was built 'to show the steady, uniform and orderly

motions of the heavenly bodies', dedicated it to the Duke of
Queensbury at nearby Amesbury House 'as a symbol of your
Grace's steady, uniform and orderly conduct through life'
(Olivier 1951: 36). Based in large measure on the formidable treatise on *Brittania* by Camden (published 1586, republished in an
enlarged edition 1695), antiquarians increasingly focused on a
regional, rather than a national, coverage.

The economic advantages reaped by the antiquarians' patrons
were real enough. The peasants were literally evicted as part of
the seventeenth- and eighteenth-century enclosure movement.
They were also evicted aesthetically. In 1726, The Duke of
Queensbury, owner of Amesbury House, near to Stonehenge,
had 30 acres; by 1773 his estate encompassed 300 acres. He
enclosed the open fields of West Amesbury and Amesbury
Countess to the East of Stonehenge, and laid great parts of the
estate down to park. He realigned the Amesbury–Market
Lavington road, landscaped the Iron Age camp and built a
'druidical' grotto. In passing, he 'preserved' Stonehenge from a
plague of rabbit warrens planted by his predecessor.

The antiquarian, William Stukeley, though a churchman and a
friend of the gentry, occasionally hints at a darker local experience of landscape. Writing, in 1740, of his survey of the
Stonehenge area, he says 'this... will...preserve the memory of it
hereafter, when the traces of this mighty work are obliterated by
the plough...that instrument gaining ground too much upon the
ancient and innocent pastoral life; ... and by destructive inclosure
beggars and depopulates the country' (Royal Commission 1979).

It is, of course, the technology that Stukeley blames, rather
than the social system. Arthur Young, professional and enthusi-
astic 'improver', writer of the *Annals of Agriculture* in forty-six
volumes, suggested, of the vast uncultivated width of Salisbury
Plain, that 'all the corn export from England would annually
grow in such a square'. But a person's engagement with the land
can change, and towards the end of his life, Young admitted: 'I
had rather that all the commons of England were sunk to the sea,
than that the poor should in future be treated on enclosing as
they have been hitherto' (Williams 1973: 66).

Stukeley, apart from his threnody about enclosure, was an
Establishment man. In his writings on Stonehenge and Avebury
there is a tension between his desire to record in meticulous 'scientific' detail and his need to validate his theological interpretation.

There has been a tendency to periodicise Stukeley's life, separating out an earlier 'scientific' fieldwork phase from a later 'druidic' phase, and lamenting his lapse into romantic fabulation (Piggott 1985: 15). More recent work suggests that, from the beginning, the two went hand-in-hand (Ucko *et al.* 1991: 53), and now that we are more prone to recognise the subjectivity that imbues all our practice, we can more readily accept the contradictions in Stukeley's work. So, on the one hand, in the early 1720s, he meticulously maps the cultural landscape of his forebears, reinvoking Stonehenge as part of a larger landscape. On the other, having read – though rather under-acknowledged – Aubrey, he promulgates a Druidic origin, and, more, attempts to place the Druids in a direct line from Moses and Abraham, and to find in their religion the lineaments of the Christian Trinity. Avebury becomes 'a landscaped model of the Trinity' in which the great circle represents 'the ineffable deity, the avenues ... his son ... in the form of a serpent', and Stonehenge a temple erected in 460 bc by Egyptian 'refugees', aided by Wessex Druids (Piggott 1985). While he held these notions from the 1720s and had 'revised' some of his plans accordingly, they were given added urgency in the 1730s and 1740s. Having moved from being a medical man to taking holy orders, perhaps in part because his hopes of patronage were disappointed, he found that Tolund and the Deists were also promoting Stonehenge as a druidical temple with the intention of relativising all religions by suggesting that 'Christianity was as old as the Creation'. In the face of this heretical intervention, Stukeley altered the title of his book from the original 'History of the Ancient Celts' to 'Patriarchal Christianity: or, A Chronological History of the Origin and Progress of True Religion, and of Idolatry'.[5]

Stukeley appropriated the Druids in the service of the Church of England. Others, particularly the Welsh nationalists in the aftermath of the French Revolution, rediscovered them as early patriots, Celtic leaders of the opposition to the Romans, symbols of resistance and liberty (Jones 1990). In both Thomas's poem 'Liberty' and in Collins's 'Ode to Liberty' (1747) the Druids figure as the apostles of freedom (Piggott 1985).

Cleric, antiquarian, landed gentry, Welsh nationalist – the number of voices increases. Each appropriates Stonehenge in

5. The first entry to the Index of the volume, published in 1740, runs:
They were of the patriarchal religion Page 1,2,17
Which was the same as Christianity 2,54

their own fashion, each creates a particular past. Some voices remain muted. The voice of the labourer, or of women of any class, most often comes down to us at second-hand. Other people talk about them, or do not talk about them. The silences are important. And often the bitterness seeps through. The radical claim to land that the Diggers and Levellers fought for in the seventeenth century were superseded, in the eighteenth century, by frustration and anger over the wholesale appropriation and enclosure of the land, as expressed, for example, in the writings of the poet-labourer John Clare.

In contemporary Britain, even with all the media available, it is still not easy to hear all the voices that contest the Stonehenge landscape. Moreover, while the stones remained 'open' right through to the beginning of this century and people could come to them with their different understandings, they are now 'closed' and Stonehenge has become a museum which attempts to 'sell', not always successfully, a particular sort of experience, a particular interpretation of the past. People with alternative views have to fight for right of entry and the right to express their views.

### Contemporary Landscapes

In the first instance, the desire to 'protect' Stonehenge sprang from radical protests at the effect of late nineteenth-century industrialisation on people and places alike. On the one hand, 'romantic' socialists like John Ruskin, appalled by the destruction wrought by the Industrial Revolution, proposed in 1854 that an inventory of 'buildings of interest' threatened by demolition be drawn up. On the other hand, a fierce intercession by working-class socialists demanding access to the countryside for the urban working class, led to the creation of the Youth Hostelling Association and the Ramblers Association (Bommes & Wright 1982). In the late 1870s, John Lubbock attempted to introduce a National Monuments Preservation Bill. Three times the bill was furiously opposed by conservative members of the the House of Commons who recognised that public amenity might come to override the rights of private ownership (Murray 1989).[6] There was, for example, a fine

6. The political implications of celebrating a Celtic past at a time when the English were putting down the Irish was not lost on the House of Commons (Murray 1989).

intercession by Francis Hervey, a Tory MP. '"Are the absurb relics of our barbarian predecessors", he clearly roared, "who found time hanging heavily on their hands, and set about piling up great barrows and rings of stones, to be preserved at the cost of the infringement of property rights?"' (Bommes and Wright 1982). Tennyson wrote a poem in which father and son are trotting across their estate. The father opens with 'Property, property, property' and the poem vindicates his obsession.

Eventually, following the precedent set by the Commons Preservation Society in the 1880s, a wonderful British blurring of the distinction between 'private' and 'public' ownership was concocted and the politicians were won over. The National Trust (founded in 1895) holds the properties and land *privately* in the national and *public* interest.

In 1894 Sir Edmund Antrobus, owner of Stonehenge, refused to allow the Ancient Monuments Commission to fence Stonehenge. He still saw it as an important public space. If they tried to fence the stones, he said, 'an indignant public might act as the London public did in regards the railings of Hyde Park, when the claim to hold meetings was interfered with' (Legg 1986: 162). His son, however, offered Stonehenge to the nation, at the excessively high price of £125,000 and with the proviso that he retain hunting and grazing rights. When this offer was turned down, he threatened to sell it to the Americans. In 1901, with the approval of the Society of Antiquaries, he erected a barbed wire fence around the monument on the specious ground that the new military camp on Salisbury Plain might result in damage. He put in two custodians and charged an entrance fee of a shilling a head (the equivalent of £5 today – obviously beyond the means of most people). Flinders Petrie and Lord Eversley (founder of the Commons Protection Society) took Antrobus to court, but as Eversley remarked, 'the judge appeared to regard with equanimity the exclusion from the monument of the great bulk of the public. He was evidently under the impression that the vulgar populace had, by their destructive propensities, disqualified themselves as visitors to a place of antiquarian interest' (cited in Legg 1986: 166).

Eversley surmised that the judge was much influenced by a line from Horace which, freely translated, runs: 'I hate the profane crowd and I exclude them.' Ninety years later things have not changed much.

In 1915, Stonehenge was put up for auction, and a Mr Chubb bought it for his wife after she remarked over breakfast that 'she would like to own it'. He paid £6,600. In 1918 he gave Stonehenge to the nation, with the express wish that access should remain free. Unfortunately he added the proviso 'unless the Ministry of Works deems otherwise' (Legg 1986). The Establishment 'deemed otherwise', and Stonehenge became a museum. Fenced in, available only to those who pay, it is no longer a lived landscape (Lowenthal 1979).

Famously, Jaquetta Hawkes (1967: 174) once wrote 'Every age has the Stonehenge it deserves – or desires.' Licking our post-imperial wounds, and in a climate of industrial decline, we commodify the past and turn Stonehenge into a tacky tourist trap. And once a year, at the Summer Solstice, it becomes an ideological and physical battleground. The arc lights go on, the razor wire unrolls, police and security men parade their dogs. For a brief moment at the Summer Solstice, the physical force that underwrites the power of the ruling classes is unmasked. In 1985 five hundred 'travellers' (a label that covers a great assortment of people who move around the countryside in old vans and buses) or 'free festivalers' were arrested and two hundred vehicles were impounded; in 1988 there was a repeat performance. In 1993 there was an eerie silence: no one, except the police and selected journalists, were there to watch the sun rise.

There is no doubt that the confrontational politics of the Thatcher years have thrown into high relief some of the conflicts that underwrite British society. It was not fortuitous that Wapping (the printers' strike), Orgreave (the miners' strike), and the Battle of the Beanfield at Stonehenge occurred within a year of each other. The same tactics, involving the deployment of non-local, unidentifiable police, were used in each encounter. The same language defines and excommunicates 'the other'. For Mrs Thatcher the miners were 'the enemy within'. Assistant Chief Constable Clement admitted that he 'would not be the slightest bit troubled if ... [the pickets] were trampled on by horses'. As for the travellers, Douglas Hurd labelled them 'medieval brigands', Mrs Thatcher brayed '[I will do] anything I can to make life difficult for such things as hippy convoys'. Sir John Cope, Tory MP, trumpeted 'we need a paramilitary police force', and Robert Key, Tory MP, gave away part of the reason for this anger and disquiet, 'two hundred nomads are squatting illegally on private land ...

there may be a sensible case for the use of troops.' Media coverage reflects similar prejudices in a characteristically hysterical form. The *News of the World* headlines read 'Sex-mad junkie outlaws make the Hell's Angels look like little Noddy' (Rosenberger 1991). In a post-Thatcher, less confrontational mode, damages against the police have been awarded to both travellers and miners.[7] There may be further conciliatory moves. They will muffle, rather than resolve, the underlying tensions.

The travellers, as an unpropertied, anarchic minority, enrage the Establishment. In particular, they enrage when they lay claim to Stonehenge. I shall return to the travellers, but I want first to consider who attempts to call the tune. In an era of flexible capitalism (Harvey 1989), who are the power-brokers at Stonehenge, what are the economics of an imagined past, who writes the scripts, who buys the product?

Who – officially – owns Stonehenge? English Heritage 'owns' the site 'for the nation'. The National Trust 'owns' 1,500 acres around Stonehenge, also 'for the nation'. *Sotto voce*, the Ministry of Defence 'owns' vast stretches of Salisbury plain, presumably for the defence of the nation. The new Visitor Centre, which we shall come to in a minute, is scheduled to be built on the edge of their terrain.

English Heritage and the National Trust act in the interests of the – admittedly heterogeneous – Establishment. Any radicalism that once existed has long faded; it is replaced, on occasion, by populist rhetoric. When, for example, in the mid-1970s, the Labour government threatened to impose a Wealth Tax detrimental to the propertied classes, the Victoria and Albert Museum put on an exhibition on the threat to country houses. This seeded the 'SAVE Britain's Heritage' campaign. The populist rhetoric that the campaign engaged in – doing 'battle' for 'our' heritage, the need to maintain 'communal values' (apolitical, organic, stable, and deeply unequal) – only thinly disguised both old and new class interests. Populist rhetoric was combined with an

7. The 'Battle of the Beanfield' took place in June 1985. Six years later, in June 1991, £23,000 was awarded to 24 plaintiffs for 'assault, damage to their vehicles and property, and for not being given the reasons for their arrest'. The judge managed to find the police not guilty of unlawful arrest and they therefore did not have to pay the costs of the trial. The plaintiffs' award was therefore swallowed up in legal costs. The miners' confrontation with the police (or vice-versa) at Orgreave in Yorkshire occurred in June 1984. In July 1985 the case against the 95 pickets was dropped. In June 1991 39 (former) miners shared £425,000 out-of-court compensation from South Yorkshire police for assault, wrongful arrest, malicious prosecution and false imprisonment (*Guardian*, 20 June 1991).

emphasis on 'green' small business economics: preservation was about re-cycling, preservation required small-scale specialised crafts (Jacobs 1990).

But beyond the rhetoric of the 'small business' and the rights of 'ordinary' people, preservation, conservation and public access have become 'big' business. In a climate of industrial decline, investment in property becomes more problematic. In the computerised age of flexible capitalism, the tourist market, which does not require heavy investment in fixed facilities, looks increasingly attractive: imaging the past is profitable.[8] In 1983 government responsibility for the preservation of ancient monuments and for scientific research was handed over to English Heritage – a quango, autonomous but state-funded. Lord Montagu of Beaulieu (author of *How to Live in a Stately Home and Make Money*) took the chair and one of the stated aims became the promotion of tourism (Hewison 1987: ch.4).

So Stonehenge has to make money. It also has to be preserved, conserved and presented. Contemporary Stonehenge is, rightly, berated for its neo-brutalist Visitors' Centre, inadequate parking, facile 'macho' historical presentation (we go back through time via an astronaut, Henry VIII, and, no doubt to the confusion of many visitors, Egypt and the Pharoahs, with not a woman in sight), and banal popularisation. It is a botched attempt to provide tourist facilities, prevent unauthorised access by those unwilling to pay, and conserve the 'sensitive' centre part of the monument. Ten million pounds is about to be invested in a new, enlarged Stonehenge Visitors' Centre. It is a reasonably inspired compromise between conservation and high-powered marketing. The Centre will probably be sited more than half a mile from the stones on Ministry of Defence land, where, screened by trees, there will be room enough for parking, shops and information facilities catering for a proposed one million people a year. Standing on high ground, the tourists can look through telescopes. They can, in time honoured fashion, spy out across the land to Stonehenge. Some, it is thought (hoped?), will not bother to make the twenty-minute walk. (A 'hands on' Foamhenge was

---

8. The takings from the Yorvik (Viking) shop at York are, per square foot, more than every Marks and Spencers in the land, except the Oxford Street branch (Baker 1988). The number of museums has increased by over 50 per cent since 1970. Roughly one museum opens every three weeks. In the late 1980s there were over 2,000 museums in Great Britain (Hewison 1987: ch.1), although, with the recession, a number have proved short-lived.

mooted, but rejected.) Down at the site, the perimeter fence will stay in place, and the stones will remain roped off. The minor road will be removed, although the locals are not happy. Interestingly, demonstrating the conflicts of interest that operate between levels of government, the County Council, in a deeply Conservative constituency, early in 1992 voted overwhelmingly against the road change. They objected, as a local newspaper put it, to 'big shots' from London trying to tell them what's good for them. They also objected to the way in which English Heritage, presumably in their search for 'authenticity', 'scalped' the trees at Old Sarum.[9]

The plan focuses on conservation, and on presentation and packaging for tourists. Other groups – Druids, travellers, free festivalers – are excluded.

There is no information as yet on how Stonehenge will be 'presented' and explained at the new Centre. What sort of image, what sort of past is to be portrayed, what history constructed and redeployed? In general, the English Heritage brief has been conservative: 'The National Heritage is remarkably broad and rich...It is simultaneously a representation of the development of aesthetic expression and a testimony to the role played by the nation in world history' (First Annual Report of the National Heritage Memorial Fund, cited in Hewison 1987). Its main focus has been the landmarks of those with power and wealth, inscribed in an aesthetic, which, as it has done for centuries, bypasses the labour that created the wealth. More recently, the net has been cast wider; the poverty and squalor of Victorian back-to-backs or the working conditions of mill or mine have been romanticised and made *bijoux*. Whether 'grand' house or back-to-back, the focus is on the locality, setting, family, rather than the socio-economic conditions that generate both wealth and poverty, people's pain or their resistance. In an industrial setting, it is always the technology, not the labour conditions, that are emphasised.

In the context of prehistoric landscapes, the focus is on 'monuments', on 'things' rather than ways of life or social practice; on 'origins' rather than historical process, even though, as Lowenthal puts it, '... things begin at all times in history' (1979).

9. English Heritage have also cut down the fine avenue of yews at Chiswick House. They did not conform to the original plan.

Stonehenge will be 'explained' in terms of roots, and of 'our' 'deep' national past. 'They' – the builders of Stonehenge – will be homogeneous. It will tell the story of those empowered to make decisions and to make claims on other people's labour – a top-down history. It will be a 'frozen' past, one that ends when the last stone went up. Hence the incongruity of the marginalised travellers or Druids laying claim to the place, their desire to make it a 'living' space, a meeting-place, a ritual centre. 'Frozen' it can be visited, excavated, become a museum exhibit. In reality, of course, it is never 'frozen', because it is always in process of appropriation. Thus 'our glorious (sanitised, de-radicalised) past' serves to justify, in a less glorious present, 'our' place in the sun, or, while being reworked as a commercial proposition, seems to provide a refuge from the forces of modernism.

The conservation and marketing lobby depend for their information and explanations of the past on the academic establishment – in the case of Stonehenge, the archaeologists. The archaeologists justify their monopoly on information in terms of the scientific rigour of their discipline. They have the artefacts, the dating material, that permit the reconstruction of the past. The fact is that archaeologists do not know why Stonehenge was built, that most of the excavation reports have never been published, and that there are widely variant explanations of the prehistoric sequence and development.[10] But as the 'official' interpreters, they, by and large, repudiate the 'alternative' theories of the New Agers, and side with the conservationists against the Free Festival on grounds of potential damage.[11] Yet they fail to protest when the police dig a trench 15 feet long and 6 feet wide across the entrance to the Free Festival field, or, in the longer term, at the much greater despoliation of the Stonehenge landscape by the Ministry of Defence firing ranges and tank runs. They attempt to eschew politics. One member of the Commission

10. One rendition of the transition from Late Neolithic to Early Bronze Age draws a contrast between those whose power derives from communal ritual expressed in collective architectural enterprises, and a new breed of thrusting individuals whose richly equipped single inhumations show their contempt both for traditional aristocratic ritual and for collective values. In an alternative reading, the Old Neolithic establishment were 'conservatives laden with gold and divine knowledge, scheming to defend their influence against local rebels and sceptics – who, in turn, chafed to get rid of the old frauds and run things in a modern way with Beaker pottery and metal tools' (Ascherson 1988). Yet another version turns Stonehenge into an 'astronomical laboratory' – Fred Hoyle, Astronomer Royal, even suggests that the astronomers were, perhaps, a genetically distinct group (Chippindale 1983: 264).

11. A rare exception, the recent book *Who Owns Stonehenge?* (Chippindale *et al.* 1990), presents, without comment, an array of mainstream and alternative interpretations.

that repudiated the Free Festival, washed his hands of the pre-dictable confrontation that would occur: '"It is most important", he said, "to draw the distinction between the defensible decisions as such and their executive consequences, largely in the hands of others"' (Fowler 1990). To the travellers the archaeologists are the 'unconscious apologists for industrial civilisation', and the loot-ers of graves (Thompson cited in Chippindale 1983: 248).[12]

Preservation and presentation for whom? English Heritage talks of '*bona fide* tourists' as opposed to the free festivalers (Golding 1989). '*Bona fide* tourists' are those who buy the past – who, since 1901, have paid their entrance fees to Stonehenge. In the 1920s there were 20,000 paying visitors, in 1955 184,000, in 1982 530,000, and in 1990 700,000. On a hot summer's day there may be two thousand visitors in one hour. Nearly three-quarters come from overseas, and of those nearly half are from the United States.

Tourism is an expression of the easefulness of long-distance communication and travel. As Jencks put it, 'why, if one can afford to live in different ages and cultures, restrict oneself to the present, the local? Eclecticism is the natural evolution of a culture with choice' (cited in Harvey 1989: 87). 'Sightseeing' is a form of symbolic capital – the emphasis on knowing where to go and what to see (however varied the decisions made may be) disguis-es both the surplus wealth required and the way in which sym-bolic capital translates into 'real' capital, increasing the 'value' of those who possess it.

Tourism at Stonehenge comes in many forms, and is used in the construction of many different identities. Those coming by car, bicycle or on foot distinguish themselves from the 'mass' tourists who arrive by bus with a 'dwell-time' of twenty-five min-utes (more than half of which, it has been ascertained, is taken up with buying souvenirs, food and going to the toilets). Those who do not come by bus may prefer to see themselves as 'travellers' (hippy or high-class) rather than 'tourists'. Just as tourists are var-ied, so are their appreciations and understandings of what they see. By and large, the 'views' of the 'footloose' traveller/tourist

12. Sir Edmond Antrobus (who protested against the fencing of Stonehenge) grumbled in the House of Commons in 1874 that 'some of the ancient barrows, through having been first rifled by antiquarians, have been carted away and levelled by farmers. For himself, he believed it was the antiquarians who had done the most mischief in England' (cited Murray 1989: 63). He wasn't far wrong: in the first decade of the nineteenth century William Cunnington and Sir Richard Colt Hoare 'ravaged' over three hundred barrows (Richards 1991: 33).

are impressionistic and comparative, formed in the 'epoch of juxtaposition, the epoch of the near and far, of the side-by-side, of
the dispersed' (Foucault 1986: 22). They must, in some measure,
subvert the English Heritage packaging of a deep-rooted and stable past.

So many landscapes. Finally, we have the 'alternative', the
unacceptable, landscapes of both the eccentric, but respectable,
Druids – people who hold down perfectly good jobs but reject
orthodox religion – and the Free Festivalers, who are more
sweeping in their rejection of Establishment orthodoxies.

The Druids take their cue from Stukeley. The Ancient Order of
Druids was founded in 1781, as part of the Romantic movement,
happy to pick up where Stukeley had left off. A splinter group,
the United Order of Druids, was founded in 1833. The Druids
worship at the Summer Solstice but they only started coming to
Stonehenge in 1905. Up to the 1970s the Druids were tolerated by
the Establishment. They were 'exotic', and quite good for the
tourist trade.

The unacceptable 'weirdos' are the New Age travellers and
myriad other groupings (hippies, punks, bikers, musicians,
clowns, jugglers, peace activists, Hell's Angels, Quakers, Hare
Krishna devotees), who have held their Free Festival in the field
next to Stonehenge since the mid-1970s, culminating in the 1985
Festival, which attracted over 50,000 people (Rosenberger 1991)
(see figure 8.4). For many of them, Stonehenge is an important
meeting-place, a place for spiritual, and less spiritual, celebrations, weddings, exchanges, part of a seasonal circuit of summer
festivals, winter park-ups on commons or derelict urban sites.
Many of them, like the Druids, believe that there are psychic
forces at Stonehenge – energy fields, ley lines – ; or believe that it
is a temple for the worship of the sun and moon, for the renewal
of seasons.[13] One traveller said:

> It's the main part of the earth energy system ... It's like a *chakra* on the
> earth's energy. You've got your acupuncture – the system of the
> human body with all the meridians and all the burial mounds mark-
> ing them. Then you've got the *chakras* of the human body which are

13. On the other hand, the messages are not always so spiritual. In 1989 four great letters
were grafittied onto the stones: L - I - V - E. They have been cleaned off, of course, but no
doubt they will still be visible under X-ray. Were they a proclamation about the life-force, or
a political credo, or – as rumoured – the unfinished logo of a certain football team?

**Figure 8.4 The Free Festival at Stonehenge (courtesy of Alan Lodge).**

Figure 8.5 The Battle of the Beanfield (courtesy of Alan Lodge).

the bigger ones like Old Jerusleum, Mecca, Egypt, Easter Island and Stonehenge ..." (Willie X: personal communication 1991)

For several years the authorities remained tolerant. After 1978 the stones were roped off, and standpipes, temporary lavatories and rubbish collection points were installed in the Festival field (Golding 1989). There was very little vandalism, and there was considerable self-policing: heroin dealers were run off the site. But by the early 1980s, government and media had turned against the travellers' self-named Peace Convoy, fearing them as anarchists and connecting them with the politically unpopular Peace Camps at Greenham Common, Molesworth, and elsewhere.[14] Despite the 1968 Caravan Sites Act which requires local authorities to provide sites for travellers, such places became fewer and fewer. In 1985 the National Trust and English Heritage took out an injunction and the police moved against them (Chippindale 1986). There were violent showdowns in 1985 and 1988 (see Figure 8.5).

The police have spent five million pounds policing Stonehenge. The government has passed a Public Order Act, permitting the police to arrest two or more people 'unlawfully proceeding in a given direction', and to create 'exclusion zones' to prevent confrontation. The antagonism towards the travellers is not surprising. At the end of the day England's landscape is a proprietorial palimpsest. The travellers own no land or houses, and pay no (direct) taxes.

## Conclusion

What I have tried to do is to chart, and to begin to explain, a cacophony of voices and landscapes through time, mobilising different histories, differentially empowered, fragmented perhaps, but explicable within the historical particularity of British social and economic relations, and a larger global economy. Rather than opting for a post-modern 'multi-vocality' which eschews explanation, I suggest that Marx, and people working in a Marxist tradi-

14. V.S. Naipaul, whose evocation of Stonehenge landscapes in *The Enigma of Arrival* were commented on in the Introduction, was not enthused by the travellers: 'not gipsies..., but young city people, some of them criminals, who moved about Wiltshire and Somerset, in old cars and vans and caravans, looking for festivals, communities, camp sites ... As a deterrent Mr Phillips had the round building wound about with barbed wire' (Naipaul 1987: 270).

tion, permit a deeper understanding. Relevant to past and present-day Stonehenge: 'What Marx depicts ... are social processes at work under capitalism conducive to individualism, alienation, ephemerality, innovation, creative destruction, speculative development ... a shifting experience of space and time, as well as a crisis-ridden dynamic of social change' (Harvey 1989: 111). This is not to say that we have to stay tightly focused on economic infrastructures and class relations, though these are of the utmost importance (Thrift 1991). There has to be a concern with cross-cutting gender relations, and with issues of ethnic identity (Deutsche 1991; Massey 1991; Gilroy 1987), and with political discourse and how people are empowered. We must accept that cultural representations (including physical structures) are not mirror images of economic and social relations. They not only possess their own autonomy, but are integral to the creation, maintenance and questioning of socio-economic conditions.

I hope that this somewhat polemic piece – in part spawned in anger at the efforts by English Heritage and parts of the Establishment to promote a socially empty view of the past in line with modern conservative sensibilities – helps to justify the study of landscape, not as an aesthetic, not as grist for the First Class Intercity poster, but as something political, dynamic, and contested, something constantly open to renegotiation.

## Acknowledgements

I would like to thank Julian Richards for sharing his knowledge and understanding of the Stonehenge region with me, and Alison Wylie, John Barrett and Mark Edmonds for encouraging me. Special thanks to John Gledhill for red-pencilling the text.

## References

Ascherson, N. 1988. *Games With Shadows*, London: Radius / Century Hutchinson.

Baker, F. 1988. 'Archaeology and the Heritage industry', *Archaeological Review from Cambridge* 7. 2, 141–44.

Bender, B. 1992. 'Theorizing landscape, and the prehistoric landscapes of Stonehenge', *Man* 27, 735–55

Bloch, M. 1962. *Feudal Society*, trans. L. Manyon, vol. 1, London:

Routledge & Kegan Paul.

Bommes, M. & Wright, P. 1982. 'Charms of residence, the public and the past', in R. Johnson *et al.* (eds) *Making Histories: Studies in History Writing and Politics*, London: Hutchinson.

Burl, A. 1979. *Prehistoric Avebury*, Yale: Yale University Press.

_____1987. *The Stonehenge People*, London: Dent.

Chamberlin, R. 1986. *The Idea of England*, London: Thames & Hudson.

Chippindale, C. 1983. *Stonehenge Complete*, London: Thames & Hudson.

_____1986. 'Stoned henge: events and issues at the summer solstice', *World Archaeology* 18. 1, 38–58.

_____*et al.* 1990. *Who Owns Stonehenge?* London: Batsford.

Daniels, S. 1988. 'The political iconography of woodland in later Georgian England', in D. Cosgrove and S. Daniels (eds) *The Iconography of Landscape*, Cambridge: Cambridge University Press.

Daniels, S. and Cosgrove, D. 'Spectacle and text: landscape metaphors in cultural geography', in J. Duncan and D. Ley (eds) *Representing Cultural Geography*, London: Routledge. Forthcoming.

Deutsche, R. 1991. 'Boys town', *Environment and Planning D: Society and Space* 9, 5–30.

Edmonds, M. 1993. 'Interpreting causewayed enclosures in the past and the present', in C. Tilley (ed.) *Interpreting Archaeology*, Oxford: Berg.

Foch-Serra, M. 1990. 'Place, voice, space: Mikhail Bakhtin's dialogical landscape', *Environment and Planning D: Society and Space* 8, 255–74.

Foucault M. 1986. 'Of other spaces', *Diacritics* 16, 22–7.

Fowler, P. 1990. 'Academic claims and responsibilities', in C. Chippindale *et al.* (eds) *Who Owns Stonehenge?* London: Batsford.

Geoffrey of Monmouth. 1966. The History of the Kings of Britain, trans. L. Thorpe, Harmondsworth: Penguin.

Gilroy, P. 1987. *There Ain't no Black in the Union Jack: the Cultural Politics of Race and Nation*, London: Hutchinson.

Gold, M. 1984. 'A history of nature', in D. Massey and J. Allen (eds) *Geography Matters!* Cambridge: Cambridge University Press in association with the Open University.

Golding, F. 1989. 'Stonehenge – past and future', in H. Cleere (ed.) *Archaeological Heritage Management in the Modern World*, London: Unwin Hyman.

Gramsci, A. 1971. *Selections from the Prison Notebooks*, New York: International Publishers.

Grinsell, L. 1976. *Folklore of Prehistoric Sites in Britain*, Newton Abbot: David & Charles.

Gurevich, A. 1988. *Medieval Popular Culture; Problems of Belief and Perception*, Cambridge: Cambridge University Press.

Harvey, D. 1989. *The Condition of Postmodernity*, Cambridge: Blackwell.

Hawkes 1967. 'God in the machine', *Antiquity* 41, 174–80.

Hewison, R. 1987. *The Heritage Industry: Britain in a Climate of Decline*,

London: Methuen.

Hill, C. 1982. 'Science and magic in seventeenth-century England', in R. Samuel and G. Stedman Jones (eds) *Culture, Ideology and Politics*, London: Routledge & Kegan Paul.

Hoskins, W.G. 1985. *The Making of the English Landscape*, Harmondsworth: Penguin.

Hobsbawm, E. and Ranger, T. 1983. *The Invention of Tradition*, Cambridge: Cambridge University Press.

Hunter, M. 1975. *John Aubrey and the Realm of Learning*, London: Duckworth.

Jackson, P. 1991. 'Repositioning social and cultural geography', in C. Philo (compiler) *Reconceptualising Social and Cultural Geography*, Aberystwyth: 'Cambrian Printers'.

Jacobs, J. 1990. *The Politics of the Past*, PhD dissertation: London University.

Johnson, M. 1993. 'Notes towards an archaeology of capitalism', in C. Tilley (ed.) *Interpreting Archaeology*, Oxford: Berg.

Jones, R. 1990. 'Sylwadau cynfrodor ar Gor y Cewri; or a British aboriginal's land claim to Stonehenge', in C. Chippindale *et al.* (eds) *Who Owns Stonehenge?* London: Batsford.

Le Goff, J. 1980. *Time, Work and Culture in the Middle Ages*, trans. A. Goldhammer, Chicago: University of Chicago Press.

Legg, R. 1986. *Stonehenge Antiquaries*, Sherborne: Dorset Publishing Co.

Lowenthal, D. 1979. 'Age and artifact', in D. Meinig (ed.) *The Interpretation of Ordinary Landscapes*, New York: Oxford University Press.

———1991. 'British national identity and the English landscape', *Rural History* 2, 2, 205–30.

Massey, D. 1991. 'Flexible sexism', *Environment and Planning D: Society and Space* 9, 31–57.

McVicar, J. 1984. 'Change and the growth of antiquarian studies in Tudor and Stuart England', *Archaeological Review from Cambridge* 3. 1, 48–67.

Murray, T. 1989. 'The history, philosophy and sociology of archaeology: the case of the Ancient Monuments Protection Act (1882)', in V. Pinsky and A. Wylie (eds) *Critical Traditions in Contemporary Archaeology*, Cambridge: Cambridge University Press.

Naipaul, V.S. 1987. *The Enigma of Arrival*, Harmondsworth: Penguin.

Olivier, E. 1951. *Wiltshire*, London: Robert Hale.

Piggott, S. 1941. 'The sources of Geoffrey of Monmouth. II. the Stonehenge story', *Antiquity* 15. 60, 305–19.

———1985. *William Stukeley. An Eighteenth-Century Antiquarian*, London: Thames & Hudson.

Richards, J. 1984. 'The development of the Neolithic landscape in the environs of Stonehenge', in R. Bradley and J. Gardiner (eds) *Neolithic*

*Studies*, Oxford: BAR.

———1991. *Stonehenge*, London: Batsford / English Heritage.

Royal Commission on Historical Monuments. 1979. *Stonehenge and its Environs. Monuments and Landscape*, Edinburgh: Edinburgh University Press.

Rosenberger, A. 1991. 'Stones that cry out' *Guardian* June 19.

Said E. 1989. 'Jane Austen and Empire', in T. Eagleton (ed.) *Raymond Williams: Critical Perspectives*, Oxford: Polity Press.

Stilgoe, J. 1982. *Common Landscape of America 1580 to 1845*, New Haven: Yale University Press.

Stuckeley, W. 1740. *Stonehenge: a Temple Restor'd to the British Druids*, London: Innys & Manby.

Thomas, K. 1983. *Man and the Natural World*, Harmondsworth: Penguin.

Thompson, E. 1974. 'Patrician society, plebian culture', *Journal of Social History* 7, 382–405.

Thrift, N. 1991. 'Over-wordy worlds? Thoughts and worries', in C. Philo (compiler), *Reconceptualising Social and Cultural Geography*, Aberystwyth: Cambrian Printers.

Ucko, P. *et al.* 1991. *Avebury Reconsidered. From the 1660s to the 1990s*, London: Unwin Hyman.

Weldon, F. 1984. 'Letter to Laura', in R. Mabey, S. Gifford and A. King (eds) *Second Nature*, London: Jonathan Cape.

Williams, R. 1973. *The Country and the City*, London: Chatto & Windus.

# Chapter 9

# Landscapes and Myths, Gods and Humans

*Denis Cosgrove*

Conventionally, landscape has been the domain of geographers, myth that of anthropologists. The landscapes that have interested cultural geographers have been ensembles of material facts – physical environments shaped by the necessities of daily life in specific regions. Anthropologists generally have examined myths the better to understand the structure and functioning of social organisation among small-scale, generally pre-modern communities. Today, as these two disciplines converge, cultural geographers recognise the significance of myth in human shaping of the physical world, while anthropologists, like other social scientists, acknowledge the importance of space, place and landscape in the constitution of social life. So landscape and myth become subjects of common theoretical interest, distinct but articulated signifying systems through which social relations among individuals and groups and human relations with the physical world are reproduced and represented (Short 1991; Duncan 1990). As a signifying system landscape is able to contain and convey multiple and often conflicting discursive fields, or sets of shared meanings, whose claims to truth are established contextually. Myths themselves constitute discursive fields or narratives purporting to represent specific human experience, but resonating across time and space. Myths may both shape and be shaped by landscapes, not only by those localised and specific landscapes visible on the ground, but equally by archetypal landscapes imaginatively constituted from human experiences in the material world and represented in spoken and written words, poetry, painting, theatre or film (Cosgrove and Daniels 1988; Olwig 1984; Eliade 1959, 1971; Tuan 1974). Landscape is taken here in its broadest sense as the surface of the physical earth, the surface upon which humans live, which they transform and which they frequently seek to transcend. In imagination, humans tend to distinguish the earth's surface (an inscription of lands and seas, variable topography, woods, rivers, rocks and streams) from the heavens which stretch unattainably above it and the elemental depths of the inorganic world below.[1] That surface is the home of active human life, the field of our relations with nature and of our interventions in natural processes. Yet the surface does not delimit our imaginative life and it is given 'depth' or meaning only in relation to what exists above and below it.

Here I shall consider certain myths of the world's landscape as surface. I shall then turn to mythical narratives which weave human life and landscape into a commentary on individual and social action in the world. The archetypal landscapes of wilderness, garden and city offer alternative, often progressive, interpretations of how human social roles should be performed on the earth's surface. As surface the landscape is not passive; it is given a constitutive role as the stage set for the human drama itself (Earle 1991; Cosgrove 1990a, 1992). The critical and enduring question concerns the bounds within which human life and action on the earth's surface should be defined. Our capacity imaginatively to escape the bounds of landscape yet simultaneously to master natural processes and turn them to our ends here and now has always been fraught with moral ambiguity. In these last years of the twentieth century the moral questions seem particularly intense with our self-proclaimed capacity for irreversible and global transformation of the earth's surface.

We should not forget, however, that historically most peoples have seen their own socially experienced world as the whole world and thus the moral questions of environmental and landscape transformation were no less 'global' in the past than they are today. Since the idea of globality is in this sense not new it is

---

1. Various terms have been used to distinguish the sphere of life which extends above and below the land and sea surface of the earth as such, the sphere of life. *Biosphere* is the most common today. It is a region of considerable depth on a human scale, but considered in relation to both the dimensions of the globe and the height of the planets and stars it is accurately described as a surface, the surface of landscape.

worth considering present global concerns in the light of myths' historical creation of landscape meanings and their implicit commentaries upon human roles in the world. Here I shall draw upon the mythological tradition of classical Greece and Rome, a tradition that has been fundamental to much of European thought, has been reinspired and reinterpretated over time (especially during the early period of European global expansion), and which is still capable of informing the cultural discourses of western society today. The personalities and narratives of classical mythology exemplify observations on issues of environment, technology and human life in our contemporary world.

## A Mantle for Gaia

Chaos was born first and after her came Gaia the broad-breasted, the firm seat of all the immortals who hold the peaks of snowy Olympos, and the misty Tartaros in the depths of the broad-pathed earth

and Eros, the fairest of the deathless gods; he unstrings the limbs and subdues both mind and sensible thought in the breasts of all gods and all men.

Gaia now first gave birth to starry Ouranos, her match in size, to encompass all of her and be the firm seat of all the blessed gods. [Hesiod: *Theogony* 116–22, 126–29 (1983)]

From the original chaos of unformed matter a three-part physical creation places the vault of heaven above and the shades of the underworld below the surface of earth or Gaia. Hesiod's creation story (and also that of Empedocles) establishes the primacy of a vertical axis in space, and Love as a force for union. As the great struggles among the sons of Earth take their course in Hesiod's account, so the surface of Gaia becomes differentiated. But his is not a clear or consistent narrative of the primal geography of earth.

In a lesser known cosmogony, the early Sage philosopher Pherecydes offers a more precise account of the horizontal surface of earth as a uniform dimension with its own unity and significance. He differentiates between the two Greek terms for Earth: Gaia and Chthon. Three things, he says, are eternal: Zeus,

Chronos and Chthon, i.e. Sky, Time and Earth. Zeus and Chthon come together in the first marriage and during its consummation naked Chthon is transformed into Gaia: 'after three days Zeus made a wide and beautiful mantle on which are woven in all colours the world's lands and seas' and with this mantle Chthon, known only in marital intimacy to Zeus, is veiled by the lightness and beauty of Gaia's surface which hides Chthon's unknowable depths.[2] Here too we have a tripartite division of Sky, Earth and Underworld. The surface veil mediates between the light of the sky above and the dark mystery below. On it alone are inscribed forms and colours, changing and refracting light, shielding the silent blackness of the unknowable. It is upon Gaia's mantle that humans dwell and from it that their material life is sustained. In the form and colour of the Gaian mantle we recognise the first notion of landscape – a terrestrial surface of beauty and life. But the myth carries hints of landscape's limitations. Gaia is perhaps superficial, both metaphorically and literally. Zeus' mantle covers a deeper, more enduring being, inaccessible to the unaided eye, while when raised from Gaia's seductive surface the eye gazes at perfection and eternity.

This notion of the earth's surface as a mantle or veil is found also in Virgil, whose account in *Georgics* II further elaborates our understanding of the relations between heavens, earth's surface and depths along a vertical axis:

> ........in spring earth swells and yearns
> For fertilizing seed. Then it is that Heaven,
> The Father omnipotent, in pregnant showers
> Descends into the lap of his glad spouse,
> and mightily mingling with her mighty body
> Nourishes every growth.
>
> Such, I would fain imagine, were the days
> That shone upon the birth of the young world;
> Such was creation's dawn.
> [Virgil: *Eclogue* II 325–30, 338–40 (1944)]

The original creative marriage of sky and earth is repeated annually in spring as the warmth of the returning sun and the rains of heaven sink into dead ground, inseminating the fertile

---

2. The fragment from Pherecydes is quoted and discussed by Farinelli (1989) to whom I owe the original stimulus for this part of the chapter.

body of Earth, renewing the cycle of seasonal life. It is the changing seasons that alter the hues of Gaia's mantle, annually
recolouring the landscape. Their representation provides an
enduring foundation of landscape art: from the pastoral poetry of
Antiquity, to late medieval illuminations of Books of Hours and
the landscape poetry and painting of the Renaissance. In the earliest European statement on the theory of landscape painting it is
the seasons that govern the artist's palate:

> In the gentle spring we see the earth dressed in the most beautiful and
> diverse shades of green, adorned in pinks and a thousand varieties of
> flowers, with the newest leaves of the trees, and with every kind of
> bush and plant which, scarcely emerged from their maternal buds but
> begin to green. In the broad fields of summer we see the oceans of
> grain bleaching as the crop ripens, and, in parts, the leaves of the trees
> turning to ochre while the earth burns in the heat, as if its vital spirit
> were exhausted. Autumn reveals other charms and varieties of
> colours, for we see the leaves turning russet and gold with age and
> beginning to fall. Then follows naked winter, bereft of all the sweet-
> ness of both colour and air, which for the most part is overtaken by
> mists and rains and the earth by frost and snow, whose horror is
> never more clearly revealed than in the blasted trees and the earth
> shorn of all beauty. (C. Sorte, *Osservazione nella pittura*, 1580 [in
> Barrochi 1960: 288–9])

The seasons are both being and becoming. Being rests in the
eternal firmament of Ouranos and the telluric depths of Chthon.
Becoming is inscribed in landscape, the surface that lies at the
mid-point between them. However, the axis that joins these three
parts of creation is turned by Chronos: time. Absolute time is also
the measure of absolute space: the starry and fathomless vault of
Ouranos. The heavens are an eternal clock, at once measuring out
days, months and years through the passage of the heavenly bodies, and giving an astronomical geometry for measuring the
earth's surface itself. With Anaximander's invention of the gno-
mon (the vertical post which allows us to measure the length and
angle of the sun's shadow), the sun's light may be used to determine the measure of earth and the pattern of its lands and seas:
the form and outline of Gaia's mantle (Harley and Woodward
1987: 132ff).

The eternal and unchanging being of the firmament is thereby
transcribed onto the surface as pure geometry, the essence of
cartography (Woodward 1987; Alpers 1983). For the ancient

Greeks the geometrical centre of earth's surface lay at Delphos,
the point where the paths of two eagles, sent in flight by Zeus
from the poles of the globe, met. Delphos was predictably also
the mid-point on the equator drawn by Anaximander across the
breadth of the *Oecumené* from the Pillars of Hercules to the
Taurus mountains (Trip 1979: 192–3). Here was the earth's
*omphalos*, place of the cosmic egg, intersection point of the horizontal coordinates of Gaia's mantle and the vertical axis joining
heavens and underworld (Eliade 1959: 36–42). Thus, at Delphos
not only was it possible to worship the gods of the unchanging
heavens, but to touch those equally powerful and potential, but
dark and immeasurable, chthonic forces that underlie the beauty
of Gaia's mantle.

Delphos is a dramatic physical landscape: it lies in a cleft on
the rocky slopes of Parnassos with views across mountains and
vales towards the Gulf of Corinth; in the lines of *Homeric Hymn* III
(To Pythian Apollo), 'a cliff hangs over it from above, and a hollow rugged glade runs under' (quoted in Scully 1962: 108). Here
was located the most important of Apollo's temples. But its
famed oracle originally belonged to the Earth itself, represented
in myth by the snakelike monster Python whom Apollo slew in
order to take possession of the site. Apollo, as a sky god, presides
over the place where telluric powers are uniquely accessible. At
Delphos, as elsewhere, Apollo's

> most important places tell us that he was usually invoked by the
> Greeks wherever the most awesome characteristics of the old goddess
> of the earth were made manifest. Wherever her symbols were most
> remote, tortuously approached, and largest in scale, and where they
> seemed to open up the interior secrets of the earth most violently or
> most dominated a thunderous view, there the temple of the young
> god was placed, and generally so oriented as not only to complement
> but also to oppose the chthonic forces. (Scully 1962: 100)

If the landscape at Delphos links heaven with earth it also
unites the two elements of Gaia's mantle: land and sea. The
Homeric Hymn telling the story of its founding relates how,
disguised as a dolphin, Apollo led Cretan sailors to the shore-
line below Delphos and there revealed his true nature before
leading them to the site which became his temple and oracular
site.

## Gods, Humans and the Mantle of Gaia

At Delphos human and cosmic time intersect. The hero goes to the oracle, bound by the past in order to seek knowledge of the future: oracular advice on being and action. Heroic being and action animate the theatre of an Earth provided by the divine powers of nature. We shall consider the mythical human drama first in terms of the individual actor, the single human personality, and in respect of the vertical axis from heaven to underworld, and then, in a more social sense, across the surface of Gaia, as the original wilderness is transformed into the social landscapes of garden and city.

Apollo, 'perhaps the most touchingly human and the most terrifyingly sublime of all the Greek gods' (Morford and Lenardon 1985: 165), is a distinctive figure – god of youth, music, prophecy, archery and healing, a son of Zeus himself. His personality as a sky god is linked to those aspects of our human spirit which are creatively rational and objective, ethical and intellectual. Using other terms, we may speak of Apollo as representing *animus*. *Animus* implies more than spirit alone, it is thought or *logos*. It is 'the breath of consciousness', an extension of the divine mind: intelligence and awareness which has to do with reason, understanding and self-knowledge, or the active outpouring of the mind and heart (Moore 1987). In classical thought humans shared personality not only with the gods but with Earth itself. Thus Earth too has *animus, animus mundi*: 'the animus of a place does not have to be taken in any spiritualistic sense, but as the geography, the climate, the history and the character of the place informing all who come into contact with it, more so, obviously, those who dwell within it. A place emanates logos, so that its specific animus is heard and perceived; animus is not merely an organ of human intelligence' (Moore 1987: 100). Thus Gaia's Apollonian life glows within the mantle of landscape.

The Apollonian is not the only form of spirit which the surface of Earth shares with both gods and humans. It is usual to contrast the Apollonian with an opposite spirit: the Dionysian. Another of Zeus's sons, Dionysus, god of vegetation and fertile organic growth, especially of wine, is very much an earth god. His spirit is much more readily associated with the changing seasonal landscape than the enduring Apollonian landscape. Dionysus speaks to the intuitive and passionate aspects of the human spirit. In

Antiquity the association of his cult with maenads and satyrs – half human, half animal – and with sexual licence, music and unrestrained dancing referred to the non-rational and mystical union of humans with chthonic earthly forces, less *animus* than *anima*. The gendering of the Latin worlds is significant: where the landscape of Apollo is harmonious, ordered and, in the terms of eighteenth-century aesthetics, 'beautiful', that of Dionysus or Bacchus is unpredictable, wild and 'sublime' – animated and animal. This is perfectly expressed in Euripides's *Bacchae* where, in opposition to the male gendering of the Apollonian *animus*, the Bacchanalian *anima* is female (Morford and Lenardon 1985: 197–227). Social life emerges and is sustained only through the union of both spirits, a manoeuvre which may reflect a *male* historical subsumption of social reproduction and thus control over the conditions of *female* biological reproduction. This occurs in 'holy' agriculture where the husbandman's skills of planting, pruning and tending subdue the wilderness while yielding to its cyclic essence. From this perceived harmony of principles emerges a middle landscape: the cultivated garden, celebrated throughout classical literature as the foundation of human community.

The contrasting spirits of Apollo and Dionysus impose upon humans the necessity of union to continue social life on the surface of Earth, and a more cosmic individual choice along the vertical axis, of either ascending to the cool intellectual order of the planets or descending to the mysterious depths of autochthonous nature. The Renaissance humanist Pico della Mirandola in his *Oration on the Dignity of Man* expressed the same choice for the individual human soul:

> He [God] therefore took man as a creature of indeterminate nature and, assigning him a place in the middle of the world, addressed him thus: 'Neither a fixed abode nor a form that is thine alone nor any function peculiar to thyself have We given thee, Adam, to the end that according to thy longing and according to thy judgment thou mayest have and possess what abode, what form and what function thou thyself shall desire. The nature of other beings is limited and constrained within the bounds of laws prescribed by Us. Thou, constrained by no limits, in accordance with thine own free will, in whose hand We have placed thee, shall ordain by thyself the limits of thy nature'. (quoted in Heller 1978: 524)

Human life is thus fixed in neither the celestial nor the terrestrial realm. We are placed 'in the middle of the world', between

Ouranos and Chthon, precisely on the surface of Gaia. But for Pico, philosopher and contemplative, such a position does not fulfil the true destiny of God's most perfect creature. He outlines two possible options, that we may either rise through reason and self-control toward the heavens and thus become as angels, or abandon reason and follow unbridled instinct, thus sinking to the level of beasts: a choice between *animus* and *anima*, Apollo and Dionysus. Pico's language indicates his own preference, indeed his *Oration* ends with three Delphic utterances which define the highest form of human conduct, through which 'we can attain to the true divine Apollo'.

Both the Apollonian and Dionysian represent ways of *being* in the world, ways in which humans, as a part of nature, define their place in the cosmos. Each in its way removes us from the changing surface of Gaia and shifts us towards the eternal worlds of either Ouranos or Chthon. Neither of these worlds speaks to the idea of *becoming*, or to the human will progressively to transform the surface of nature, to 'engineer' the mantle of Gaia. This third, mundane, role is captured in Greek mythology not by a god, nor indeed a hero, but by the curiously ambiguous figure of Daedalus: inventor, craftsman and crafty man.[3] Daedalus is not an agriculturalist. He works with less labile aspects of the natural world so as to exploit its potential, but always risking the danger of forcing it into *un*natural paths by seeking to contain it or to overcome the limitations it imposes. His is what Renaissance thinkers would come to describe as *natural magic*, which is dependent upon the human understanding of inherent natural powers. It is neither angelic nor demonic – the dualistic terms with which Christian orthodoxy would often seek to taint experimental interventions into natural processes.

Daedalus's legend speaks of three great inventions, each located along the axis from sky to underworld. His craft begins, appropriately, on the surface, literally bringing together human and animal life in his construction of the hollow cow in which Pasipha, wife of King Minos, hides in order to be impregnated by the white bull of Poseidon with whom she has fallen in love. The hideous offspring of this unnatural union is the Minotaur,

---

3. The Greek God Hephaestus, who forges Achilles's shield and armour in the *Iliad*, is certainly a craftsman and is occasionally represented as an inventor. Significantly his club foot and ugliness suggest something of human imperfection rather than divinity.

the shadow that attends human interference with the natural order. The Minotaur is returned by Daedalus's art to the chthonic realm in the form of the Labyrinth, to be fed every nine years by the youth of Athens. For assisting Ariadne and Theseus in killing the Minotaur and escaping the Labyrinth, Daedalus and his son are imprisoned. Their escape is facilitated by the best-remembered of Daedalus's inventions, wings fashioned from wax which allow father and son to overcome the terrestrial bonds and fly across the skies. The fate of Icarus serves to remind us of the hubris which attends human invention. The indeterminacy of our place in creation imposes limits not only upon human craft but upon our capacity to behave truly as gods, and the shadow of nemesis falls even on the greatest engineer and natural magician. Each of Daedalus's inventions leads to that conclusion. Practical action is subject to the danger of hubris: Zeus and Chthon shadow the Gaian surface and only through flirting with demonic or angelic powers can we escape them. Such powers move us beyond natural magic to other, more dangerous forms of magic. More controversially, we might say that when we ignore the limits inherent in the constant and seasonal self-renewal of Gaia we *become* demonic. No specific figure emerges from classical mythology to embody such an idea. We have to await the dawn of the modern age to discern the mythical personality of Faust. We shall return to Faust, for his dilemma is especially that of our own times. In the pre-modern world the mythical transformation of Gaia's surface into ideal human landscapes always claimed to respect the cycle of life, love and generation inherent in Gaia's own relations with the moving heavens and vital chthonic forces.

### Reweaving the Gaian Mantle

Pico's view that the moral direction of individual human striving should be towards Apollo rather than Dionysus has precedents within classical theories of nature and culture.[4] Both in time and

---

4. A point which may (or may not) reflect the phallocentrism of classical patriarchy, in that the Apollonian is normally gendered male while Dionysus is frequently represented with female characteristics and accompanied above all by a chorus of lascivious women. In this respect it is worth recalling that it is the Dionysian or Bacchanalian iconography which places the phallus, quite literally, at the centre. Feminist interpretations of Earth myths are discussed in Diamond and Orestein (1990)

space the progress of social life and its corresponding landscapes are seen to move from the organic, wild and unformed towards the inorganic, controlled and ordered as ever-greater human intervention reweaves the Gaian veil. But this movement, although apparently progressive, is cyclical, returning ultimately to its point of origin and thus uniting being and becoming.

In both Hesiod and Virgil (as well as in Hebrew and Zoroastrian texts) we can trace a narrative which moves through time and space from nature towards culture (see figures 9.1 and 9.2). The narrative adopts different guises (some of them still informing the terminologies of modern archaeology and anthropology) but is best known through its metallic imagery of 'ages'. The first humans find the earth in a state of natural perfection, a perfect landscape:

> At first the immortals who dwell on Olympos
> created a golden race of mortal men.
> That was when Kronos was king of the sky,
> and they lived like gods, carefree in their hearts, shielded from pain
> and misery. Helpless old age
> did not exist, and with limbs of unsagging vigor
> they enjoyed the delights of feasts, out of evil's reach.
> A sleeplike death subdued them, and every good thing was theirs;
> the barley-giving earth asked for no toil to bring forth
> a rich an plentiful harvest. They knew no constraint
> and lived in peace and abundance as lords of their lands,
> rich in flocks and dear to the blessed gods.
> (Hesiod: *Works and Days*, 110–21 [1983])

The golden age landscape is Edenic: climatically perfect and naturally fertile, requiring no intervention on the part of humans to sustain life. According to the myth this golden race was superseded by silver and iron races who were obliged to apply progressively greater inputs of labour on the earth as its free-flowing abundance declined, and each more prone to social violence and war. Time's cyclical turning, moving through ages as it moves through days and seasons, ensures senescence in nature and its constituent elements, even as culture progresses, eventually returning nature to its primeval state (Glacken 1967). Virgil's poetic *opus* echoes this natural cycle. The *Eclogues* deal with the simplest social form: a pastoral life where humans live harmoniously with flocks and gain their sustenance with minimal invention and violence to earth, animals or each other. The

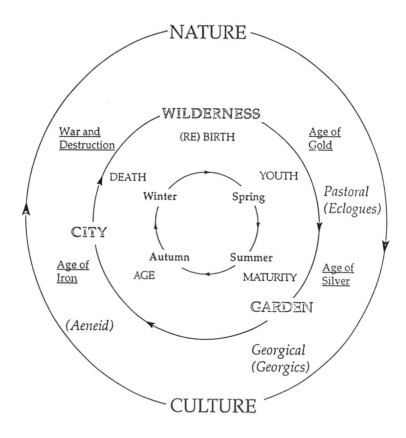

**Figure 9.1  Mythical histories of nature/culture and landscape in the classical tradition**

*Georgics* concern agricultural life where the iron ploughshare, heaved by the sweat of human and animal labour, wounds the body of earth but brings forth its harvest. Finally, the *Aeneid* deals with sophisticated and inventive urban life and the warfare that comes with competition, trade and commerce (Olwig 1984: 3ff). Warfare will ultimately lead to destruction and a return to primitive society and the wilderness state.

This temporal narrative moves from nature to culture via increasing human invention and social sophistication. Its spatial dimension is a series of symbolic landscapes from the wilderness of pristine nature, through the glades and meadows of the pastoral and the cultivated agrarian garden, to the walls and buildings of the city with its market for commerce and forum for political discourse. The social landscape itself evolves in accordance with the revolution of the natural landscape. Their common temporal cycle is rendered spatially through a concentric, cosmic pattern of the three mythic landscapes, each representing a progressively greater intervention by human design and labour in the forms and patterns of Gaia's surface (See Figure 9.2). At the centre of this mythic geography is the city, its immediate environs gardened and cultivated, and beyond the georgical landscape the more extensive pastoral economy of animal husbandry, grading finally into untouched wilderness. Nature thus passes geographically into culture: the Dionysian landscape becomes progressively Apollonian.

The metaphorical potential of this mythical geography is revealed in Figure 9.3, where its tripartite archetypal landscape is mapped across a series of discourses – spatial, social, gendered, physiological and artistic – in a hierarchy of ideal types that governed classical cultural theory from Aristotle to nineteenth-century Romanticism. Thus the realm of culture belongs to the city, above all to its central space, conventionally occupied by the forum, the theatre of power, rhetoric and political discourse. In European patriarchy this has been gendered as male space (often exclusively so) and related physiologically to the head and thus the Apollonian *animus*. In the hierarchy of the human arts the highest form of drama was tragedy; of poetry, the epic; and of painting, *historia*: picturing great historic or religious events.[5] In

5. The hierarchy of genres originates in Aristotle's *Poetics*, but was elaborated further in the Renaissance with respect to painting by Leon Battista Alberti in his *Ten Books of Architecture* and to theatre by Sebastiano Serlio and Daniele Barbaro in their books on perspective. Serlio's text is illustrated by woodcuts showing the tragic, comic and satyric scenes as, respectively, classical forum, medieval Gothic street scene and woodland glade with thatched huts.

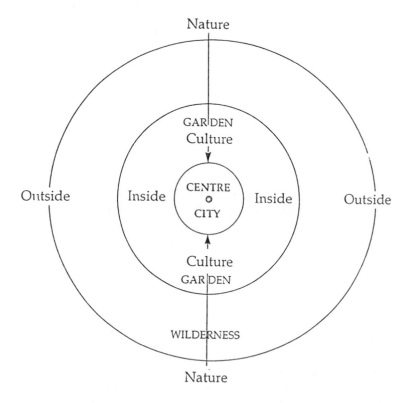

**Figure 9.2 Mythical geography of nature/culture and landscape in the classical tradition**

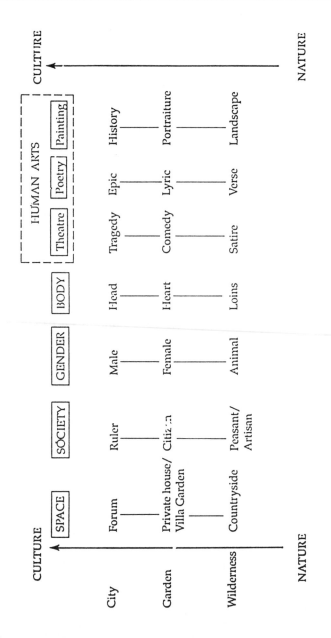

**Figure 9.3  Nature/culture homologies in life and art in the classical tradition**

each of these the proper subject matter was 'the great deeds of great men': great art was to express the rhetoric and exercise of power and authority in human society. The tragic scene is a landscape divorced from organic life, a world of stone, columns and monuments, of words, of texts. Its pattern archetypally is modelled on the pure intellectual geometry of the heavens as we see consistently in the plans of ideal cities and urban utopias.[6]

The middle landscape is that of the garden, of cultivated and lovingly controlled nature which, as we have noted, represented the marriage of Apollonian and Dionysian forces and thus the firmest basis of human community. The garden can be differentiated into its Georgical and Pastoral types, but both share common characteristics. These are landscapes of domestic economy, of the loving family and the private life of citizens. They are landscapes of labour, to be sure, but of labour that honours and complements natural processes, at one with the hours and seasons. Physiologically, this fulcrum between nature and culture is represented by the heart and it is gendered female. It provided the location for comedy in the theatre, for lyrical poetry, and for portraiture as the second-ranked genre of painting. Each of these arts was concerned with matters of love, affection and generation. The middle or garden landscape has appealed historically as an ideal for balanced and happy social life. It is landscape of the courtly pastoral: mannered conceit of those feigning weariness with the sophistication and intrigues of power; the landscape too of utopian idealists: Thomas Jefferson seeking to build America from virtuous family freeholders cultivating their individual farms across the geometric Midwestern garden; and the landscape of communalists and new-age dreamers to our own day (Rosand 1988; Marx 1962; Peebles-Smith 1988). Time's movement causes each of these three mythological landscapes to pass into the next; thus, paradoxically, the harmonious middle landscape is at once balanced and unstable, a feature long noticed by artists who from Virgil's original representation in *Eclogue* I placed funerary symbols in the pastoral landscape: 'Et in Arcadia Ego'

6. The application of Euclidean geometry to urban planning is consistent in the West from classical Greece to our own century. For an interpretation of its use in medieval new town design see Friedman (1988). Relating the pattern of streets and walls to the cardinal points is recommended by the Augustan Roman architect Vitruvius whose *Architecture* achieved particular influence among Renaissance and Baroque architects and urban theorists, while the specific representation of the celestial pattern in the order of the city is to be found in Tomasso Campanella's utopian work *City of the Sun* (1623).

(Panofsky 1970). Thus, more than wilderness or city, the middle landscape is the locus for a yearning nostalgia, a place of fleeting youthful wonder balanced between childhood innocence and cynical age.

The wilderness landscape is furthest removed from the city and civil life. It lies at both the beginning and at the end of the cycle of nature. It is the wild wood, the moor and waste, the mountain fastness and the trackless desert or marsh. If the city is gendered male and the middle landscape female, then wilderness is neuter because it is pre-social. It is the home of the animal and its inhabitants regarded as such by their more sophisticated and cultured peers in farm and city. This attitude is reflected in the physiological mapping of wilderness in the loins. Here is kept the seed which will ultimately become society; but it requires the union of male and female to become the middle landscape. In the traditional hierarchy of theatre, wilderness was the appropriate stage for the lowest genre – for satire (from those half human/half animal satyrs that accompanied Dionysus/Bacchus) or farce. We need only think of Bottom in *A Midsummer Night's Dream*, with his buffooneries and, appropriately, his ass's head, to recognise that this hierarchy is also mapped across social classes: the lowest orders are confined to the wilderness status. It is little wonder that rural *contadini* in Renaissance Italy were referred to as 'beasts'. In poetry the lowest genre was blank verse, the uncouth speech of the common people; while in painting it was 'landscape', the representation of the natural world and the idiocies of the peasants.[7] Landscape was considered suitable fresco decoration for villa walls rendered in tempera or in watercolour, but certainly not for oils on the walls of the public building or the urban palace.

Each of these archetypal landscapes is ambiguous and interpretatively open. Wilderness itself may be gendered female, the place of *anima* which requires the male Apollonian *animus* to bring forth the marriage of a middle landscape. Each landscape type takes much of its meaning from its contextual relations to others in the hierarchy/cycle. Thus the wilderness may be both scorned as the place of uncouth nature and yet honoured and

7. Wordsworth's poem 'Michael', which was consciously revolutionary in its attempt to give dignity to the voice of the shepherd (repository of moral value in his wilderness landscape), uses blank verse to reflect the intonations of everday speech, an argument made explicitly by Wordsworth and Coleridge in their *Preface to the Lyrical Ballads* of 1798.

preserved as the seedbed of social life. By the same token the city is both the pinnacle of civil society, cultured sophistication and power, and the seat of corruption and guile, even violence. Apollo and Dionysus are never truly removed from each other. It is the role of the middle landscape to keep them in harmony, but, as we have seen, here too the instability is palpable.

## The Theatre of Nationhood

The mythical frameworks and landscapes we have been considering may be less removed from contemporary life than they appear. They are perhaps so deeply rooted in the cultural unconscious of Europeans that we simply take them for granted as ways of reading our world. To give a brief example, the state and status of Britain has been the subject of sustained critical debate over the past decade, in response to a number of events and phenomena: the resurfacing of chauvinist nationalism generated by the Falklands War of 1982 and its encouragement by the Thatcher government; growing demands for cultural and political separatism in Scotland and Wales; and the fear of British national submergence within a supranational Europe. Commentators have recognised the importance of landscape in these debates over the foundation and state of the nation (Wright 1985; Lowenthal 1986; Daniels 1993). The 'landscape' of Britain does have a broad mythical structure which accords with that outlined above. At the centre is London whose dominance over provincial cities has increased consistently over the course of the century and which is unchallenged as a seat of power, culture and social privilege in Britain. Ultimately its claim to power resides in parliament, whose structure has been compared to that of the 'men's house' in other cultures (Ardener 1981; repr. 1993). Recent debates over London's townscape have been dominated by the interventions of Prince Charles: crown prince and arbiter of Establishment culture, promoting an architectural Classicism for London that represents the city as a princely capital. Charles's is the architecture of the tragic scene as conceived by Sebastiano Serlio or Inigo Jones. Equally, London has always fulfilled the other side of its mythical role: a place of corruption in both high and low places, of the arrogant court and the unprincipled speculator, of the mob and the ghetto.

Beyond London lies the *English* – significantly, not British – landscape, subject of unending study, both celebratory and critical. But the mythical English landscape is drawn from a highly localised region: the lowland counties in the south and east of the island, from 'Constable Country' in Suffolk or from the home counties such as Kent (the *garden* of England), at best from the 'clouded hills' and dales of northern limestone. It is an ordered and domestic scene of country house, cosy cottage and herbaceous border. Its small-scale lanes and hedged fields with their half-hidden villages and sentimentally 'wild' life have to be protected from the ravages of scientific farming and urban encroachment (Daniels 1991; Cox 1988). Significantly, the group most directly concerned with its conservation is the Society for the *Protection* of Rural England, the fragile middle landscape of mythical harmony between society and nature, frequently projected as the authentic landscape of all Britain.

Beyond rural England landscape lies the third archetypal landscape: the upland areas of Britain, including Wales, Scotland, and even Ireland. Here are the peripheral wilderness areas, the *national* parks. Since at least the eighteenth century, it is here that the monuments and symbols of 'ancient' Britons are located: the dolmens and henges, the speakers of original Celtic tongues. Here lie the seedbeds of the nation, areas to be *preserved* rather than protected. It is to the uplands that people trek from the metropolis to rediscover contact with supposedly untouched nature in both the landscape and themselves. The culture of the wilderness is that of the individual hiker, rambler and backpacker, its dress codes differentiated from those of both city and lowland countryside. Again, however, there is ambiguity, for the native peoples of these regions, for all that they may preserve the original spirit of the nation, are deemed rude and uncultivated, even brutish and bestial.[8]

To disclose this archetypal landscape of Britain we have stripped away much of the subtlety and ambiguity that English and British, like all other national myths, have woven into the

8. See Pringle (1988) and Gruffudd (1990). Some of the biggest of the henges of course lie safely within the confines of lowland England's garden landscape, but they have been read as relics of that first nation, left behind as the primeval wilderness was transformed and indigenous peoples were pushed to the mountainous western margins. Reference to the brutish, wild and animal characteristics of the Welsh, Scots and Irish is consistent in English representations of these peoples, for example from Cruikshank's simian-faced caricatures of Irishmen to contemporary tabloid reference to IRA 'animals'. See the papers presented at the session 'Celtic identity, national separatism and the European past', Institute of British Geographers, Annual Conference, Swansea, 1992

discourse of nature and landscape. But the bare bones thus revealed gesture towards the enduring power of a mythical tradition. Undoubtedly, parallels may be found in the other nations of Europe and perhaps beyond. The changes currently taking place in the map of European nations, especially in the east of the continent, give these myths a renewed relevance worthy of concentrated attention, for they promote powerful and often bloody passions.[9] Rather than follow these narratives here, I wish to return to the global stage of Gaia where we began, for reviving nationalism in the contemporary world parallels a debate on the appropriate ways in which humankind as a whole should live on the earth's surface, a surface now familiar to us as a single landscape represented from the depths of space in satellite images.

### Living with Gaia

The classical name of Gaia is now familiar from the thesis developed by James Lovelock (1979), positing terrestrial nature as a self-sustaining homeostatic system acting in the manner of a single organism to sustain its own life. Whatever the scientific validity of the 'Gaia thesis', its impact on popular environmental debates in the West about human interventions on the earth's surface has been very considerable. The idea that the terrestrial surface of lands and seas, existing at the mid-point between the cold majesty of space and the molten interior of Earth, is unitary and vital returns modern consciousness directly to the narratives of Earth told in classical mythology and this may account in some measure for its appeal. The vitalism implicit in the Gaia thesis reinstates a natural teleology that is fundamentally denied in the mechanical philosophy and that has been dominant in modern

9. It is worth remembering that the key legislative decade for defining national parks in the USA was 1900–10, especially under the presidency of Teddy Roosevelt. This was exactly the same decade in which the first tide of non-Anglo-Saxon immigrants peaked. Considerable fear was expressed about the pollution of America's bloodstream, especially in the cities where most of the Slavs, Italians, Jews and others settled (see Short (1991: 110–14) for a selection of quoted responses to this immigration). As far as I know the idea that the national parks should, metaphorically, preserve the 'seed' of the American nation in the face of urban racial corruption has never been examined. It is, however, noticeable even today that the cult of wilderness experience in the USA, which is to be had above all in the national parks, is dominantly a middle class WASP phenomenon. As this chapter is being written signs are appearing of boundary debates between the constituent nations of the former Soviet Union. A rich terrain for observing the contemporary power of national and landscape myths is presented there. On aspects of Russian territorial mythology see Bassin (1991).

thought since the scientific revolution (Cosgrove 1990b; Merchant 1980; Matless, 1991). The Faustian myth, elaborated by Marlowe at the dawn of the scientific revolution and again by Goethe during the Romantic revolution, offers the image of the individual human subject raised high above the Gaian surface with a gaze which masters the globe. But Faust's separation from Gaia is not achieved in order to participate in the Apollonian life celebrated by Pico (for Faust's contract recognises his ultimate mortality and damnation), but to gain a controlling perspective over terrestrial materiality during the span of an his own lifetime. Only by sundering the limiting bonds that tie human life with that of a living landscape can Faust achieve his dream of total control, and to do so requires a direct and damning embrace of the shadow recognised but feared in the Daedalan myth of classical thought, and rendered diabolical in the Christian tradition.

The vitalism implied by Lovelock's Gaia hypothesis undermines the mechanistic vision of nature found in the Faustian myth. It allows for both 'technocentric' and 'ecocentric' responses, each claiming a degree of sensitivity, absent from the Faustian dream, to the limits imposed on human action by a living nature itself. Technocentrism emphasises the capacity of human reason and intellect to guide human interactions with the natural environment, ecocentrism places greater emphasis on an intuitive grasp of our unity with nature (Pepper 1984). In this way the Gaian theory reactivates those Apollonian and Dionysian narratives so deeply rooted in our culture. Attention to those narratives within contemporary debates would require acknowledgement that neither was ever a fully adequate guide to practical daily life in the world; rather, they represented deep creative forces and continuously motivating currents in our thoughts and passions. In their marriage was to be sought a degree of harmony that, like the middle landscape, would always be unstable, contingent, and threatened with the inevitable progress and decay of time.

Thus Daedalus the craftsman, rather than Faust, perhaps represents an approriate model of practical human life within Gaia. Daedalus achieved his successes in invention, to be sure, working a natural magic through those vital forces of the surface that mediate between the cosmic and the chthonian. But his craft was, and remains, a risky business, making social landscapes out of the Gaian original. All of Daedalus's engineering feats were accompanied by the shadow: the cow promoted an unnatural sexual union, the Labyrinth hid the terror of cannibalism, conquest of the air led to the death of his son. Hubris leading to nemesis was the final act of the hero regularly played out against the tragic scene of classical theatre.

We find a powerful contemporary restatement of this theme in Paul Theroux's *The Mosquito Coast*. Its hero, Allie, is a paradigm Yankee in his practical inventiveness, resourcefulness and belief in intermediate technology. He is equally contemptuous of high-tech modernity, advertising, government, big business, and of 'savages' living in a state of nature:

> ... savagery was seeing and not believing you could do it for yourself, and that was a fearful condition. The man who saw a bird and made it into a god, because he could not imagine flying himself, was a savage of the most basic kind. There were tribes of people who did not have the sense to build huts. They went around naked and caught double-pneumonia. And yet they lived in the same neighborhood as birds which made nests and jack rabbits which dug holes. So these people were savages of utter worthlessness who did not have the imagination to come out of the rain.
>
> I'm not saying all inventions are good. But you notice dangerous inventions are always unnatural inventions. You want an example? I'll give you the best one I know. Cheese spread that you squirt from an aerosol on your sandwich. That's about as low as you can go. (Theroux 1982: 165–6)

Allie's story progesses from the metropolitan core of New England to the Olancho and Mosquitia wildernesses of Honduras. Its high point is the garden landscape of Jeronimo where his Daedalan craft brings Gaia under control, precisely by working a natural magic based upon human inventiveness in using her own rhythms and processes. But Allie's hubris, transporting the ice he has made from fire across the jungle as rhetorical proof of his power, leads, like a Greek tragedy, to the ruin of the garden, his own madness and final destruction by the nature he sought to conquer.

However, it was such heroes who strode the tragic scene, not the cautious husbandman of the middle landscape. The shadow always accompanied the heroic character. So his own humanity pushes Allie ever further, beyond the perfection of his utopian garden landscape. His story strikes a note in the contemporary world because he recognises the Faustian aspects of modernity's beliefs in conquering the Gaian surface. He rejects the Faustian bargain offered by unrestrained technology and uncontrolled markets to sell our souls in exchange for a cornucopia of material goods and thereby threaten Gaia's delicate veil. To rule Gaia, Faust substituted for patient, crafty manipulation of the surface demonic, unnatural powers that belong properly only in the heavens and the underworld. Allie seeks always to work with what can be seen and measured here on the surface of Earth. But all such landscapes of human striving are shadowed and must pass away. The nature of Gaia is surface, an intermediate point in space, its landscapes characterised precisely by their between-ness in time. Our most valid actions here on Gaia will always be contingent, even if our heads will ever incline to the certainties of the heavens and our loins to the comforts of the body of Earth.

## References

Alpers, S. 1983. *The Art of Describing: Dutch Painting in the Seventeenth Century*, London: John Murray.

Ardener, S. (ed.) 1981. *Women and Space*, London: Croom Helm. Revised edition, Oxford: Berg, 1993.

Barrochi, P. (ed.) 1960. *Trattati d'arte del cinquecento: fra manierismo e contrariforma*, Vol.1, Bari: Laterza.

Bassin, M. 1991. 'Russia between Europe and Asia: the ideological construction of geographical space', *Slavic Review* 50. 1, 1–17.

Cosgrove, D. 1990a. 'Landscape as theatre in pre- and post-modern cities' in P. Groth (ed.) *Vision, Culture, Landscape*, Working papers from the Berkeley Symposium on Cultural Landscape Interpretation, U.C. Berkeley: Department of Landscape Architecture, 221–40.

_____1990b. 'Environmental thought and action: premodern and postmodern', *Transactions, Institute of British Geographers* n.s. 15, 144–58.

_____1993. *The Palladian Landscape: Geographical Change and its Cultural Representations in Sixteenth Century Italy*, Leicester: Leicester University Press.

_____and Daniels, S. 1988. *The Iconography of Landscape: Essays on the Symbolic Representation, Design and Use of Past Environments*, Cambridge: Cambridge University Press.

Cox, G. 1988. 'Reading nature: reflections on ideological persistence and the politics of the countryside', *Landscape Research* 13. 3, 24–34.

Daniels, S. 1991. 'The making of Constable Country', *Landscape Research* 16. 2, 9–18.

Diamond, I. and Orestein, F. (eds) 1990. *Reweaving the World: the Emergence of Ecofeminism*, San Francisco: Sierra Club.

Duncan, J. S. 1991. *The City as Text: the Politics of Landscape Interpretation in the Kandyan Kingdom,* Cambridge: Cambridge University Press.

Earle, J. 1991. 'Landscape in the theatre', *Landscape Research* 16. 1, 21–30.

Eliade, M. 1959. *The Sacred and the Profane: the Nature of Religion,* New York: Harcourt Brace and World.

_____1971. *The Myth of the Eternal Return, or Cosmos and History,* Princeton NJ: Princeton University Press.

Farinelli, F. 1989. 'Pour une theorie generale de la geographie', *Georythmes* No.5, Geneva: Recherches geographiques.

Friedman, D. 1988. *Florentine New Towns: Urban Design in the Late Middle Ages,* Cambridge MA: MIT Press.

Glacken, C. 1967. *Traces on the Rhodian Shore: Nature and Culture in Western Thought from Classical Times to the End of the Eighteenth Century,* Berkeley: University of California Press.

Gruffudd, P. 1990. '"Uncivil engineering": nature, nationalism and hydro-electrics in North Wales', in D. Cosgrove and G. Petts (eds) *Water, Engineering and Landscape: Water Control and Landscape transformation in the Modern Period,* 159–73, London: Belhaven.

Gruffudd, P., Daniels, S. and Bishop, P. (eds) 1991. 'Landscape and national identity', theme issue, *Landscape Research* 16. 2, 1–48.

Harley, J. B. and Woodward, D. (eds) 1987. *The History of Cartography,* Vol.1: Cartography in prehistoric, ancient and medieval Europe and the Mediterranean, Chicago: University of Chicago Press.

Heller, A. 1978. *Renaissance Man,* London: Routledge & Kegan Paul.

Hesiod, 1983. *Theogony, Works and Days, Shield,* trans. Apostolos N. Athanassakis, Baltimore: Johns Hopkins University Press

Lovelock, J. 1979. *Gaia, a New Look at Life on Earth,* New York: Oxford University Press.

Lowenthal, D. 1986. *The Past is a Foreign Country,* Cambridge: Cambridge University Press.

_____1991. 'British national identity and the English landscape', *Rural History* 2.2, 205–30.

Marx, L. 1962. *The Machine in the Garden: Technology and the Pastoral Ideal in America,* Oxford: Oxford University Press.

Matless, D. 1991. 'Nature, the modern and the mystic: tales from early twentieth century geography', *Transactions, Institute of British Geographers* n.s.16, 272–86.

Merchant, C. 1980. *The Death of Nature: Women, Ecology and the Scientific Revolution,* London: Wildwood House.

Moore, T. 1987. 'Animus mundi, or the bull at the center of the world', *Spring* 14, 116–31.

Morford, M. P. O. and Lenardon, R. J. 1985. *Classical Mythology,* New York and London: Longman.

Olwig, K. 1984. *Nature's Ideological Landscape,* London: Allen & Unwin

Panofsky, E. 1970. '"Et in arcadia ego": Poussin and the elegaic tradition', in *Meaning in the Visual Arts,* 340–67, Harmondsworth: Penguin.

Peebles-Smith, R. 1988. *Landscape and Written Expression in Revolutionary America*, Cambridge: Cambridge University Press.

Pepper, D. 1984. *The Roots of Modern Environmentalism*, London: Croom Helm.

Pringle, T. 1988. 'The privation of history: Landseer, Victoria and the highland myth' in Cosgrove and Daniels 1988, 142–61.

Rosand, D. 1988. *Places of Delight: the Pastoral Landscape*, London: Weidenfeld and Nicolson.

Scully, V. 1962. *The Earth, the Temple and the Gods: Greek Sacred Architecture*, New Haven and London: Yale University Press.

Short, J. R. 1991. *Imagined Country: Society, Culture and Environment*, London: Routledge.

Taylor, P. 1991. 'The English and their Englishness: a curiously mysterious, elusive and little known people', *Scottish Geographical Magazine* 107, 3. 146–61

Theroux, P. 1982. *The Mosquito Coast*, Harmondsworth: Penguin.

Tripp, E. 1979. *The Meridian Handbook of Classical Mythology*, New York: Meridian.

Tuan, Y. F. 1974. *Topophilia: a Survey of Environmental Perception, Attitudes and Values*, Englewood Cliffs: Prentice Hall.

Virgil, 1944. *The Eclogues and the Georgics*, trans. R. C. Trevelyan, Cambridge: Cambridge University Press.

Woodward, D. (ed.) 1987. *Art and Cartography, Six Historical Essays*, Chicago: University of Chicago Press.

Wright, P. 1985. *On Living in an Old Country: the National Past in Contemporary Britain*, London: Verso.

# Chapter 10

## Sexual Cosmology: Nation and Landscape at the Conceptual Interstices of Nature and Culture; or, What does Landscape Really Mean?

*Kenneth Robert Olwig*

The Hebrews were forbidden to utter the name of God, so they used the word 'Yahweh', which is thought to mean something like 'that which we may not say'. The word landscape, like Yahweh, also contains meanings which, because they are left unsaid, mystify and increase their power. 'Landscape', I will argue, along with 'nature', 'nation' and 'culture', is integral to an ongoing 'hidden' discourse, underwriting the legitimacy of those who exercise power in society. All four concepts are linked, furthermore, by a sexual cosmology which is fundamental to the very notion of 'legitimacy'.

It is characteristic of the four words that despite their multiplicity of value laden meanings, they tend to be used as if their meaning were unambiguous and God-given, thus 'naturalising' the particular conception which remains hidden behind a given usage. There would even seem to be a direct relation between the frequency with which a word is used, and its ambiguity. In the case of 'landscape', for example, there is no agreement, even among scientific users of the word, whether it refers to 'the land-forms of a region in the aggregate' or 'a portion of area that the eye can comprehend in a single view, vista, prospect' (Webster 1963: landscape; Hard 1970). This is not, however, an argument for the elimination of such polyvalent words, and their replacement by supposedly more neutral, univalent concepts. It doesn't help to keep adding 'Yahweh' words to the language. When we use words like environment and ecology instead of words like landscape and nature, it is only that much more difficult to elucidate the concealed, congealed, layers of meaning in the discourse of power. The significance of the difference between the conception of landscape as scenery, and landscape as enclosed area, thus becomes surprisingly intelligible when the different meanings are traced to their origins in separate, if related, discourses on landscape and the legitimacy of power, which had their intellectual epicentres in different parts of Europe, in differing periods of history. Close attention to the wealth of information in a common etymological dictionary greatly facilitates such an endeavour. The definitions of the key words used here are printed in the appendix.

The first part of this chapter analyses the transformations undergone by the concepts of landscape, nature, culture and nation working together as a 'synergism', in which each concept is seen to define and colour the other. In this context, I make considerable use of textual examples, because they serve to explicate the way the different terms work together in 'poetic synergy'. The second part exemplifies the significance of these transformations in the context of several pivotal, historical examples. My point of departure is the poetry of the classical author Virgil, because his work has played a definitive role in discourse on nature, nation, culture and landscape throughout the history of western civilisation (Olwig 1984: 1–10). The other key figure, discussed in part two, is Thomas Jefferson who, it has been argued, attempted to create a new nation in the image of the Virgilian pastoral (Marx 1964). Put briefly, it can be said that Virgil linked the concepts one to the other on an abstract poetic plane, whereas Jefferson sought to reify *poesis* in the context of a concrete place. Both, in my view, were notable because they compressed so many tendencies of their time in their life's work. As a means of exemplifying the pivotal transition in the concepts of landscape, nation and nature occurring between Jefferson and Virgil I have focused on the eighteenth-century landscape garden at Stourhead.

## I

### Landscape, Nature, Nation

The word landscape is often used interchangeably with the word nature, and nature is, as Raymond Williams laconically puts it, 'perhaps the most complex word in the language' (Williams 1976: 184). The two concepts have had a long and somewhat parallel lexical development within the Germanic (landscape) and Romance (nature) languages respectively.

Nature shares its root *nat* with words like *nat*ive and *nat*ion. It is this cognate linkage, I would venture, which subtly informs the history of these words, giving them a synergistic power which they would not have on their own. Consider the way Shakespeare links natural inheritance and nation to legitimise power over the social commonalty in a scene where the emissary from 'brother England' demands the French throne for King 'Harry' which:

> By law of *nature* and of *nations*, 'longs
> To him and to his heirs; namely, the crown,
> And all wide-stretched honours that pertain
> By *custom* and the ordinance of times
>
> He sends you this most memorable line,
> In every branch truly demonstrative;
> Willing you overlook this pedigree:
> And when you find him sevenly derived
> From his most famed of famous ancestors,
> Edward the Third, he bids you then resign
> Your crown and kingdom, indirectly held
> From the *native* and true challenger.
>   (Shakespeare, *Henry V*, (Act II, scene iv), 1948: 466; my italics )

The English philosopher R.G. Collingwood tells us that the word nature, in its original classical sense, referred primarily to a cosmological 'principle' of 'development, growth or change' which takes successive forms so that 'each is the potentiality of its successor' (Collingwood 1960: 43–8). This process of growth, however, is, in turn, the product of a nascent birthing process, as the Australian philosopher, John Passmore, reminds us: 'The word 'nature' derives, it should be remembered, from the latin *nascere*, with such meanings as 'to be born', 'to come into being'. Its etymology suggests, that is, the embryonic, the potential rather than the actual' (Passmore 1974: 32). The inborn natural nature of native and nation, claimed by King Henry, is thus a product of a natural in*nate* creative birthing principle which makes growth and development, and the rebirth inherent in these processes possible. [1]

This notion of nation as being constituted by the native born precedes the idea of nation as territory. The nation is essentially a people to which you belong by virtue of being born into that people. The way in which people interact culturally affects, however, the character of the place where they dwell. This, in turn, can lead to the development of a more permanent bond between the nature, or character, of the culture of a particular people and the nature, or character, of the particular areas where they dwell.[2]

The word landscape shares many features of the twin words, nation and nature. The word 'scape' has been spelled in a myriad of ways in various times and places in the Germanic languages. The most common spellings still in use in modern English are 'ship', as in the word 'township' and, as a verb, 'shape', in the sense of creating by shaping, or, more precisely, 'carving out'. Another permutation of the suffix is 'shaft', a word which can be applied in various Germanic languages, including English, to objects with a shape which is suitable for carving something out. Other permutations of the suffix, however, are applied to objects which have a hollowed-out shape, such as 'ship' or, in Danish,

1. It is also, however, a principle which is naturally most apparent at the time of actual birth, or origin. This is why nature came to refer to: '7a: man's original or natural condition, b: a simplified mode of life resembling this condition' (Webster 1963). This definition, however, represents a more modern and simplified concretisation of the classical meaning of the term, which referred to a cyclical (or spiral), rather than a linear process where nature is located at the beginning of the process, and culture at the end.

2. It is this bond which makes it reasonable to term a particular area a nation, and to call the particular character of its environment its 'nature' in the physical sense. But it is not before the Renaissance, or even the Enlightenment, that this usage of nation becomes particularly evident in English (Williams 1976: 178). Note the subtle way, in the definition of nature quoted in the appendix, in which the meaning shifts from that of a people defining an area to that of an area defining a people.

*skab*, meaning closet. The word, as might be expected, also has been applied to both the male and female procreative organs (*Ordbog over det Danske Sprog* 1931: *'skab'*, *'skabe*; Oxford English Dictionary 1971: 'shape'), as well as to the physical fitness necessary to engender sexual desire, as in 'get in shape' and 'shapely'. The word nature has likewise been applied to the procreative organs, as well as to the various secretions identified with them (semen, menstrual blood) (Oxford English Dictionary 1971: 'nature'). Like nature, 'shape' is a word which is applied not only to such literal dimensions of the birthing process, but also, as in the following Danish, German and English definitions, to more abstract notions of 'organic growth' 'determined by nature' (*Ordbog over det Danske Sprog* 1931: *'skab'*, *'skabe'*), or 'the creative power of nature' (Collins-Klett 1983: *'schaffen'*) or 'to create, fashion, form . . . (said of God or Nature)' (Oxford English Dictionary 1971: 'shape').

Whereas the suffix 'scape' has parallels to the original sense of the word nature, the words land and landscape bear similarities to the word nation. The word 'land', of course, is used synonymously with the word nation to this day. It refers to a territory belonging to a people and is present in the name of a number of nations, such as England and Holland. In a Germanic language such as Danish the prefix 'land' refers both to an 'open space' or 'parts of the surface of the earth which have been taken into use by people; particularly to (parts of) the surface of the earth used for . . . agriculture', and, reflexively, to a place identifiable with the people who have taken it into use (*Ordbog over det Danske Sprog* 1931: *'land'*). The medieval Danish landscape laws were based upon the customary law of particular areas of the country identified with particular peoples, much as a township is the area belonging to a town. Swedish landscapes, such as Gotland (land of the Gots, or 'Goths'), remain loci of Swedish regional identity, though they have lost political importance. Natives from a given landscape will thus join their landscape's 'nation' (a brotherhood, something like an American fraternity) while attending the university.

The various usages of the term landscape thus suggest that the landscape is an area carved out by axe and plough, which belongs to the people who have carved it out. It carries the suggestion of being an area of cultural identity based, however loosely, on tribal and / or blood ties, and thus bears, with the word nation, a counterpositional relation to the concept of the state as a more formal governmental organisation. It is thus characteristic of this distinction that the Aaland Islands, which have a semi-autonomous status as a culturally Swedish territory under the Finnish state, are officially 'called' a landscape. The word nation is similarly used, for example, to refer to peoples, such as the Croatians or the Scots who, at various times in history, have retained a certain amount of autonomous identity even though they may have existed within an encompassing state.

We are dealing here, however, with connotative rather than denotative meaning; with the traces of meaning which are the stuff of poetry more than of science. At one time and place the word landscape, in the territorial sense, may be as neutral and straightforward as the word 'township'. At another time such a word can, by devious etymological routes, gather together an ideologically potent plethora of meanings. These are all the more powerful because the scientific mind tends to ignore them rather than confront them, belonging as they do more to poetic than scientific rationality. This sort of lexical renaissance occurred in the course of the nineteenth century when, in the context of nationalistic political movements, landscape became something of a ruling passion in many nations, particularly Germany. This resulted, among other things, in the emergence of a geographic science of 'landscape'. The concept of landscape used here was a conscious return to a revived ancient Germanic conception of landscape as territory (Hard 1970). This landscape was, however, analysed primarily as the tangible, physical surface of the earth. The landscape was dichotomised into a 'natural' landscape, preceding man, opposed to a cultural landscape which man superimposes upon the areal surfaces defined by nature. This kind of geography provided a justification for a *Blut und Boden* ideology which was important to an emergent state seeking to incorporate Germanic peoples from within the boundaries of other states (Gröning and Wolschke-Bulmahn 1987). Oswald Spengler's reference to 'cultures that grow with original vigor out of the lap of a maternal natural landscape, to which each is bound in the whole course of its existence' (quoted in Sauer 1969: 325), amply illustrates the metaphoric, and ideological, potency of the term landscape when linked to that of nature and culture in this way. The use of the word landscape, in English, to mean the physical topography of an area in the landscape history approach of writers such as W.G. Hoskins (Hoskins 1955) is identifiable with this revived Germanic use of the term. The political implications of this approach to landscape are less pronounced in Britain, but such works participate, nevertheless, in a subtle discourse on the nature of the nation.

## Nature, Nation, Culture

In its original, classical sense nature and culture were not polar opposites, quite the contrary. Culture was, if anything, the worship of nature. The meaning of the word has changed, along with many changes which have occurred in the meaning of nature, making it, along with nature, 'one of the two or three most complicated words in the English language' (Williams 1976: 76; see also appendix to this chapter).

The ultimate root meaning of culture is the Latin word *colere* which had a range of meanings such as 'inhabit', 'cultivate', 'protect', 'honour with worship'—the word cult meant 'care' or 'adoration'. It was also related to the Greek *kyklos* which refers to circularity and cyclicality, and thus contains an implication of wheel-like reciprocity through time. The notion of culture as a means of developing the potentiality of the soil is then quite close to the concept of nature as elucidated by Passmore above. Culture, in the classical sense, was society's way of participating, via care (e.g. of the land), in a cyclical natural process in which the natural, in-born potentiality of society and its environment was made manifest. In the classical texts, human beings ceased being barbaric animals when they formed a settled community which shared its common resources in the breeding and grazing of tamed animals on the common fields of a given area. These activities required the pruning and felling of trees, the planting of grass, and the regulation of watercourses. The pastoral economy shaped the environment. The nature, or character, of the 'pastoral' environment, with 'no fence or boundary-stone' (Virgil, *Georgics* I: 151–2, 1946: 69), was expressive of the cultural breeding of the community which created it. The next stage in this natural process of development was believed to be the cultivation of the soil through agriculture. Agriculturalists were seen to preserve the community values of their pastoral predecessors, even though fields were cultivated individually. The next stage in this process was the development of the city, which enabled a natural exchange of products between areas producing different things (Olwig 1984: 2–10). This cycle was seen as being repeatable, and it is this sort of notion, of course, which is latent in the concept of Renaissance–rebirth.

Pastoral society was widely believed, in classical times, to have originated in a rugged and chilly area of Greece called Arcadia. The historian Polybius (?205–?125 bc), himself a native of Arcadia, made an account of the region which illustrates how the various meanings of culture linked together. Life in Arcadia was thus characterised by 'common assemblies and sacrifice . . . in common for men and women, and choruses of girls and boys together'. These collective cyclical 'cultic' rites, involving competitions in athletics and what we would call 'the arts' (especially music and dance), had the effect of 'smoothening and softening' the effects of a harsh environment, much as the Arcadians smoothed and softened their physical environment (quoted in Lovejoy and Boas 1935: 345–8, from Historia IV: 19–21; see also: Olwig 1984: 2–10). Here we see an expression of the full range of meanings identified with culture, such as 'inhabit', 'cultivate', 'protect' and 'honour with worship'. These meanings, furthermore, were quite parallel to those generated, in the ancient Germanic languages, in connection with the idea of agricultural land 'scaped' by a people, thereby generating an identity between people and lands. The Old Norse word 'dyrka' is similarly used to refer both to the cultic devotion to a deity, and the cultivation of the soil, and modern day equivalents can still be applied, like the word 'cultivate', to the 'arts' (*Ordbog over det Danske Sprog* 1931: 'dyrke').

Polybius's account is, according to the geographer Clarence Glacken, 'the first full exposition . . . of the idea that an environment produces a certain kind of ethnic character, which by conscious, purposive, and hard work, can be counteracted by cultural institutions (such as music) which are all-pervasive. Here the transition from a primordial state (probably of barbarism, induced by the environment) to civilisation is made by the conscious decision of a body of culture-heroes or elders' (Glacken 1967: 96). The natural nature of the natives is thus not a direct product of the environment (which merely creates barbarism), but of a process of cultivation which is expressed in the culture of the Arcadians. Virgil built upon this by linking the idea that

Arcadia was the birthplace of cultured society with ancient myths concerning the origin of man in a paradisiacal Golden Age. Arcadia was thereby transformed into an idyllic pastoral birthplace for lyric song, poetry and love. Culture thus became, in Virgil's tender hands, distinctly linked to the origin of the arts and hence to 'high culture', as well as to more lowly forms such as agriculture, and related rural seasonal cultic ritual.

Virgil is a key 'classical' figure in subsequent western discourse on nature, culture and nation because his writings represent an apparently conscious attempt to create a body of literature which would play, for the Roman nation, the same ideological role which the work of Homer played for the Greek. His image of the pastoral genesis of the nation in the *Eclogues*, or its further development into an agricultural society, as described in the *Georgics*, or the birth of the Roman state itself, as chronicled in the epic *Aeneid*, is thus loaded with symbolic meaning concerning the relationship between nature, culture and nation. Thus, even though the word landscape is not present in his writing, it became one of the primary sources of inspiration for the modern concept of landscape.

Later conceptualisations of culture as representing an educational process and a stage of civilisation, were thus nascent in the most influential, 'classic' literature of the ancient past. The original identification of culture with agriculture, furthermore, tended to persist, as we shall see, well into modern times, though it is seldom so apparent as in Francis Bacon's pungent reference from 1605 to 'the culture and manurance of minds' (quoted in Williams 1976: 77).

## Sexual Politics

We have been dealing with metaphors which are heavily laden with psychological power, and which seem to be able to generate an entire cosmology. This is the thrust of the argumentation of the seminal authority on this subject, Sigmund Freud:

> The female genitalia are symbolically represented by all such objects as share with them the property of enclosing a space or are capable of acting as receptacles; such as pits, hollows, and caves . . . . The complicated topography of the female sexual organs accounts for their often being represented by a landscape with rocks, woods, and water . . . . If you

have chanced to wonder at the frequency with which landscapes are used in dreams to symbolize the female sexual organs, you may learn from mythologies how large a part has been played in the ideas and cults of ancient times by 'Mother Earth' and how the whole conception of agriculture was determined by this symbolism (quoted in Shepard 1967: 97).

This statement is interesting not only because of the way in which Freud has taken possession of a sexual cosmology, but equally for the way in which that cosmology has taken possession of him! It could just as well have been the concept of (agri)culture which determined the symbolism of Mother Earth as the reverse. It is not necessary to posit a primitive 'natural', subliminal, psychological mother fixation, to explain the potency of the notion of Mother Earth. It is readily apparent to any farmer that there is something going on between the sky and the earth which is critical to the fertility of the land. Much as the fertility of women is periodic, so too is the fertility of the soil, and both seem to be determined by the cyclical movements of the heavenly bodies. In spring, the heavens supply the rains from which the seed emerges from the dark and moist earth as from a womb, and the spring lambs and hares are born on grassy slopes. The metaphorical power of this symbolism is given poetic force by Virgil:

> Spring showers her leafy blessings on the trees,
> Spring clothes the woods; in spring the swelling
>     earth
> Demands the seed of life. Then Father Air
> With fruitful rains omnipotent descends
> Upon the bosom of his smiling bride,
> And with her greatness mingling greatly feeds
> Her teeming womb. Then pathless brakes
>     resound
> With birds in full song; cattle seek their kind
> On certain days; the gravid earth brings forth,
> And to warm Zephyr fields unbind their
>     breasts;
> The gentle moisture freely flows
> . . . .
> Thus dawned, I trow, the birthday of the
>     world.
> (Virgil, *Georgics* II: 380–420, 1946: 106–107)

As sexual beings we participate, vicariously, in the cosmic coitus described in such a poem. We also, however, 'cultivate' our sexuality by giving it cultural form, thereby giving shape to our interior psychological environment much as the Arcadians 'smoothed and softened' their exterior environment. The predominant theme of love in pastoral poetry is no accident, it is part and parcel of its natural theme. The cultic ritual, dancing, for example, around a springtime maypole, is a physical way of participating in the cosmic natural generative process while, at the same time, physically cultivating one's body, and one's impulses, by giving them cultural form. Ploughing the earth provided yet another means of doing so. This can be seen in the earliest record of the ancient Scandinavian rock carvings, as well as in the cultivated writings of the American founding fathers, who saw themselves carving a nation out of a land which they saw to be:

> Like a faire virgin, longing to be sped,
> And meete her lover in a Nuptiall bed.
> (quoted in Kolodny 1975: 12)

The process of carving out a landscape from 'virgin' nature, and thereby giving it cultural form creates an 'enclosed' topological space, which not only has Freudian implications, but which defines an organic territory, shaped from within, becoming thereby the *place* of belonging of the people who shaped it. This is the sort of organic space to which we naturally relate in very fundamental ways. Bonds of this 'natural' sort, like bonds of kinship, therefore provide the model for a myriad of systems of social control and government, from tribal chieftains to kings, as was seen in the quotation from *Henry V*.

## Nature and Landscape Scenery: The 'Semiotic Shift'

The word nature, as a statement of the inborn character of something, implies a norm. It is natural to conform to that inborn character, unnatural to deviate from it. Nature, in this sense, has been said to be the most powerful normative concept in western thought (Lovejoy 1927: 444). A culture, whether it be that of a field, nation or organic yoghurt, is thus natural and normal when it conforms to the natural generative creative principle, and abnormal, and unnatural, when it does not.

The central motif of Virgil's art was the counter-position of some form of 'natural' rural society to the 'unnatural' urban imperial power which Rome had become. Virgil often conveys this natural or unnatural quality through the symbolic medium of the environment. A healthy fertile environment is the expression of a natural society, and a desiccated desertified one (the 'negative pastoral', see Williams 1973)) is the expression of an unnatural society.

A number of transitions occured in the meaning of the words nature, nation and landscape in the course of the Renaissance which, taken together, were the prerequisite for the generation of the modern meanings of these words. This involved, in the case of the word nature, a gradual process of reification in which nature became one with the environments used to symbolise the natural. The first step in this process was signalled by a passage in Dryden's translation of Virgil's *Georgics* of 1697, in which he writes: 'Surveying Nature with too nice a view' (Oxford English Dictionary 1971: 'nature' def. 13). Nature, hereby, for the first time in history, becomes scenery.

The term which came to be applied at this time to such scenic depictions of nature was 'landscape'. Landscape thus became virtually synonymous with the word nature, in the scenic sense: 'a picture representing a view of natural inland scenery'. Landscape was the word the Dutch applied, quite naturally, to paintings of the countryside. When English connoisseurs imported them, they were not called 'countryside pictures', or 'natural scenes of the land', but 'landscapes'. In this way, landscape came to mean '1a: a picture representing a view of natural inland scenery'. In the course of time the word underwent a further process of transition from '1b: the art of depicting such scenery' to '2a: the landforms of a region in the aggregate', '2b: a portion of land that the eye can comprehend in a single view', and '3: VISTA, PROSPECT' (Webster 1963). There is thus a transition from a term referring to a painting, to a way of painting, to the material subject matter of the painting. Thus, as in the case of nature, the meaning of the word landscape is reified. Its meaning is transferred from an artistic symbol, to the concrete world depicted in that symbol. One consequence of this process is that the original Germanic meaning of landscape, as an enclosed area identifiable with a people, is replaced by a meaning in which landscape becomes a scene, projecting into infinity, defined by a given individual viewpoint.

The language of semiotics helps clarify the significance of the transformations occurring in the words nature and landscape. We are not simply dealing with an external accretion of meaning, but with a 'semiotic shift' which occurs within the very means by which we express ourselves, and which is responsible for much of the difficulty which we have in interpreting the meaning of landscape and nature (see Figure 10.1). A painted landscape is a concrete thing, a 'signifier' which signifies an abstract meaning, often a normative conception of the way things 'naturally' ought to be if they are to conform to the natural order of things (see figure 10.2). The painting does this, however, by *referring* to some familiar external concrete phenomenon, e.g. a pastoral environment, which in a given culture is identified with the abstract meaning which the signifier (the painting) signifies, e.g. a 'natural' form of society. The artwork 'refers' to this external 'reality' usually through some form of artistic convention, such as that of the pastoral. The pastoral environments depicted in artworks thus need not have any direct correlation with environments in the 'real' world. A shift in meaning occurs here, in which the meaning of the word landscape ceases to be applied primary to the signifier (the painting), or to an artistic genre, but is transferred to the external referent of that painting e.g. the concrete pastoral environment. At the same time, we see that the use of the word nature changes so that it ceases to be applied primarily to the signified abstract meaning, and comes to be applied first to the artistic signifier (a scene described by Virgil), and then to the artistic referent (a given physical environment). This process is facilitated, furthermore, by an increasing 'realism' in art, by which the artistic signifiers (e.g. landscape paintings) come to resemble, more and more, actual places. The ultimate 'realism' is achieved, as shall be seen in part two, when the artistic signifier is a landscape garden which is virtually indistinguishable from the surrounding countryside (see Figure 10.3).

When landscape and nature become one with a physical environment, this environment does not cease to bear value-laden, normative meanings concerning the natural. On the contrary, those meanings become even more naturalised because they no longer appear to derive from an artistic scene composed by a subject, an author or artist, but from objective physical reality itself.

In the same period that nature and landscape become a physical scene the meaning of the word nation is also imperceptibly transformed so that it comes to be applied to a politically defined territory, rather than to the native race of people inhabiting that territory. It thus seemed 'natural' for the young American state to

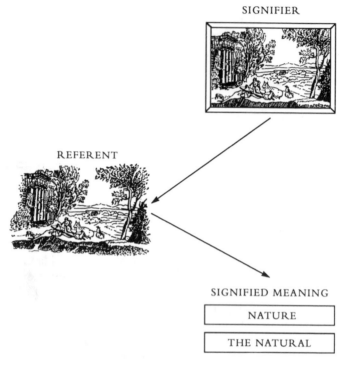

Figures 10.1–10.4 Figures 10.1, l0.2, 10.3, and 10.4 illustrate what I have termed a 'semiotic shift.' They should be studied in conjunction with the definitions of nature and landscape in the appendix.
Figure 10.1 The landscape painting is, in the terminology of semiotics, a 'signifier'. It is a 'landscape' in the earliest sense of the word in modern English, i.e. it is 'a picture of natural inland scenery' (see Appendix 1a). To generate meaning the signifier *refers* to something external to itself which is familiar to the person looking at the signifier, in this case a pastoral environment. The meaning connoted by the signifier is a matter of interpretation, but historically such scenes often symbolised the abstract meanings of nature listed under numbers one to four – e.g. 'inherent character', 'creative force' etc. A 'semiotic shift' occurs when the term 'landscape' ceases to be applied, first and foremost, to the signifier, the painting, and becomes applied to the referent, an actual environment (see Appendix, 'landscape' definitions 2 and 3, e.g. 'landscape' 2b: 'a portion of land that the eye can comprehend in a single view'. A 'trace' of the original meaning persists, however, in so far as 'landscape' still tends to be defined as something seen from the perspective of someone viewing or painting a picture. At the same time as this shift in the meaning of landscape occurs, the meaning of the word 'nature' also shifts so that it is also applied to the referent, conceived of as landscape – i.e. 'nature,' 'natural scenery'. Fig. by Ulla Hoffman for K.R. Olwig.

**Figure 10.2** The drawing of Claude Lorrain's painting from c. 1660, *'Landscape with Mercury and Argus'*, signifies an ideal nature inspired by the ancient poets. It is found in the National Gallery, London.

Figure 10.3 Henry Hoare's park at Stourhead was inspired both by the poetry of the ancient poets, particularly Virgil, and by landscape painting in the style of Claude. It is an artwork, and, as such, as much a signifier as Claude's painting, but it represents a subtle shift towards meanings 2 and 3 in the definition of landscape (see Appendix). It is an artwork, but it is also an actual place and it is difficult to know to what extent that actual place is a signifier, or the referent for a signifier. Photo K.R. Olwig.

Figure 10.4 Yellowstone, from 1872, is the first national park. The environment was not shaped by an artist, but it was bounded and framed and protected from change by people who perceived it as park landscape in the tradition of landscape park architecture. They also saw it as a signifier of natural values. In this case, it is almost impossible to distinguish the signifier from the referent. The semiotic shift is now virtually complete because most people, no doubt, would apply the words landscape and nature primarily to the concrete place, i.e. the 'natural scenery' of Yellowstone, and not to the park as a landscape signifier of abstract natural values. Photo Thomas Vale.

pass a law requiring that to be president one must be born in the U S A, (and therefore be native born), regardless of parentage, but it would have been unthinkably unnatural for Henry V, in Shakespeare's play, to be denied his 'native' right to the throne of France because he was not born there. For him, and for Shakespeare, his legitimacy as heir to the throne of France was primarily an issue of birth and breeding, not a question of where he happened to be born.

The final shift which I see taking place within this whole interrelated constellation of meanings is the shift, implied in the notion of nature as landscape scenery, to an essentially terrestrial, and hence feminine, concept of nature. The key to understanding this further semiotic shift lies in the way landscape is represented as scenery. There is a sleight of hand whereby the very structure of landscape perceived as scenery, as in a landscape painting, becomes a means of representing a concept of nature in which both the male and female poles are present, but only the female is visible to the naked eye in the form of the represented terrestrial shapes. The male principle is present, on the other hand, as the invisible structuring geometries which create the illusion of infinite spatial depth.

II

### The Structure of Nature

Virgil expressed his concept of the natural creative process of nature via a poetic retelling of a myth in which nature is conceived, in the most literal way, through intercourse between a celestial male principle and a terrestrial female principle. It is the sort of ancient mythic material to which Freud also referred, but I do not believe the myth should be interpreted entirely as a kind of cultural sublimation of basic human psychological relations. It is more useful to see this myth, in Lévi-Strauss's sense, as a means of resolving structurally unresolvable oppositions of both an experiential and an ontological sort (Lévi-Strauss 1967). This seems to be the way Virgil saw the problem, and this may explain why his works remained so central to western discourse on nature, culture, nation and landscape, through many centuries of historical change.

The opposition between the celestial and terrestrial concepts of the nature of being is expressed in a passage where Virgil asks the

Muses to instruct him in the power of celestial nature, and hence:

> In all the ways of heaven and the stars,
> The sun's eclipses and the travailings
> That vex the moon; what makes the earth to shake,
> What power persuades the mighty sea to swell.
> Break bounds and refluent on himself recoil;
> Whence is that eagerness of winter suns
> To plunge in ocean, whence the long delay
> That binds the lingering nights.

But he then appears to acknowledge that this quest for knowledge runs counter to a very different kind of natural wisdom:

> But if the blood
> Run cold about my heart, nor suffer me
> To touch these mysteries of Nature's realm,
> Green fields and stream-fed valleys be my joy,
> Rivers and woodlands be my humble love.
> Happy was he whose wit availed to grasp
> The origin of things . . . .
> Blest too is he who knows the rural gods,
> (Virgil, *Georgics* II: 570–89; 1946: 114–15)

These last lines point up the divergence between a mode of rational, mathematical and geometrical knowledge, identifiable with the perfect, timeless celestial spheres, and a sort of organic, biological wisdom, identifiable with terrestrial existence. We are dealing, it would seem, with the same sort of epistemological impasse which not only divides physics from biology as science, but which also characterises entire historical eras. The notion that 'the book of nature was written in mathematical figures' expressed by the astronomer Galileo (quoted in Collingwood 1960: 94), was appropriate to an age which learned to interpret nature in terms of a giant celestial clock or machine, ticking away within an infinite Newtonian space. Yet, by the nineteenth century, nature tends to be described in terms of organic, terrestrial forms. The concept of nature can thus, in Arthur O. Lovejoy's words, 'slip more or less insensibly from one ethical or esthetic standard to its very antithesis, while nominally professing the same principles' (Lovejoy 1927: 444). The reason that it can do this is that the meaning of nature was, in fact, merely slipping from one pole to another within a nature which is a unity of opposites. The unity is the sexual cosmology in which a female earth and a male sky are conceptually linked in a seminal process of cosmic intercourse.

The knowledge of the nature of the heavens, for Virgil, is linked to the sorts of knowledge cultivated in cities for use in trade, war and imperial dominance. The worshipper of rural nature is happy because:

> He regards no lictor's rod;
> No royal robes distract his gaze
> Nor Rome's own turmoil and the doom that
>         broods
> O'er other kingdoms; never pitied he
> Him that hath not, nor envied him that hath.
> What fruits the branches, what the willing earth,
> Freely afford, he gathers, nor beholds
> State archives, ruthless laws and city broils. . . .
> And gloats o'er buried gold.

Rural community provides a natural antidote to the celestial extremes of unnatural imperial urbanism. Thus, while some dwellers of imperial Rome 'wade through brothers' blood, triumphant, changing all the sweets of home for exile kingdoms 'neath an alien sky':

> Meantime the husbandman with crooked plough
> Has cleft the earth: hence labour's yearly meed,
> Hence feeds he little child and fatherland.
> Such was the life the Sabines lived of yore,
> Such Remus and his twin; 'twas this, in sooth,
> That made Etruria strong, and Rome herself
> The fairest thing the world hath ever seen.
>    (Virgil *Georgics* II :589–641; 1946: 115–17)

The modern anthropologist Victor Turner operates with a set of oppositions similar to Virgil's in his discussion of the relationship between the structured, hierarchical world of the city and state, and that of *'communitas'*, which builds upon a feeling of egalitarian brotherhood. The two forms of social organisation are, conceptually and experientially, mutually incompatible, with the result that they must be mediated by myth and ritual. The passage from one to the other takes place via a rite which allows one to cross the limen, or invisible boundary between them. A pilgrimage is a very literal form of such passage in which people often move from urbanised core areas of the state, to rural areas which are often perceived to be the core of the ancient national homeland of a given people within a state. Through the process of travelling together by primitive means and in common dress, people form ties which cross social boundaries. Such pilgrimages are necessary, particularly at times of crisis, such as war, Turner argues, because without a feeling of community solidarity societies cannot survive (Turner 1974: 166–230). Virgil's emphasis upon the natural terrestrial community virtues of the shepherds Romulus and his twin brother Remus was thus quite appropriate given the fact that he was writing at a time of devastating civil war in the urban Roman *imperium*.

It is this structural opposition which explains, I believe, the particular ideological power of the prefix land in landscape. Like the word 'country', a vital part of its meaning is tied to its structural opposition to city and state. It is the locus of communitas, or community identity, and it is in organic, biological terms of breeding and cultivation that power within the community is legitimated. This is why the feudal ideology that linked political legitimacy to land has remained so powerful up to the present day, and why we continue to oppose the country to the city (Williams 1973).

Much of the ideological power of landscape and country must be understood in terms of their opposition to city and state, and so related terms, such as culture and community, must also be understood as being 'counter', in the sense that they are 'more direct, more total and therefore more significant relationships', to 'the more formal, more abstract and more instrumental relationships of *state*, or of *society*' (Williams 1976: 66).

## The Colonisation of Nature by Landscape Scenery

One way of resolving the oppositions between the two poles of nature is through myth and cultic ritual, or by creating works of culture, or art, which build upon myth and ritual. Landscape paintings, as has been seen, were often inspired by, or represented scenes from, such works of art. Landscape painting, however, represented nature not only in its subject matter, but through its very structure, which can be seen to resolve the oppositions within the concept of nature itself.

Landscape painting involves a framework within which that subject is painted, the framework of perspective drawing. Perspective drawing emerged in the context of urban commercial growth which characterised cities such as Florence and Venice in the Renaissance. Its proponents were frequently Neoplatonists who saw the godhead in the geometries of the celestial spheres (Edgerton 1975; Cosgrove 1984, 1988). The significant development in Renaissance cosmology in this context, however, is not the notion of a higher, celestial, nature, divorced from terrestrial existence, but the belief that this higher nature was present, behind the scenes, in terrestrial nature. Newton was given similar significance because of the way he showed that the immutable, rational, timeless, laws of celestial nature applied on earth (Nicolson 1963). Or, as Alexander Pope, put it:

> Nature and Nature's laws hid in night;
> God said, Let Newton be! and all was light!
>         Now o'er the one half world
> Nature seems dead.
> (quoted in Williams 1972: 164)

The Ptolemaic map provided an exemplary metaphor for a concept of nature in which the rationality of celestial nature infuses terrestrial nature, giving structure and meaning to it. The map was the vehicle which facilitated the transition from the vertical cosmology, which Virgil described, to the horizontal cosmology of the landscape scene (Tuan 1974: 129–36). Upon the celestially coordinated geometric grid work plan, the cartographer projects the shapes of the earth (see Figures 10.5 and 10.6). It is this same framework which provided the basis for the technique of projection, through a square frame (or 'window') which made landscape painting possible. The history of landscape painting is thus concomitant with that of cartography, involving the same circles and philosophies which produced cartography (Edgerton 1975; Cosgrove 1984, 1988; Olwig 1987). Where cartography made possible an urban and regional planning in which the earth was bounded and reformed according to the quadratic net of the map, landscape painting provided a means of visualising the world which the landscape architect used to reshape the topography according to his designs (Olwig 1990). It is this same basic cosmology which continues to inform the work of modern landscape architects when they write:

Figures 10.5 This is a woodcut which illustrates how the cartographic grid, within a 'window' frame, provided the structure for the earliest perspective drawings. It is the drawing of a woman by Albrecht Dürer from 1525, the artist is using a pointed object, resembling a monument, to make his sightings. The same technique was used by surveyors, using actual monuments, in the field. It is interesting to note that the first use of the term 'nature' in the scenic sense listed in the Oxford English Dictionary is a sentence from John Dryden's 1697 translation of Virgil's *Georgics*, which reads: '*Surveying* Nature with too nice a view' (my italics).

Figure 10.6 This is a woodcut which illustrates how the cartographic grid, within a 'window' frame, provided the structure for the earliest perspective drawings. This woodcut is from a book on drawing technique by Johann II of Bavaria and Hieronymus Rodler, and dates from 1531

... man's destiny being to rise above the animal state, he creates around him an environment that is a projection into nature of his abstract ideas. . . . . The mind of intellectual man, for instance, has always responded to the tranquillity and assurance of certain geometrical forms such as the square and the circle, although the manifestations of these in the landscape vary according to geography, society, economics, morals and philosophy, all of which are local and transitory (Jellicoe and Jellicoe 1975).

The structure of the landscape painting represents a concept of nature which subtly colonises the earlier concepts of nature, nation, landscape and, even, culture. A sexual cosmology based on a 'vertical' intercourse between two natural poles is colonised by a 'horizontal' cosmology in which the celestial infuses and controls the terrestrial. It is, thus, a notion of landscape which privileges an intellectually and physically distanced, visual perception of the world, reducing the bodily participation in land 'shaping' (be it ritual/cultural or physical) to scenery. It is a cosmology which, in other contexts, resulted in a degrading of not only the terrestrial and feminine, but – more generally – the organic and the bodily (Merchant 1980). Within the painting we find enframed images of particular enclosed, organic, topological, carved out, spaces, but these spaces are illusory for they have been projected and structured within the framework of a geometric, 'absolute' space, an undifferentiated and unbounded physical space that is independent of what occupies it (Edgerton 1975: 161; Tuan 1977).

Landscape was framed and reified as a cultural object, to be bought and sold as cultural capital on the burgeoning new art market, much as land itself was being divided up according to the geometric coordinates of the map, to be sold and traded on the property market. This whole process, in turn, went hand-in-hand with a transformation by which reciprocal, inherited, customary cultural relations, rooted in the organic cosmology of feudalism, were replaced by money relations in which the particular was commodified through a universal system of quantifiable monetary value that was independent of that which was exchanged. There is thus a certain poetic appropriateness to the fact that the first representations of landscape scenery in painting tended to be views seen from the window of the urban patron whose protrait was being painted, and that the same persons who imported Dutch surveyors and engineers to England to restructure and rationalise their properties, imported landscape paintings and hired landscape architects.

An example of the colonisation of nature by landscape as scenery is Henry Hoare's eighteenth century landscape garden at Stourhead (see figure 10.3). The Hoare family made their money in London trading in gold, slaves, and other commodities at a time when the rise of merchant capitalism was dramatically shifting the balance of economic and social power between the landed aristocracy and the urban bourgeoisie. But the economic power generated by urban capital did not confer cultural legitimacy. This could only be obtained by buying a country estate, and, if possible, a title. The Hoares purchased the estate of an ancient noble family, the Stourtons. They then proceeded, like so many others in their situation, to tear down the Stourton family home and build a new one in the Palladian style. It was a style embodying the sort of natural ideal which the architect, and stage designer, Christopher Wren espoused when he wrote: 'There are two causes of Beauty – natural and customary. Natural is from Geometry, consisting in Uniformity . . . . Geometrical Figures are naturally more beautiful than any other irregular; in this all consent, as to a Law of Nature'(quoted in Miller 1988: 117). Note how 'custom,' which lay at the heart of Henry V's 'natural' claim to the throne of France, is here counterposed to nature. The natural has become unnatural, and vice-versa.

Henry Hoare, who had inherited the estate, did not leave matters here; like many other landowners of the time he took the further step of providing the estate with a landscape park. In this park the very material substance of the estate was shaped into a physical replica of the landscape images of Virgilian Arcadian natural ideals painted in the style of a Claude. Much as Virgil celebrated the birth of Rome, Hoare appears to have been celebrating the birth of the family estate (Woodbridge 1970: 36). One technique commonly used in such parks to create the Virgilian impression that there was 'no fence or boundary stone to mark the fields' was to erect 'ha-ha's, (fences or walls buried in ditches so that they could not be seen from the mansion). They blurred the fact that these artful scenes of classical Arcadian commons were being created at a time when English commons, and the inherited customary rights which underlay their use, were being enclosed as saleable properties, cut according to the geometries of the map by surveyors (Williams 1973). The land was literally being transformed from a landscape in the original sense to a landscape in the modern sense, while maintaining the illusory image of the values identified with the original concept. The reification of nature represented by the landscape park both naturalised a power relation and obfuscated the source of that power. The legitimacy of the right to control the use of the land, and hence to communal cultural leadership in the nation, was 'naturalised' according to a subtly redefined notion of nature and nation in which property relations rather than 'blood' relations grant legitimacy.

These developments involved, furthermore, not only an upwardly mobile urban gentry, but also a rural aristocracy that was busy replacing the customary moral economy of the feudal system with one based on the money economy (Bushaway 1982). The significance of the 'ha-ha' in this process is that the laugh – engendered by the sudden discovery of the deception – belongs to the estate owner, not the dispossessed. The fence is only invisible from the estate house, and only amusing when it is abruptly discovered while strolling therefrom. From the outside it is obvious, and not funny. This sort of ideology is not so much a product of conscious deceit, as of self-deception, the need to rationalise one's own position of power, especially when that power is based on forms of economy (usury, land speculation etc.) long condemned as unnatural within one's society. The way to do this is to redefine terms, to make the natural unnatural and vice-versa, and to shift the terrain of discourse, so that landscape becomes a question of the aesthetics of the scenic surface created by the illusion of perspective, rather than the nature of the cultural relations which created it.

No one was more conscious of the 'duplicity' (Daniels 1989) of the situation than the staunch defender of customary rights, Oliver Goldsmith. In his 'negative pastoral,' the *Deserted Village* (1770), the construction of just such a park is made to symbolise the death of the natural English national virtues:

> . . . The man of wealth and pride,
> Takes up a space that many poor supplied;
> Space for his lake, his park's extended bounds,
> Thus fares the land, by luxury betray'd
> In nature's simplest charms at first arrayed,
> But verging to decline, its splendours rise,
> Its vistas strike, its palaces surprise;

> While scourged by famine from the smiling land,
> The mournful peasant leads his humble band;
> And while he sinks without one arm to save,
> The country blooms—a garden, and a grave.

(Goldsmith 1773)

The mournful exiled peasant sinks, as fate would have it, in the swamps of America, an *uncultivated* place without landscape in the original sense, only horrid wilderness.


## Jefferson and the American Landscape

It was no accident that the architecture and landscapes of places like Stourhead were the preferred style of the founders of the new American republic, who were equally inspired by Virgilian values. The American experience amply illustrates the ideological problems engendered by the reification of nature and nation as physical landscape.

The United States became the first western nation to be defined almost solely in terms of birthplace (the territory of America) rather than natural rights of lineage. This was appropriate because it was a nation which was literally defined in counterdistinction to the national ideology which made Americans the 'natural' subjects of the British king. This notion is captured in Robert Frost's lines:

> The land was ours before we were the land's.
> She was our land more than a hundred years
> Before we were her people. She was ours
> In Massachusetts, in Virginia,
> But we were England's, still colonials.

(quoted in Kolodny 1975:10)

An added problem was that the land belonged to another nation (or nations) long before the land was colonised by the British, and these 'Native Americans' are still inclined to see white Americans as colonials. Unlike the natives in Goldsmith's poem, the American native was of a different race and culture from the colonists. In an imperial situation, when one is taking the patrimony from the natural, native born people of an area, the status of those who were 'native' by lineage of birth ceases to provide

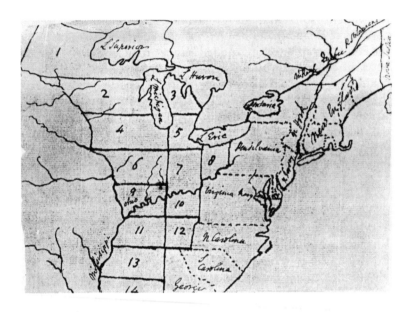

**Figure 10.7 The lines of longitude and latitude which Jefferson projected directly on to the soil of America in the form of administrative boundaries, determined the future structure of America. Jefferson-Hartley map of the Western Territory. William L. Clements Library, University of Michigan.**

legitimacy, but rather becomes a badge of degradation. The definition of America as a nation by its territory was a way of making a nation out of the entire multi-ethnic hotchpotch which settled in America. The nation was to be defined by its land, but it was also to be defined by people who were conscious of their role as 'Founding Fathers', fathers who were steeped in European cultural values and deeply aware of the fact that they were creating a new nation in a territory which the Europeans did not deem to be *cultivated*. The task was thus to redefine the nature of America as landscape according to a new concept of nature, much as Henry Hoare redefined the nature of his estate as landscape.

The architect of the American landscape was, first and fore-most, Thomas Jefferson, who was also the architect of its consti-tution. Jefferson had made a meticulous study of the landscape gardens of England and he lavished considerable attention upon the Palladian architecture and landscape architecture of his estate at Monticello, built by the labour of slaves who, in principle, could have been sold to his estate by the Hoares. Jefferson solved the problem of the wild 'uncultivated' American nature by giving America its own special architect, God. America became, as one nation under God, God's own country. Jefferson, however, did not call God 'God', or even 'Yahweh', he called God 'Nature', and nature was the pre-eminent word in his vocabulary (Miller 1988: 1–20).

As a child of the Enlightenment, Jefferson's nature was, first and foremost, the celestial nature of reason. He loved geography and his proudest accomplishment in his geographical study of Virginia was his map (Miller 1988: 18, 120). Later, when, as President, he purchased the Northwest Territory, he had the pleasure of taking this virgin Virginia writ large, and projecting upon it the geometrical structure of the map (fig. 3), thereby pre-determining the structure of its colonisation and cultivation (Miller 1988: 138–9; Cosgrove 1984: 161–88)(see Figure 10.7). It was upon the undifferentiated geometric space of this materi-alised map (rather than upon the national territory of the native Indians) that the national landscape was to be carved out by the ploughs of the farmers whom he, like Virgil, saw as being the backbone of the nation. But in America there was no obvious equivalent of Romulus and Remus, the shepherds who created the landscape which the Roman farmers transformed into agri-cultural land. Instead there was God, or 'Nature'. The uncultivat-ed wilds of Virginia thus became, under Jefferson's pen, a natural, God-given pastoral paradise which, in fact, owed it ori-gins more to Virgil than to Virginian reality (Marx 1964: 73–144). In this respect, Jefferson was building on an already well estab-lished European tradition of seeing America as paradise (Marx 1964: 34–72).

Rather than move tons of earth to create an appropriately Arcadian scene, as landscape architects in England had done, Jefferson incorporated the existent God-given landscape, seen from his Monticello, into his garden. The 'ha-ha' became super-fluous when all of America was a pastoral garden. Rather than build a sham bridge, as had Hoare, he purchased a bridge built by 'Nature' – the natural bridge of Virginia – and gave it to the nation. He thereby set a precedent which would reach full flower with the establishment of the American National Parks, which were essentially landscape gardens architected by God, or 'Nature', and enframed by the state. Jefferson himself, however, did not see nature predominantly as landscape in the modern sense of scenery. As the father of what he hoped would be a new nation of independent farmers, Jefferson was more interested in creating a landscape in something approaching the original sense of the word, than in scenery (Clark 1989). The notion of America as a sort of virginal *tabula rasa* (Smith 1970), upon which civilisation has the chance to begin anew, retracing the natural cycle of development, is a theme which persists throughout American history through the writings of Henry David Thoreau (1817–1862) and the history of Frederick Jackson Turner (1861–1932). They created thereby the central American myth, which is played out daily in endless films and books about the heroic pioneers who carved out America, and the (singing) cowboy shepherds who paved the way for them (Nash 1973). This strand of the American landscape tradition thus represents something of an atavistic return to the original meaning of the term, with a people defining, in their image, a 'vernacular landscape', as J.B. Jackson terms it (Jackson 1986).

Jefferson's landscape was the creation of cultivators, it was not picturesque scenery, but his concept of American nature begged for landscape painting. A 'cult of landscape', with Church's painting of *The Natural Bridge of Virginia* its foremost example, soon became a national passion. As Barbara Novak has documented in her book *Nature and Culture*, the visual image of landscape played an extraordinary role in the development of the American national identity at a time when its material reality was beginning to belie the 'natural' ideals of the founding fathers (Novak 1980). It was thus a logical consequence of this interest in landscape that, when explorers on the western frontier discovered vast areas that had the appearance of pastoral parkland, many felt that the American concept of American landscape as the creation of God or 'Nature', had been made manifest. The enclosure of these areas as the world's first natural parks, in the modern sense, set a pattern which has since become paradigmatic for such 'national' natural parks. The fact, however, that the first tourist pilgrims to the first of these parks, Yellowstone, had to be protected by troops from the native Indians, counterpointed the birth of these parks with a note of Goldsmithian irony (Olwig and Olwig 1979). The ultimate expression of the American concept of nature, nation and landscape, was achieved when Jefferson's visage (along with that of other founding fathers) was carved into the side of a mountain in Mt Rushmore National Park.

There was no need for 'ha-ha's' when 'Nature' itself was architect of the park, for nature serves the same purpose by obfuscating the true origin of the point of view which is naturalised in the landscape. In Jefferson's case we are dealing with a point of view which sees agri*culture* as the process which brings out the natural potentiality of the land. There was no place for either slaves, cities or industry in his natural pastoral paradise. The existence of the former, as he feared, rent asunder the American national fabric, and they have yet to be accorded, in practice, full native citizenship. America, itself, went on to become a heavily urbanised and industrialised society. The commercial colonisation of the continent was facilitated, ironically, by the very grid system which Jefferson imposed upon it. Increasingly, in this process nature came to be regarded, not as the home of pastoral and agricultural culture, but as a study object for naturalists, a raw material for industry and as a recreative proving ground for rugged individualists. Once nature became one with the God given physical environment, and detached from culture, it could be used to serve any number of Gods, including those who see nature as being in fundamental opposition to culture. Nature, in this way, now excludes from its parks the very agriculturalists whom Jefferson saw to be the scapers of his land. It is a place, in the words of the Sierra Mountain Club, where we can 'take only pictures, and leave only footprints'—unless, that is, we are bulldozing the footprints in the topsoil away in search of coal (Olwig and Olwig 1979).

## Conclusion

Though the American concept of landscape and nature was rooted in Europe, America was the first modern nation in the sense that it was the first nation to define itself in terms of the land from which it grew, relatively unencumbered by feudal notions of the nature of the nation. Western Europe is now also in the process of (re)defining its collective identity in terms of a territorial unity which is expected to transcend traditional national barriers. It is in this context that landscape has become a fetishised concept which allows people to discourse about a national identity which no longer is supposed to exist in the multi-ethnic society which the European Economic Community is already well on the way to becoming (Gilroy 1987). This is not only apparent in the growth of the heritage industry, and the burgeoning interest in everything from landscape painting and landscape history to countryside conservation (Daniels 1991; Lowenthal 1985), it is also apparent in the movement among conservationists to eradicate 'opportunistic' and 'alien' natural plant and animal species which push the 'native' species out of their countryside habitats (Agyeman and Hare 1988). In eastern Europe, on the other hand, the nation, in the original sense of a people or race, is re-emerging as an explosive element in a dissolving state system which long tried to suppress national identity by, among other things, destroying the pre-existent bond between the nations of the area and their territory. The difficulty of re-establishing national territorial units in such a fragmented situation is resulting in considerable suffering and bloodshed, and it is questionable whether even 'all the king's horses and all the king's men' can create a semblance of landscape unity between community and territory again. In such a situation, it is not enough to take our inherited concepts of nature, culture and landscape for granted as being God- or 'Nature'-given. We will need, once again, to redefine these concepts to suit our times. To do so, we need a clear understanding of the ideologies and taboos (including sexual and racial taboos) which lie concealed under present usage. Unless we are cognisant of the complex of meanings which inform these concepts we will only be using landscape in the way the Hebrews used Yahweh, as a way of expressing that which we cannot, or will not say openly about nation, nature and culture.

## Appendix

**land.scape** , *often attrib* (D *landschap, fr. land* + *-schap* -ship)
**1a:** a picture representing a view of natural inland scenery
**b:** the art of depicting such scenery
**2a:** the landforms of a region in the aggregate

**b:** a portion of land that the eye can comprehend in a single view
**3:** VISTA, PROSPECT.

**na.ture** *n* (ME, fr. MF, fr. L *natura*, fr. *natus*, pp. of *nasci* to be born
– more at NATION)
**1a:** The inherent character or basic constitution of a person or
thing: ESSENCE
**b:** DISPOSITION, TEMPERAMENT
**2a:** a creative and controlling force in the universe
**b:** an inner force or the sum of such forces in an individual
**3:** a general character: KIND
**4:** the physical constitutions or drives of an organism
**5:** a spontaneous attitude (as of generosity)
**6:** the external world in its entirety
**7a:** man's original or natural condition
**b:** a simplified mode of life resembling this condition
**8:** natural scenery.

**cul.ture** (ME, fr. MF, fr. L *cultura*, fr. *cultus*, pp.)
**1:** CULTIVATION, TILLAGE
**2:** the act of developing the intellectual and moral  faculties esp.
by education
**3:** expert care and training
**4:** enlightenment and excellence of taste acquired by intellectual
and aesthetic training
**5a:** a particular stage of advancement in civilization
**b:** the characteristic features of such a stage or state
**c:** behavior typical of a group or class
**6:** cultivation of living material in prepared nutrient media, *also*: a
product of such cultivation.

**cult** (F & L; *culte*, fr. L *cultus* care, adoration, fr. *cultus*, pp. of *colere*
to cultivate – more at WHEEL)
**1:** formal religious veneration: WORSHIP
**2:** a system of religous beliefs and ritual; *also* its body of adherents.

## References

Agyeman, J. and Hare, T. 1988. 'Towards a cultural ecology . . . ', *Urban
    wildlife*, (June), 39–40.
Bushaway, B. 1982. *By Rite: Custom, Ceremony and Community in England
    1700–1880*, London: Junction.

Clark, R. 1989. 'The absent landscape of America's eighteenth century' in
M. Gidley and R. Lawson-Peebles (eds) *Views of American Landscapes*
81–99, Cambridge: Cambridge University Press.

Collins-Klett. 1983. *German-English Dictionary*. London: Collins.

Collingwood, R.G. 1960. *The Idea of Nature*, Oxford: Oxford University
Press.

Cosgrove, D. 1984. *Social Formation and Symbolic Landscape*, London:
Croom Helm.

———1988. 'The geometry of landscape: practical and speculative arts in
sixteenth-century Venetian land territories', in D. Cosgrove and S.
Daniels (eds) *The Iconography of Landscape*, 254–76, Cambridge:
Cambridge University Press.

Daniels, S. 1989. 'Marxism, Culture and the Duplicity of Landscape', in
R. Peet and N. Thrift (eds) *New Models in Geography*, 196–220, London:
Unwin and Hyman.

———1991. 'Envisioning England', Journal of Historical Geography 17,
1, 95–9.

Edgerton, S. Y. jr. 1975. *The Renaissance Rediscovery of Linear Perspective*
New York: Basic Books.

Gilroy, P. 1987. *There ain't no black in the Union Jack*, London: Hutchinson.

Glacken, C. 1967. *Traces on the Rhodian Shore: Nature and Culture in
Western Thought from Ancient Times to the End of the Eighteenth Century*,
Berkeley: University of California Press.

Goldsmith, O. 1773. *The Deserted Village*, Leipzig: Altenburgh.

Gröning, G. and Wolschke-Bulmahn, J. 1987. 'Politics, planning and the
protection of nature: political abuse of early ecological ideas in
Germany, 1935–45', *Planning Perspectives* 2, 127–48.

Hard, G. 1970. *Die 'Landschaft' der Sprache und die 'Landschaft' der
Geografien: Semantische und forschungslogische Studien. Colloquium
Geographicum*, Bonn b.11, Bonn: Ferd. Dümmlers Verlag.

Hoskins, W.G. 1955. *The Making of the English Landscape* London: Hodder
& Stoughton.

Jackson, J.B. 1986. 'The vernacular landscape', in E.C. Penning-Rowsell
and D. Lowenthal (eds) *Landscape Meanings and Values*, 65–81,
London: Allen & Unwin.

Jellicoe, G. and S. 1975. *The Landscape of Man: Shaping the Environment
from Prehistory to the Present Day*, New York: Viking.

Kolodny, A. 1975. *The Lay of the Land*, Chapel Hill: University of North
Carolina Press.

Lévi-Strauss, C. 1967. *Structural Anthropology*, trans. C. Jacobsen and B.
Grundfest Schoepf, Garden City: Anchor.

Lovejoy, A.O. 1927. '"Nature" as aesthetic norm', *Modern Language Notes*
42, 444–50.

Lovejoy, A.O. and Boas, G. 1935. *Primitivism and Related ideas in
Antiquity*, Baltimore: Johns Hopkins Press.

Lowenthal, D. 1985. *The Past is a Foreign Country*, Cambridge: Cambridge University Press.

Marx, L. 1964. *The Machine in the Garden*, Oxford: Oxford University Press.

Merchant, C. 1980. *The Death of Nature: Women, Ecology and the Scientific Revolution*, San Francisco: Harper & Row.

Miller, C. 1988. *Jefferson and Nature: an Interpretation*, Baltimore: Johns Hopkins University Press.

Nash, R. 1973. *Wilderness and the American Mind*, New Haven: Yale University Press.

Nicolson, M.H. 1963. *Mountain Gloom and Mountain Glory*, New York: Norton.

Novak, B. 1980. *Nature and Culture: American Landscape and Painting 1825–1875*, New York: Oxford University Press.

*Ordbog over Det Danske Sprog*. 1931, Copenhagen: Gyldendal.

*Oxford English Dictionary*. 1971. Oxford: Oxford University Press.

Olwig, K. R. 1984. *Nature's Ideological Landscape*, London: Allan & Unwin.

———1987. 'Art and the art of communicating geographical knowledge: the case of Pieter Brueghel', *Journal of Geography* 86, 47–50.

———1990. *Nature, Structure, and Daily Life: Planning, Landscape, and the Idea of Nature*, Stockholm: Nordic Institute for Studies in Urban and Regional Planning (Nordplan).

Olwig, K. F. and K. R. 1979. 'Underdevelopment and the development of "natural" park ideology', *Antipode* 11, 16–25.

Passmore, J. 1974. *Man's Responsibility for Nature*, New York: Charles Scribner.

Sauer, C.O. 1969. 'The morphology of landscape' in J. Leighly (ed.), *Land and life*, 315–50, Berkeley: University of California Press. First published 1925.

Shakespeare, W. 1948. *Major Plays, and the Sonnets*, New York: Harcourt, Brace & World.

Shepard, P. 1967. *Man in the Landscape*, New York: Ballantine.

Smith, H. N. 1970. *Virgin Land: the American West as Symbol and Myth.*, Cambridge, MA: Harvard University Press.

Tuan, Yi-Fu. 1974. *Topophilia: A Study of Environmental Perception, Attitudes, and Values*, Englewood Cliffs, N. J.: Prentice-Hall.

———1977. *Space and Place*, Minneapolis: University of Minnesota Press.

Turner, V. 1974. *Dramas, Fields, and Metaphors: Symbolic Action in Human Society*, Ithaca: Cornell University Press.

Virgil. 1946. *Eclogues and Georgics*, trans. T.F. Royds, London: Dent.

*Webster's Seventh New Collegiate Dictionary*. 1963. Springfield, MA: Merriam.

Williams, R. 1972. 'Ideas of nature', in J. Benthall (ed.) *Ecology , the Shaping Enquiry*, 146–64, London: Longman.

———1973. *The Country and the City*, New York: Oxford University Press.

_____1976. *Keywords: a Vocabulary of Culture and Society,* London: Fontana.
Woodbridge, K. 1970. *Landscape and Antiquity: Aspects of English Culture at Stourhead 1718 to 1838,* Oxford: Clarendon Press.

# Notes on Contributors

**Barbara Bender** is Reader in Material Culture in the Department of Anthropology, University College, London.

**Barbara Bodenhorn** is Fellow and College Lecturer in Social Sciences at Pembroke College, Cambridge.

**Denis Cosgrove** is Reader in Geography at Loughborough University.

**Felicity Edholm** is Staff Tutor at the Open University.

**Neil Jarman** is a Postgraduate in the Department of Anthropology, University College, London.

**Susanne Küchler** is Lecturer in Material Culture in the Department of Anthropology, University College, London.

**Howard Morphy** is Curator of Anthropology at the Pitt Rivers Museum, Oxford, and Lecturer in Ethnology at the Institute of Social and Cultural Anthropology.

**Kenneth Olwig** is Associate Proffessor at Norplan, Stockholm, Sweden.

**Julian Thomas** is Lecturer in the Department of Prehistory at the University of Wales.

**Christopher Tilley** is Lecturer in the Department of Prehistory at the University of Wales.

# INDEX

American landscape, 335–8

Anaximander, 285–6

Apollo, 286–9
see also landscape, natural ... cultural;

archaeological landscapes, 20, 25–6, 29–44, 55–82, 269–70

archaeological perspective, 19–20, 25–6, 270–1

archaeology, see monuments;

art,
colonial context of 'indigenous' traditions, 90
gender and, 24–5, 296–7
murals and, 109, 118–25
relationship to land, 90–7
Western, 21–2, 85, 285, 297, 318–9, 327–31

Aston, Michael, 25–6

Aubrey, John, 261

Australian landscapes,
aboriginal, 2–3, 14, 205–7, 230–40
colonial, 206–30
conflicting notions of what constitutes, 234–6, 239–40
see also landclaims;

Avebury area, 30–44 passim, 254–5, 263

Bakhtin, Mikhail, 248

Baudelaire, Charles, 139–41, 147–52, 154–5

Belfast, 11–2, 107–34,
see also art, murals; social control; social identity;

Bentham, Jeremy, see Panopticon;

Bohuslan, 65–71, 78–9

British landscapes, 245, 298–300

cities, the urban as negative, 143–4, 298, 326–7

see also Belfast; Paris;

Clare, John, 2

class, 109–10, 140–65 passim
see also gender; landscape, contested;

colonialism, see Australian landscapes; Malangan;

commerce, 115–7, 131, 144–6, 148, 151, 164

Cosgrove, Denis, 21–2

culture, concept of, 313–5

Daedalus, 289–90, 301–2

Davis, Mike, 23

death, see mortuary practices;

Degas, 154, 156

Dionysus, 287–9
see also landscape, natural ... cultural;

Druids, 263, 272

dwelling, see Heidegger;

economic appropriation of landscape, see commerce;

enclosures, 262–4, 332–4

Engels, Frederick, 169–71

English Heritage, 267–76 passim

'Enigma of Arrival, The', 3–10

Faust, 301–3

feminist perspectives, 24, 169

food, see social identity;

Foucault, Michel, 22–3

Freud, Sigmund, 315–6

funerary rites, see art; mortuary practices;

Gaia, 283–93 passim, 300–3

gatherer-hunters, 169, 172
see also Inupiat;

gaze, the, 22–5
see also gender; landscape, the

347

term;
gender, 109, 129
    defined in relation to class,
    153–5
    gaze and, 24–5, 324
    gendering of space, 16, 142, 169,
    178, 184, 198–200
    public and private spheres, 140,
    142, 153, 159, 169–71, 176, 293
    *see also* sexual division of
    labour; social organisation;
    *see also* art; kinship; landscape,
    the idea of the objective view;
    women;
globalism, 282–3

habitus, 248
Haussmann, Baron, 141–51 *passim*
health, public, *see* cities;
Heidegger, Martin, 27–9
    concept of dwelling, 28–9
heritage industry, 267–8
    *see also* monuments;
Hesiod, 283, 291
history, totalising notions of, 23,26
Hoare, Henry, 332
hunter-gatherers, *see* gatherer-
    hunters;
Huysmans, G., 154–5

identity, *see* social identity;
Inupiat, 13–14, 169–201

Jones, Inigo, 261
Jefferson, Thomas, 336–8

kinship, 95–6, 175–7, 181, 183
    *see also* social organisation, pro-
    visioning strategies;

land claims, 209–10
    oppositional strategies to,
    218–9, 226–9

landscape,
    as cosmology, *see* Australian
    landscapes, aboriginal; mythic
    landscape;
    changing perceptions over time
    209, 222–3
    contested, 112, 114, 128–32,
    144–6, 215–6, 218, 224, 248,
    255–8, 262–4, 266–7, 269–75,
    erasure and removal of the
    working class, 145–6
    erasure and rewriting of
    indigenous landscapes,
    16, 206–9, 334–8
    naturalisation of a political,
    7–8, 78, 224–6, 236, 245–6, 307,
    333
    resistance and, 29, 125–8, 206
    *see also* commerce; enclosures;
    land claims; monuments,
    changes in use and meaning,
    & contestation, & in relation to
    the human scale;
    differing relationships to, 2–3,
    140–1, 150, 161–2, 246, 259, 333
    emergence of in Western Art,
    21–2
    *see also* landscape, the idea of
    the objective view;
    naming, the power of, 123,
    224–6, 236
    natural...cultural, 293–303, 312,
    319, 327
    *see also* British landscapes;
    cities; wilderness;
    property relations and, 246,
    264–7, 333
    social control and, 110, 116,
    144–5, 269
    *see also* class; social control;
    social mapping of, 134, 261, 328
    *see also* mortuary practices;
    the idea of the objective view,
    85–6, 259, 261, 318–24, 328–31
    alternatives to, 86

*see also* Australian landscapes, aboriginal; Heidegger;
the term;
  ambiguity of, 307–9
  ideology implicit in, 246, 307–8, 311–2, 331
  origins of, 1–2, 309–11, 318–24
  time and movement through, 179–82
*see also* American landscape; archaeological landscapes; art; Australian landscapes; heritage industry; memory; monuments; mythic landscapes;

Lévi-Strauss, Claude, 324
linear perspective, 21–2, 328
Lovelock, James, 300–1

Malangan, 86–104
  *see also* art; mortuary practices;
mapping, *see* landscape, the idea of the objective view; memory, landscape as;
material culture, 32–3, 35–8
  funerary rites and, 35–6, 74, 77
  *see also* art; mortuary practices;
Mauss, Marcel, 179
megaliths, *see* monuments;
memory,
  landscape as, 86, 91–2, 96–103
  landscapes of, 86
  *see also* landscape, the idea of the objective view;
  political economy of, 101–2
  smell and, 95–6, 99–100
  *see also* material culture;
migration, rural/urban, 142, 146
Monmouth, Geoffrey of, 254–5
modernity, 140
  *see also* Haussmann;
monuments,
  aesthetic character of, 50–1
  appropriation of meaning for political ends, 249–51, 261–3,

269–71
  changes in use and meaning over time, 34, 37–8
  contestation of the right to determine meaning 267–75,
  in relation to habitation sites, 69, 74, 78–9, 251, 253
  in relation to human phsyical scale, 30, 34–8, 41–4, 56, 73, 81–2
  in relation to landscape, 51–2, 54–61, 65, 69–82, 145
  marketing of, 265–6
  symbolic encoding of social identity, 77–8, 82, 270
  symbols of antiquity, 50, 52–4, 265–6
  tourism and, 271
  *see also* archaeological landscapes; Stonehenge;
mortuary practices, 34–6, 77, 90–2, 94, 97–100
  associated depositions, *see* material culture;
  burial sites, 98
  food and, 99
'Mosquito Coast, The', 302–3
Mulvey, Laura, 24
murals, *see* art;
mythic landscape, Western, 15, 283–303, 328–31
  *see also* landscape, natural ... cultural;

Naipaul, V.S., 3–10
Napoleon III, 144–5
Nation, concept of, 309–11, 319–24, 334–5
National Monuments Preservation Bill, 264–5
National Trust, The, 267
nature, 325–6
  as a normative principle, 317–9
  *see also* culture; landscape, the term;
New Ireland, 11, 86–95

Ngalakan, 209–10, 230–8
nomadism, 176
'Origin of the Family, Private Property and the State', 170

Panopticon, 22–3
Paris, 12–3, 139–65
    commune, 141, 146
    *see also* landscape, contested, & social control and; migration; monuments, in relation to landscape;
Parks, National, 337–8
past, manipulation of the,
    *see* heritage industry; landscape; monuments;
pastoral poetry, 315–7
pastoralism, 313–4
Pherecydes, 283–4
Pico della Mirandola, 288–9, 301
politics of art, *see* art;
Polybius, 314
Postmodern perspectives,
    Materialist versus, 23–5
    feminist alternatives to, 24
power relations and the built environment, *see* landscape; monuments, in relation to human scale; social control;
production, *see* social organisation;
prostitution, 155–8
    *see also* women;
public/private spheres, *see* gender;

Realism, *see* art, Western;
reciprocity, 181
    *see also* kinship; social organisation; women;
Roper Bar, 209–41
Rosaldo, Michelle, 169–71

'Seasonal Variations of the Eskimo', 179
sexual division of labour, 169–71, 183–6, 198–201

differences between indigenous and wage labour, 184
ritual elaboration of hunting, 187–95
    *see also* gender; social organisation, provisioning strategies;
Skane, 56–9, 74–6
Silbury Hill, 38
social control, 112–7
    *see also* class; gaze; landscape, contested, & social control and; monuments, in relation to human scale;
social identity,
    cultural elaboration of, 118, 120–4, 178, 181–2
    *see also* memory, landscape as; social organisation;
    expressing class differences, 109–10, 118, 120, 127–8
    food and, 182–3
    politicisation of, in relation to landscape, 174
    *see also* Australian landscapes, Aboriginal;
    re/created through landscape, 109–11, 114, 132–4, 206, 230–6
    *see also* art; gaze; landscape, contested; memory, landscape as; nation;
social organisation,
    access/distribution of resources, 175, 177, 185–7, 193–5, 201
    disruption of residence patterns, 88–90, 237–9
    *see also* mortuary practices;
    domestic unit, fluidity of, 176–8
    matrilineal, 89
    non-kin relations, 178–9
    provisioning strategies, 183, 192–5, 200
    *see also* kinship; sexual division of labour; social identity; women;
space, *see* gender; monuments;

social identity;
Stonehenge, 14–5, 248–76
    Battle of the Beanfield, 266
    free festival, 270–1
    tourism, 271–2
    *see also* archaeological perspective; English Heritage; monuments;
Stukeley, William, 262–3, 272
surveillance, *see* gaze;

Theroux, Paul, 302
travellers, 272–5
    *see also* Stonehenge;
Turner, Victor, 326–7

Valadon, Suzanne, 12–3, 139–41, 152, 160–2
Vastergotland, 59–65, 76–8
Virgil, 284, 291–3, 308, 314–32 *passim*

vision,
    politics of, *see* gaze;
    privileging of, 22, 85–6, 331
    *see also* art, Western; gaze; landscape, the term, & the idea of the objective view; monuments, in relation to human scale;

West Kennet long barrow, 33–8, 43
wilderness, 297
    *see also* British landscapes; landscape, natural ... cultural;
Williams, Raymond, 327
Wolff, Janet, 140
women,
    hunting and, 175, 184, 187–95
    representations of, 152–9
    support networks amongst, 159–60